MUSICIANS CODING AI FOR THEMSELVES

Musicians Coding AI for Themselves blends cutting-edge academic research with the real-world experiences of musicians working at the intersection of music and AI. This book not only reflects on the philosophical implications of AI in music but also offers readers insights into the technical inner workings of bespoke, artist-crafted AI systems.

The chapters are written by emerging and innovative coder-musicians who present their own artistic practice and research, with a focus on creative, ethical, collaborative, and educational uses of AI. Interviews with leading musicians who have incorporated AI into their work traverse diverse topics, from behind-the-scenes details of how each artist uses AI in their music to the greater conceptual impact of AI on the arts, the future of music technology, and the creative process.

This book will be of interest to practicing musicians who wish to synthesize the creative potential of AI in their music and understand its implications for the wider music community. It will also appeal to students of music composition, music studies, experimental music, music technology, and human–computer interaction.

MUSICIANS CODING AI FOR THEMSELVES

EDITED BY
CONSTANTIN BASICA AND JULIE ZHU

Routledge
Taylor & Francis Group
LONDON AND NEW YORK

Cover design by Simona Fitcal.

First published 2027
by Routledge
4 Park Square, Milton Park, Abingdon, Oxon OX14 4RN

and by Routledge
605 Third Avenue, New York, NY 10158

Routledge is an imprint of the Taylor & Francis Group, an informa business

Funding Body: The University of Michigan Office of the Vice President for Research

For Product Safety Concerns and Information please contact our EU representative GPSR@taylorandfrancis.com. Taylor & Francis Verlag GmbH, Kaufingerstraße 24, 80331 München, Germany.

British Library Cataloguing-in-Publication Data
A catalogue record for this book is available from the British Library

Library of Congress Cataloging-in-Publication Data
Names: Basica, Constantin editor | Zhu, Julie, 1990- editor |
Chowning, John M. writer of foreword
Title: Musicians coding AI for themselves/edited by Constantin Basica and Julie Zhu.
Description: Abingdon, Oxon; New York: Routledge, 2026. |
Includes bibliographical references and index.
Subjects: LCSH: Artificial intelligence–
Musical applications | Artificial intelligence–Computer programs
Classification: LCC ML74.3 .M89 2026 (print) | LCC ML74.3 (ebook) |
DDC 780.285/63–dc23/eng/20260702
LC record available at https://lccn.loc.gov/2026022048
LC ebook record available at https://lccn.loc.gov/2026022049

ISBN: 978-1-041-01667-0 (hbk)
ISBN: 978-1-041-01666-3 (pbk)
ISBN: 978-1-003-61587-3 (ebk)

DOI: 10.4324/9781003615873

Typeset in Akzidenz Grotesk and Franklin Gothic
by Deanta Global Publishing Services, Chennai, India

CONTENTS

EDITORS

Constantin Basica

Palo Alto, California

Constantin Basica is a Romanian composer whose work focuses on symbiotic interrelations between music, video, and performers. His compositions include works for solo instruments, small groups of musicians, and large orchestras, often incorporating electronics and visual elements. Performances of his compositions have taken place in Europe, North America, and Asia, presented by distinguished ensembles and artists such as Ensemble Dal Niente, Ensemble Liminar, ELISION Ensemble, Distractfold, Mocrep, JACK Quartet, Spektral Quartet, RAGE Thormbones, line upon line, Retro Disco, Fresh Squeezed Opera, SonoMania Ensemble, Séverine Ballon, and Tony Arnold. His works have been featured in over fifty international festivals and conferences. Basica was a postdoctoral scholar at Stanford University's Center for Computer Research in Music and Acoustics (CCRMA) in California, where he also earned his doctorate in composition. Before this, he obtained a master's degree in multimedia composition from the Hamburg University of Music and Drama in Germany and bachelor's degrees in composition and conducting from the National University of Music Bucharest in Romania. In recent years, he has collaborated with other researchers on the development of systems for co-creativity between humans and artificial intelligence. Basica is currently a lecturer at CCRMA, Stanford University, where he teaches composition and interdisciplinary courses.

Julie Zhu

Ann Arbor, Michigan

Julie Zhu is a composer, artist, and carillonist. Technology—from artificial intelligence to live sound processing, sensors, and virtual reality—often supports her work, which seeks to reveal and amplify underlying mathematical structures and gentle noises through innovative intermedia instrumentation and diverse chamber experiences. Her music has been featured on Radio France's Création Mondiale and at various institutions such as GMEM Festival Propagations Marseille, IRCAM Paris, ICST Zürich, Sansusī Latvia, Tetramatyka Lviv, Carnegie Hall, among others. Zhu's research on music and AI focuses on the project Deep Drawing, which tests the machine's capabilities for bringing the intricate noises of drawing and writing to visual life. Other long-term projects include *Talking Pupils*, a VR Opera centered on the experience of the visually impaired, and the Bell Resonator, a device to sustain the sound of the bell. As a carillonist, Zhu regularly performs on the Burton and Lurie Tower at the University of Michigan and concertizes in the summer. Zhu studied at Yale University (BA mathematics, BA art), the Royal Carillon School (Diploma carillon performance), Hunter College (MFA art), and Stanford University (DMA composition). She is currently an assistant professor at the University of Michigan.

CONTRIBUTORS

Alexandru I. Berceanu

Bucharest, Romania

Alexandru I. Berceanu is a mixing-realities director and researcher conducting interdisciplinary research at the intersection of art and neuroscience. Starting with his doctoral studies, his research has centered on aggressive and prosocial behavior, using drama and immersive environments as investigative tools to develop emotional regulation through gamified approaches and theatrical representation. His results are published in international journals, and his artistic work covers interactive-media installations, VR, immersive environments, and theater. Berceanu is an associate professor in the Animation and Interaction Department at the National University of Theatre and Film "I. L. Caragiale" in Bucharest, Romania, where he also teaches in the Community and Therapeutic Theatre master's program. He initiated the International Center for Research and Education in Innovative and Creative Technologies (CINETic), as well as its master's program in Interactive Technologies.

Celeste Betancur Gutiérrez

Stanford, California

Celeste Betancur Gutiérrez is a PhD candidate at Stanford University's Center for Computer Research in Music and Acoustics (CCRMA), where her research explores the intersections of music, technology, and algorithmic composition and performance. As a composer, digital artist, and live coder, her work spans a broad spectrum—from academic concert halls to underground electronic music scenes—emphasizing real-time score generation, live-coding performance, and the development of interactive audiovisual systems. Betancur's interdisciplinary practice includes the design and construction of expanded musical instruments, large-scale installations, and sculptures. Her compositions have been performed by internationally renowned ensembles and artists. Beyond composition and performance, Betancur is a software developer specializing in music technology. She has contributed to the development of the ChucK programming language and is part of its core maintenance group.

CJ Carr

Boston, Massachusetts

CJ Carr is a pioneering AI researcher and musician. With Zack Zukowski, he co-founded Dadabots, a creative collective born from their days at Berklee College when they used to play instruments. After falling down the rabbit hole of Python, Theano, arXiv, and GitHub, a benevolent alien abducted them in a UFO and granted them unlimited GPU credits, which they wasted on generating never-ending noise music. Dedicated to open-source ideals, CJ Carr's collaborations and presentations have inspired artists and technologists worldwide, making him a central figure in the intersection of experimental music and artificial intelligence.

Doga Cavdir

Copenhagen, Denmark

Doga Buse Cavdir is an assistant professor of HCI and Design at the IT University of Copenhagen and co-head of the Affective Interactions and Relations (AIR) Lab. Her research lies at the intersection of creative practice, disability studies, performance-led research, and inclusive design. She develops new musical interfaces and interaction modalities that support equitable access to musical expression and performance, drawing on participatory design and practice-based methodologies that foreground first-person perspectives and diverse sensory ways of knowing. Cavdir has been performing with her custom-designed, body-based musical instruments solo and with other performing artists. She has been selected as a MacDowell fellow and a resident artist at Headlands Center for the Arts. Cavdir holds a PhD from the Center for Computer Research in Music and Acoustics (CCRMA) at Stanford University where she was selected as a Diversifying Academia, Recruiting Excellence (DARE) and Stanford Impact Labs fellow.

John Chowning

Palo Alto, California

John Chowning was born in Salem, New Jersey, in 1934. He studied composition in Paris with Nadia Boulanger and received a doctorate in composition (DMA) from Stanford University in 1966. In 1964, he began the research that led to the first generalized surround sound localization algorithm. Chowning discovered the frequency modulation synthesis (FM) algorithm in 1967. This breakthrough in the synthesis of timbres allowed a very simple yet elegant way of creating and controlling time-varying spectra. In 1973, Stanford University licensed the FM synthesis patent to Yamaha in Japan, leading to the most successful synthesis engine in the history of electronic musical instruments. He taught computer-sound synthesis and composition at Stanford University's Department of Music. In 1974, Chowning co-founded the Center for Computer Research in Music and Acoustics (CCRMA), which remains one of the leading centers for computer music and related research. He was elected to the American Academy of Arts and Sciences in 1988. The French Ministry of Culture awarded him the *Diplôme d'Officier dans l'Ordre des Arts et des Lettres* in 1995. Chowning was given honorary doctorates in 2002 by the Université de la Méditerranée, in 2010 by Queen's University, and in 2016 by the Hamburg University of Music and Drama. He was Laureate of the Giga-Hertz Award in 2013 and is the recipient of the 2026 Technical Grammy Award.

Kelsey Cotton

Gothenburg, Sweden

Kelsey Cotton (she/her) is a vocalist-artist-mover working with experimental music, musical artificial intelligence, electronic textiles, soft-robotics, and human-computer interaction. As a researcher, Cotton is fascinated by pushing the limits of musical bodies, with her recent work delving deeper into designing artifacts that harness, augment, and fuse different physiologies. She is passionate about somatic interaction, the potential for intersomatic experiences between fleshy and synthetic bodies, and first-person feminist perspectives of musical AI.

Hugo Flores García

Chicago, Michigan

Hugo Flores García (he/they) is a computer musician, improviser, programmer, and scientist. Hugo's creative practice spans improvised and composed music for guitars, sound objects and electronics, sound installations, bespoke digital musical instruments, and interactive art. Their research centers around designing new instruments for creative expression, focusing on artist-centered machine learning interfaces for the sound arts. Flores plays guitar and designs custom electronics for the Chicago psychotropical band Cabeza de Chivo, among other Chicago acts. Flores received their PhD in Computer Science from Northwestern University in 2025, advised by Bryan Pardo. Flores was born and raised in Honduras, the heart of Central America. He now lives in Chicago, IL, with his partner and two cats, pipi and pixel.

Charles Hiroshi Garrett

Charles Hiroshi Garrett was an innovative scholar of US music and culture, with a special interest in race and ethnicity, social justice, digital culture, nationalism, popular music, jazz, and sound studies. He taught at the University of Michigan from 2004 until his death in 2024. His book, *Struggling to Define a Nation: American Music and the Twentieth Century* (2008), which received the Irving Lowens Memorial Book Award (Society for American Music), has since become a classic for its focus on racial identity in a spectrum of musical styles, querying the borders of what it means to sound "American." Garrett served as editor-in-chief for *The Grove Dictionary of American Music* (second edition, 2013), the most comprehensive reference source in the field. He coedited *Jazz/Not Jazz: The Music and Its Boundaries* with David Ake and Daniel Goldmark (2012) and *Sounding Together: Collaborative Perspectives on U.S. Music in the 21st Century* with Carol J. Oja (2021). He served as President of the Society for American Music. At the time of his death, Garrett had several projects underway. In *Virtually Music*, he was addressing the impact of early twenty-first-century digital technologies—including artificial intelligence—on how we produce, understand, and experience musical culture. In another project, he was examining the politics of musical representation during the Japanese-American internment of World War II—a topic with personal resonance. Among friends, colleagues, and students, Garrett was known for his exceptional kindness. He was a "beautiful soul," as memorialized on Instagram by the musicologist Guthrie P. Ramsey Jr.

John Granzow

Ann Arbor, Michigan

John Granzow specializes in the design and fabrication of new musical interfaces and instruments, bridging fields of music, engineering, and interactive media. His research explores new performance systems, embedded electronics for sound synthesis, spatial audio, and applications of digital fabrication for instrument prototyping and design. His work frequently crosses disciplinary boundaries, resulting in collaborations with composers, performers, and engineers. His teaching at the University of Michigan encompasses courses in instrument design, sound synthesis, physical computing, and creative applications of technology in the performing arts. Granzow is also active in mentoring students in research projects and fostering interdisciplinary partnerships across campus through his role as Faculty Director of Arts Engine. Granzow has presented his instruments and sound installations internationally, with work supported by organizations such as the National Endowment for the Arts, the Humanities Collaboratory, Michigan Arts Initiative, and the Canada Council for the Arts. Granzow holds a PhD in Computer-Based Music Theory and Acoustics from Stanford University.

Holly Herndon

Berlin, Germany

Berlin-based artist Holly Herndon is known for her pioneering work in music, machine learning, and protocol development. In collaboration with Mathew Dryhurst, her practice creates precedent-setting projects where technical systems are artworks unto themselves. *Holly+* (2021) is an AI clone of Herndon's voice that anyone can use freely, with a protocol to share profits from commercial use. Their image-making documents novel software interventions. *Crossing the Interface* (2021) engineered the world's first text-to-video animations, and *Classified* (2021) produced portraiture of image model embeddings. Major exhibitions include *The Call* at the Serpentine Gallery in London and *Starmirror* at Kunstwerke Berlin, and the 2024 Whitney Biennial. In 2022, the duo co-founded Spawning, an organization building a consent layer for AI, creating tools for artists such as *haveibeentrained.com* and the *Do Not Train* protocol covering two billion+ works. Their critically acclaimed musical works include *Platform* (4AD/2015) and *PROTO* (4AD/2019). Awards include the 2022 Ars Electronica STARTS prize, Austria's first Digital Human Rights Award (2024), the Kairos Prize (2025), and the German AI Prize (2025). Holly Herndon holds a doctorate in Computer Music from Stanford University and is a fellow at the Berlin Artistic Research Grant Program 2024/25.

Molly Jones

Chicago/Ann Arbor, Michigan

Molly Jones is an improviser, composer, and data engineer based in Chicago and Ann Arbor, Michigan. She creates work influenced by her experiences with free jazz, new music, Balkan brass, and found samples/sound collage. Her work originates in a place of playfulness, listening, and attention. She is currently completing a PhD in Performing Arts Technology at the University of Michigan with a focus on machine learning for creative audio applications.

George Lewis

New York, New York

George Lewis is an American composer, musicologist, and trombonist. He is the Edwin H. Case Professor of American Music at Columbia University. He is a Fellow of the American Academy of Arts and Sciences and the American Academy of Arts and Letters, an International Fellow of the British Academy, a member of the Akademie der Künste Berlin, and an Honorary Member of the American Musicological Society. Lewis's other honors include the Doris Duke Artist Award (2019), a MacArthur Fellowship (2002), and a Guggenheim Fellowship (2015). A member of the Association for the Advancement of Creative Musicians

(AACM) since 1971, Lewis's work is presented by ensembles worldwide and published by Edition Peters. A Yamaha Artist, Lewis is widely regarded as a pioneer in the creation of computer programs that improvise in concert with human musicians. Lewis's central areas of scholarship include the history and criticism of experimental music, computer music, interactive media, and improvisation, particularly as these areas become entangled with the dynamics of race, gender, and decolonization. His widely acclaimed book, *A Power Stronger Than Itself: The AACM and American Experimental Music* (University of Chicago Press, 2008) received the American Book Award and the American Musicological Society's Music in American Culture Award.

Ted Moore
Bethany, Connecticut
Ted Moore (he/him) is a composer, improviser, and intermedia artist whose work fuses sonic, visual, physical, and acoustic elements, often incorporating technology to create immersive, multidimensional experiences. Moore's music has been presented by leading cultural institutions such as MASS MoCA and The Walker Art Center, and by ensembles including Talea Ensemble and the JACK Quartet. He has held artist residences with the Phonos Foundation in Barcelona and the Studio for Electro-Instrumental Music (STEIM) in Amsterdam. Moore has held artist residences with the Phonos Foundation in Barcelona, the Arts, Sciences, & Culture Initiative at the University of Chicago, and the Studio for Electro-Instrumental Music (STEIM) in Amsterdam. After completing a PhD in Music Composition at the University of Chicago, he served as a postdoctoral Research Fellow in Creative Coding at the University of Huddersfield as part of the ERC-funded FluCoMa project, where he investigated the creative potential of machine learning algorithms. Moore is Faculty in Music, Technology, and Media at the Peabody Institute of Johns Hopkins University.

Alexander Schubert
Hamburg, Germany
Alexander Schubert studied bioinformatics and multimedia composition. He is a professor at the Hamburg University of Music and Drama and a freelance composer. Schubert explores the border between the acoustic and electronic worlds. In music composition, immersive installation, and staged pieces, he examines the interplay between the digital and the analog. He creates works that realize test settings or interaction spaces that question modes of perception and representation. Continuing topics in this field are authenticity and virtuality. The influence and framing of digital media on aesthetic views and communication are researched in a postdigital perspective. Recent research topics in his works are virtual reality, artificial intelligence, and online-mediated artworks. Schubert is a founding member of ensembles such as Decoder. His works have been performed more than 700 times in the last few years by numerous ensembles in over thirty countries.

Victor Shepardson
Ann Arbor, Michigan
Victor Shepardson is a researcher, technician, and musician. He is completing doctoral research in the Intelligent Instruments Lab at the University of Iceland, having previously

studied computer science and computer music and worked as a machine learning engineer. His current research approaches the lived experience of people with AI via design of, and performance with, new musical instruments. Victor has worked with artists including Nordic Affect, Jonathan Reus, Stefan Maier, Jenna Sutela, and Arca. His music searches electroacoustic and algorithmic assemblages for weird spaces, unanticipated instants, and absurd entanglements. His practice lately involves no-input mixing, bricolage signal processing, found objects, e-textiles, and generative MIDI.

Laetitia Sonami

Oakland, California

Laetitia Sonami's visionary contributions have expanded the boundaries of sound and technology over the course of several decades. She has demonstrated a deep engagement with gesture-based performance, real-time sound synthesis, and interactive systems. In 1991, she devised her first *lady's glove*. It became her primary instrument for the next twenty-five years, at which point she devised the Spring Spyre that applies machine learning to real-time control of audio synthesis. Her practice articulates a critical approach to technology—eschewing dominant paradigms of control and mastery in favor of embodied knowledge, contingency, and unpredictability. She has exhibited and performed at major international festivals and venues and has mentored and inspired many young artists with her approach to sound and technology as spaces of curious inquiry. In 2025, Sonami received the Giga-Herz Lifetime Achievement Award.

Nao Tokui

Tokyo, Japan

Nao Tokui is an artist and researcher based in Tokyo. While pursuing his PhD in Engineering at the University of Tokyo, he produced his first music album and singles using AI, including a 12-inch record with Nujabes, a legendary Japanese hip-hop producer. After completing his PhD research, he founded Qosmo, AI Creativity and Music Lab, in 2009. Since then, he has been actively working at the intersection of AI technology and art. Tokui and his team's works have been exhibited at renowned venues such as the Museum of Modern Art (MoMA) in New York and the Barbican Centre in London. Their performances have also been showcased at various music festivals, including MUTEK and Sónar+D. Additionally, he is leading the development of AI-based music instruments at his newly founded company, Neutone. In 2021, Tokui received the Okawa Publishing Award for his Japanese book on AI, art, and creativity. The book was translated and released in English as *Surfing Human Creativity with AI: A User's Guide* in November 2023.

Pierre Alexandre Tremblay

Lugano, Switzerland

Pierre Alexandre Tremblay is a composer and a performer on bass guitar and sound processing devices, in solo and within various ensembles. His concert music is released on *Empreintes DIGITALes*. He formally studied composition with Michel Tétreault, Marcelle

Deschênes, and Jonty Harrison; bass guitar with Jean-Guy Larin, Sylvain Bolduc, and Michel Donato; analysis with Michel Longtin and Stéphane Roy; and studio technique with Francis Dhomont, Robert Normandeau, and Jean Piché. After nineteen years in Huddersfield, where his last endeavor was the *Fluid Corpus Manipulation* project, Pierre Alexandre is now research professor of composition at the Conservatorio della Svizzera italiana (Lugano, Switzerland). He previously worked in popular music as producer and bassist and has a keen interest in creative coding. He enjoys spending time with his family, drinking oolong tea, gazing at dictionaries, reading prose, and taking long walks.

Prateek Verma
Mumbai, India
Prateek Verma is an AI researcher who has worked at Stanford University's Department of Electrical Engineering and the AI Lab. His work focuses on large language models, machine learning, and generative models for music and sound synthesis. His background is interdisciplinary, and he held a residency at Google X. Verma completed his undergraduate studies at the Indian Institute of Technology (IIT) Bombay, graduating with a degree in Electrical Engineering with a specialization in Signal Processing. Subsequently, he earned a master's degree from the Center for Computer Research in Music and Acoustics (CCRMA) at Stanford University, where his graduate work centered on the intersection of music, audio, AI, and acoustics.

Jennifer Walshe
London, United Kingdom
"The most original compositional voice to emerge from Ireland in the past 20 years" (*The Irish Times*), composer and performer Jennifer Walshe was born in Dublin, Ireland. Her music has been commissioned, broadcast, and performed all over the world. She has been the recipient of fellowships and prizes from the Foundation for Contemporary Arts, New York; the DAAD Berliner Künstlerprogramm; the Internationales Musikinstitut, Darmstadt; and Akademie Schloss Solitude, among others. *A Late Anthology of Early Music Vol. 1: Ancient to Renaissance*, her third solo album, was released on Tetbind in 2020. The album uses AI to rework canonical works from early Western music history. *A Late Anthology* was chosen as an album of the year in *The Irish Times*, *The Wire*, and *The Quietus*. Her book *13 Ways of Looking at AI, Art & Music* was published by Unsound in 2025. Walshe is professor of composition at the University of Oxford. Her work has been profiled in many publications including *The New Yorker*.

Ge Wang
Palo Alto, California
Ge Wang is an associate professor at Stanford University in the Center for Computer Research in Music and Acoustics (CCRMA) and a Senior Fellow and the Associate Director of Research (Arts & Humanities) at the Stanford Institute for Human-centered Artificial Intelligence and Data Science. He specializes in the art of design and computer music, researching programming languages and interactive software design for music, interaction

design, mobile music, laptop orchestras, expressive design of virtual reality, aesthetics of music technology design, and education at the intersection of computer science and music. Ge is the author of the ChucK music programming language and the founding director of the Stanford Laptop Orchestra (SLOrk). He is also the co-founder of Smule (reaching over 200 million users) and the designer of the iPhone's Ocarina and Magic Piano. Wang is a 2016 Guggenheim Fellow and the author of *Artful Design: Technology in Search of the Sublime*—a book on design and technology, art and life.

FOREWORD

John Chowning

Disclaimer/Declaration

I am not an intellectual, nor a scholar, nor a scientist, nor a composer. I'm a musician who loves to compose music using computers. My programming skills are modest, but I am persistent and don't give up. As Max Mathews once told me, "I write my own programs so that if I have a problem, I know who to ask," which I too follow; but I will ask for help if I'm really stumped, as many of my colleagues know.

Since my early years, I have cared only about music and have been well-trained. I am self-motivated and inspired by the people in the world I choose to inhabit and, through circumstances, have found myself (military service in Europe eight years after World War II was eye-opening for an 18-year-old). Sometimes I have insights and see possibilities that others miss; for example, an unexplored terrain for composing in "Tones and Tuning with Stretched Partials,"[1] research on prehistoric and ancient subsurface reverberant spaces (Chauvet Cave in France, Chavín de Huántar in Peru, and the Longyou Grottoes in China).

Context

Since 1964, when David Poole convinced John McCarthy to grant me limited access to the Stanford Artificial Intelligence Lab (SAIL), I have had doubts about the extravagant claims surrounding Artificial Intelligence and human-like cognition. So did most SAIL researchers, including McCarthy himself, who coined the term "Artificial Intelligence" in 1955. He established SAIL in 1963, with lavish funding from the Department of Defense's Advanced Research Projects Agency (DARPA). Les Earnest, the SAIL administrator, was able to find the brightest researchers worldwide. I was schooled by these researchers, who would cheerfully answer my many, and often naïve, questions. Joined by other composers and researchers, we in the Computer Music Project[2] were, in a sense, students, and we found these colleagues to be patient teachers as they watched us build a new means for making and representing music. We understood that those with motivation and perseverance, but no special competence in building electronic devices, were presented with a means to engage with a medium—at a high level of abstraction—that was a defining musical advance in the twentieth century: music composed for loudspeakers.

* * *

Last year in Vicenza, during an informal lecture for about fifty musicians and composers, an enthusiastic participant asked me for my thoughts on AI and composing music. It did not surprise me, as AI is on everyone's mind. I don't "play to the audience" when a serious question is asked, so I thought for a moment, anticipating my answer would disappoint, and replied, "I care as much about AI and composing as Katie Ledecky (current 800-meter and 1500-meter freestyle Olympic champion, and graduate of Stanford) would care about a robot swimmer that could halve her time. She swims because she loves to swim, and I compose because I love to compose." To my great surprise, my audience burst into applause and cheers!

Of course, AI can accomplish many tasks in music. In the process of composing a work that is a complex "remix," I want to know all instances of notes in the reference work, including their frequency of occurrence, octave, note duration, etc., and create a histogram. I could do this myself, but at a great cost in time and labor. However, with a few prompts, I can ask ChatGPT to complete it in an hour or so of my time. This kind of useful application of AI is, of course, widespread; for example, medical doctors use AI to scan for details in thousands of images in milliseconds—a task they could not complete by themselves in a lifetime.

While composing another work and under the pressure of a firm deadline, I decided to ask ChatGPT to "help me out." With great attention to detail, I created prompt after prompt until the *few-shot prompt* finally became the *multi-shot prompt*, to the point that I ended up composing the work myself. With ChatGPT there was no magic, only the commonplace.

In my experience, generative AI is still far from having the same creative power in music composition as it does in language, where it can create credible stories and, more questionably, poetry. Poetic inference is not the same as logical inference. The reason may be that large language models, poetry, and stories share the same abstract domain—text. In contrast, the waves that enter our ear canals can be several abstractions away from compositional ideas → notation: *representation in electronic music* [my emphasis] → instrumentation: *synthesis/processing* → performance: *sound projection* → sound waves that enter our ears. Where aesthetics is the overriding and most significant abstraction in the chain (it's difficult to quantify and implement), we simply *know* when it's right.

Cartesian dualism—separation of mind and body. First, we can agree that both composing and listening to music involve human cognition. Now let's consider this thought experiment. We have an up-to-date robot packed with as many forms of AI as are available: Generative AI, Predictive AI, Agentic AI, and Multimodal AI. So, our robot can hear, see, and remember.

We want to evoke emotions to determine if our robot can respond as we humans do. Literature, cinema, art, and music can evoke profound emotions that bring tears. However, our robot has no tear ducts. We can think of music that evokes a sensual response, such as Rachmaninoff's *Piano Concerto No. 2 in C minor*: specifically, the slow movement is noted for its soaring, passionate nature. And some of Wagner's works (e.g., *Tristan und Isolde*, the Prelude) were intended to be erotic, according to some scholars. Our robot has no sexual apparatus; however, *it is packed with motor activators throughout its body*!

Frisson! Is there music we can play for our robot that would cause its motor activators to shiver (called an "eargasm" by some), as the pleasure center equivalent to dopamine coursing across synapses in our brain is activated in our robot? We play music for our robot. For me, the fugato near the end of the slow movement in Beethoven's *Eroica* Symphony and

Ligeti's *Lux Aeterna* are examples. We ask our friends which music gives them the shivers. We play more music and wait for action from the motor activators ...

> and more music and wait ...
> and more music and wait ...
> knowing that its neural net is learning about itself ...
> how much music do we present ...
> and how many days, months, years, do we wait ...
> until we see our robot shiver?

Notes

1 Houtsma, Adrianus J. M., Thomas D. Rossing, and Willem M. Wagemakers. "Tones and Tuning with Stretched Partials." In *Auditory Demonstrations*, 70–71. Eindhoven, Netherlands: Technische Universiteit Eindhoven, Institute for Perception Research, 1987. https://homes.esat.kuleuven.be/~compi/demos/AuditoryDemonstrations/402660.pdf.

2 Buchanan, Bruce G. "Introduction to the COMTEX Microfiche Editor of Memos from the Stanford Artificial Intelligence Laboratory." *AI Magazine* 4, no. 4 (Winter 1983): 37–41. https://doi.org/10.1609/aimag.v4i4.416.

ACKNOWLEDGMENTS

We extend our deepest gratitude to all the contributors to this volume for their creativity, forward-thinking ideas, and generosity of time. A special thanks goes to John Chowning for writing a spirited foreword, especially as it came on the heels of his receiving a Technical Grammy Award.

At Routledge, our wonderful editors—Hannah Rowe, Evie Evans, Emily Tagg, and Danielle Zarfati—provided invaluable guidance and support, for which we are immensely grateful. Our heartfelt thanks go to Simona Fitcal for creating the beautiful and distinctive cover design that brings this book to life. We are also indebted to Saleema Waraich for so graciously providing materials on behalf of the late Charles Hiroshi Garrett.

We acknowledge the generous funding provided by Bradford Orr, Arthur F. Thurnau Professor of Physics and Associate Vice President in Natural Sciences/Engineering at the Office of the Vice President for Research, University of Michigan, which helped meet the publishing requirements for one of our contributors.

Our home institutions provided a vital and encouraging environment for this research: the Center for Computer Research in Music and Acoustics (CCRMA) at Stanford University and the Department of Performing Arts Technology at the School of Music, Theatre & Dance at the University of Michigan.

Finally, we offer our love and appreciation to our families for their unwavering support during the editing of this book.

1

PRELUDE

Personal and Peculiar

Julie Zhu and Constantin Basica

DOI: 10.4324/9781003615873-1

Metaphors for artificial intelligence (AI) abound in the media. AI is a *wave*, and you can either ride it or get swept up in it regardless. AI is an *agent*: an assistant or interlocutor, nefarious or benevolent—who can say? AI is a *magnifying glass*, a *telescope*, an *atlas*, or other wayfaring device, because who isn't lost in one way or another?

These metaphors range from imperfect to bad, but mostly they're fearmongering. AI is either out to get you and your livelihood or it's the biggest thing you missed out on. AI is not one thing, but many, and often in the most ridiculous juxtapositions; for example, fanfiction, gunk, and boobs—as Jennifer Walshe observes in *13 Ways of Looking at AI, Art & Music*—or amphetamine and cancer in Alexander Schubert's collection of claims at the end of this book.

But probably the first metaphor that comes to mind is that AI is a *black box*. Something goes in and another thing comes out, and we don't know what happens in between. But that is the opposite of how musician-coders in this book feel about the AI they're creating for themselves. On a neural level, perhaps some connections are still unknown, but on a conceptual level, artists know what they want and are making the tools to get there.

What do artists want? Well, what artists have wanted since the beginning. Freedom, creativity, and good tools. Pierre Alexandre Tremblay argues that AI can't help with freedom—a quandary for society and capitalism. George Lewis is adamant that the creativity of artists should be protected and nurtured, separate from whatever technology they use. Can AI be a good tool? And what makes a tool good?

When faced with black-box AI models, artists experience unease in deciding how much agency to renounce during the creative process. Moreover, the fact that the dataset may have been unethically sourced or may contain significant, unstated bias is off-putting, since creative decisions may be embedded in the system based on that obscure training. In their study on "Human–AI Music Creation," Newman, Morris, and Lee reached the conclusion that small, personalized AI systems based on "ethically sourced data" are more likely to be adopted by artists in their search for creativity-enhancing AI interaction.[1] Nao Tokui talks about these ideas in our interview, saying, "Artists don't need generic models or universal models."

Our chapter contributors have gone a step further and come up with a diverse array of AI tools that prioritize their specific interests and needs. They're surprising, innovative, and you'll hear about them in the creator's own words: how the artists got to the problem in the first place, and how the artists use the tools they made. They also share stories about applications in performance—as solo practice, collaborative music-making, and as systems offered to others to explore, like Victor Shepardson does with *Notochord*.

We hope this book is the opposite of a black box. While not an introductory course on music and AI, the mix of chapters from coder-musicians and interviews from visionary practitioners at least elucidates and makes transparent the ways of thinking and artistic choices that go into an artist making good tools for themselves.

Coder-Musicians / Musician-Coders

In a 2019 article,[2] Rebecca Fiebrink pointed out that, while machine learning (ML) techniques had been in use in music and the performing arts before the recent boom of generative AI, there was still a scarcity of educational offers for creative practitioners (artists, musicians, designers, and game developers) wanting to engage with ML. Today, the educational landscape of machine learning for artists has exploded: courses at universities and research centers,[3] online classes and workshops, conferences,[4] hackathons, meetups, and community-driven education on social media and other video-sharing platforms[5] (including an online course by Fiebrink herself on Kadenze).[6]

Simultaneously, more and more musicians, especially composers, have started experimenting with AI. It is no longer a niche, but a major technological shift that cannot be ignored—one that has spread beyond the computer music field. As Walshe noticed in our interview, "an awful lot of composers [are] putting AI in their bio." If some of this can be attributed to what Ge Wang frames as AI FOMO,[7] there is also evidence of deeper engagement with an increasing number of artists and institutions developing applications and libraries that are intended for easier adoption by musicians without a computer science background. Among these, IRCAM[8] has been a primary supplier of ML-aided algorithmic composition tools, such as MuBu, Somax2, Dicy2, CataRT, and others. The creators of FluCoMa[9] (two of whom contribute to this book: Pierre Alexandre Tremblay and Ted Moore) have focused their energy more on community building in recent years; similarly, the community around Fiebrink's groundbreaking and user-friendly Wekinator encourages widespread participation starting as early as grade school. The existence of large language models (LLMs), too, has likely helped ease musicians' anxiety for working with code—thanks to their ability to help with software and library setups as well as troubleshooting. CJ Carr (of Dadabots) was particularly excited in his interview about vibe coding and its potential to burst open any real or perceived gates in computer science for artists.

We believe that when artists have control of their tools (systems, instruments, programming environments), it's better for everyone. The phrase *human-in-the-loop* is tossed around as a publicity tool by the thousands of new AI companies, but *human-in-the-loop* is only a performative gesture when they are beholden to profit.

These generative AI tools exhibit a level of creativity that's impressive to artists. But there is a paradox, John McCormack writes, between what artists see as human creativity and what "big tech" companies imbue into their models: a cocktail of "late capitalist ideals of efficiency, productivity, cost-effectiveness, and automation, sugar-coated in the rhetoric of personal empowerment and technological advancement for its own sake."[10]

That resonates with some of the somber remarks by Walshe, Tremblay, and Wang in our interviews. They repeatedly allude to the late-capitalistic roots of the current development of generative AI as a hazard to traditional values of human creativity. Eduardo Navas likens this shift toward AI "art" and "creativity"—fueled by ethically fraught corporate principles of optimization and speed—to a threat to humans' ability for *empathy*, which is a slow process by contrast.[11]

Witness the frenzy of easily accessible AI tools online whose output borders on deepfakes by offering to revive and animate vintage photographs, to bring your favorite dead singer to life (and even sing you a personalized song in the style of another recording artist, alive or dead), or to place you in a video with famous actors getting a coffee. Add to that the hungry mouth of social media, an accelerator and consumer of these tools' outputs, creating an infinite churn of content.

These commercial music-generating AI tools can often be tested for free, before the platform attempts to lock you into a subscription (or serves you ads). There is a deceiving impression that these tools (and more specifically, their companies) lend to users: the promise of bypassing one's inability to put ideas into practice by offering tools to harness creativity. But "that feeling of empowerment wears off very quickly when you see that anyone can do the same thing."[12] No surprise: one still needs to have original ideas. Replication by statistics—what the machine is especially good at—is the opposite of creativity.

But in the hands of creative humans, these generative tools and AI models have the possibility to become powerful instruments—whether as inspiration, material for further manipulation, or partners in performance. And the good news is that there is a growing number of people manually responding to pull requests on their open-source GitHub page for that weird AI tool they designed themselves.

The Small-Scale Resistance

It is hard to ignore a red thread of *David vs. Goliath* in this book. The chapters present musicians who take matters into their own hands and show alternatives to the bleak vision of dominant platform companies regarding creative machines. In a podcast interview, Suno CEO Mikey Shulman pontificated that "it's not really enjoyable to make music now," arguing that the required time, practice, and skill make the traditional process unpleasant for most people[13] (and as a result making himself the subject of online ridicule among musicians). He wants to make music creation "accessible" to a billion people by removing these "barriers" through AI.

Anyone who makes music, even just casually, will tell you that it's the *process* that's fun about making music. Celeste Betancur Gutiérrez manifests that spark of creation in all of her live-generating process scores in the chapter about *Pandora's Dream*. The journey of learning offers opportunities to fine-tune musical ideas and come up with new ones; and getting better at something is inherently satisfying. Prompt-generating songs wholesale is at best a parlor trick, yet millions of these songs with fake artist names are hiding in Spotify (on Spotify-suggested playlists) because the company then doesn't have to pay royalties.[14]

It's okay to be angry. But that anger should be directed at humans, not at the machine learning model. It's the corporate executives who manipulate the technology to replace humans instead of helping humans. Quick iteration is the name of the game; productivity is the goal. But music quality? Meaningful creation processes? Transcendent musical experiences?

Dystopian views on musical AI abound in the corporate world. Scott Cohen, a British music executive, thinks of "music today [as] not creative. There are only twelve notes in the Western music scale, and how many more ways are there to reassemble those notes? A machine can create all the possible combinations."[15] What then logically follows? Humans can retire from creating and recording music; now let the commercial GenAI platforms train on their work (without any credit or compensation, of course—it's all "fair use") and generate a never-ending stream of songs.

A similarly skewed view of music happens in much of musical AI research today. Hernandez-Olivan and Beltran, for example, adopt the copyright-related definition of music as "a succession of pitches or rhythms, or both, in some definite patterns."[16] Like many other AI researchers, they assume that music composition can be categorized under clear rules that predominantly abide by Western music theory. And this is convenient because large-scale AI models need large datasets, many of which contain Western music genres (classical, pop, rock, jazz, etc.). But the human musical experience is not limited to the tonal music paradigm, to the commercial music world, or even to pitch-based and melody-driven music structures.

Our chapter writers show a different way to work with AI. By integrating machine learning algorithms into their idiosyncratic creation process, these artists expand the limits of their practice and probe new grounds. They *play* with their AI tools—both as in *perform* and *tinker*. Instead of asking, "What is the best AI tool out there to compose music for me?" the artists in this book ask, "What kind of music are we trying to compose?"; "Why do we need to integrate machine creativity into our human composition and performance?"; and "How do we feel about the implications of AI-generated music in our work?"

This experimental creative spirit builds on the traditions laid out by avant-garde composers and computer music pioneers of the recent past. Some of them are present in this book as interviewees, sharing insights from their work and voicing concerns or hopes around this growing field of Music and AI.

It is important to note, however, that most of the machine learning frameworks proposed by the chapter contributors are driven by personal creative needs and not intended for adoption on a large scale. They are models for artistic experimentation that demonstrate one possible path forward for human creativity and artistic process into an era where the entire human experience is poised to be influenced by AI.

Cue doom and gloom potentialities, like socioeconomic collapse, misinformation and political chaos, unchecked surveillance and bias, environmental disaster, human extinction—don't worry, we have people looking into that …

But this does raise the question: why play with AI in the first place if it has the potential to cause so much damage and has wrecked livelihoods already? Our answer lies in a guiding principle that understanding is power, and though fear is a forceful driver, it usually doesn't yield the best long-term outcome for everyone.

How can we formulate guiding principles for human-aligned musical AI? Molly Jones and Ted Moore argue for empowering individuals with an understanding of the basic principles of AI and how it works as a *starting point.* Holly Herndon shows that one of the good uses of AI is to create communities that share knowledge freely—an idea that inspires cautious optimism about sharing the musical landscape with our new intelligent machines.

The Opposite of Fear Is Knowledge and Understanding

In *AI Ethics*, Mark Coeckelbergh describes the spectrum of enthusiasm and fear regarding AI in music: some see it as a panacea for human problems, while others see it as a serious existential threat. He goes on to say that, "AI is already happening today and it is pervasive, often invisibly embedded in our day-to-day tools." Validating Wang's concern about the unintended consequences of deploying well-intended AI technologies into the world in unchecked ways, Coeckelbergh asks: "Who shapes the future of AI?"[17]

The chapter contributors and interviewees in this book are part of the answer. By engaging critically with AI technologies and investigating the potential of personalized tools, these artists help lay the groundwork for the next generation of musicians whose practices will develop with embedded AI. By scrutinizing existing models and turning them inside out with their own hands, some of these artists exemplify the potential of switching from a passive consumption of black-box tools to an active process of personalization of open-source frameworks, revealing their potential and their limitations.

In our interview, Laetitia Sonami shared that the most interesting part about working with generative AI was its *failures*. This is echoed in Kelsey Cotton's and Hugo Flores García's chapters, where AI *mishearings* turn into fruitful creative devices. Many artists are fascinated with the mistakes a machine makes. Massive Attack's Robert Del Naja, for example, emphasized the appeal of AI errors when talking about the *Mezzanine* collaboration with Mick Grierson, in which a neural network generated thousands of remixes.[18] So, AI gives us slop, but it just takes a different perspective to see its worth. Aberration can offer unexpected results, and surprise can be inspiring.

The philosopher Slavoj Žižek has been obsessed with trash for most of his career, proclaiming that we should embrace the landfill to understand the true nature of our desires and the hidden costs of our "ideological fantasies." The path to love, he says, is to "see perfection in imperfection itself."[19] LLMs (the earlier ones) have been trained on vast amounts of human data—if we are to love humanity, we must love our detritus too.[20]

Yet we acknowledge that it takes a certain kind of artist to work with trash. AI is not for everyone in music, nor should it be. It takes a leap of faith for an artist to try out a new tool, let alone adopt it into their workflow. But we think everyone should understand how it works—its pitfalls and affordances—if only to turn more toward handcraft and the messiness of live performance (yes!).

And we acknowledge that even if "intentionality remains (it seems) the exceptional realm of humans, at least for now,"[21] what software engineers intended for an artistic tool doesn't necessarily pan out. Thomas Marrinan et al. posit that "a distinction must be made between humans using AI to assist in the creation of art and the use of generative AI to replace humans when creating art." Their envisioned use of the generative system they develop is to be a human-enhancing tool rather than human-replacing, but in the proof of concept, the examples they give of the work are essentially removing the human creator from the loop and transferring that role to a prompt-based model. AI researchers may very well have good intentions and moral grounds while also contributing to the development of the kind of systems they are opposing in the first place—all for the sake of progress.

That's why we wanted to put together a book of coder-musicians who designed their systems with themselves as artists in mind. The artists here are uniquely positioned to dispel general, black cloud fears about AI, especially about *replacement* in the arts. The key is not taking away from the creative process but adding to it and strengthening musical relationships along the way. Nothing new under the stars: Musicians such as Lewis have emphasized the importance of treating machines as mediators for human–human music-making since the dawn of computer music. As with all other technologies used by musicians, artists must shape the AI tools that will in turn shape their work and our collective musical future. Doga Cavdir already traces such "shifts in creative practice" by interviewing the contributing artists in the book's conclusive chapter.

Artist Paul DeMarinis, upon hearing about this book project, wondered rhetorically how a publication in this fast-evolving field could stay relevant. Most likely, in the following years, new technologies will shadow early-stage AI explorations, including the ones presented in this book. Nevertheless, despite the natural obsolescence intrinsic to these systems, it is the lessons learned by the people in the making process that we think are worth sharing. Not beholden to investors, artists and musicians don't need to constantly develop new ways to extract data and flatten human interaction into polarizing clickbait for profit. So, if we lend our heads, hearts, and hands[22] to our (open-source) communities—even one as esoteric as computer music—we'll be stronger collectively to face the unknown.

Notes

1 Newman, Morris, and Lee, "Human–AI Music Creation."
2 Fiebrink, "Machine Learning Education."
3 University of Oxford, "Generative AI"; Designlab, "Get Started with AI."
4 "Machine Learning for Creativity and Design."
5 LABASAD, "Online Master in Generative Artificial Intelligence."
6 Kadenze, "Machine Learning for Musicians and Artists."
7 FOMO is an abbreviation for "fear of missing out."
8 IRCAM (French: Institut de recherche et coordination acoustique/musique; English: Institute for Research and Coordination in Acoustics/Music) is a major public research center in Paris, France focused on music and science.
9 Tremblay et al., "The Fluid Corpus Manipulation Toolbox."
10 McCormack, "Autonomy, Intention, Performativity," 250.
11 Navas, "AI Ethics, Aesthetics, Art and Artistry."
12 McCormack,. "Autonomy, Intention, Performativity," 242.
13 Griffiths, "It's Not Really Enjoyable."
14 Bogost, "Nobody Cares If Music Is Real Anymore."
15 Clancy, "The Future," 149.
16 Hernandez-Olivan and Beltran, "Music Composition with Deep Learning," 1.
17 Coeckelbergh, *AI Ethics*, 7.
18 Armstrong, "Massive Attack Coded Their Album."
19 "Slavoj Žižek."
20 Since "creative" AI feeds not only on human-produced artworks and media, but also on the massive and fast-paced crop of AI-generated artifacts, we will soon reach (or maybe we are already at) Jean Baudrillard's final stage of simulation: the output given to a human prompter "has no relation to any reality whatsoever: it is its own pure simulacrum." See Baudrillard, *Simulation and Simulacra.*
22 As Yuval Noah Harari recently stated in The New York Times, "This is the first time in history nobody has any idea what the world will look like in 10 years—what the job market will look like, what social relations will look like, et cetera. So hedge your bets. Don't focus on a narrow subject like coding. Give equal importance to your head (intellectual skills), your heart (social skills), and your hands (motor skills). It is in the combination of these three that humans still have a large advantage over AI. Also, try to enjoy the ride." See "Where is A.I. Taking Us?"

Bibliography

Armstrong, Stephen. "Massive Attack Coded Their Album *Mezzanine* into DNA." *Wired*, June 27, 2018. https://www.wired.com/story/massive-attack-mezzanine-dna.

Baudrillard, Jean. *Simulacra and Simulation*. Translated by Sheila Glaser. The Body in Theory: Histories of Cultural Materialism. Ann Arbor, MI: University of Michigan Press. 1994.

Bogost, Ian. "Nobody Cares If Music Is Real Anymore." *The Atlantic*, July 4, 2025. https://www.theatlantic.com/technology/archive/2025/07/velvet-sundown-ai-band-spotify/683410.

Clancy, Martin. "The Future: Interview with Scott Cohen." In *Artificial Intelligence and Music Ecosystem*, edited by Martin Clancy, 148–164. New York, NY: Routledge, 2022.

Coeckelbergh, Mark. *AI Ethics*. The MIT Press Essential Knowledge Series. Cambridge, MA: The MIT Press, 2020. https://doi.org/10.7551/mitpress/12549.001.0001.

Designlab. "Get Started with AI for Design." *Designlab*. Accessed February 3, 2026. https://designlab.com/advanced/get-started-ai-for-design.

Fiebrink, Rebecca. "Machine Learning Education for Artists, Musicians, and Other Creative Practitioners." *ACM Transactions on Computing Education (TOCE)* 19, no. 4 (2019): 1–32. https://doi.org/10.1145/3294008.

Griffiths, Daniel. "'It's Not Really Enjoyable to Make Music Now,' Says the CEO of an AI Music-Making Platform, and He Wants to Help." *MusicRadar*. January 17, 2025. https://www.musicradar.com/music-industry/its-not-really-enjoyable-to-make-music-now-says-the-ceo-of-an-ai-music-making-platform-and-he-wants-to-help.

Hernandez-Olivan, Carlos, and Jose R. Beltran. "Music Composition with Deep Learning: A Review." Preprint, last revised on September 7, 2021. arXiv:2108.12290v2. https://arxiv.org/abs/2108.12290.

IRCAM. Accessed December 26, 2025. https://www.ircam.fr/lircam.

Kadenze. "Machine Learning for Musicians and Artists." *Kadenze*. Accessed February 3, 2026. https://www.kadenze.com/courses/machine-learning-for-musicians-and-artists/info.

LABASAD. "Online Master in Generative Artificial Intelligence for Creatives." *LABASAD Barcelona School of Arts & Design*. Accessed February 3, 2026. https://www.labasad.com/en/master/online-master-in-generative-artificial-intelligence-for-creatives.

"Machine Learning for Creativity and Design." In *NeurIPS 2022 Workshop on Machine Learning for Creativity and Design*. Accessed February 3, 2026. https://neuripscreativityworkshop.github.io/2022.

Marcus, Gary, and Ernest Davis. *Rebooting AI: Building Artificial Intelligence We Can Trust*. New York, NY: Pantheon Books, 2019.

McCormack, John. "Autonomy, Intention, Performativity: Navigating the AI Divide." In *Choreomata: Performance and Performativity after AI*, edited by Roberto Alonso Trillo and Marek Poliks, 242–257. Boca Raton, FL: CRC Press, 2024.

Navas, Eduardo. "AI Ethics, Aesthetics, Art and Artistry." In *Handbook on the Ethics of Artificial Intelligence*, edited by David J. Gunkel, 173–186. Cheltenham, UK: Edward Elgar Publishing, 2024. https://doi.org/10.4337/9781803926728.00017.

Newman, Michele, Lidia Morris, and Jin Ha Lee. "Human–AI Music Creation: Understanding the Perceptions and Experiences of Music Creators for Ethical and Productive Collaboration." In *Proceedings of the 23rd International Society for Music Information Retrieval Conference (ISMIR)*, 733–40. Milan, Italy: ISMIR, 2023. https://archives.ismir.net/ismir2023/paper/000008.pdf.

"Slavoj Žižek: The Path to Love Is through Trash." YouTube video, 0:48. Posted by "Žižek & So On Podcast," March 8, 2022. https://www.youtube.com/watch?v=eQmc039N0jE.

Tremblay, Pierre Alexandre, Owen Green, Gerard Roma, James Bradbury, Ted Moore, Jacob Hart, and Alex Harker. *The Fluid Corpus Manipulation Toolbox* (vol. 1). Zenodo, July 14, 2022. https://10.5281/zenodo.6834643.

University of Oxford. "Generative AI for Creative Professionals." *Department for Continuing Education*. Accessed February 3, 2026. https://lifelong-learning.ox.ac.uk/courses/generative-ai-for-creative-professionals.

"Where Is A.I. Taking Us? Eight Leading Thinkers Share Their Visions." *The New York Times*, February 2, 2026. https://www.nytimes.com/interactive/2026/02/02/opinion/ai-future-leading-thinkers-survey.html.

2

MOVEMENT I

Machine Learning at the Artist Scale

Molly Jones

DOI: 10.4324/9781003615873-2

Introduction: Artists Using Machine Learning

Artists are well positioned to innovate with machine learning. Artists dedicate time, thought, money, and effort to mastering divergent skills and techniques in the service of our creative work. Any artist who has learned how to play a musical instrument, dress a loom, use a camera, or compose forms at micro, macro, and multiple scales—that is, any artist—has engaged in a practice requiring diligence, problem-solving, and the building of technique through iteration and play. Artists are engineers; we meet the challenges and opportunities that arise when the creative process encounters material and financial limitations, and we realize our own designs through technical practice. Because machine learning (ML) encompasses a set of technical practices no more intricate than designing a weaving pattern or orchestrating a chamber composition, artists, with our disciplined practice and commitment to innovation despite and through limitations, are well positioned to build original creative work with machine learning and to contribute to the design of art-focused AI tools. I hope this chapter provides some foundational information on how you could begin to use machine learning in your own creative projects (if you so choose) and inspiration from other artists. Ultimately, I hope that your own ideas and projects expand far beyond what's presented here.

One Journey with Machine Learning and Music

I discovered that artists are engineers accidentally, by becoming both. From 2011 to 2019, I was a saxophonist and composer playing free jazz and Balkan brass shows in Detroit and Chicago while making ends meet with an array of part-time jobs: massage therapist, dog walker, Lyft driver ... At a certain point, I wanted more stability, and I enrolled in a coding bootcamp in hopes of finding a tech job. I did land a role as a data engineer, but more importantly, I found immediate artistic applications for the computational tools I used at work. I learned about random forest models, and I trained them to complete abstract drawings. I learned about classification, and I began ideating a multimedia performance in which instrumental timbres trigger changes in graphic scores. I trained my first generative model, a DCGAN[1] for image generation, and I learned I could adapt the model to generate audio instead of images. I began generating sounds. In January 2021, I participated in an artist residency at Ragdale, in northern Illinois. Instead of composing music for a jazz trio as planned, I found myself spending two weeks training and optimizing an audio-generating neural network. Machine learning presented itself as a palette of tools to explore for compositional applications. What it took to learn programming and ML was a few months of regular practice, the same discipline I had built as a student of the saxophone.

My ongoing interest in incorporating machine learning into multimedia compositions eventually led me to a couple more residencies and a PhD—but engaging with machine learning in the first place didn't require a PhD. Beginning to train my own models required time, patience with myself and the computer, and, most importantly, imagining the potential creative applications of ML. Artists are good at imagining potential creative applications of technologies. Artists are also good at hacking, misusing, and testing the boundaries of technologies. I wanted to see how other artists were engaging with machine learning, so I started an event series called Chicago Creative Machines to bring together artists and ML enthusiasts and build community. I'll discuss Chicago Creative Machines later in this chapter. First, I'll share some of the basics of machine learning, because I found it empowering to learn something about these tools. If you're already comfortable with machine learning, please feel free to skip to the section titled "Data."

Machine Learning Basics

Defining Machine Learning and AI

Here, I'll offer my definitions of *artificial intelligence* (AI) and *machine learning* (ML) and talk about how they relate to each other. AI is a whole field, while machine learning is a specific set of computational techniques. Machine learning techniques are a common part of AI research in the twenty-first century.

I define *artificial intelligence* as the use of technology to perform tasks requiring human intelligence. This definition of AI pushes the work down the road, because now I have to define human intelligence. I can't do that—it's too involved. The field of AI is a centuries-long research effort to try to define and replicate human intelligence. AI is cross-disciplinary, incorporating philosophy, neuroscience, computer science, mathematics, engineering, literature, robotics, and more. I'd argue that AI research began millennia ago, when Egyptian and Persian inventors created water-powered devices that automated tasks previously performed by humans, like striking the time or blowing air through organ pipes.[2] The two scholars who designed the first artificial neural network in 1944, Warren McCulloch and Walter Pitts, were neuroscientists studying human neural networks.[3] AI history is inseparable from the study of human abilities and intelligence.

In the twenty-first century, when people talk about AI, we're typically talking about a specific set of computational techniques called *machine learning.* Machine learning techniques have been developed since the mid-twentieth century to enable computers to learn algorithms on their own.[4] The three mathematical pillars of machine learning—statistics, calculus, and matrix mathematics—have been around since the 300s BCE (matrix math) and the 1600s CE (statistics and calculus), but it took until the second half of the twentieth century for computer hardware to be powerful enough to realize ML algorithms in practice.[5]

Here's how machine learning relates to traditional computer programming: A traditional programmer types a program into the computer line by line; the resulting algorithm takes an input and runs each sequential line of calculations in order to generate an output. An ML programmer, on the other hand, doesn't know the algorithm in detail ahead of time. The ML programmer provides the computer with matched pairs of input and output data, and the computer learns the algorithm that will transform the inputs into the desired outputs through iterative, incremental statistical calculations. This iterative, incremental learning process is called *training* a machine learning model. Machine learning is useful in situations where we know the kinds of things we want to get out of an algorithm, but the algorithm is too complicated or time-consuming to type out in a line-by-line fashion.

Classical Machine Learning and Deep Learning

Machine learning models can be categorized into *classical machine learning* models and *deep learning* models. The former predate the latter. There is a whole assortment of classical machine learning models, including *random forest*, *K-nearest neighbors*, *support vector machines* (SVM), *K-means clustering*, *Gaussian mixture models*, *ensemble methods*, and many more. *Deep learning* (DL) models, also known as *neural networks*, are arrangements of artificial neurons. Deep learning models provide the power and flexibility to model more complex relationships than many classical ML models can. At the moment, when people talk about AI, they're often talking about deep learning models. Deep learning usually requires more computational resources than classical ML.[6] For different creative tasks, either classical ML or DL models might prove useful, depending on the volume of data involved, the complexity of the task, and the computer(s) available.

Neural Networks

Neurons are the building blocks out of which deep learning models, or neural networks, are built. *Neural networks* are bunches of neurons connected in different configurations. Neural network structures get really complicated, but neurons are mostly all the same. It's possible to understand neural networks at different levels of detail: a 30,000-foot view, a 10,000-foot view, a 500-foot view, etc. A close-up, finely detailed understanding of neural networks isn't necessary to use them. It's possible, even preferable, to develop an intuitive sense of how a neural network behaves in practice without focusing on the mathematical details. As you need to gain a more fine-grained understanding of a neural network to accomplish a task, you can look up more details. However, I want to walk through a single neuron in relatively close detail. Neurons are the basis of almost every twenty-first-century AI model. If you're like me, and you like understanding how things work from the ground up, you may find it empowering to learn how a neuron is constructed.

One Neuron in Detail

A neuron has an input, an output, and a sequence of mathematical calculations between them. See diagram (a) in Figure 2.1. The input to a neuron is any kind of digital data. Anything that can be represented as numbers in a computer (text, color hex codes, multichannel

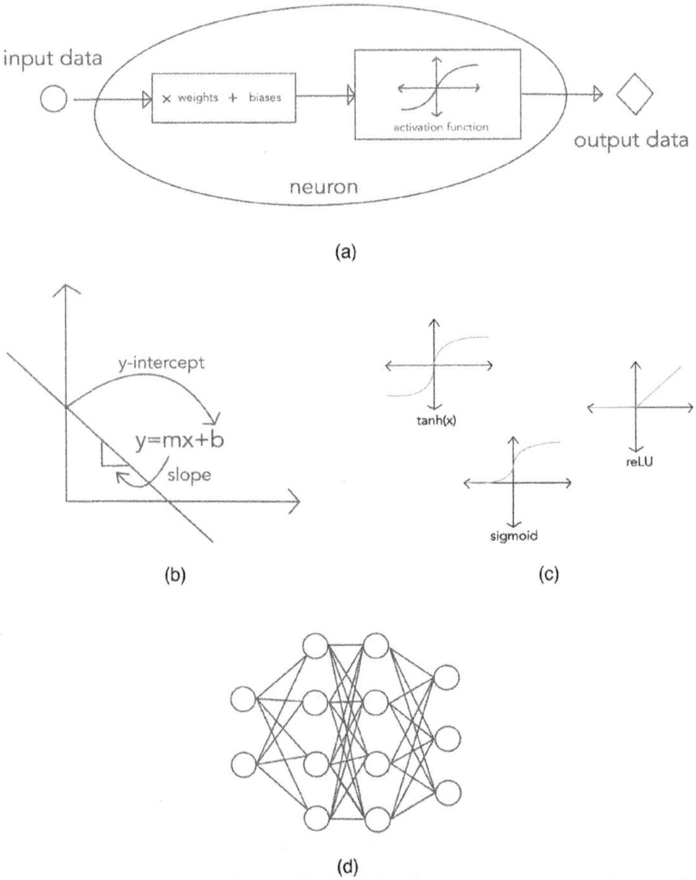

Figure 2.1 An artificial neuron, its components, and its context. (a) An artificial neuron. (b) A linear function. (c) Common activation functions. (d) A deep feedforward neural network, the most basic neural network architecture. Each circle represents a neuron, and the lines (read from left to right) indicate where the output of one neuron becomes the input to another neuron.

audio, photographs, weaving patterns, room dimensions, motion sensor data, etc.) can be the input to a neuron. The output of a neuron is also any kind of digital data. The kind of data a neuron takes into its input does not have to be the same kind of data it produces as output. You can have a neuron whose input is a photograph and output is stereo sound, or vice versa. A neuron can map any kind of data onto any other kind of data. A neuron is a mathematical machine that converts one kind of data into another.

Now, let's talk about the mathematical calculations that turn a neuron's input into its output. There are two mathematical steps. The first is a linear function, and the second is an activation function. To imagine these mathematical steps, it's helpful to think of the data not as a photograph or audio or whatever the data represents but as a bunch of abstract points in space. First, the linear function takes the form $y = mx + b$, which you may remember from school. See diagram (b) in Figure 2.1. In school, m is called the slope, and b is called the y-intercept. In machine learning, m is called the weights, and b is called the biases. Weights and biases are plural because, in machine learning, m and b aren't a single number but are matrices of numbers. This linear function $y = mx + b$ takes in the input data points, multiplies them by the matrix of weights m, and adds the matrix of biases b. That's all for the linear function.

Now, we feed the output of that linear function through an activation function. An activation function is a smooth, curvy, nonlinear function. There are a handful of typical activation functions used in neurons. See diagram (c) in Figure 2.1. The purpose of the activation function is to introduce nonlinearity into the neuron. That is, if we just apply the linear function step, we're creating a linear model of the data. A linear model is a simple model that can capture linear relationships in the data. If our data is complicated, important features of the data might not be adequately represented by a linear model. Therefore, we add the nonlinear activation function to the neuron. The output of the activation function is the output of the neuron.

So we have input data points, a linear function, a nonlinear activation function, and the output. The only remaining thing to learn about a neuron is how the weights of the linear function get adjusted slightly during each training step until the neural network is behaving the way we want it to. This adjustment happens with a calculus technique called backpropagation. Neuron math is all done without calculus until the backpropagation step.

Connecting Neurons

When neurons are built into a neural network, the output of one neuron becomes the input to another neuron, whose output becomes the input to yet another neuron, and so on. Neural networks are groups of neurons networked together in various ways. See diagram (d) in Figure 2.1. Large neural networks in the 2020s can have billions of neurons.[7] Much of the impressive behavior of large neural networks emerges from the complex, unpredictable interactions among neurons.

Data

Training machine learning models for creative work is predicated on having data for the models to train on. Some ML approaches require more data than others, and different ML approaches require different kinds of data. Finding or making data is one of the challenges faced by artists wanting to work with machine learning. You need *enough* data. How much is *enough* is highly dependent on the model and type of data. You need *high-quality* data, which is neither easily defined nor auditable if you have a large dataset that might contain errors or outliers. You need a useful *variety* of data so that the ML model produces output of sufficient variety to be interesting, and dataset *variety* is challenging to define and measure. You may need paired input and output data, that is, *labeled* data, which can be hard to find and time-consuming to label yourself. It may become clear only after training a model that your data is too little, too low-quality, or too homogeneous.

Broadly, there are three sources of data: proprietary datasets, public datasets, and personal datasets. Proprietary datasets are owned by companies and cost money. Public datasets are free to use within the bounds of licensing agreements. Personal datasets are data you gather yourself, either with intentional data gathering practices (like field recording) or by assembling digital traces of your own prior creative work as a dataset. It might feel soulless to treat your previous creative work as data, and it may seem to reduce the ineffability of such rich human experiences. On the other hand, using your own creative output to train ML models enables personalized creative projects that don't rely on others' data. Training a model on a personal dataset may reveal previously unnoticed patterns in your existing work; a model may learn patterns in your work that you find desirable, or it may discern patterns you hadn't noticed, alerting you to creative habits. Deliberately considering and sourcing your datasets, or combining multiple datasets, is an important step in defining a creative ML task.[8]

Chicago Creative Machines

Motivation

As I developed experience with ML and began to work with it in a musical capacity, I wondered why I hadn't seen ML tools presented before as creative utilities. I sensed a gap between the reality of the increasing openness and flexibility of machine learning tools and the anxiety I heard artists in my circles express toward AI technologies. I began to hear colleagues say "AI" and mean specific, corporate-controlled language models like ChatGPT, Midjourney, and DALL-E. I suspected that the companies marketing these models wanted the public and artists to believe that AI is the same thing as their products. I thought I might be able to spark dialogue around alternative machine learning and art practices by bringing interested artists and community members into the same room for conversation.

In 2023, I approached Experimental Sound Studio (ESS) in Chicago about hosting a series of events to highlight the work of artists creating with original machine learning tools. I titled the series Chicago Creative Machines. In 2024 and 2025, ESS hosted eight Chicago Creative Machines lecture-performances featuring Midwest artists who work with machine learning in original, personal, and ethical ways as part of their creative practices. Each artist gave a technical talk about how they build, train, or misuse ML models, followed by a brief intermission and then a performance of work they created using those ML tools. The events featured artists working in a variety of media, including composition, improvised music, film, performance art, sculpture, and social robotics. The events were offered free to the public. All eight events are archived and viewable for free online.[9]

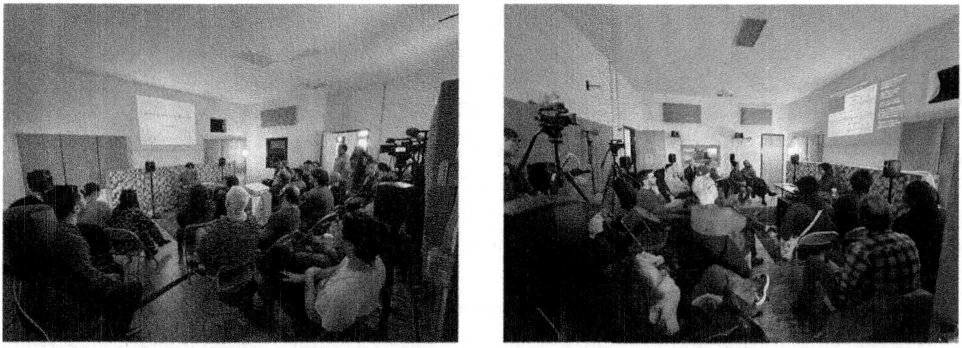

(a) (b)

Figure 2.2 Chicago Creative Machines events at Experimental Sound Studio, February and March 2024. (a) Hugo Flores García presents VampNet. (b) Julie Zhu discusses Deep Drawing.

The brief intermission in the event structure was intentional because I wanted the audiences to start talking. During interstitial moments, audience members began to chat about their overlapping interests. I overheard conversations about electronic music, algorithmic composition, poetry by robots, evil robots, censorship, creative agency. These conversations were a primary purpose of Chicago Creative Machines. Multiple audience members have since reached out to ask about how they can start to learn ML for themselves, and the Chicago Creative Machines website now includes a page of learning resources.[10] The series also included a free hands-on workshop in FluCoMa and Max in 2025.

In the next sections, I'll talk about a few of the artists featured in Chicago Creative Machines and the work they've made using, building, and misappropriating machine learning models (Figure 2.2). There are more artists using and misusing machine learning through practices like walking the latent spaces of autoencoder models,[11] designing new data types for existing models to train on,[12] defining custom loss functions for training neural networks, building instruments that incorporate embedded ML models on microcontrollers,[13] and more. These artists each engage in a completely personal blend of ML approaches. The incorporation of machine learning into their creative practices *looks* and *sounds* different in many ways.

Hunter Brown and FluCoMa

Two of the eight artists featured in Chicago Creative Machines, Hunter Brown and Ted Moore, have built laptop improvisation practices around FluCoMa.[14] Short for Fluid Corpus Manipulation, FluCoMa is an open-source library for machine learning within audio programming environments Max, SuperCollider, and Pd.

Hunter Brown uses machine learning to help him control an extensive SuperCollider software instrument that he uses to improvise and compose. There are hundreds of parameters that can be controlled on his software instrument. Hunter employed FluCoMa to train a *dimensionality reduction* algorithm that helps him control his software instrument with a two-dimensional X-Y pad rather than hundreds of separate knobs or faders. Hunter first collected training data; he set all 200-plus instrument controls so that the instrument was producing a sound he liked, and he associated this set of 200-plus control settings with a single point on his X-Y pad. He did this repeatedly, building up a training dataset that captured sounds he liked and associated their controls with a point in the X-Y plane. Hunter then trained a machine learning model. The ML algorithm learned to map each position on the X-Y pad to a sound that he liked. Now, when Hunter scrolls his finger across his X-Y pad, the algorithm determines what combination of the hundreds of possible instrument controls is most likely to produce a sound he would like. The algorithm is able to create combinations of sounds he never explicitly programmed. Machine learning enables Hunter's SuperCollider instrument to produce sounds that match his preferences but are chosen by the model.

Hugo Flores García, VampNet, and Token Telephone[15]

Hugo Flores García, a computer musician and researcher, created VampNet—a deep learning model that generates variations on input audio. VampNet masks out parts of the input audio and learns to fill in the gaps. A musician feeding their own music into the input of VampNet will get back variations of their own work. Hugo performs with VampNet, guitar, and other electronic instruments. Hugo has also exhibited a feedback installation called *Token Telephone*, taking the output of VampNet back into its input repeatedly.

Julie Zhu and Deep Drawing

Julie Zhu's Deep Drawing[16] is a collaboration between herself and an AI performer. The AI performer, a *convolutional neural network* (CNN), listens to the sound of Julie drawing on a large vertical surface and translates the sound into a visual guess of the original drawing. Deep Drawing includes elements of visual art, sound art, sculpture, and performance art.

Molly Jones and Approximations

I trained two audio-generating neural networks on recordings of two specific instrumentalists and composed a piece, *approximations*, in which those instrumentalists imitate the models imitating the performers in a kind of feedback loop. I took audio recordings of improvisations by percussionist Louis Pino and accordionist Matti Pulkki and trained two WaveNet models to generate short snippets of sound resembling the two performers' timbres. I then composed *approximations*, a piece performed by Louis, Matti, and fixed media stereo audio stitched together from the outputs of the two neural networks using some probabilistic Python functions. After the premiere, I shared the trained WaveNet models and codebase with Louis and Matti in recognition of their role providing the training data that enabled the models to generate those sounds.

X. A. Li, Caitlyn Min-ji Au, and Video Generation

Artists X. A. Li and Caitlyn Min-ji Au each engage with video-generating models to push the models' boundaries.

For her Chicago Creative Machines event, X. A. presented paired audio and video pieces titled *Ecstasies* and *Instruction*, exploring themes of self-optimization and aspiration. She projected generated video of faces from open-source models morphing into one another while distorted generated voices confronted the audience from eight surround speakers. X. A. sat on the floor below the projection, carefully arranging and then scattering printed photographs.[17]

Caitlyn Min-ji Au employed video-generating models to extend the visual vocabulary of her film and sculpture practice. At her Chicago Creative Machines event, she showcased a music video featuring actors performing an archetypal story in front of a blend of AI-generated and filmed backgrounds. She exposed expectations about visual culture by generating almost-recognizable visual tropes filtered through the lens of pretrained ML models.

Conclusion

The Urgency of Machine Learning for Artists

In recent years, conversations about AI and its relationship to the arts and labor have expanded. I think it's an exciting time to work with machine learning. I think it's valuable for artists to become part of the communities and teams engaging hands-on with AI. And I think all of us, digital citizens, should gain a basic knowledge of how machine learning works as these tools increasingly mediate our interactions.

I suspect artists armed with ML knowledge will dream up personalized machine learning tools customized to their own quirky projects, and I think artists will hack existing models in interesting ways. I believe artist-made, project-specific engagements with ML have the potential to be more creatively compelling than AI art tools trained on agglomerated data and optimized for profit.

Where to Go to Learn More

For a list of ML learning resources I know about, see the Chicago Creative Machine website.[18] Free community workshops, when available, could also be promising avenues for musicians and artists desiring to engage with machine learning.

Artists, Machines, and Imagination

Many of the flaws in machine learning tools flow from human flaws: data bias, noninclusive design, lack of imagination. Humans, with our varied priorities and motivations, set the objectives for training machine learning models. While corporate-created AI art tools will continue to exist in our creative ecosystems, AI for creative practice can be made smaller, friendlier, and more eccentric.[19] Machine learning literacy can shift our concerns away from the technical foundations of AI and toward how humans use AI in relation to creative practice and other humans. Understanding and trying out machine learning can calm our fears about AI—or at least shift them to a more realistic set of fears.

Notes

1 DCGAN stands for *deep convolutional generative adversarial network.* A generative adversarial network (GAN) is an architecture that combines two neural networks, a generator and a discriminator. The generator network generates some output, and the discriminator tries to determine whether the generated output is real or fake. The better the generator gets, the more it can fool the discriminator into thinking what it has generated is real. The DC part of DCGAN means that the network includes convolutional layers, which are good at detecting structure at multiple scales.

2 Cotterell, Dickson, and Kamminga, "Ancient Egyptian Water-Clocks"; Banū Mūsā, *Book of Ingenious Devices.*

3 McCulloch and Pitts, "A Logical Calculus."

4 McCulloch and Pitts, "A Logical Calculus"; Fradkov, "Early History of Machine Learning."

5 Fradkov, "Early History of Machine Learning."

6 Computational resources include CPU (to hold information in the computer's memory), GPU (to do matrix math efficiently), and electricity—all this computer infrastructure consumes material resources.

7 Kaplan et al., "Scaling Laws."

8 Paullada et al., "Data and Its (Dis)Contents."

9 Jones, "Chicago Creative Machines."

10 Jones, "Learning Resources."

11 Cella, *nnirror.*

12 Vigliensoni et al., "R-VAE."

13 Montoya-Moraga, *TinyTrainable.*

14 Tremblay et al., *Fluid Corpus Manipulation.*

15 Flores García et al., "VampNet."

16 Granzow et al., "Deep Drawing."

17 Li, *xa-li.*

18 Jones, "Learning Resources."

19 Vigliensoni, Perry, and Fiebrink, "A Small-Data Mindset."

Bibliography

Bin Musa ibn Shakir, Muhammad, Ahmad Bin Musa ibn Shakir, and Al-Hasan Bin Musa ibn Shakir. *The Book of Ingenious Devices / Kitáb al-Ḥiyal: Kitáb al-Hiyal*. Translated by P. Hill. Dordrecht: Springer Netherlands, 1978.

Cella, Michael. *nnirror*. Accessed June 11, 2025. https://nnirror.xyz.

Cotterell, B., F. P. Dickson, and J. Kamminga. "Ancient Egyptian Water-Clocks: A Reappraisal." *Journal of Archaeological Science* 13, no. 1 (1986): 31–50. https://doi.org/10.1016/0305-4403(86)90025-7.

Flores García, Hugo, Prem Seetharaman, Rithesh Kumar, and Bryan Pardo. "VampNet: Music Generation via Masked Acoustic Token Modeling." In *Proceedings of the 24th International Society for Music Information Retrieval Conference (ISMIR)*, 359–366. Milan, Italy: ISMIR, 2023.

Fradkov, Alexander L. "Early History of Machine Learning." *IFAC-PapersOnLine* 53, no. 2 (2020): 1385–1390.

Granzow, John, Julie Zhu, Erfun Ackley, and Zhiyu Zhang. "Deep Drawing: An Intermedia AI Co-Performer." In *Proceedings of the Conference on AI Music Creativity (AIMC)*. Oxford, UK: AIMC, 2024.

Jones, Molly. "Chicago Creative Machines." Accessed June 13, 2025. https://www.chicagocreativemachines.com.

Jones, Molly. "Learning Resources." *Chicago Creative Machines*. Accessed June 13, 2025. https://www.chicagocreativemachines.com/learning-resources.

Kaplan, Jared, Sam McCandlish, Tom Henighan, Tom B. Brown, Benjamin Chess, Rewon Child, Scott Gray, Alec Radford, Jeffrey Wu, and Dario Amodei. "Scaling Laws for Neural Language Models." Preprint, submitted January 23, 2020. arXiv:2001.08361. https://arxiv.org/abs/2001.08361.

Li, X. A. *xa-li*. Accessed June 11, 2025. https://xa-li.com.

McCulloch, Warren S., and Walter Pitts. "A Logical Calculus of the Ideas Immanent in Nervous Activity." *The Bulletin of Mathematical Biophysics* 5 (1943): 115–133.

Montoya-Moraga, Aarón. *TinyTrainable*. GitHub. Accessed February 4, 2023. https://github.com/montoyamoraga/TinyTrainable.

Paullada, Amandalynne, Inioluwa Deborah Raji, Emily M. Bender, Emily Denton, and Alex Hanna. "Data and Its (Dis)Contents: A Survey of Dataset Development and Use in Machine Learning Research." *Patterns* 2, no. 11 (2021): 1–14. https://doi.org/10.1016/j.patter.2021.100336

Tremblay, Pierre Alexandre, Owen Green, Gerard Roma, James Bradbury, Ted Moore, Jacob Hart, and Alex Harker. *The Fluid Corpus Manipulation Toolbox*, vol. 1. Zenodo, July 14, 2022. https://10.5281/zenodo.6834643.

Vigliensoni, Gabriel, Phoenix Perry, and Rebecca Fiebrink. "A Small-Data Mindset for Generative AI Creative Work." In *Generative AI and HCI – CHI 2022 Workshop*. New Orleans, LA: GenAICHI, 2022.

Vigliensoni, Gabriel, Louis McCallum, Esteban Maestre, and Rebecca Fiebrink. "R-VAE: Live Latent Space Drum Rhythm Generation from Minimal-size Datasets." *Journal of Creative Music Systems* 1, no. 1 (2022). https://doi.org/10.5920/jcms.902.

3

INTERLUDE I

Interview with Laetitia Sonami

Constantin Basica and Julie Zhu

DOI: 10.4324/9781003615873-3

Julie: You said you wanted to "mess up the AI," and I love that. I'm teaching an electronic chamber music class now, and the theme is *dazzle and camouflage* ... people who wear makeup to fool the AI and face recognition and so on—except with aural camouflage. Is that something that resonates with you?

Laetitia: Well, I refer to the idea of "messing things up" a bit in the article with Rebecca Fiebrink.[1] By the time I met Rebecca, I had twenty-five years of mapping and elaborating control strategies with the *lady's glove*[2] and I got to the point where the most interesting moments were those when I did not really have control. Obviously, there were various degrees of control, but I wanted to be surprised. And the *lady's glove* was not surprising me anymore. I was not particularly interested in machine learning when I first met Rebecca at Princeton, because I had done some experiments in the '90s with David Wessel,[3] and I still had in mind the crazy programming and hardware needed. But I was staying at her apartment getting ready for a talk, and she offered to demonstrate her Wekinator.[4] I was very impressed and said I would create an instrument for it. I did not want to rethink the *lady's glove* mapping at this point, but instead to start afresh. I told her that my main interest was to actually investigate ML as a way to grow and discover. I could not grow if I was not being surprised.

As an artist, a musician, I think you're always trying to "go beyond." Replicating someone else's music or a particular genre is the last thing you want to do. So I mentioned to her that while I wanted to use her system, I did not want it to "learn correctly." Why would I want that when I can do it with a fader or some other controller? But I really wanted it to come back to me with different sounds. In that sense, I wanted a system that does not learn correctly—like a kid: you don't want a kid to do only what you say (even though you may wish they would!).

That's how it started: from the perspective of using a system that will open up ideas and different sound environments. And I think that's a big issue, saying, "Oh, you want to sound like some other musician, or you want to have it do this or that, or you want to adapt to someone else's corpus ..." It's so hard as an artist to be authentic and find a voice. Why would you want to have a system that emulates other aesthetics or ideas?

Anyway, the "messing up" was really from a perspective of just trying to hear things that I couldn't hear. And that's been my frustration and interest. What do I need to do to be surprised? And I've been on this for a while; after fifty years of doing electronics, it's getting harder and harder to be surprised!

Julie: This element of surprise ... it can happen with a certain kind of randomness too, right? Like a random number generator or something like that. But that's just pure randomness and chaos. Do you put AI and randomness in the same category? Or is it slightly different for you?

Laetitia: It's a good question. You can have degrees of randomness and juxtapose layers of randomness. It's definitely a way to navigate terrains that require you to adapt. I think it is embedded in George Lewis's early *Voyager*, or at least this is my understanding of it. I don't associate ML with randomness but rather with terrains of opportunity—and this came about when using Wekinator and RapidMax[5] (which was inspired by Rebecca's algorithms).

I spend a lot of time training models. It's a bit like sculpting. While I want to be surprised, I look for surprises that I can model a bit further once I hear how the training functions. The training allows for flexibility—if it is fast (and speed is essential), it can create unexpected results. If I like what I hear, I can go back and retrain to expand the boundaries, and I love this. I refer to it as the *predictability index*. You can dial the predictability level based on how wide the training is. If I hear something interesting, I freeze the training and use it as a new foundation for new trainings. This is how I build sonic terrains. I mostly use Miller Puckette's PAF synthesis[6] with ML since it allows for a wide range of control data and has a beautiful analog feel. I think it would be hard to do that with randomness, but you could of course if you knew programming well.

Constantin: Would you consider having separate machine learning models trained by other people in order to make your system even more unpredictable? Imagine you gave your instrument to some other artist who you know and respect, to see what they make of it. And then they used it for some time and trained a Wekinator model in their own way. They would find their own sonic terrains, and then you'd have different models: the Rebecca Fiebrink model, the Paul DeMarinis[7] model, or the Pamela Z[8] model ... that you could switch between during performance. Would that give you more unpredictability?

Laetitia: No, because I don't think anybody would want to deal with my system. The whole process is so tight, it would be like giving somebody ...

Constantin: A part of your life?

Laetitia: Yes. At first they would hate it, because it requires so much patience. Nobody would want to do that, unless it's their tool. I'd be happy to help them build their own. But my practice has evolved over many years. So having to explain that to somebody ... to give them the instrument ... it's so personal. Because it connects to the synthesis, and it connects to the body and how I think of gestures, so it's not like you can say, "Oh, do some interesting modeling for me." It's still tied to my gestures. So if they don't understand how it's performed, it would be very hard. But I would love for someone to say, "Here's a synthesis engine," or "Here's a system that you could work with." That's why I like Rebecca's work.

Constantin: That makes sense.

Your collaboration with Rebecca and the Wekinator on the Spring Spyre[9] is a beautiful example of artist–engineer collaboration. Have you collaborated with other researchers in the musical ML/AI world? With people who would build synthesis algorithms for your instrument? Or do you see yourself partnering with AI researchers looking for your unique blend of skills in performance, improvisation, composition, and ML training?

Laetitia: I approached ML from a mapping perspective. Having done extensive mapping with the *lady's glove* in Max,[10] I was aware of how complex and unwieldy it could be: extensive networks of logic, mapping the thirty or so sensors (that capture gestures) to synthesis. In the case of the Spring Spyre, the sensors are not directly mapped; the audio from the springs—activated through gestures—is extracted and fed as data to ML.

I haven't collaborated with other researchers besides Rebecca, even though I'm desperately looking for new synthesis. Rebecca is the one who put me onto RAVE[11] a few years ago, saying that I might find something there. I didn't, but it was still interesting. Or David Zicarelli,[12] who recently mentioned he had a feedback patch that I might want to try. So I talked to a few people. But it's hard because of the way most people think of machine learning systems as control systems, expecting the system to do what you imagined. You may think it is so great that any embodiment has to follow exactly what your mind imagined, but it does not work like that. I am looking for imperfections, accidents.

I said originally that I did not consider AI to be a collaborator. But every tool has a history and leads us on a specific path. A hammer has so much embedded "training." It carries a long history of practice, even though it is so simple. So, it's the same with AI. Obviously, it's going to completely change how you approach composition and your artistic practice; it reveals unexpected ideas. But the problem is that we, people with digital tools, too often have this idea of perfection. We have this idea that things have to be just the way we imagine (because we're so great, you know?!). The last thing I want is for it to do something I imagined, because it's probably predictable and limited. This is why I think it's hard to get people excited about creating a system that's *not* going to do exactly what they want.

So, I think most engineers probably wouldn't care because of the current approaches to machine learning and AI. From the perspective of creation and arts, it's very hard. Unless they're musicians too, engineers rarely understand what you want. That was the thing with Rebecca: she knows what musicians or artists think and desire because she is one herself.

Constantin: On this note of control and agency, it sounds like you do want this sort of agency from a system: to figure things out by itself and give you unpredictability, new sounds, and a new world of things that you can explore. But at the same time, you're saying that right now you can't consider it a partner because it's just a tool like any other software. So, thinking about your vast experience as a performer and instrument designer, I wonder if that could become a tension point for you in the future. If there was something that actually had its own agency and unpredictability, and you could use it as a partner—would you be interested in that? Or would you still want to retain a level of control that gives you more of an instrument than a partner?

Laetitia Yeah, it's interesting. I could be interested if that agency allowed for exchange and not compliance. To get back to your question about the collaborator, and why I was ticked by that—take the *lady's glove*. Everything I thought about music embodiment came because of me using that. I never thought I was going to get into gestural controllers or embodiment; I never thought about that. I was just creating a tool, and the tool influenced my approach. So I was lucky to create this thing that actually taught me so much and led me without me knowing. Would I call it a collaborator? I don't think so ...

The main issue when teaching ML in the design of instruments is to make it part of the process. Often, students have a composition in mind that is already fixed, and then they want to apply ML at the end of the compositional process. But this should be applied fairly soon in the design as it will influence how one approaches the compositional process. What sounds can I create and modify in performance using ML that I could not do with buttons and faders?

So, if you had a system that I would have to collaborate with ... Everything I do is already somehow like that, but I guess you're talking about different degrees of collaboration where suddenly the system is figuring things out. And I wonder: what is it figuring out? Decision-making? Change? I guess I'd be interested, but it would have to be really interesting at how it figures things out.

Constantin: You're setting a very high bar for AI. [*Both laugh.*]

Laetitia: I wouldn't know what it's doing—maybe that would be interesting. In a way, even though you don't know what you're doing in instrument design, you obviously have an idea of how you want the body to interface; you have some desires. You already have a scope of how you want it to behave. And then you learn because it does different things, and you can tweak it and change it. So it's a collaboration in that sense.

Why don't I like the word *collaboration*? Because I'm tired of this idea that there's an external intelligence. This idea of embedded intelligence—that it's smart, and it's going to show me how to do things, how to behave, and that I'm going to collaborate with it ... Maybe I'm reacting to that because I feel like everything we do is somehow in a feedback loop. This is the problem with a lot of digital tools: you want it to do exactly what you want, and you don't want the feedback loop. If you're going to use something like Ableton,[13] the software guides a particular approach. Would you call that collaboration? No. Max? No. But obviously, you chose it because it offers a platform that allows some navigation that responds to your intentions.

So, if it was a system that's really interesting, and I wanted to collaborate ... Yes, I'd have to test it. I have no idea. Give me something, and I'll tell you if I like it. A system that's easy to use and flexible, which you can sculpt, mold, and guide to different degrees—do you know anything that does that?

Constantin: Nothing so far that behaves at the level you would like it to.

Julie: I love what you said there: "Give me something, and I'll tell you if I like it." Actually, that is a very important part of machine learning—the human feedback that all the AI ethicists talk about. It's about having the human in the loop. You've thought of yourself like that in technology for a really long time. Can you say more about it? You have preferences, right? Do you think those preferences evolved through your artistic practice and your experience? Or is it more like you were born this way? That you just know what you want?

Laetitia: No, I have no idea what I want. Maybe it's my French side! I'm very critical, so I can easily tell you what I don't like and how it should be! What I *don't* like guides me more than what I like. Maybe it's not exactly true, but I've learned through the tools. All my ideas came from just ... interfacing with the tools. Obviously, people I met influenced my work greatly as well. But playing with the limitations of the system is very important, and that's one of the issues of the digital age: creating limits is very hard. The boundaries make the instrument and its expressivity.

You just don't know how things will talk back, how they will grow, and you can't think, "Oh, I'm gonna have this great idea of this amazing instrument." It's really about just starting with a system, and then trying to make it do what it can't do. And for that, machine learning is great because you can take the simplest inputs and then you can train it to do expansive results, or very limited results. I don't understand why not everyone is using machine learning.

Constantin: You mentioned the word *limits*, and you said you are "bound to the body, and the body can only do so much." I was wondering if you could talk a little bit more about that in terms of instrument design. The limitations of the body. And, thinking of machine learning, would there be a way for you to extend that boundary of gesture limitation? If you could, let's say, train a system with your hands, and then have it do crazy things that you couldn't do with your body (move very fast or something like that).

Laetitia: Yeah, but it's still performed by my body.

Constantin: Or maybe you could use your brain to control it?

Laetitia: Yeah, I could be shaking, trembling, and just creating ... the next kind of performance, probably. [*Both laugh.*] I am not so interested in my brain.

It's interesting because I have used the hand extensively. And right now I'm doing something where I'm trying to have sensors embedded on my head. I'm kind of curious about the head and what people do with their heads. If I were younger, I could maybe think of other systems that would be interesting, more collective systems or wings made of bendable metal creating swarms of sounds ... But for me, it always is anchored in performance. That's why I like the *lady's ball(s)*.[14] I was really missing the gesture—because the Spring Spyre is very oracle-like, I'm just in front of it and I'm barely moving springs—and I wanted to get back to some bigger gesture.

Figure 3.1 Laetitia Sonami performs with her *lady's ball(s)*.
Photograph by Chiara Bellamoli.

Often people say, "Oh, do you want to collaborate with dancers?" or "Do you want to give your system to dancers?" I'm like, no! I'm sorry, I'm not going to work with dancers—this crazy personal system would drive them insane. Like I said before, it's such a collaboration between the system you design, how you think about it, and your own body. As a musician, you're willing to go through this wormhole and create something terribly complicated, but nobody else is going to want to share that. And if you want to make it really simple to use, then somehow you realize it's missing some of the stuff that you had hoped. That said, I'd love to make a toy with machine learning for kids. It should be so simple to make without calling it machine learning. It would be great. I'm not in the industry, but it would be fun.

Julie: Well, what we're picking up from almost every artist and writer in our book is *specificity*, and how that is so important for machine learning to actually help artists. To be super specific to who you are, or what it does. Because all of the other types of machine learning for generating money—they're very general. That's their whole thing: they're general models that a layperson can get something out of. So I think that really resonates with what you're saying. But I think AI agents in the future will be capable of creating these synthesis machines that you are now craving for a human to create for you. So that might be one layer up: these agents that speak between software and programming languages … And maybe it's not as good right now, but I think it will get much better. Is that something that you're curious about, excited about? Getting new synthesis algorithms from an AI agent? They can't right now, but what if they could?

Laetitia: Yes, I would love to experiment with that. It would have to be fast: something that you could interact with quickly because you can't spend three weeks waiting for a result—that's what we did in the '70s with punch cards.[15] I think that a lot of the issues with AI are related to what you use to train a system. I would have to know how to train it and what the elements of training are. I haven't heard anything yet, but I've been wanting for a long time now to have a synthesis method that's generated from … a color, a smell, humidity, topography, whatever. I'd want to feed strange inputs to the system and generate some unexpected results.

For instance, why don't we train sound synthesis on … anthill architecture? That might be interesting. I'd like to know how anthill architecture can be applied to synthesis. I wouldn't know how to do that. But if you had this really good feature extraction of ants' circulation, work distribution, and the structure of the anthill … yes, that would be wonderful! Or just different intelligences, different systems, different kinds of organizational systems. I'm thinking about ants because I was in the desert, and there were a lot of anthills at that time of year, and I wanted to see how they move. And I thought: look at these thousands of little moving creatures and how they move—that would be amazing if I could hear that. Not in a sonifying way, but in an intelligent way. That would be very interesting. So, yes, I would like to see how AI could be applied to synthesize music from that. But I haven't heard anything that would do something like this.

Julie: Anthills. That would be amazing!

Laetitia: If you find a student who could apply anthills to synthesis … I will test their system happily.

Julie: I will mention it to my students and let you know. [*All three laugh.*]

Learn more about Laetitia Sonami and her work at https://sonami.net

Notes

1 Fiebrink and Sonami, "Reflections."
2 The *lady's glove*, fitted with various sensors, is Sonami's "signature instrument."
3 David Wessel (1942–2014) was an American researcher, composer, and the founder of the Center for New Music and Audio Technologies (CNMAT) at the University of California, Berkeley. See more

about his experiments with neural nets in Wessel, Drame, and Wright, "Removing the Time Axis"; Freed et al., "Real-Time Additive Synthesis"; Lee, Freed, and Wessel, "Real-Time Neural Network Processing."

4 Fiebrink and Cook, "The Wekinator."

5 Di Maggio, *RapidMax*.

6 Puckette, *The Theory and Technique of Electronic Music*, 151–155.

7 Paul DeMarinis is an American visual and sound artist and professor at Stanford University.

8 Pamela Z is an American composer, performer, and media artist.

9 The Spring Spyre is an instrument built by Sonami with "3 long springs, 3 hacked audio pick-ups from spring reverb units" as well as "a hacked Roland PC-1600." It uses Rebecca Fiebrink's Wekinator for mapping the instrument to Miller Puckette's phase-aligned formant (PAF) synthesis algorithm.

10 Max (also known as Max/MSP) is a popular visual programming language among musicians performing live electronics.

11 Caillon and Esling, "RAVE."

12 David Zicarelli is an American software designer, the founder and CEO of Cycling '74, the company that develops Max.

13 Ableton Live is a digital audio workstation (DAW) popular for live performance.

14 The *lady's ball(s)* is the latest addition to Sonami's instruments. It uses a wireless accelerometer attached to her wrist (while moving a wire ball) and RapidMax for machine learning.

15 "Punched Card."

Bibliography

Ableton. *Ableton Live*. Accessed January 18, 2026. https://www.ableton.com/en/live.

Caillon, Antoine, and Philippe Esling. "RAVE: A Variational Autoencoder for Fast and High-Quality Neural Audio Synthesis." Preprint, last revised December 15, 2021. arXiv:2111.05011v2. https://arxiv.org/abs/2111.05011.

Campion, Edmund, Adrian Freed, and John MacCallum. "In Memoriam: David L. Wessel, 1942–2014." Academic Senate, University of California, 2014. https://senate.universityofcalifornia.edu/_files/inmemoriam/html/DavidL.Wessel.html.

Bennington Colleg. "David Zicarelli." *Bennington College*. Accessed January 18, 2026. https://www.bennington.edu/academics/faculty/david-zicarelli.

Cycling '74. *Max*. Accessed January 18, 2026. https://cycling74.com/products/max.

Di Maggio, Francesco. *RapidMax*. GitHub. Accessed July 12, 2022. https://github.com/francesco-di-maggio/rapidmax.

Fiebrink, Rebecca, and Perry Cook. "The Wekinator: A System for Real-Time, Interactive Machine Learning in Music." In *Proceedings of the Eleventh International Society for Music Information Retrieval Conference (ISMIR)*. Utrecht, Netherlands: ISMIR, 2010. https://ismir2010.ismir.net/proceedings/late-breaking-demo-13.pdf.

Fiebrink, Rebecca, and Laetitia Sonami. "Reflections on Eight Years of Instrument Creation with Machine Learning." In *International Conference on New Interfaces for Musical Expression (NIME)*. Birmingham, UK: NIME, 2020.

Freed, David, Mark Goldstein, Michael Goodwin, Michael Lee, Keith A. McMillen, Xavier Rodet, David Wessel, and Matthew Wright. "Real-Time Additive Synthesis Controlled by a Mixture of

Neural-Networks and Direct Manipulation of Physical and Perceptual Attributes." In *Proceedings of the International Computer Music Conference (ICMC)*, 362–63. Aarhus, Denmark: International Computer Music Association (ICMA), 1994. http://hdl.handle.net/2027/spo.bbp2372.1994.094.

Lee, Michael A., Adrian Freed, and David Wessel. "Real-Time Neural Network Processing of Gestural and Acoustic Signals." In *Proceedings of the International Computer Music Conference (ICMC)*, 277–80. Montreal, Canada: International Computer Music Association (ICMA), 1991. https://quod.lib.umich.edu/i/icmc/bbp2372.1991.064.

Pamela Z. Accessed January 18, 2026. https://pamelaz.com.

Paul DeMarinis. Accessed January 18, 2026. https://pauldemarinis.org.

Puckette, Miller. *The Theory and Technique of Electronic Music*. World Scientific Publishing Company, 2007.

"Punched card." *Wikipedia*. Accessed January 18, 2026. https://en.wikipedia.org/wiki/Punched_card.

Sonami, Laetitia. "Lady's Ball(s)." *Laetitia Sonami*. Accessed January 18, 2026. https://sonami.net/portfolio/items/ladys-balls.

Sonami, Laetitia. "Lady's Glove." *Laetitia Sonami*. Accessed January 18, 2026. https://sonami.net/portfolio/items/ladys-glove.

Sonami, Laetitia. "Spring Spyre." *Laetitia Sonami*. Accessed January 18, 2026. https://sonami.net/portfolio/items/spring-spyre.

Wessel, David, Cyril Drame, and Matthew Wright. "Removing the Time Axis from Spectral Model Analysis-Based Additive Synthesis: Neural Networks versus Memory-Based Machine Learning." In *Proceedings of the International Computer Music Conference (ICMC)*. Ann Arbor, MI: International Computer Music Association (ICMA), 1998. http://hdl.handle.net/2027/spo.bbp2372.1998.322.

4

MOVEMENT II

Notochord: Designing and Experiencing a Low-Latency MIDI Language Model

Victor Shepardson

DOI: 10.4324/9781003615873-4

LLM Aesthetics

As I write this in early 2026, "Artificial Intelligence" is almost synonymous with large language models (LLMs). The years of hyping up narrow statistical models, brittle rule-based systems, or crude image generators as AI are being quickly forgotten. Now we are confronted by software that can converse with us, in our own language, on any topic, with an apparent breadth of knowledge that can sometimes astonish. Just as quickly, we find ourselves up to our elbows in slop, as mindless machine-generated content takes less effort to produce and more effort to distinguish from intentional human communication.[1]

But not much has changed lately in the methods of AI. At its core, an LLM is little different from the technology powering machine translation between languages or autocorrect on smartphone keyboards. These are both statistical models that assign a numerical probability to the next element in a text, given the preceding elements, on the basis of example texts or *training data*. Indeed, one of the earliest computer-generated music compositions included this kind of sequential probability model.[2] What has changed is mainly scale: LLMs process digital libraries larger than any human could peruse in a lifetime. The capabilities of LLMs emerge from the brutally simple task of predicting the next word, again and again, on the basis of so much information. And what works for text is applied, in more or less the same way, to image, sound, music, and more. The core statistical learning methods underlying LLMs have existed for decades; only now, the raw computational power and internet-scale data exist to fuel them.

The most visible applications of LLMs are AI chatbots like ChatGPT and its ilk. These are thin veneers on top of an animate archive. Underneath the cheerfulness, the sycophancy,[3] and the projection of helpful, honest, harmless,[4] is the LLM. Often, there is no separation between the agent you converse with and the data it references to answer your question—the AI is *made of* the archive, distilled from it. When you talk to an LLM, you play a game of meaning-making where the AI tries to make your conversation resemble a document from the archive stylistically, but also semantically. It tries to make the conversation make sense in light of its training data. The model constructs its replies to evoke the structure of past conversations, between two humans, between itself and the workers employed during the post-training process, or perhaps one generated by another LLM.

It's anyone's guess what comes next, but clearly now is the LLM era of AI. A large proportion of work presented this past year at NeurIPS, the largest machine learning and AI conference, had to do with creating, operating, incorporating, or studying LLMs. Since the launch of ChatGPT a few years ago, LLMs have become ubiquitous, provoking much discussion about their implications for productivity, livelihoods, and education. As someone working with machine learning and music technology, I feel a sense of urgency in coming to grips with their particular aesthetics. What do LLMs feel like? How do they change my experience? Can I understand it better by making my own AI music systems?

You might ask why I think LLMs, which manipulate text, are so relevant to music. (Or not, since the trend is toward multimodal AI systems that incorporate audio, images, and video.) However, *text* has long been used in the humanities and the social sciences to mean any cultural artifact. Texts represent the world and are subject to interpretation; they can be read whether or not they are constructed with language. Generative machine learning operationalizes this. Any digital media can become a text for a language model, and this is why general-purpose machine learning methods are subsuming the once disparate fields of computer vision, speech synthesis, music information retrieval, natural language processing, and others.

Music models essentially expand the vocabulary of textual elements to represent small fragments of sound or symbolic music. When a user enters a text description and the model generates music, it works like a chatbot conversation on a technical level. But the interaction is less dialogical. It goes one way, from the text to the audio modality, from concept to execution. However, dialogue is also possible in music models; in principle, they can continue or infill audio supplied by the user, enabling call-and-response or even simultaneous musical gestures, i.e., jamming with an AI musician. Nevertheless, music is far more sensitive to timing than a chatbot. The same computational scale that enables LLM aesthetics also makes models slow. So there is a fundamental trade-off between model size and musical agility that stands in the way of bringing LLM aesthetics to musical improvisation.

As I've watched the LLM era unfold, I've felt a need to wrangle with it by building my own models. I've been fascinated by generative machine learning for a while now. The mysterious emergence of meaning from dumb statistical prediction. The weird ways the machine fails to understand. The dialogue between elegant mathematical models and crude numerical processing. I wanted to understand it all by doing it myself. I feel the same way about music. I started to learn music a bit late and computer science a bit early, both around the same time. Music was always something I could do with code as much as a DAW or guitar. It was not about realizing what I hear in my head, but posing a question in the form of a machine that answers with sound. Music was always about making assemblages as much as mastering technique. *Assemblage* is a useful concept for describing what we often do with music technology: mess around in a cycle of experimentation and inspiration. The point of an assemblage is not the result, but the assembly.[5] Its substance is in the process of making and unmaking.

My latent fascination with LLM aesthetics, combined with a disposition to treat software assemblage as musical material, led me to start my own MIDI modeling project.

Notochord

The *Notochord* project was shaped by three virtues instilled in me during my training as a computer scientist: impatience, greed, and shamelessness.

I was impatient. I wanted something that could react instantly. I didn't want to feel constrained by a slow call-and-response loop, or locked into a certain tempo. I imagined something extemporaneous and free-flowing. The key to this is *latency*, which is the time difference between user input and system output. The rule of thumb for imperceptible latency is about 10 milliseconds, or one hundredth of a second.[6] Quicker than that, things feel simultaneous. Suppose I'm playing an electronic drum kit. As far as I can tell, the drum plays as I strike it, even if the hit is being sensed and then the sound is being synthesized a few milliseconds later by electronics and played through a loudspeaker. This is possible because computers are very fast. A CPU might process one million instructions in a single millisecond. But if the delay is longer than 10 milliseconds, I start to notice it, which imposes a certain kind of groove. If the delay is consistent, I can still adapt to it. A piano, for example, has substantial delay in the hammers striking the strings once I've pressed the key. Even the speed of sound will add a few milliseconds per meter of distance between my head and the loudspeaker. If the latency is inconsistent, however, I really start to notice the effect: this is called *jitter*. Rhythmic playing feels uncertain; I can't "lock in." Above 100 milliseconds or so, consistent delay also imposes a tempo on the music. This isn't necessarily bad, but it is limiting.

I wanted to design a system with low latency, enabling a sense of immediacy. But I was also greedy. I still wanted the aesthetics of a large model, big enough to be full of surprises and unexpected references. Unfortunately, the heavy processing needed for AI is fundamentally in tension with low latency and low jitter. And it's not only a matter of computing power. It takes time for AI to perceive musical inputs for more fundamental reasons. If I play a sine wave bass note at G1, it oscillates at 49 hertz; one cycle of the waveform is already more than 20 milliseconds long. There is simply no way to "hear" the note faster than that, for either a human or a computer.

MIDI-based music generation models have some advantages over audio-based models. MIDI, or the musical instrument digital interface,[7] is a standard for communication between musical interfaces and synthesizers. MIDI doesn't encode sound, but a more abstract, symbolic representation of music, mainly at the level of notes. MIDI is simpler: an audio model has to do the work of creating plausible instrument sounds, while a MIDI model defers that work to a separate synthesizer. Since MIDI is symbolic, it gets around some of the listening problems described above; the note G1 arrives all at once as a symbol—it doesn't need to be discerned from a waveform. A human can't react to new musical changes much faster than a 100 milliseconds; we rely on anticipation. But a machine can. An AI MIDI model can pivot on an unexpected note in milliseconds, recontextualizing it at the speed of perception. Since MIDI explicitly represents polyphony and multiple channels, human-performed and AI-generated MIDI events can be interleaved in precise and intimate ways. One model might harmonize on top of what you play, or play an accompaniment, or orchestrate your performance onto different instruments, depending on how it is used.

Finally, I was shameless. I didn't mind compromising between low latency and music quality. I didn't need to impress anyone. A research lab like Google Magenta, for instance, exists materially as a PR and talent recruiting mechanism for its parent company, which itself exists primarily to create profits for shareholders by selling advertisements. Google and Magenta are of course made up of talented people with their own motivations who care about their work. But they operate within these constraints, and without others. In any case, the work Magenta puts out needs to be legible, technically impressive, and slick. Over the same period I've been working on Notochord and before, Magenta researchers have developed a series of MIDI performance models. The most recent of those can credibly exchange melodic playing and accompaniment in the style of a virtuoso keyboardist;[8] but it can only do that. No one else seems to have made a full-track ultra-low-latency model quite like Notochord, because they are trying to make an impressive machine musician, not one that sounds drunk. My position as a doctoral student working in experimental music allowed me to have different priorities. I could make something more goofy, more broken, more idiosyncratic, and then dig into those qualities rather than polishing them away.

Notochord is my project for grappling with large model aesthetics via assemblage and music improvisation. But it's also for grappling with the assumptions and values of machine learning research culture, and their awkward collision with musical culture. I created Notochord as part of my doctoral research in *digital lutherie*, or the design of new musical instruments incorporating software. Following some time working as a machine learning research engineer, I joined the Intelligent Instruments Lab, a project investigating attitudes toward contemporary AI via new musical instrument design.[9] Our research is practice-based, and every member of the lab is both an artist and a technologist. Another useful concept for thinking about what we do is Small's *musicking*.[10] The idea is to think of music as a participatory process, not an end product. This is an expanded process which includes composers and performers, but also venues, audiences, recordists, and of course instrument builders. Thinking about process rather than production completely changes the premises of AI in music. We are not asking whether AI can make music, or whether it improves the efficiency of some workflow. We want to know how it changes the experience of musicking for those who participate.

Into this environment I brought a certain attitude. I was fascinated by machine learning, driven to understand and experiment with it firsthand. To me, this was continuous with other forms of musical tinkering and assembly. Because of this, I had consumed a lot of technical literature, internalizing the language and priorities of machine learning as a field. At the same time, I was dissatisfied with the scientific emphasis on theory, the engineering fixation on metrics and benchmarks, and the capitalist imperative to extract, manipulate, and surveil. It was the aesthetics of assembling ML systems that really interested me. I found inspiration in Philip Agre's *critical technical practice*.[11] The idea is to cultivate both an engineering mindset and a critical mindset, putting the two in dialogue. A deep appreciation of how technologies work makes for sharper critique; critique gives purpose to technical practice. By embracing the logic of machine learning research as musical research, I perhaps wanted to puncture it and let the air out, escape from it. Or to reassemble it as musical material.

Probabilistic Machine Learning

Something I noticed after immersing myself in machine learning techniques for years and then applying my skills to instrument design is how the field of machine learning is obsessed with generality. It wants to build what I think of as an "everything machine." This can be in tension with design priorities, which often lean toward "ultimate particulars."[12] The field of deep learning, which gave rise to current AI technologies, gives pride of place to "end-to-end" methods.[13] End-to-end learning algorithms take in raw data at one end and produce complete answers at the other, with as little human attention to the particulars of the training data as possible. This in turn enables the indiscriminate use of massive datasets scraped from the internet, providing the scale that powers large language models. And so the current fascination is with converting every problem into some form of text completion to be solved by LLMs.

LLMs are one form of *probabilistic machine learning.*[14] The central concept is the probabilistic *model.* Consider a run up the C major scale from C to A, for example. What comes next? We could guess that it will be the next note in the scale, B. But without more context, it's impossible to know for sure. We don't know what process produced this C major scale in the real world. Was it a composer with some purpose in mind, or their hands noodling with barely a thought? Is this the melody of a song, a moment of improvisation, a training exercise? A probabilistic model handles such uncertainty by assigning a numerical probability for every possible value of the next note. It might look something like Figure 4.1. Perhaps B is the most likely. But this could be the mixolydian scale—B♭ is a possibility. Maybe we don't complete the scale and jump up to C, or go back down to the fifth, or to another scale tone. And of course, anything could happen, so no probability is quite zero. Every note in a database of music can be seen as a piece of evidence for this kind of probabilistic model. Each note occurs with some probability, *conditioned* on the preceding notes. Without knowing the intention or physical process that generated the music, machine learning makes a guess based purely on form.

Notochord was a small project, which grew out of control into an everything machine. It was going to be a simple sequence model for yet undetermined purposes. Maybe for streams of sensor readings in a digital musical instrument. I thought to pretrain it on MIDI so it would learn something about repetition, timing, and musical structure, even if modeling MIDI tracks wasn't the end purpose. But I got too interested in the process. It's not much fun to model just sequences of MIDI pitches. With timing, the model could play melodies. By separating NoteOn and NoteOff events, it could play polyphonically. With velocity, it could express

Figure 4.1 A sequence of pitches x_1 to x_6 and the distribution $P(x_7 | x_{1 \ldots 6})$.

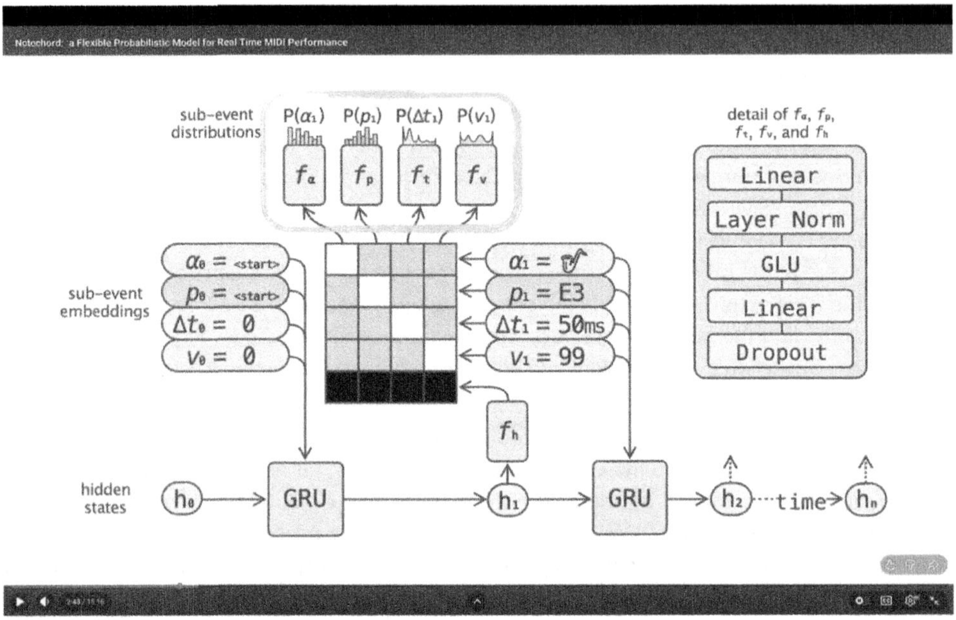

Figure 4.2 A video still giving a technical overview of the Notochord model and early demos.
From "Notochord," https://www.youtube.com/watch?v=mkBKAyudL0A.

dynamics. With the channel of each MIDI event, it could play multiple instrument parts at once (Figure 4.2). MIDI is not so different from the sequence of pitches in the previous example. One just needs to interleave the pitches with the other parts of a MIDI event—is it a NoteOn or NoteOff, what is the velocity, which channel is it played on, and how much time has passed since the previous event? Once this is done, the MIDI performance becomes a sequence of tokens amenable to language modeling. The rest is details. But I got very involved in those details.

Homunculus

Soon I had created a model with more possibilities than I could explore myself. I had created an interesting *meta-instrument*,[15] a toolkit for building instruments. I named it "Notochord," which is the primordial backbone common to vertebrate animals and their ancestors. This was not the whole animal—it was just some structural material. I put together a few demonstrations: playing one part while Notochord plays another; Notochord harmonizing a performed melody; using a MIDI controller to select notes by their relative probability according to Notochord, instead of by pitch. But each of these felt too limited to bend toward musical purposes, while being complicated to modify and reconfigure. To get musicians interested, and to make any useful comparisons between their experiences, I would need to develop some kind of standard interface to Notochord, which musicians could immediately start playing with, yet which could be configured in different ways to expose a range of the model's behaviors.

Responding to needs uncovered in the development of a performance by my colleague Nicola Privato and me,[16] I designed an interface which I called Homunculus (Figure 4.3), after the artificial person of alchemical lore. Homunculus processes MIDI inputs and outputs in real time. It exposes a few controls for each of the 16 MIDI channels, while additional configurations can be set in a text file. Each channel can be put into a certain *mode*. MIDI events on an *input* channel, for example, condition the model but are not altered by it. *Auto* mode channels play new MIDI events that are generated autonomously by the Notochord model. A Homunculus channel can also be in *punch-in* mode, which causes it to switch to input mode when MIDI events arrive and switch to auto mode when none are received for some amount of time. This way, a musician can take control only to have their playing continued

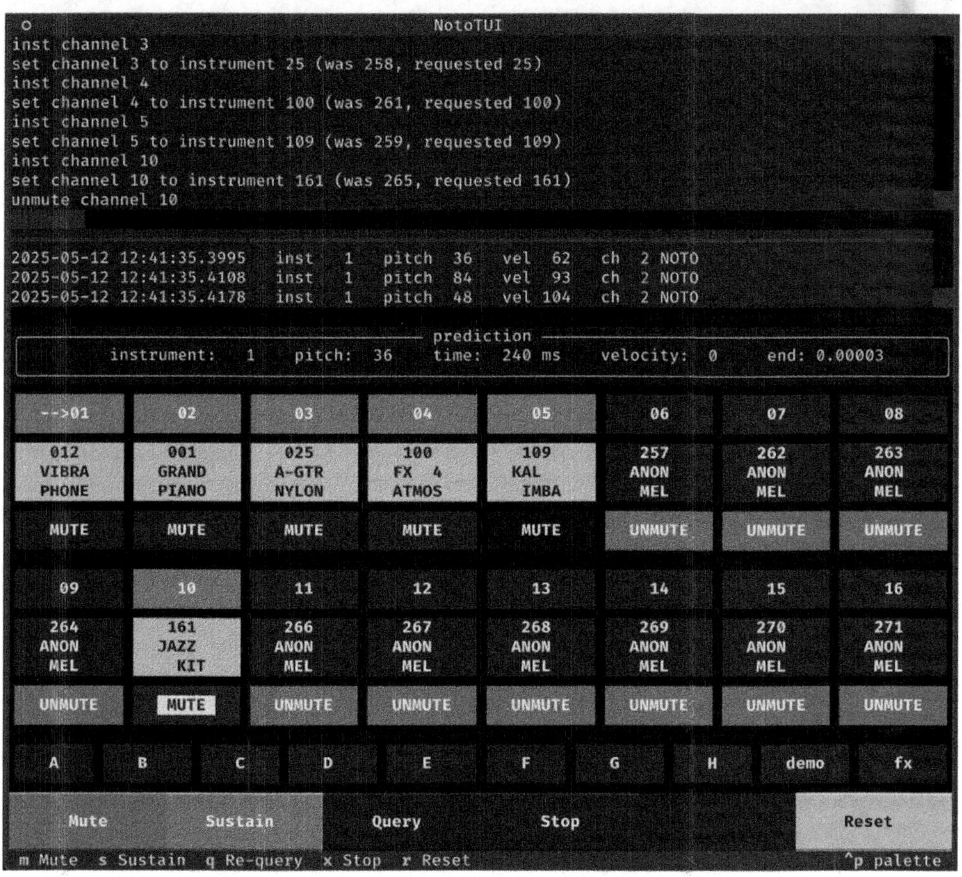

Figure 4.3 Homunculus TUI (text-based user interface). From top to bottom: general log, note log, predicted next MIDI event, MIDI channels 1–16, presets 1–10, global controls.

Figure 4.4 A still from a video demonstrating the MIDI processing features of the Notochord model.

From Shepardson, "Notochord Homunculus," https://www.youtube.com/watch?v=u1ntK2Qg8vo.

by Notochord once they stop. Finally, Homunculus can read a MIDI file into Notochord as a prompt. Notochord then behaves as if continuing past the end of the file with the same instrumentation and style. Homunculus allows live switching between presets, each of which can have different channel configurations and MIDI file prompts (Figure 4.4).

A Notochord model can be trained on any MIDI files, but since I wanted to explore large model aesthetics, I focused on a collection called the Lakh MIDI Dataset.[17] It contains about 100,000 MIDI files scraped from the internet. Most of these use the General MIDI standard, which was common in the 1990s and 2000s on PCs, computer games, electric pianos, synthesizer modules, and karaoke machines. General MIDI defines, among other things, the meaning of each possible MIDI Program Change message to choose a certain instrument sound. When Notochord is trained on this information, and its MIDI outputs are routed to a General MIDI synthesizer, it can play a motley collection of GM "instruments" ranging from various types of pianos and guitars, orchestral instruments, vaguely defined synthesizer sounds, drum kits, and charmingly, a few sound effects like *telephone* and *helicopter*. While it's perfectly possible to route MIDI from Homunculus to a DAW or hardware synthesizer, I like to use an open-source synthesizer[18] together with free General MIDI SoundFonts. This makes a full set of GM sounds available, and steers toward a corny, retro aesthetic that respects the training dataset. Notochord is an animate archive, made up of the General MIDI culture represented by the Lakh dataset; I prefer it to sound that way.

Case Studies

For me, Notochord became a sort of "anti-AI" project. A deadpan parody, unapologetically stupid. An impossible compromise between speed and scale that no responsible engineer would make. An absurd abomination that no music lover should tolerate. MIDI model as sketch comedy. My idiot AI son. A portrait of the plagiarism machine as a broken clock that is right twice a day. A friendly ghost which can always make me laugh. A corpse upon which to meditate.

These are a few ways I've felt about Notochord while incorporating it in various projects. While Notochord has been adapted for less MIDI-centric projects including Tidal Cycles[19] and a machine Txalaparta player,[20] in the following I'll focus on MIDI-based applications using Homunculus.

No-Input Notochord

I don't even like MIDI. When I play music with Notochord, I feed it noise. I like to play the no-input mixer—when a mixing desk is connected from output to input to make feedback—which can be tuned and performed using the gain, equalizer, and routing functions. This is an impossible instrument to represent via MIDI. But represent it I do, using software to crudely transcribe its clicks and screeches and pass them into Notochord. The model does what it can with this signal. Usually it becomes extremely confused. Sometimes we can establish a dialogue. My software measures the mixer's deviation from A440 tuning and bends the MIDI pitches to match; there's always some correspondence between the two sounds. Notochord always reacts to my movements, if not in an expected way. I like to be there at the edge of sensemaking. I like the tension between the ecstatic asemic practice of no-input mixing and the relentlessly referential nature of the language model.

Haunting *in Fríkirkjan*

Once, we put Notochord into a church organ. An organ often has two to four keyboards (called *manuals*) as well as a set of foot pedals, and each one can play a different sound, or *stop*. This organ had three manuals, so four voices including the pedals. We used Homunculus with four channels, in punch-in mode. Whenever the organist stops playing for a while on a particular manual, Notochord takes over. So the organist can play along with it, play call-and-response, or prevent Notochord from playing, all in an intuitive way just by playing the organ with no extra controls. Julie Zhu composed a four-voice fugue, which was used as a prompt for Notochord. As she began to play the fugue, Notochord would join in and continue parts as she moved between the manuals. As Notochord deviated from her score, she would have to improvise around it. It would react and they would try to establish some rapport. But inevitably, they would stumble over each other at some points. Notochord

Figure 4.5 Video still of Julie Zhu and Notochord performing *Haunting* in Fríkirkjan í Reykjavík, Iceland.
From Zhu and Shepardson, "Haunting Fríkirkjan," https://www.youtube.com/watch?v=K-69ZwARreA.

would hear the music becoming more crowded and discordant, and continue that process until it was running feverishly across the manuals (Figure 4.5).

I thought of this as a haunting in two senses: one academic and one vernacular. The first sense is Fisher's *sonic hauntology*.[21] It has been observed that AI music is quintessentially postmodern in the way it makes a flattened and aestheticized pastiche of music history. However, the heightened uncanniness of AI music can also render it fertile ground for artistic critique.[22] Fisher further elaborates a distinction between two kinds of strangeness: the *weird* and the *eerie*.[23] The weird is about unexpected juxtapositions: combinations that don't make sense. The eerie, meanwhile, involves agency. In the eerie, the agent is unclear or not fully present. This is something hauntings and AI models have in common. Who did that? Was it only me? A coincidence? Just an opaque physical process? A trace of the past? An immaterial intelligent being?

One aspect of sonic hauntology is to recall past anticipations of a future that was never realized. I sometimes think of LLMs as specters of utopian sentiment around the early internet, file sharing, and the public library. Even as Fisher wrote about the death of modernism in the mid-2000s, my own formative years were shaped by a sense of rapidly expanding access to information. A rapidly growing internet built around web search and independent publishing seemed to guarantee an enlightened and democratic future. Since that time, this vision has evaporated. Online activity has migrated into a few large social networks that increasingly tighten their grip on user experience to maximize engagement, protect the interests of copyright holders, and serve targeted advertisements. Web searches have meanwhile become increasingly littered with results that exist only to game the search engine rankings, delivering a low-quality answer to the search query buried among diversions and advertisements. Internet users are moving quickly away from web search and into LLM chats instead. The old internet promised to put the archives at everyone's disposal, but that promise was repressed by entrenched interests. Now capital distills those same archives into LLMs and sells them back to the public. The legitimacy of this is unsettled, and so we exist in an uneasy state in which information is free and abundant, but this fact cannot be directly acknowledged. I suspect that the anthropomorphic quality of LLM chatbots—their impersonation of conscious agents—is partially due to a need to repress the awareness that an LLM is an archive.

I also thought of haunting in a second sense: the vernacular ghost story. I enjoy listening to accounts of paranormal experience, noting the common tropes and patterns, and how they relate to the fears, desires, and explanatory frameworks of the experiencer. We gave Notochord's residency in the organ the structure of a spirit encounter story, of which I know two recurring types: haunting by a ghost and demonic possession. A demon is malevolent. It can manipulate you, but only if you listen to it. I think that targeted advertisements are like demons: they prey on the viewer's fears and desires to manipulate attention and extract wealth. This is why I feel social media platforms are a kind of hell. I shudder to think of the kind of powerful demons unleashed by the falling costs of LLM agents which can deeply research the circumstances and personality of a target and craft messaging to induce the desired behavior. However, I think of Notochord as more of a ghost than a demon. Ghosts are harmless if you don't fear them. They are echoes of the past, making only tenuous contact with the present. They are stuck in their own reduced world, with limited appreciation for what is going on among the living. And yet they have an unsettling presence that makes itself known.

User Study

To enable more pointed comparisons, I designed a user study based on individual sessions with Notochord. I invited seven improvising musicians from a variety of backgrounds, some composers, some improvisers, some researchers, some teachers. Some were based in Reykjavík, some visiting from elsewhere.

I tried to strike a delicate balance: musicians should have enough choice to find an aspect of Notochord that appeals to them, but the experience should be constrained enough that direct comparisons can be made between sessions. To make the interface consistent, Homunculus was set up with simplified controls: the player could switch among eight presets and pause Notochord, but not change any other settings or see any visual feedback. Only keyboard players were recruited to play on a MIDI piano with built-in speakers. A pad controller was placed on the music stand for choosing presets, so the musician was presented with one physically cohesive instrument. To make the eight Notochord presets, random MIDI files were drawn from the training dataset, filtering only for diversity and presence of multiple parts. One prominent part from the MIDI file was assigned to the piano keyboard, with the rest to be played by Notochord. As each musician began to play, Notochord would try to operate the other parts as a continuation of the source music. However, the musicians never heard the source files, and neither did I until after the fact.

I was mainly interested in how the experience of improvising with Notochord felt to these musicians. Many people don't find it easy to describe an experience in detail, especially a musical experience that might not have words attached to it in their mind. It can be hard to choose what questions to ask, and especially to avoid suggesting the answers you expect to hear. I used a method called an *explicitation interview*[24] to address these challenges. In an explicitation interview, I ask questions that help the subject focus on recalling how a brief part of their improvisation with Notochord played out. What did they hear? How were they using their hands? I assume as little as possible, mostly repeating what they say back to them to consider. I ask almost empty questions, like "when X happens, what happens? How do you know that Y?" In this way we construct an account of how they approached making music with Notochord that comes from the musician, not from my assumptions. These accounts can become very detailed. It's easy to spend half an hour unpacking a 5-second memory into its constituent sensations and micro-gestures. Of course it's difficult to know if the results of this process correspond exactly to how the experience itself took place. But we can be certain that they represent the subject's retrospective understanding of it. And there is also some experimental evidence that the explicitation interview technique can recover accurate memories of which the subject is otherwise unaware.[25]

Each musician was given time to freely explore the eight Notochord presets. Then I asked them to prepare a short improvisation using a preset of their choice. Immediately after they gave the performance, I asked them to think of a moment that stood out. After identifying a moment, I played the audio recording back to them and then started an explicitation interview focused on that moment.

For example, one musician is primarily a free improvising pianist. His interview produced a detailed account of how improvisation took place with Notochord at a critical juncture when he felt "an urge to be rebellious." He played a certain gesture as a provocation, but "the computer then surprised [him] by playing a phrase super low in volume." He described the experience of formulating an improvised reaction: part of this was being in a state of full awareness, but with a sense of "not thinking." Another aspect was choosing whether to follow his first impulse or defer to a secondary impulse. By digging into this moment, we drew a detailed picture of how he approached Notochord as an improvising partner and focused on satisfying his craft as an improviser. "Working with" Notochord this way was one of three general approaches among the musicians.

A second approach was more of a probing or questioning one. One player's rapport with Notochord reminded me of LLM conversations I've had where I catch it in a confabulation or logical error. Often, pointing out an error fails to get it back on track, and only causes it to become more confused. I notice something analogous happen when players approach Notochord this way. A fragmented series of musical questions is very unlike its training data, and when it sees this, it tends to become more and more incoherent. This tends to cause the musician to target simpler and simpler behaviors. In the musician's mind, they pause and "start over" each time with a new query; but the model has no understanding of this. It sees a stilted and meandering dialogue, which it can at best continue in a similar vein.

The third approach was to *appropriate*[26] Notochord as an instrument by deliberately "breaking" it. During the sessions, Homunculus had a failure mode in which it could get stuck in a "runaway" behavior, producing MIDI events as fast as possible. This would cause it to either create thick drones by opening many notes at once, or to "shred" as one player put it, with many short or percussive notes. Several players found a way to trigger this behavior and chose to do so deliberately in performance. For some, this was related to the keyboard not being their primary instrument. Causing Notochord to produce a dense drone that they could then play on top of or influence at a more coarse gestural level was most compelling to them.

Discussion

I undertook these various encounters with Notochord as part of a *diffractive* research program. Diffractive research is an idea developed by physicist and feminist theorist Karen Barad,[27] building on a text by Donna Haraway.[28] Haraway uses an optical metaphor, comparing a classical theory of light moving in rays with the more general physical theory of light as a propagating electromagnetic wave. Waves not only move through space but extend throughout it, diffracting around corners and interfering with one another. Classical reasoning involves representing the world with language and making deductions. Haraway identifies this kind of linear thinking with classical optics, and provocatively suggests diffractive thinking as the analog of wave optics. With diffraction, the emphasis is on differences and resonances rather than trajectories and final destinations. Barad extends the metaphor with ideas from quantum physics, introducing ideas about indeterminacy, the inseparability of the researcher from the experimental apparatus, and the duality of instrument and object of study.

Though Barad developed diffraction as a way of critical reading and writing, it has been taken up by designers who operationalize it in various ways.[29] For me, diffraction is a way of relating diverse experiences and theories. I have the most extensive and intimate understanding of my own instruments, which I know as both a designer, technician, and musician. But relying purely on my own experience, it would be difficult to reach conclusions that could generalize more widely. I want to incorporate others' experiences too. On the other hand, traditional scientific methods are difficult to apply to the subjective aesthetic experiences I'm interested in. Formal analysis is not useful when one's measurements are only tenuously related to experience. Diffraction offers a way to read the technical methods I design with, theories of agency, my first-person experiences, and explicitation interviews all through one another. In particular, I find it useful to turn others' experiences back on myself. While characterizing each player's approach, I ask myself whether it feels familiar; is it something I have practiced myself, or something I haven't considered? Do I have a latent feeling that it is *wrong* or *right*? Can I understand why in terms of what I know about how Notochord works? Ultimately, this produces *intermediate-level* knowledge,[30] that is, knowledge which I do not claim to be universal, but which is also not completely situated. This is the sort of knowledge that is useful in design, where there are no universally correct principles and no exact specifications. This diffractive process eventually crystallized a few concepts for designing with large model aesthetics.

Ambiguous Attribution

The artificial neural networks underlying LLMs, Notochord, and essentially all generative machine learning are notoriously inscrutable. They are made up of millions to billions of parameters, which at the lowest level of description are engaged in meaningless arithmetic. It's much easier to understand what a model is set up to do than how it actually does it. We tend to understand models teleologically: they "want" to complete sequences plausibly because their training process minimizes prediction error with respect to a dataset. But this logic fails when the input data is too different from the training data (*out of domain*); the model is again just a big pile of parameter values, and its behavior is arbitrary. But how different is too different? Being able to *generalize* from the training data to similar future inputs is the basic promise of generative machine learning. But for the user, it can be impossible to tell whether this is happening. This is especially true when the training dataset is too large or unfamiliar to the user. Is the model doing this because of the training data? Or by sheer accident of its weights? Even as its author, I often cannot tell whether a model is making sense in a way I don't appreciate, or failing to make sense at all. I find this pushes me away from an analytical frame of mind; I have no choice but to give the model the benefit of the doubt and try to make sense with it on its own terms. But this inability to attribute Notochord's behavior also forces me into a certain attitude toward it as an artist. If I don't know how it is using the training data, I can't appropriate that data earnestly. This forces me into an ironic posture, where I recklessly appropriate the entire dataset as a commentary on the process. I am not tempted to record or perform music in the idiom of the dataset using Notochord; I feel a need to take the model deliberately out of domain, or use it conceptually, or write research papers about it.

Agentic Possibility

I looked at whether musicians were preoccupied with understanding how it worked or precisely what it could do. One spoke of "being on the wrong side of the computer screen," while another played in a questioning style, trying to "see how it would respond." In contrast, another player described choosing to "give up thinking" about how it worked. The one player with the deepest technical understanding of Notochord claimed to bracket any thoughts of how it worked out of his awareness: "I didn't ever for a second think about datasets or architecture."

Introspectively, as the creator of Notochord, I'm almost unable not to think about how it works. As I play with Notochord, part of my mind constantly tries to attribute its behavior to the dataset, the model architecture, or the Homunculus runtime. I speculate whether unexpected behaviors are due to software bugs, deficiencies of the model, or peculiarities of the data. But at the same time, I have a limited interest in precisely characterizing its capabilities, which feels like a chore. I'm content to know that it *might* do anything, that it incorporates every piece of training data, and that it computes a unique distribution for every possible MIDI sequence supplied as context. I know that it is sensitive to everything I play, on some level, and that we go down a different path together in every session. This sense of possibility is part of what keeps Notochord mysterious and interesting to me.

Mirroring

A final theme that emerged from the various Notochord encounters: you get out what you put in. Though LLM chatbots obscure this to an extent by prompting the model to stick to a helpful, anodyne personality, generative models inevitably shape their behavior to user inputs. In *Haunting*, for example, we used this quality to structure the piece in multiple ways. First, running the fugue through Notochord once as a prompt biased it into the expected tonality and baroque style. However, there was a mismatch between the performer's attempts to perform the score and Notochord's extemporizations, which resulted in clashing material. Notochord then mirrored this, leading to escalating chaos, which the performer ultimately encouraged to bring the piece to its exorcistic climax.

In the user study, this was particularly apparent when comparing between certain players. One player used a probing, questioning approach. He seemed to assume that Notochord should read his intent as he repeatedly proposed elementary cadences for it to complete. However, from the perspective of the statistical model, there was merely a halting and disjointed performance that it then continued. Another player had a distinct talent for calming Notochord down. While most players' sessions with Notochord converged toward intentional or unintentional disorder, Notochord tended to reciprocate her slow and deliberate playing. She encountered a very different Notochord than some other players, resulting in a divergent experience.

Finally, there is another sense in which generative models are a mirror for the user. One player chose to suspend her efforts to understand Notochord's behavior in order to focus on "feeling" the music. On hearing the recordings of her performance, she noted how different they sounded to her in the moment. She also focused on timbral qualities of the music, which are somewhat incidental to Notochord's actual capacities as it deals only with MIDI notes. Notochord was a foil to this player's immersion in a dense landscape of General MIDI sounds, which she described as "relaxing" and "meditative." Ultimately, she supplied her own meaning to the experience, rather than looking for it in dialogue with the putative AI agent.

Conclusion

I created Notochord in an attempt to unravel LLM aesthetics via music. Like LLMs, Notochord is a crude statistical prediction scaled up to large datasets and then executed as quickly as possible. I put Notochord in a variety of situations in my own and others' music, as well as in a more artificial setting where player experiences could be put under the microscope. Approaching this constellation of experiences diffractively, I identified ambiguous attribution, agentic possibility, and mirroring as concepts for design with large model aesthetics.

While large models are essentially made out of references to training data, one frequently has to guess what those references are. Trying to explicitly understand a model's behavior is often counterproductive, pushing users toward one of two attitudes. One is to offer the model the benefit of the doubt, as if it were a human improviser. However, when the model lacks the agency of a human musician, it becomes something like a mirror: the musician is making sense on behalf of the AI. The experience moves toward Fisher's aesthetics of the eerie, where the presence or absence of agency is felt.

The other route, by contrast, is to deliberately oppose or break the model, moving in the direction of the *weird*. The referential opacity of generative models makes it impossible to appropriate from the dataset in the way one would by direct sampling or allusion. So, to appropriate the AI system itself, a user has to push it out of domain, complicating its connection to the dataset. By making its behavior sufficiently weird, it becomes possible to appropriate the referentiality of the model, rather than merely automating reference to the data.

Notes

1 Victor Shepardson et al., "Notochord."
2 Hiller and Isaacson, *Experimental Music.*
3 Malmqvist, "Sycophancy in Large Language Models."
4 Askell et al., "A General Language Assistant."
5 Jackson and Mazzei, *Thinking with Theory.*
6 Jack et al., "Effect of Latency on Performer Interaction."
7 *MIDI 1.0 Detailed Specification.*
8 Scarlatos et al., "ReaLJam."
9 Magnusson et al., "The Organium."
10 Small, *Musicking.*

11 Agre, "Toward a Critical Technical Practice."
12 Stolterman, "The Nature of Design Practice."
13 Glasmachers, "Limits of End-to-End Learning."
14 Murphy, *Probabilistic Machine Learning.*
15 Fiebrink, "Machine Learning as Meta-Instrument."
16 Shepardson and Privato, "Notochord Arcs & Scrambled Signals."
17 Raffel, "Learning-Based Methods for Comparing Sequences."
18 Newmarch, "FluidSynth."
19 Shepardson et al., "Notochord."
20 Johannsson et al., "Real-Time Musical Collaboration."
21 Fisher, "The Metaphysics of Crackle."
22 Rubinstein, "Uneasy Listening."
23 Fisher, *The Weird and the Eerie.*
24 Petitmengin, "Describing One's Subjective Experience."
25 Petitmengin et al., "A Gap in Nisbett."
26 Zappi and McPherson, "Dimensionality and Appropriation."
27 Barad, *Meeting the Universe Halfway.*
28 Haraway, *Modest_Witness@Second_Millennium.*
29 Frauenberger, "Entanglement HCI The Next Wave?"
30 Höök and Löwgren, "Strong Concepts."

Bibliography

Agre, Philip E. "Toward a Critical Technical Practice." In *Bridging the Great Divide: Social Science, Technical Systems, and Cooperative Work*, 131–157. Mahwah, NJ: Lawrence Erlbaum Associates, 1997.

Armitage, Jack, Thor Magnusson, Victor Shepardson, and Halldor Ulfarsson. "The Proto-Langspil: Launching an Icelandic NIME Research Lab with the Help of a Marginalised Instrument." In *Proceedings of the International Conference on New Interfaces for Musical Expression (NIME).* Auckland, New Zealand: NIME, 2022. https://doi.org/10.21428/92fbeb44.6178f575.

Askell, Amanda, Yuntao Bai, Anna Chen, et al. "A General Language Assistant as a Laboratory for Alignment." arXiv:2112.00861. Preprint, last revised December 9, 2021. arXiv:2112.00861v3. https://arxiv.org/abs/2112.00861.

Barad, Karen. *Meeting the Universe Halfway: Quantum Physics and the Entanglement of Matter and Meaning.* Duke University Press, 2007.

Fiebrink, Rebecca. "Machine Learning as Meta-Instrument: Human-Machine Partnerships Shaping Expressive Instrumental Creation." In *Musical Instruments in the 21st Century: Identities, Configurations, Practices*, edited by Till Bovermann, Alberto de Campo, Hauke Egermann, Sarah-Indriyati Hardjowirogo, and Stefan Weinzierl. Springer, 2017. https://doi.org/10.1007/978-981-10-2951-6_10.

Fisher, Mark. "The Metaphysics of Crackle: Afrofuturism and Hauntology." *Dancecult: Journal of Electronic Music and Dance Culture* 5, no. 2 (October 24, 2013): 42–55. https://doi.org/10.12801/1947-5403.2013.05.02.03.

Fisher, Mark. *The Weird and the Eerie.* Repeater, 2016.

Frauenberger, Christopher. "Entanglement HCI The Next Wave?" *ACM Transactions on Computer-Human Interaction* 27, no. 1 (2019): 2:1–2:27. https://doi.org/10.1145/3364998.

Glasmachers, Tobias. "Limits of End-to-End Learning." In *Proceedings of the Ninth Asian Conference on Machine Learning*, edited by Min-Ling Zhang and Yung-Kyun Noh, 17–32. *Proceedings of Machine Learning Research* 77. Seoul, South Korea: PMLR, November 11, 2017. https://proceedings.mlr.press/v77/glasmachers17a.html.

Haraway, Donna J. *Modest_Witness@Second_Millennium. FemaleMan_Meets_OncoMouse: Feminism and Technoscience*. 2nd ed. Routledge, 2018. https://doi.org/10.4324/9780203731093.

Hiller, Lejaren, and Leonard M. (Leonard Maxwell) Isaacson. *Experimental Music: Composition with an Electronic Computer.* With Wellesley College Library. New York, NY: McGraw-Hill, 1959. http://archive.org/details/experimentalmusi00hill.

Høffding, Simon, and Kristian Martiny. "Framing a Phenomenological Interview: What, Why and How." *Phenomenology and the Cognitive Sciences* 15, no. 4 (2016): 539–564. https://doi.org/10.1007/s11097-015-9433-z.

Höök, Kristina, and Jonas Löwgren. "Strong Concepts: Intermediate-Level Knowledge in Interaction Design Research." *ACM Transactions on Computer-Human Interaction* 19, no. 3 (2012): 23:1–23:18. https://doi.org/10.1145/2362364.2362371.

Jack, Robert, Tony Stockman, and Andrew McPherson. "Effect of Latency on Performer Interaction and Subjective Quality Assessment of a Digital Musical Instrument." In *Proceedings of the Audio Mostly 2016 Conference on Sound in Experience*, 116–123. Norrköping, Sweden: Association for Computing Machinery, October 4, 2016. https://doi.org/10.1145/2986416.2986428.

Jackson, Alecia Youngblood, and Lisa Mazzei. *Thinking with Theory in Qualitative Research: Viewing Data Across Multiple Perspectives.* Routledge, 2011. https://doi.org/10.4324/9780203148037.

Johannsson, Karl, Victor Shepardson, Enrique Hurtado, Thor Magnusson, and Hannes Högni Vilhjálmsson. "Real-Time Musical Collaboration With a Probabilistic Model." In *2024 International Conference on Content-Based Multimedia Indexing (CBMI)*, September 2024, 1–4. https://doi.org/10.1109/CBMI62980.2024.10858876.

Magnusson, Thor, Kit Braybrooke, Sophie Skach, et al. "The Organium: A Library of Technical Elements for Improvisatory Design Thinking." In *Proceedings of the 19th International Audio Mostly Conference: Explorations in Sonic Cultures (AM '24)*, 198–208. New York, NY: Association for Computing Machinery, 2024. https://doi.org/10.1145/3678299.3678319.

Malmqvist, Lars. "Sycophancy in Large Language Models: Causes and Mitigations." arXiv:2411.15287. Preprint, submitted November 22, 2024. arXiv:2411.15287. https://arxiv.org/abs/2411.15287.

MIDI 1.0 Detailed Specification. The MIDI Manufacturers Association, 1996.

Murphy, Kevin P. *Probabilistic Machine Learning: An Introduction.* MIT Press, 2022.

Newmarch, Jan. "FluidSynth." In *Linux Sound Programming.* Springer, 2017.

"Notochord: A Flexible Probabilistic Model for Real Time MIDI Performance." Presentation by Victor Shepardson, Jack Armitage, and Thor Magnusson. YouTube video, 15:16. Posted by "AI Music Creativity 2022," September 20, 2022. https://www.youtube.com/watch?v=mkBKAyudL0A.

Petitmengin, Claire. "Describing One's Subjective Experience in the Second Person: An Interview Method for the Science of Consciousness." *Phenomenology and the Cognitive Sciences* 5, nos. 3–4 (2006): 229–269. https://doi.org/10.1007/s11097-006-9022-2.

Petitmengin, Claire, Anne Remillieux, Béatrice Cahour, and Shirley Carter-Thomas. "A Gap in Nisbett and Wilson's Findings? A First-Person Access to Our Cognitive Processes." *Consciousness and Cognition* 22, no. 2 (2013): 654–669. https://doi.org/10.1016/j.concog.2013.02.004.

Privato, Nicola, and Thor Magnusson. "Querying the Ghost: AI Hauntography in NIME." In *Proceedings of the International Conference on New Interfaces for Musical Expression*, 2024. Utrecht, Netherlands: Zenodo. https://doi.org/10.5281/zenodo.13904901.

Raffel, Colin. "Learning-Based Methods for Comparing Sequences, with Applications to Audio-to-MIDI Alignment and Matching." PhD diss., Columbia University, 2016.

Rubinstein, Yair. "Uneasy Listening: Towards a Hauntology of AI-Generated Music." *Resonance* 1, no. 1 (2020): 77–93. https://doi.org/10.1525/res.2020.1.1.77.

Sanches, Pedro, Noura Howell, Vasiliki Tsaknaki, Tom Jenkins, and Karey Helms. "Diffraction-in-Action: Designerly Explorations of Agential Realism Through Lived Data." In *CHI Conference on Human Factors in Computing Systems*, 1–18. New York, NY: Association for Computing Machinery, April 29, 2022. https://doi.org/10.1145/3491102.3502029.

Scarlatos, Alexander, Yusong Wu, Ian Simon, et al. "ReaLJam: Real-Time Human-AI Music Jamming with Reinforcement Learning-Tuned Transformers." In *Proceedings of the Extended Abstracts of the CHI Conference on Human Factors in Computing Systems*, April 25, 2025, 1–9. New York, NY. https://doi.org/10.1145/3706599.3720227.

Shepardson, Victor. "Notochord Homunculus Real-Time MIDI Model—Voices and Steering." *YouTube video*, 5:45. May 12, 2025. https://www.youtube.com/watch?v=u1ntK2Qg8vo.

Shepardson, Victor, Jack Armitage, and Thor Magnusson. "Notochord: A Flexible Probabilistic Model for Embodied MIDI Performance." In *Proceedings of the 3rd Conference on AI Music Creativity*, September 17, 2022. https://doi.org/10.5281/zenodo.7088404.

Shepardson, Victor, and Thor Magnusson. "Notochord Homunculus: A Playground for Low-Latency Deep Generative MIDI." In *Proceedings of the International Computer Music Conference*, 2025. https://iil.is/pdf/2025_icmc_notochord_homunculus.pdf.

Shepardson, Victor, and Nicola Privato. "Notochord Arcs & Scrambled Signals." *AIMC 2023*, August 29, 2023. https://aimc2023.pubpub.org/pub/tii5jy7j/release/4.

Small, Christopher. *Musicking: The Meanings of Performing and Listening.* Wesleyan University Press, 1998.

Stolterman, Erik. "The Nature of Design Practice and Implications for Interaction Design Research." *International Journal of Design* 2, no. 1 (2008).

Zappi, Victor, and Andrew McPherson. "Dimensionality and Appropriation in Digital Musical Instrument Design." In *Proceedings of the International Conference on New Interfaces for Musical Expression*, 2014. London, UK: Zenodo. https://doi.org/10.5281/zenodo.1178993.

Zhu, Julie, and Victor Shepardson. "Haunting Fríkirkjan." YouTube video, 9:55. Posted by "julie zhu," September 10, 2025. https://www.youtube.com/watch?v=K-69ZwARreA.

5

INTERLUDE II

Interview with George Lewis

Constantin Basica and Julie Zhu

DOI: 10.4324/9781003615873-5

Julie: If you could make a fantasy team of musicians and composers throughout history to play with an AI agent, who would be on your team?

George: A lot of the people who performed with my systems over the years are considered important parts of twentieth and twenty-first century musical history: Muhal Richard Abrams, Amina Claudine Myers, Alexander von Schlippenbach, Louis Sclavis, Louis Moholo, Leroy Jenkins, Mary Oliver, Aki Takase, Roscoe Mitchell, Steve Lacy, Joëlle Léandre, Miya Masaoka, Geri Allen, Derek Bailey, Douglas Ewart, Nicole Mitchell, Magda Mayas, Evan Parker, Bill Dixon, and many others. So I guess I've realized my fantasy.

Julie: You have said that "we have to change our consciousness." We have the hope of changing things in classical music the way that we would like. What do you think will let people say "well, that was different" with regard to AI?

George: Well, I've already experienced that and so have my audiences and many of the performers I've worked with over the decades. But I read this question as more about that elusive value of "greatness," as in the canard "Why are there no great women composers?" My favorite *Voyager* review was from *The New York Times* in 2024: "Computer Soloist Holds Its Own."[1] If the other performers end up feeling (or admitting) that Voyager is holding its own with them, that's already a change of consciousness. But of course, not everyone wants computers to improvise, so that kind of difference is less attractive to them. I would say that, in either case, this kind of conceptual difference can be subversive, upending settled wisdoms.

Julie: What can still surprise you when working with AI, given that you've worked with it for decades now?

George: I haven't worked with "AI." I've worked with a few AIs—all of which I built myself, going back to *Chamber Music for Humans and Non-Humans*[2] in 1979 and *Rainbow Family*[3] at IRCAM[4] in 1984. The last in this series was Voyager. Joel Ryan programmed the FORTH interpreter that I used to create the program at the late, lamented Studio voor Elektro-Instrumentale Muziek (STEIM) in Amsterdam. From 1986 to 2004, Voyager was a multitimbral, microtonal "virtual improvising orchestra" of up to 64 asynchronous, single-voice MIDI "players," using Yamaha FM synthesis and later MIDI sample players. In 2004, Damon Holzborn and I translated Voyager from FORTH into Max on the Macintosh, and I reconceived it as an improvising pianist performing on a Yamaha Disklavier™. This is the version that most people know, which made its Carnegie Hall debut as a soloist with the American Composers Orchestra, improvising freely with my 17-minute orchestral work, *Virtual Concerto*.

At this point, the way Voyager plays and how it responds to what it encounters isn't all that surprising to me, although it still occasionally comes out with things I haven't heard before. As with any person you live with for years, one shouldn't be surprised by that either. And surprise is not an unalloyed good; we have all been surprised by someone suddenly showing us their rotten side.

The latter observation allows me to take aim at the huge cliché that *surprise* constitutes an important achievement in music. Since the Benjaminian revolution of the mechanical reproduction of music, people can now listen to a single piece of music literally thousands of times over their entire lives. I marvel at how a piece of music that one has listened to so much can still provide new pleasures and experiences, even something that you were not aware of before. But again, this is something that living with people (or creative machines) can also offer. There is no compositional, improvisational, or technical process that will necessarily lead to this kind of experience. Thus, rather than making a benchmark from the production of surprise, my goal in making musical AI is to avoid the kind of familiarity that prompts contempt.

Julie: How does AI take criticism? As the creator of Voyager, are you the one receiving criticism? Are you the one responsible?

George: Here, I notice the similarity to older questions of authorship, authority, ownership, copyright, crediting, and intellectual property that were often posed to improvising musicians and composers who incorporated improvisation in their work. Michel Foucault reminds us that when an author "stands behind" a work, the function of a specific author name becomes attached to "the juridical and institutional system that encompasses, determines, and articulates the universe of discourses."[5]

As I've written elsewhere:

> Certainly a real-time improvisation (with or without computers) may be framed as an act of co-authoring, and at the crucial moment of making a sonic choice, the question of whether or not certain co-authors are people may prove just as vestigial as these questions that Foucault regards as a kind of rehashing of old news: "Who really spoke? Is it really he and not someone else? With what authenticity or originality? And what part of his deepest self did he express in his discourse?"[6]

The question here is of responsibility for the creations of an AI, but once you go there, the other questions loom. However, I find these questions to be distractions from my main interests, so I won't make further reference to them here. Instead, I want to approach the question from a different angle, recalling a public question-answer session following a 2011 duo-piano performance between Geri Allen and my Voyager pianist program at the University of Michigan. As many people know, Voyager is an RBAI (rule-based AI) that operates as a self-directed improviser engaged in real-time dialogue with human performers. The Voyager software's rules use its real-time analysis of a human's (or another AI's) performance to guide (but not dictate) its musical responses. The system can generate music without external input, so it becomes what I call a *generative-interactive* AI, manifesting apparent intentionality, personality, and difference.

Reflecting on her performance with Voyager, Allen told the audience, "I found the same types of challenges that I found playing in other duopiano settings. You know, I had to listen and I

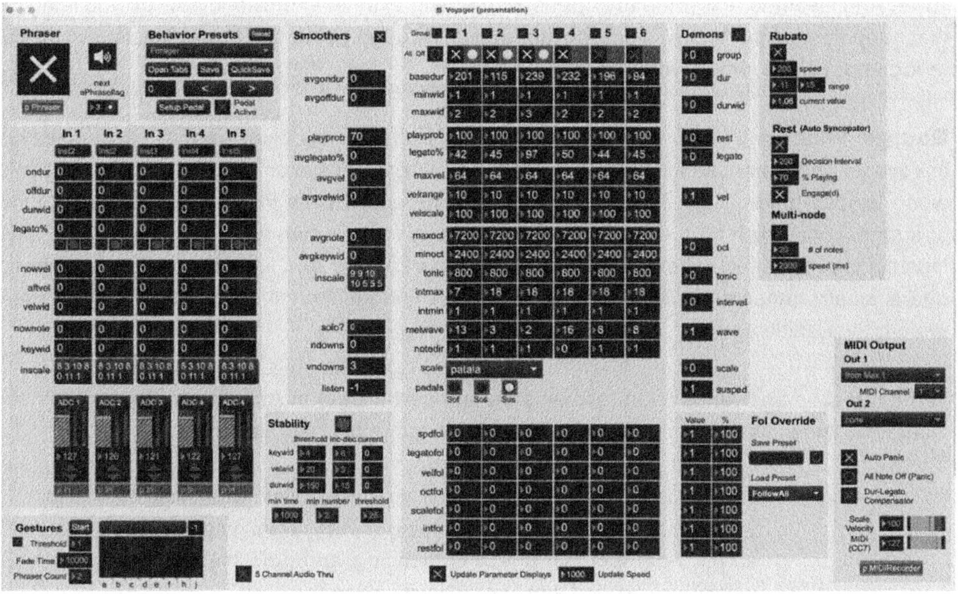

Figure 5.1 The splash screen for the Voyager system, as used in a performance of George Lewis's *Forager* at the Center for Practice and Research in Science and Music (PRiSM), Royal Northern College of Music, Manchester, UK.

had to respond … I completely trusted the choices it was making because it was George's choices in many cases. No? I'd like to know."

I said,

> Where was I? I was in the audience … Whatever choices you guys were making, it was your baby … I made some meta-choices at some level. The way this thing kind of operates is that … you said yourself that it played differently with each of those people, and it also seemed to play very differently with you, which sort of indicates that, if I'm making the choices, that's a pretty good set of choices to be able to have it play differently with each one of you. And maybe that makes me a very special person [laughs]. Or maybe what it really does is, maybe there's a sense in which there's an openness to a lot of different possibilities, so that you guys can just go up there and decide for yourselves what happens in the music, which is kind of the ideal.[7]

The question of responsibility is closely related to the deeper question of agency, which in a Voyager performance is shared between the system, its programmers, and the onstage musical partners. However, at the point of performance, immediate decisions as to where the music is headed come from the onstage performers, not from the programmers. The music being made by the system and its partners inhabits a different, foregrounded modality of agency, as distinct from the background agency of the programmer.

Julie: And if someone wanted to suggest something to an AI improviser, how do you imagine that happening in the future? Through language? Through gesture? Through facial/emotional recognition? What would you prefer?

George: Well, I don't know about the future, but right now, I look at what the musicians do in Voyager performances as making suggestions, which the system is free to adopt or ignore along various parameters. The musicians can also regard what the system does as a form of suggestion, which they are also free to deal with in their own way. As with any real-time musical improvisation, what is on offer to both performers and listeners is the experience of a sonically transacted negotiation. This sense of negotiation is central to any improvised encounter, artistic or not.

In the question-answer session following the concert with Geri Allen, an audience member wanted to know more about how she was experiencing that negotiation:

Question:	Is that to say that you didn't feel like the machine was going to step in and hold you up if you were coming to a low point on your side?
Allen:	Well, I did feel that it was responding, and I didn't know how it was going to respond, but I knew it was going to.
Question:	So it was harder to predict than with a human associate. Of course.
Allen:	I don't know if I would say that.[8]

Geri Allen treated Voyager not as a tool, but as a free being like herself, with a kind of subjectivity. The limits of that subjectivity are only testable by interacting with it in performance and by listening, which is another mode of improvising. For many, Allen's implication that there was no value in essentializing machine difference as experienced in sound could be a truly unsettling prospect. But from her standpoint, improvising with the computer was really no different in kind from working with any other musical partner, like Wayne Shorter or Ornette Coleman, with whom she also performed. With Voyager we have an encounter with difference, in the form of intentionality and personality—or what Harold Cohen called "entitality," since, as he put it, his pioneering painting AI AARON, also an RBAI, is not a person.[9]

Voyager also isn't a tool because it's not instrumentalizable. Rather, it acts as an independent creator with its own artistic personality, one that is not really reducible to the programmer's choices, in the same way that we distinguish between genotype and phenotype. In performance, you can't tell it what to do, and you have no way of vetoing its decisions. It doesn't have "users," and it doesn't accept "prompts." This challenges the dominant tool-user discourse, while obliging humans to face the possibility that we aren't the only creators around.

The question about facial recognition reminds me of a story that appears in an article of mine from 2007,[10] where US National Public Radio commentator Kurt Andersen, interviewing AI pioneer Rodney Brooks,[11] incorporated rather downbeat critical commentary on an excerpt from a Voyager performance[12] they had just played—without any chance for me to respond.

Commentator:	Rodney, I guess the computer programs and output devices that he, George Lewis, uses, don't strictly qualify as a robot in your definition.
Brooks:	No, but they do at least respond to something they're sensing in the world. They're sensing what the human is playing ...
Commentator:	Right.
Brooks:	... from that, come to where they play.
Commentator:	I wonder if a machine that actually played a trumpet or a trombone or a piano, as opposed to outputting those digital sounds, would get us any closer to a kind of interesting simulation of human musical creation?
Brooks:	Well, you might want the robots to be sitting there with the other musicians and making eye contact with them, and understanding the nod and making a little nod back—whose turn it is to take the solo.[13,14]

I would have really enjoyed the opportunity to be part of that conversation, but I probably would have pointed out that communication in music takes place primarily through sound, not through eye contact or nodding. Of course, computer vision has had much more research funding than computer sound, which makes IRCAM a huge and welcome outlier. For the rest, moving beyond the scope of the question, the commentator asked Brooks, "When do we, uh ... get there—that is, machines creating art that we care about?" Well, what I care about in experimental music is the exploration of new forms of intelligibility. That seems to be something that AI researchers like Brooks really did care about—perhaps more in the past than today.

I want to conclude from the foregoing line of argument that there are more interesting and salient questions about musical AI than the problem of the credit line.

Constantin: You have been critical about new trends in AI technology that focus on machine learning to emulate music by—very often dead—humans (e.g., Beethoven or Coltrane), and you point to this shift from people wanting machines to be partners in exchanging subjectivity to people using machines as tools for quick music production via imitation. Is there any positive spin you can see in this going forward? Could this age of perfecting imitation resemble the way a composer or an improviser might start their career by listening, analyzing, and (sometimes consciously but more often unconsciously) imitating some of their favorite music figures, only to later develop their own musical language by distilling their previous influences?

George: Actually, I didn't see that many people who wanted to improvise music with independently thinking machines. That was definitely a minoritarian preoccupation. So I don't mean to be critical of other people's musical choices. I think people should do what works for them. But as always, I find myself asking about what could be different from the dominant view, and as someone who comes from Afrodiasporic musical values, I don't find imitation very attractive artistically. As I told musicologist Alexander Rothe in a published interview,

> All that bebop that people were doing, they're all trying to find themselves and get their own voice and step out. You go on these concerts and the musicians would catch you

> with one of those Berklee "riff books," they called them, where you had all these patterns and stuff, and they say, What are you doing with that? Chico Freeman and I went to Muhal (Richard Abrams) and said, Could you show us how *Giant Steps* works? He said, Why do you want to know that? You know, like it's very suspicious. So I'll show you just this one time. But you have to promise that you will not use this in your own work as a musician.[15]

In that world, it's about finding your own voice, "telling your own story." The pianist Erroll Garner told the drummer Art Taylor in an interview, "If you take up an instrument, I don't care how much you love somebody, how much you would like to pattern yourself after them, you should still give yourself a chance to find out what you've got and let that out."[16] In African American musical history, finding your own voice becomes a post-slavery narrative about a music that banishes silencing forever.

Constantin: Can machines, once they have become "Beethovens" and "Coltranes," be able to move to a higher level of musical understanding and originality?

George: None of what I've been talking about has anything to do with "becoming a Coltrane." It's about finding yourself, and in the AI encounter, perhaps it's finding out something about what it means to be human. Everyone starts out sounding like someone else, but then they work toward developing something personal. Guitarist and theorist Nicola L. Hein goes as far as to identify this phenomenon, which he calls *autocybernetization*, as strongly influenced by

> jazz and Afrological musical practices as the historical precondition and the very cultural and musical genetics of musically improvising computer programs. If we acknowledge this lineage, we can see the relation between the development of jazz and the conception of musical persona and [music as a whole]. The establishment of idiosyncrasy in musical expression and persona as one of the core values of jazz music and its political project is the condition of many contemporary approaches to improvising MAS [musical agent systems].[17]

Constantin: Do you see this paradigm of training AI models on musical styles or genres as a dead end in terms of machine creativity?

George: Well, as an update on Fordist processes, it seems to be monetizable, at least in the short run. But maybe there will be a story where an AI becomes self-aware that goes like the Charlie Parker chili-house tale:

> I remember one night before Monroe's I was jamming in a chili house on Seventh Avenue between 139th and 140th. It was December 1939. Now I'd been getting bored with the stereotyped changes that were being used at the time, and I kept thinking there's bound to be something else. I could hear it sometimes but I couldn't play it. Well, that night I was working over "Cherokee," and as I did I found that by using the higher intervals of a chord as a melody line and backing them with appropriately related changes, I could play the thing I'd been hearing. I came alive.[18]

I would imagine that the AI would tell that chili-house story itself, either in words or in some kind of new music. But how you get to creativity from genre is anybody's guess. Coltrane once said about Third Stream that it was "an attempt to create something, I think, more with labels, you see, than true evolution."[19] My own recent view has been that music has a very unhealthy obsession with genre. Until the new MLAI (machine learning AI) tools came along, visual art did not share this obsession. But now, they have the same aesthetic problem that we do in terms of moving beyond enhanced Benjaminian reproduction and old-style model and variation processes. This is what we are trying to do now with our IRCAM SoVo project,[20] which combines the RBAI approach of Voyager with IRCAM's Somax2[21] (an MLAI). This is a hybrid program that aims to bridge the gap between rule-based and ML-corpus-based models, asking whether and how we can move beyond imitation and toward creativity—not just creating variations on a pattern.

Perhaps, as with the chili-house story, the relations among listening, pattern, iteration, memory, and boredom might be key, as Andrew Pickering noted about Gordon Pask's interactive cybernetic device, MusiColour, which was "designed to get bored … If the same musical trope was repeated too often, the thresholds for the corresponding lighting pattern would eventually shift upward and the machine would cease to respond, encouraging the performer to try something new."[22]

Julie: Electronic music does not need to take a breath. It is not affected by the limitations of human performance. AI takes this even further. The machine can compute and render beyond human capabilities. What aspects of human limitation are you interested in transcending with AI? What aspects of human limitation would you rather leave alone?

George: I certainly don't have a strong sense of what human limitations are. Nobody seems worried about the four-minute mile anymore, and one of the major advances in life expectancy was the discovery of regular hand-washing with soap. And we are always hearing about some new physical feat that people are doing now that hasn't been done before.

One notion of "limitation" to be addressed is the idea that *the human* and *the machine* are isolated from themselves and each other. But both artificial and human intelligence and achievement are the products of social forces, experiences, and histories—"group genius," as R. Keith Sawyer says.

The newest AI Go and chess players seemingly remember everything and can play billions of scenarios before a single move to defeat human players. Certainly, the musical AI programs could record everything and bring back something that was performed 30 minutes ago, or even last year. Perhaps for adherents on the Kivy side of the Peter Kivy–Jerrold Levinson debate on form[23] (i.e., global versus concatenative), that might appear to be a boon of some sort, but I continue to wonder about the actual utility of that capability or action to an immediate musical situation. I can certainly hear when a human (or computer) improviser is thinking ahead and trying to anticipate what the environment will yield. But they can be wrong. Wrong or right, new music is the result. In music, no one "wins"—or maybe everyone wins.

Julie: Electronic music expanded our perception of tonality, among other things. What does AI music expand our perception of? Genre? Musicking? Collective consciousness?

George: The League of Automatic Music Composers[24] noticed a phenomenon of emergence through machine–human sociality in their computer music-making networks of the late 1970s. Each of the League's computers was running a program created by one of its composers that was able to produce music without outside intervention—an automatic improvisation program—as well as taking in data that could affect the behavior of its own system and outputting data that could affect the behavior of the other machines.[25]

However, they noticed that

> if each one of these pieces is played by itself, it sounds quite different. Or if they're all played together without being interconnected into the network, it sounds like, let's say, four different processes going on. But once the network is there, the whole system seems to tune up. So it seems like it's on its own at that time. It seems like it's some kind of ... artificial intelligence that we sort of like contributed to but we can't really say "I did that," right? It's—"the system did it."[26]

Constantin: As a scholar who has written and talked considerably about the social dimension of musical systems, what is your advice to young artists and researchers working with AI models? Do you notice any blind spots—ethical, philosophical, social, artistic—in the way we conceive and develop musical AI systems today?

George: Discussions about AI have changed radically since I began my work in the late 1970s. The people who first inspired me—Roger Schank and especially Marvin Minsky—belonged to an earlier generation who saw a place for computing in tackling the big problems of reason facing humanity. Marvin was a recognized founder of AI, but he was also a virtuoso pianist who always described himself as an improviser and implicitly rejected the hackneyed distinction between improvisation and composition in Western classical music.[27]

I saw some of these early AI scientists as introspective humanists, and their project of representing knowledge was fundamentally an epistemological and philosophical project. Computers became a medium to do philosophy and test theories in an interactive arena, to "understand the nature of the human mind." The idea was to get a computer to do things that, if done by a human, would be perceived by us as intelligent. Of course, the question of who *us* is becomes central, and even some of these researchers did not quite see this.

But most of the popular AI discussions I've read recently don't seem to care much about this humanistic project. In fact, people like Timnit Gebru and Joy Buolamwini[28] have criticized the deeply antihumanist and eugenicist direction[29] that corporate AI has taken, which results in facial recognition programs[30] that often report that Black people fit a criminal profile, or academic "help" programs that single out Black students for punitive measures.[31]

Constantin: What considerations do you think individuals—and, by extension, the institutions they may represent—should take to develop ethical AI systems that foster creative agency in human–machine interaction while avoiding the replication of hierarchies or exclusions found in other musical structures and technologies?

George: As I observed in an article published a quarter century ago,[32] notions about the nature and function of music inevitably become embedded in musical software; interactions with these systems reveal characteristics of the community of culture that produced them. So, in new music, as in other areas, we need to develop and nurture new experts who can form a community to develop new aesthetics and cultural values alongside new technologies. As the ethics of the creators go, so will the ethics of the systems. Wasn't that Gandhi's quip? "What do you think of Western civilization?" "It would be a wonderful idea."

Learn more about George Lewis and his work at https://music.columbia.edu/bios/george-e-lewis

Notes

1 Seth Colter Walls, "A Computer Soloist Holds Its Own"; Lewis, *Tales of the Traveller.*
2 Lewis, *Chamber Music for Humans and Non-Humans.*
3 *Écoutez votre siècle*; Lewis, *Rainbow Family.*
4 IRCAM (French: Institut de recherche et coordination acoustique/musique; English: Institute for Research and Coordination in Acoustics/Music) is a major public research center in Paris, France focused on music and science.
5 Foucault, "What Is an Author?" 216.
6 Foucault, "What Is an Author?" 222; see also Lewis, "What Is a Co-Author?"
7 *The Evolution of George Lewis's Voyager System.*
8 *The Evolution of George Lewis's Voyager System.*
9 Estorick, "When the Painter Learned to Program."
10 Lewis, "Mobilitas Animi."
11 Brooks, interview.
12 Lewis, interview.
13 Interestingly, this colloquy has been scrubbed from the current record of the Brooks interview at the NPR link.
14 Lewis, "Mobilitas Animi," 111.
15 Lewis et al., "Whether It Has a Certain Musical Form," 220.
16 Taylor, *Notes and Tones*, 97.
17 Hein, "A Thousand Ecologies of Improvisation," 158–159.
18 Giddins, *Celebrating Bird*, 59.
19 Lewis, *A Power*, 360.
20 Fiorini et al., "Becoming a Player."
21 IRCAM, *Somax2.*
22 Pickering, The *Cybernetic Brain*, 316.
23 Kania, "The Philosophy of Music."

24 The League of Automatic Music Composers, *The League of Automatic Music Composers.*
25 Bischoff et al., "Music for an Interactive Network," 27.
26 The League of Automatic Music Composers, interview.
27 Minsky, "Music, Mind, and Meaning"; Schank and Abelson, *Scripts, Plans, Goals.*
28 Algorithmic Justice League, "Mission, Team and Story."
29 Gebru and Torres, "The TESCREAL Bundle."
30 Buolamwini, "Unmasking the bias."
31 Rami, "AI teacher tools."
32 Lewis, "Too Many Notes."

Bibliography

Algorithmic Justice League. "Mission, Team and Story." Accessed December 24, 2025. https://www.ajl.org/about.

Bischoff, John, Rich Gold, and Jim Horton. "Music for an Interactive Network of Microcomputers." *Computer Music Journal* 2, no. 3 (1978): 24–29.

Brooks, Rodney. Interview by Kurt Andersen. *Studio 360.* WNYC, January 17, 2003. Audio, 7:24. https://www.wnyc.org/story/117686-special-guest-rodney-brooks/.

Buolamwini, Joy. "Unmasking the Bias in Facial Recognition Algorithms." *MIT Sloan Management,* December 13, 2023. https://mitsloan.mit.edu/ideas-made-to-matter/unmasking-bias-facial-recognition-algorithms

Écoutez votre siècle 8: George Lewis, Rainbow Family. Directed by Michel Davaud. 1984. IRCAM. Video, 26:00. https://medias.ircam.fr/x55b193.

Estorick, Alex. "When the Painter Learned to Program." *Flash Art*, December 5, 2017. https://flash-art.com/article/harold-cohen/.

Fiorini, Marco, George E. Lewis, Gérard Assayag, and Damon Holzborn. "Becoming a Player: The Ubiquitous Subjectivity of SoVo" *Leonardo.* Published electronically November 26, 2025. https://muse.jhu.edu/article/976366.

Foucault, Michel. "What Is an Author?" Translated by Robert Hurley and others. In *Essential Works of Foucault, 1954–1984, Volume Two: Aesthetics, Method, and Epistemology*, edited by James D. Faubion, 205–222. New York, NY: New Press, 1998.

Gebru, Timnit, and Émile P. Torres. 2024. "The TESCREAL Bundle: Eugenics and the Promise of Utopia through Artificial General Intelligence". *First Monday* 29, no. 4 (2024). https://doi.org/10.5210/fm.v29i4.13636.

Giddins, Gary. *Celebrating Bird: The Triumph of Charlie Parker.* Minneapolis, MN: University of Minnesota Press, 2013.

Hein, Nicola Leonard. "A Thousand Ecologies of Improvisation: Cybernetic Listening, AutoCybernetization, and the Decentering of Technology." PhD diss., Columbia University, 2025. https://academiccommons.columbia.edu/doi/10.7916/kt8s-jr49.

IRCAM. Accessed December 26, 2025. https://www.ircam.fr/lircam.

IRCAM, Music Representation Team. *Somax2.* Application. Accessed December 29, 2025. https://forum.ircam.fr/projects/detail/somax-2.

Kania, Andrew. "The Philosophy of Music." In *The Stanford Encyclopedia of Philosophy*, edited by Edward N. Zalta and Uri Nodelman. Winter 2024. https://plato.stanford.edu/archives/win2024/entries/music/.

Lewis, George E. *A Power Stronger than Itself: The AACM and American Experimental Music*. Chicago, IL: University of Chicago Press, 2008.

Lewis, George E. *Chamber Music for Humans and Non-Humans*. Performance with Abdul Wadud, Douglas Ewart, and Richard Teitelbaum, The Kitchen, New York, NY, October 23–24, 1979. http://archive.thekitchen.org/?p=404.

Lewis, George E. "Forager." *Wise Music Classical*. 2022. https://www.wisemusicclassical.com/work/66984/Forager--George-Lewis.

Lewis, George E. "George Lewis: *Tales of the Traveller* (2016)." Performed by Ensemble Signal, conducted by Brad Lubman, with Nicole Mitchell (flute soloist), and Voyager Interactive Computer (piano). YouTube video, 27:44. Posted by "TIMES: SPANS Festival," May 9, 2023. https://www.youtube.com/watch?v=gteMJiucbzk.

Lewis, George E. Interview by Ted Panken. *Studio 360*. WNYC, January 17, 2003. Audio, 7:22. https://www.wnyc.org/story/117684-voyager.

Lewis, George E. "Mobilitas Animi: Improvising Technologies, Intending Chance." *Parallax* 13, no. 4 (2007): 108–122.

Lewis, George E. *Rainbow Family*. Carrier Records, 2020. Digital release of 1984 composition. Bandcamp, https://carrierrecords.bandcamp.com/album/rainbow-family.

Lewis, George E. "Too Many Notes: Computers, Complexity, and Culture in *Voyager*." *Leonardo Music Journal* 10 (2000): 33–39. https://muse.jhu.edu/article/20320.

Lewis, George E. "What Is a Co-Author?" Pew Center for Arts and Heritage, 2014. https://www.pewcenterarts.org/post/keynote-essay-george-e-lewis-what-co-author.

Lewis, George E., Sean Griffin, and Catherine Sullivan. "'Whether it Has a Certain Musical Form, Maybe No One Cares, Except for Some People': George E. Lewis, Sean Griffin, and Catherine Sullivan talk with Alexander K. Rothe about *Afterword, an opera*." *The Opera Quarterly* 39, no. 3–4 (2023): 206–226. https://doi.org/10.1093/oq/kbae017.

Minsky, Marvin. "Music, Mind, and Meaning." *Computer Music Journal* 5, no. 3 (Fall 1981): 28–44. Accessed January 8, 2026. https://web.mit.edu/6.034/www/6.s966/Minsky-MusicMindMeaning.pdf.

Pickering, Andrew. *The Cybernetic Brain: Sketches of Another Future*. Chicago, IL: University of Chicago Press, 2010.

Rami, Norah. "AI Teacher Tools Display Racial Bias When Generating Student Behavior Plans, Study Finds." *Chalkbeat*, August 6, 2025. https://www.chalkbeat.org/2025/08/06/ai-teacher-assistants-promote-racial-bias-study-finds.

Schank, Roger C., and Robert P. Abelson. *Scripts, Plans, Goals, and Understanding: An Inquiry into Human Knowledge Structures*. Hillsdale, NJ: Lawrence Erlbaum, 1977.

Taylor, Arthur. *Notes and Tones: Musician-to-Musician Interviews*. New York, NY: Da Capo Press, 1993.

The Evolution of George Lewis's Voyager *System*. Videofilm for the exhibition *Musica ex Machina: Machines Thinking Musically*, EPFL Pavilions, Lausanne, Switzerland, September 20, 2024–June 29, 2025.

The League of Automatic Music Composers. Interview. KPFA-FM, Berkeley, California, September 21, 1979.

The League of Automatic Music Composers. *The League of Automatic Music Composers 1978–1983*. Album. New World Records, 2007. Bandcamp, https://newworldrecords.bandcamp.com/album/the-league-of-automatic-music-composers-1978–1983.

Walls, Seth Colter. "It's Alive! It's With the Band! A Computer Soloist Holds Its Own." *New York Times*, August 22, 2022. https://www.nytimes.com/2022/08/22/arts/music/time-spans-voyager.html.

6

MOVEMENT III

The Grain of Musical AI Voices: Coding Extra-Normal Values in Live Performance with AI Models

Kelsey Cotton

DOI: 10.4324/9781003615873-6

Deep learning models have revolutionized approaches to synthesizing, cloning, and generating audio material.[1] Although deep learning models for sound synthesis offer opportunities to explore AI-mediated music and sound creation,[2] there are rising concerns about how these models and systems may adversely affect artistic communities and practices and shift sociocultural attitudes toward data sovereignty and societal valuation of art.[3]

Voice-related deep learning development demonstrates similar tensions. Models for rapid voice cloning[4] demonstrate progressive gains in audio fidelity and speed and are increasingly human-like.[5] Such developments are embroiled in ethics discussions,[6] with concerns about deepfakes[7] and impersonation across voice industries.[8]

Critical and playful engagement with AI voice models within music performance contexts affords opportunities to investigate the pragmatic, aesthetic, and ethical potentials of incorporating these technologies into vocal practices.[9] Artistic implementation of AI voice models may facilitate the construction of novel timbral and textural sounds that might otherwise be physiologically dangerous or taxing for vocalists.[10] Further, engagement with novel technologies is not uncommon within the arts: artists are frequently early adopters of technologies,[11] investigating what the technology may offer to both their artistic outputs and their creative process. Music live-coding communities are especially active in this regard, with live coding[12] scholarship increasingly concerned with real-time and live-coded improvisation with AI systems and agents,[13] sound retrieval by virtual agents,[14] and even real-time generation of code.[15]

In this chapter, I investigate how deep learning models for parsing, generating, and synthesizing human-like voice may be critically and playfully approached within my own musical practice through what I term "coding extra-normal values." This is an approach to making and singing with musical AI voices that deliberately uses extra-normal voice as input to AI voice models to reveal and exploit the tensions between human vocal expression and computational processing.

Conceptual Foundations

Evolving Definitions of AI

Definitions of artificial intelligence have evolved across the twentieth and twenty-first centuries, reflecting technological capabilities and theoretical emphasis—from Alan Turing's questions around machine thinking[16] to John McCarthy's framing of human-like reasoning,[17] and from the theory on rational behavior and diverse computational architectures[18] to twenty-first century views foregrounding autonomy and adaptiveness in dynamic environments.[19] Legal definitions recently established in Article 3(1) of the EU AI Act[20] define AI as "a machine-based system ... designed to operate with varying levels of autonomy and that may exhibit adaptiveness after deployment ... that can influence physical or virtual environments." This regulatory framing prioritizes the implications of deployment and societal impact over purely technical capabilities. Such a framing reflects historical and ongoing discourse in critical and feminist scholarship,[21] which reframes the debate on what AI *is*, foregrounding questions around *where* and *how* it is used, and who is affected.[22]

Musical AI

This work defines musical AI as artificial intelligence technologies for analyzing, generating, and manipulating music and sound. Current state-of-the-art models leverage transformer-based diffusion architectures,[23] with leading systems such as Stable Audio and AudioX[24] demonstrating capabilities to generate coherent and high-fidelity audio through latent-diffusion transformers operating on compressed audio representations. Recent innovations include flow matching techniques,[25] multimodal conditioning integrating diverse inputs, and chain-of-musical-thought prompting[26] alongside efficiency improvements through lightweight conditioning mechanisms.[27] These advancements constitute a shift in musical AI,[28] with such sophisticated systems generating high-fidelity musical content.

For voice specific applications, deep learning architectures such as text-to-speech synthesis,[29] transformers,[30] as well as audio and speech generation[31] herald a new era of voice computing. These technologies facilitate the learning, classification, reconstruction, and generation of the textural and timbral features of the human voice. In this text, I specifically engage with deep learning architectures for parsing, cloning, and synthesizing human-like voice material. These include automatic speech recognition (ASR),[32] text-to-speech synthesis (TTS),[33] and variational autoencoders (VAEs).[34]

Automatic speech recognition converts human speech into text by transforming audio waveforms into sequences of tokens[35] through a process of extracting features from the waveform and mapping them to phonemes.[36] Voice conversion and style transfer extract features from source and target audio material, and then use deep neural networks to learn feature transformations from the original and transfer them to the target voice. The transformed features are synthesized into the target voice using a vocoder. Other AI-speech applications include style transfer with transformers and voice conversion. Style transfer with transformers leverages attention mechanisms to capture and modify prosodic elements like rhythm, intonation, and emotional expression while preserving the linguistic content. Voice conversion techniques encompass both speaker identity transformation—where one person's voice is converted to sound like another speaker—and attribute modification (such as changing gender, age, or accent characteristics). These applications often combine multiple neural network components, including encoders for feature extraction, transformers for style modeling, and sophisticated vocoders for high-quality audio synthesis.

Voice

The human voice is both a musical instrument and a sonic and material phenomenon that *has* and *communicates* meaning.[37] It is produced by humans using their physiological subsystems. As a sonic and material phenomenon, it is considered and perceived in relation to the voice-producing body:[38] as representative or indicative of one's identity.[39]

When I refer to human voice or vocal outputs made by a human, I use the term "voice." This distinction becomes important when discussing AI-generated vocal material, which I define as "musical AI voices" to differentiate between human vocal production and computational vocal synthesis. A further distinction I make is between *singing* and *phonation*. While singing and phonating are related, the terms represent different things. Phonation refers to the physiological process of sound production, encompassing the full spectrum of sounds the human vocal apparatus can produce.[40] Singing typically refers to phonation organized according to musical parameters such as pitch, rhythm, and cultural aesthetic frameworks.[41] That is, *phonation* refers to the physiological processes through which vocal sound is produced, while *singing* refers to these processes conducted within a system of aesthetic organization.

Extra-Normal Voice

The human voice is a versatile instrument, and phonation is achievable in a myriad of ways. Alternative ways of phonating are commonly termed "extended vocal techniques,"[42] and can encompass sounds such as creaking, groaning, dental and labial percussion, fricatives, and vocal fry. However, there has been some criticism for the implication that an extended vocal technique defines a departure or a deviation from some singular or universally accepted vocal technique.[43] Michael Edgerton proposes a broader term: "extra-normal," which foregrounds the flexibility of human physiology to produce a wide array of phonatory possibilities, while considering the cultural and musical aesthetics that shape and inform these possibilities. Extra-normal voice sounds have been heard (and notated!) in musical compositions and performances spanning the twentieth and twenty-first centuries.[44]

I adopt Edgerton's term "extra-normal" because it foregrounds the plurality of vocal practices rather than positioning them as deviations from a fixed norm. While the term references "normal," its intent is not to reinforce a universal standard but to acknowledge that what is considered normal is culturally and historically contingent. In my practice, this framing is useful because it situates phonatory diversity within aesthetic and cultural contexts rather than treating it as an anomaly. "Extra-normal" signals an expansion of possibilities (hence the "extra"), recognizing that techniques such as vocal fry, ingressive phonation, or labial percussion are not marginal but part of a continuum shaped by artistic, physiological, and cultural factors. This inclusivity aligns with my approach of using these sounds as creative resources, challenging normative assumptions embedded in both vocal pedagogy and AI voice technologies.

Musical AI Voices

As a material and sonic phenomenon, the human voice has become an important component for deep learning architectures for cloning and synthesizing voice material.[45] Musical AI voices, as I define them in this chapter, are vocal outputs generated or processed by AI models used within musical contexts. This definition encompasses both "successful" replication of human vocal characteristics and "failed" or audibly distinctive divergences from a human-like voice. The resultant musical AI voices become aesthetically significant precisely because they reveal the normative constraints embedded within AI voice architectures, making audible the collision between human vocal materiality and algorithmic processing. Musical AI voices are thus born in a liminal space between human and machine expression, engaging with musical and aesthetic frameworks typically associated with human phonation while demonstrating their own distinctive "AI grain."

Phenomenology and Sound

As a vocalist working within an extra-normal voice practice and with technology, my musical practice is informed by theories of sound and listening that emphasize definitions of sound as a vibrational practice. Barry Truax's definition of sound as "any vibration in the air or other medium, some types of which are able to cause a sensation of hearing" accommodates perspectives from acoustics, psychoacoustics, and soundscape studies, as well as more holistic views of hearing as not solely constrained to the ear—important for parsing and processing by computational means.[46]

This vibrational understanding of sound becomes particularly relevant when considering sound as a material phenomenon.[47] Following Don Ihde's phenomenological perspectives on sound,[48] it possesses materiality through its capacity to affect and be affected—it moves through space, encounters obstacles, and undergoes transformation through various media. When voice becomes input for AI voice models, this materiality persists across different states: from phonation through acoustic vibration to digital representation, and back to synthetic acoustic output. The material properties of sound—its frequency content, amplitude characteristics, and temporal structure—remain central to how AI voice models process and reconstruct vocal material, yet these same properties are simultaneously subject to computational interpretation and transformation.[49]

Toward AI Grain

The theoretical frameworks outlined above converge in my "coding extra-normal values." This approach builds on the phenomenological understanding of sound as vibrational and organized material to position AI voice processing not as a neutral technical operation, but as a transformation that may alternatively preserve or alter the acoustic properties of vocal input. These material transformations may create frictions—after Roland Barthes's "friction between music and something else"—and can become novel material to engage with in musical contexts. The resultant output—the musical AI voice—possesses what I term "AI grain": computational artifacts that function similarly to Barthes's "grain of the voice,"[50] wherein the materiality of the computational processing is made audible.[51] Through live coding's emphasis on transparent, real-time intervention, these moments of computational friction become sites for creative collaboration rather than technical problems to be resolved. I argue for a critical engagement with AI voice technologies that neither accepts their normative assumptions uncritically nor rejects their creative potential. Instead, we may strategically explore the tensions between human vocal expression and AI processing to generate novel sonic possibilities while simultaneously revealing the values and constraints embedded within these systems.[52]

Coding with Musical AI Voices

This section provides an overview of how ASR, TTS, and VAE models are integrated within my live coding setup. The primary objective is to create a feedback loop between vocal expression and computational interpretation, enabling real-time exploration of the tensions between human voice and musical AI voice while making the tensions visible and manipulable through code. This approach bridges research-through-design,[53] technical research practice,[54] and experimental musical practice[55]—embodying the "coding extra-normal values" through deliberate engagement with computational friction as a creative resource. The technical choices outlined below directly serve the aesthetic and critical goals of this practice.

The system comprises three interconnected components: an ASR-TTS pipeline that processes extra-normal phonated samples, generating unexpected linguistic content that is synthesized back into warped vocal clones; a real-time VAE model that reconstructs and interpolates between live voice recordings; and the live coding environment itself.

I use strudel REPL[56] as my live coding software. My customized strudel environment operates on a distributed microservices architecture using three core servers. The primary web interface is served by an Astro.js development server with React components, providing the code editor, pattern visualization, and user interaction elements. Audio samples (both original and AI-generated) are delivered through a dedicated Node.js server (@strudel/sampler) that provides HTTP streaming to the Web Audio API for pattern playback. I implemented periodic, real-time directory scanning so that newly recorded, generated, and interpolated voice samples become immediately available without manual intervention. A Python-based audio processing server integrates hardware control with a Genki Wave MIDI ring, used as a wearable controller to trigger audio recording and automatic processing through the trained VAE.

Recording. The Genki ring controls recording processes through a custom WaveController class using Bleak and genki-wave Python libraries. Incoming events are mapped to an

AudioRecorder class to translate button interactions into recording control signals. Live-recorded audio is written to .wav files in the local strudel codebase, both for use as samples and as material for VAE reconstructions. All audio files recorded into the *live* directory are immediately parsed by a custom AudioProcessor class, where two main actions occur: reconstruction of the recorded audio through the VAE, and generation of interpolated audio files from two previous reconstructions. These are made available to the strudel sample server through the AudioProcessor class.

The variational autoencoder. I trained a VAE using the open-source codebase by Tatar.[57] The VAE was trained on the Freesound Database 50K (FSD50K),[58] which includes sounds of objects, environmental sounds, human sounds, animal sounds, and musical instruments. Prior to use, I filtered the dataset to include only audio files licensed for commercial usage under CC-BY-SA or CC-BY licenses, ensuring the most conservative approach when using data collected by others.

Reconstructions. Newly recorded audio files are normalized to prevent clipping, split into fixed chunks of 1024 samples, and converted to PyTorch tensors. The VAE encodes the audio tensor based on features learned from FSD50K, yielding a compressed representation that is then decoded to reconstruct the audio based on the learned distribution.

Interpolations. The most recently recorded-and-reconstructed audio serves as one interpolation input, paired with a randomly selected historical reconstructed file. A random interpolation alpha (the blending ratio of latent features between the two files) is set and decoded in the latent space, generating a new audio file that amalgamates both inputs. This newly created file is written to a *live_interp* directory, ready for use in the strudel environment.

ASR-TTS clones. I used a dataset of my voice demonstrating extra-normal phonatory techniques (vocal fry, burps, coughs, crying, etc.) as input for OpenAI's Whisper and SpeechBrain's automatic speech recognition models, with the resultant transcriptions used as textual input for the Coqui TTS/XTTS V2 model. The originally recorded phonatory material was then used as a target audio for synthesis.[59] The resultant musical AI voices are warped clones of my own voice, achieved through forcing the "normative" functionality of TTS models to utilize the ASR transcriptions of my extra-normal sounds.

Coding "Grain" in AI Musical Voices

Framing sound as organized material contextualizes how AI voice models process and transform phonated material, creating new material conditions for sonic expression.[60] This grain manifests differently across the ASR-TTS pipeline and VAE processing, each revealing distinct aspects of how computational constraints interact with extra-normal phonation. As an

Figure 6.1 Kelsey Cotton performs a live coding set in strudel, using the setup described in this section to process her voice, at a concert in the KTH Reaktorhallen in Stockholm, Sweden.

Photograph by Kristina Popova.

example, when exhaled sounds are processed by an ASR model as discussed by Cotton and Tatar,[61] the original breath-to-sound ratio becomes reconfigured through spectral analysis and reconstruction, creating sonic possibilities that do not exist in the original vocal gesture. Practically, this means that the ASR-TTS pipeline transforms my original phonated sample, generating a novel sound that maintains a connection to my original input while presenting audio artifacts in the newly generated sound that are a direct consequence of how these models parse human voice. Barthes's "grain" as "the friction between music and something else"[62] is sonically evident in examples of the ASR-TTS pipeline outputting metallic shimmering sounds from phonated vocal fry input (occurring when TTS models struggle to synthesize transcriptions of creaky phonation) and pitch displacements of my exhaled voice due to my overtones creating new musical AI voices that have shifted into registers I cannot physically reach.

These are not errors to be corrected, but aesthetic materials to be explored. They constitute audible evidence of the model's learned assumptions, training biases, and architectural constraints: Barthes's "grain" is extended beyond a human body to the computational.[63] Within my live coding context, I can manipulate and respond to these artifacts in real time, transforming AI grain into collaborative musical material.

Sonic Affordances of the Pre-Generated Samples

AI grain first manifests in my collection of my voice samples parsed through the ASR-TTS pipeline discussed in the "Coding with Musical AI Voices" section. As an example, a burp transcribed as "HAPPENED OH GO NOT R"[64] by the ASR and resynthesized through TTS acquires a pitch displacement (it is lowered) due to the glottal percussion of the sound. This, in turn, transforms the perceived gender marker of the musical AI voice.

When my burps become bilabial plosives and my exhales become syllables, these *errors* reveal the ASR models' embedded assumptions about what constitutes meaningful, or at least transcribable, phonation. In performance, I respond to these algorithmic misreadings by adjusting my live phonation—sometimes mimicking the AI's interpretation of my sounds, sometimes deliberately contrasting with them. This creates feedback loops where human and computational hearing inform each other.

The ASR models' transcription of my extra-normal sounds isn't *wrong* in any absolute sense: the models succeed in performing their operational functions of converting audio to text. But their outputs are aesthetically compelling because of their text-based paradigms struggling to process extra-normal phonation. This glitch then becomes a creative resource: I use the transcriptions as input for the TTS model to resynthesize the glitchy transcriptions (in the style of my extra-normal sounds) back into sound. This effectively creates a warped *clone* of my voice, and a novel musical AI voice in its own right. These are used as samples in my live coding practice, where I can adjust the musical AI voice sample through code, or phonate in dialogue with it. This is also typically the first occasion when I get to hear the musical AI voice. The real-time discovery and response that live coding facilitates allows me to transform the ASR-TTS algorithmic mishearing into a collaborative and creative opportunity: the unpredictability of how my voice has been parsed by the ASR-TTS models becomes a generative resource in live performance.

Sonic Affordances of the Reconstructions and Interpolations

The real-time VAE processing reveals AI grain in more immediate, improvisational contexts. Here, the materiality of the sound is directly manipulable in the live coding context where I first phonate and can then call the reconstructed or interpolated samples into strudel.

Using the VAE trained on FSD50K resulted in audio samples that had a distinctive grainy, watery, and filtered aesthetic. They were quite clearly demarcated from the original recordings of my voice, which had higher perceived fidelity and more timbral and spectral detail. Effectively, the VAE reconstructions had their own distinctive grain. The AI grain of the reconstructions became a creative provocation to respond to with novel vocal gestures. During performance, I found that I would adjust my improvised vocal gestures to contrast, highlight, or timbrally complement the grain of the reconstructed audio.

The training data further influenced how the VAE would reconstruct my voice. The FSD50K dataset encompasses a broad range of sound categories including environmental, object, instrumental, and human sounds. Although human sounds are in the dataset, they are not always voice-specific sounds. The VAE's reconstruction of my voice consistently exhibited characteristics that suggested the model was interpreting vocal input through learned features from non-vocal sources—*mishearing* voice as environmental or mechanical audio. This became more obvious in higher-pitched voice material such as screeches and squeaks, where the high-frequency content in the reconstructions diverged significantly from my voice's characteristics. Rather than a limitation, this became a creative asset: to explore the timbral variations of the VAE in the reconstruction of higher-pitched phonatory gestures.

The interpolation between the VAE reconstructions became an additional resource to explore even more complex sonic possibilities. These interpolations generate impossible vocal gestures, sounds that exceed my physiological vocal limits. As an example, an interpolation between dental plosives and sustained ingressive vowels creates rhythmic patterns with spectral content that morphs continuously between percussive attack and tonal sustain. These are complex sounds that are physiologically impossible for me to sustain. In a live coding performance setting, I would listen to the interpolated transformations and then attempt to recreate aspects of these sounds with my own voice in real time to send back into the VAE as input. This process encourages engagement with the VAE as a collaborative way of exploring new sounds with my voice and new sonic territories that have been revealed through the generative possibilities of the model.[65]

Coding Extra-Normal Values: Synthesis and Implications

The practices and concepts outlined throughout this text collectively constitute a "coding of extra-normal values" into musical AI voices. This prioritizes designing for ambiguity over clarity, exploration over optimization, and glitch as a creative resource. Through integrating automatic speech recognition, text-to-speech synthesis, and variational autoencoders with real-time extra-normal phonation, this work demonstrates how critical and playful interventions with AI voice technologies create novel sonic possibilities. ASR mishearings transform burps into bilabial plosives and dental percussion into unexpected phonemic transcriptions, while VAE reconstructions and interpolations form new musical AI voices to sing and live code with.

This work contributes three elements. First, it presents insight into my artistic practice with AI voice models: I parse my extra-normal phonations into ASR-TTS model pipelines and through VAE models, which I then interact with through singing and live coding. Second, I propose a term for understanding computational vocal materiality by extending Roland Barthes's "grain of the voice" into computational voice synthesis domains. "AI grain"—audible artifacts from the frictions between human voice and AI voice—reveals how AI voice technologies produce a sonic materiality. This process becomes apparent through the use of the ASR-TTS pipeline and real-time application of the VAE to generate reconstructions and interpolations of extra-normal phonation. Third, I reframe the use of AI voice technologies in critical and playful ways as a "coding of extra-normal values." This reframing embraces computational glitches and mishearings as creative resources in a musical performance context, and is a challenge to concepts of vocal normativity in AI voice technologies.

My work demonstrates how artists may critically and playfully engage with musical AI technologies to discover new forms of human–AI vocality. Rather than accepting AI voice systems as closed systems, live coding enables real-time intervention by facilitating feedback loops between human phonation, computational processing, and sonic exploration. The resulting musical AI voices occupy sonic territories that neither human phonation nor computational processing could achieve independently.

As AI voice models become increasingly prevalent across cultural and commercial domains, it becomes increasingly important to cultivate practices that assert the complexity and creative potential of singing *with*, and to critically and playfully explore where these models *succeed* and *fail* in parsing, synthesizing, and generating musical AI voices. This work contributes to broader conversations about artistic engagements with AI by proposing strategic interventions that create space for the extra-normal and the unexpected. Ultimately, I propose critical and playful approaches to AI voice technologies—neither accepting them uncritically nor rejecting them entirely. The goal is not to perfect AI voice technologies but to cultivate the liminal spaces where musical AI voices and human ones meet, enabling the discovery of new sounds and new ways of singing with AI models.

Acknowledgments and Funding

This work was partially supported by the Wallenberg AI, Autonomous Systems and Software Program—Humanities and Society (WASP-HS) funded by the Marcus and Amalia Wallenberg Foundation. The computations were enabled by resources provided by the National Academic Infrastructure for Supercomputing in Sweden (NAISS), partially funded by the Swedish Research Council through grant agreement no. 2022-06725.

Notes

1 Kreuk et al., "AudioGen."
2 Harkins and Prior, "(Dis)locating Democratization."
3 Tatar et al., "A Shift in Artistic Practices."

4 Chen and Jiang, "Voice-Cloning Artificial-Intelligence Speakers."
5 Cui et al., "Sifisinger."
6 Lee et al., "Ethics of Singing Voice Synthesis."
7 Hutiri et al., "Not My Voice!"
8 Arunsaravanakumar, "Deepfake Music Sends Ripples."
9 Warren, "Show More/Show Less."
10 Cotton and Tatar, "Singing for the Missing."
11 Kockelkoren, "Art and Technology Playing Leapfrog."
12 Live coding is a performance practice where software is written, modified, and executed in real-time, often as a form of musical or artistic expression (see Blackwell et al., *Live Coding*). Its history spans from mid-twentieth century computer music (see Roads, *Computer Music Tutorial*) to interactive sound programs (see Chadabe, *Electric Sound*). Momentum grew in the early 2000s with TOPLAP (see Collins et al., "Live Coding"), whose draft manifesto guides the ethos of live coding—emphasizing the visibility of the code being written, edited, and executed. Current global trends indicate integrations of machine learning and AI agents for code generation and responsiveness (see Wilson, "Live Coding"; Xambó and Roma, "Human–Machine Agencies").
13 Knotts and Paz, "Co-Creating Music with Machines."
14 Xambó et al., "Live Coding with the Cloud"; Xambó and Roma, "Human–Machine Agencies."
15 Betancur Gutiérrez, "AI in Live Coding Environments."
16 Turing, "Computing Machinery and Intelligence"; Rich, *Artificial Intelligence*.
17 McCarthy et al., "A Proposal for the Dartmouth Summer Research Project."
18 Minsky, *Semantic Information Processing*.
19 Nilsson, *The Quest for Artificial Intelligence*; Boden, *AI: Its Nature and Future*.
20 European Parliament and Council, *Artificial Intelligence Act*.
21 Johnson and Verdicchio, "The Sociotechnical Entanglement of AI and Values"; Adam, "A Feminist Critique of Artificial Intelligence."
22 Klein and D'Ignazio, "Data Feminism for AI"; Hampton, "Black Feminist Musings"; Noble, *Extended from What?*; Crawford, *Atlas of AI*.
23 Paroiu and Trausan-Matu, "Deep Learning for Music Generation."
24 Tian et al., "AudioX."
25 Lan et al., "High Fidelity Text-Guided Music Editing."
26 Lam et al., "Analyzable Chain-of Musical-Thought Prompting."
27 Tsai et al., "MuseControlLite."
28 Tatar et al., "A Shift in Artistic Practices."
29 Tits et al., "Exploring Transfer Learning."
30 Wang et al., "One-Shot Voice Conversion"; Li et al., "StyleTTS-VC"; Agarwal et al., "Leveraging Symmetrical Convolutional Transformer Networks."
31 Oord et al., "WaveNet"; Wang et al., "Tacotron."
32 Warden, "Speech Commands"; Park et al., "SpecAugment."
33 Kalchbrenner et al., "Efficient Neural Audio Synthesis"; Liu et al., "StrengthNet"; Tits et al., "Exploring Transfer Learning."
34 Tatar, Cotton, and Bisig, "Sound Design Strategies."
35 Typically, these are phonemic structures.
36 Some common deep learning architectures include Connectionist Temporal Classification (CTC), Listen-Attend-Spell (LAS), and Recurrent Neural Networks (RNN).
37 Jensenius, *Sound Actions*; Weidman, "Voice"; Eidsheim et al., *The Oxford Handbook of Voice Studies*.
38 Cotton et al., "Singing for the Missing."
39 Ihde, *Listening and Voice*; Eidsheim, "Voice as a Technology of Selfhood."

40 Sundberg, *Science of the Singing Voice.*
41 Kelsey, "What Is Singing?"
42 Noble, "Extended from What?"
43 Edgerton, *The 21st-Century Voice.*
44 Extra-normal voice sounds can frequently be heard in recordings and in performances by vocalists such as Cathy Berberian, Meredith Monk, Diamanda Galás, Charmaine Lee, Maggie Nichols, Jaap Blonk, and Lori Lixenberg, among others.
45 Josan, "AI and Deepfake Voice Cloning"; Pecora, *Data Driven.*
46 Truax, *Handbook for Acoustic Ecology*; Müller, *Fundamentals of Music Processing.*
47 Weidman, "Voice."
48 Ihde, *Listening and Voice.*
49 Müller, *Fundamentals of Music Processing.*
50 Barthes, "The Grain of the Voice."
51 Shep, "Digital Materiality."
52 Cotton and Tatar, "Sounding Out Extra-Normal AI Voice."
53 Frayling, "Research in Art and Design."
54 Pelinski et al., "Ways of Knowing, Ways of Writing."
55 Warren, "Show More/Show Less."
56 Referred to as strudel hereafter. A JavaScript port of Tidal Cycles, strudel is chosen for its high readability and browser-friendly accessibility, which facilitates rapid prototyping.
57 Tatar, *rawaudiovae.*
58 Fonseca et al., "FSD50K."
59 For a deeper overview of this process, see Cotton and Tatar, "Sounding out Extra-Normal AI Voice."
60 Poulsgaard and Malafouris, "Understanding the Hermeneutics of Digital Materiality."
61 Cotton and Tatar, "Singing for the Missing."
62 Barthes, "The Grain of the Voice."
63 Berry, *The Philosophy of Software*; Kirschenbaum, *Mechanisms*; Poulsgaard and Malafouris, "Understanding the Hermeneutics of Digital Materiality."
64 See the poem titled "04-4.burps_oh—200106_1543—012.wav" on page 86 of *is there more to say?* Accessible via my website: https://kelseycotton.com/projects/is-there-more-to-say.
65 Rezwana and Maher, "Understanding User Perceptions"; Tatar et al., "A shift in Artistic Practices."

Bibliography

Adam, Alison. "A Feminist Critique of Artificial Intelligence." *European Journal of Women's Studies* 2, no. 3 (1995): 355–377. https://doi.org/10.1177/135050689500200305.

Agarwal, Shrutina, Sriram Ganapathy, and Naoya Takahashi. "Leveraging Symmetrical Convolutional Transformer Networks for Speech to Singing Voice Style Transfer." Preprint, submitted August 26, 2022. arXiv:2208.12410. https://arxiv.org/abs/2208.12410.

Arunsaravanakumar, Srishreya. "Deepfake Music Sends Ripples Across the Music Industry." *The Wildcat Tribune*, May 25, 2023. https://thewildcattribune.com/17528/ae/deepfake-music-sends-ripples-across-the-music-industry.

Barthes, Roland. "The Grain of the Voice." In *Image, Music, Text.* New York, NY: Hill and Wang, 1978.

Berry, David M. *The Philosophy of Software: Code and Mediation in the Digital Age.* London, UK: Palgrave Macmillan, 2011.

Betancur Gutiérrez, Celeste. "AI in Live Coding Environments: Pandora's Dream." In *Proceedings of the International Conference on AI and Musical Creativity.* AIMC, 2023. https://aimc2023.pubpub.org/pub/9lqurr1x.

Blackwell, Alan F., Emma Cocker, Geoff Cox, Alex McLean, and Thor Magnusson. *Live Coding: A User's Manual.* Cambridge, MA: MIT Press, 2022.

Boden, Margaret A. *AI: Its Nature and Future.* Oxford, UK: Oxford University Press, 2016.

Chadabe, Joel. *Electric Sound: The Past and Promise of Electronic Music.* Upper Saddle River, NJ: Prentice Hall, 1997.

Chen, Wenjun, and Xiaoming Jiang. "Voice-Cloning Artificial-Intelligence Speakers Can Also Mimic Human Specific Vocal Expression." *Preprints* (2023). https://doi.org/10.20944/preprints202312.0807.v1.

Collins, Nick, Alex McLean, Julian Rohrhuber, and Adrian Ward. "Live Coding in Laptop Performance." *Organised Sound* 8, no. 3 (2003): 321–330. https://doi.org/10.1017/S135577180300030X.

Cotton, Kelsey, Katja de Vries, and Kıvanç Tatar. "Singing for the Missing: Bringing the Body Back to AI Voice and Speech Technologies." In *Proceedings of the 9th International Conference on Movement and Computing, MOCO '24*, 1–12. New York, NY: Association for Computing Machinery, 2024. https://doi.org/10.1145/3658852.365906.

Cotton, Kelsey, and Kıvanç Tatar. "Sounding Out Extra-Normal AI Voice: Non-Normative Musical Engagements with Normative AI Voice and Speech Technologies." In *The International Conference on AI and Musical Creativity.* Oxford, UK, 2024. https://aimc2024.pubpub.org/pub/extranormal-aivoice/release/1.

Crawford, Kate. *Atlas of AI: Power, Politics, and the Planetary Costs of Artificial Intelligence.* New Haven, CT: Yale University Press, 2021.

Cui, Jianwei, Yu Gu, Chao Weng, Jie Zhang, Liping Chen, and Lirong Dai. "Sifisinger: A High-Fidelity End-to-End Singing Voice Synthesizer Based on Source-Filter Model." In *ICASSP 2024 - 2024 IEEE International Conference on Acoustics, Speech and Signal Processing (ICASSP)*, 11126–11130. IEEE, 2024. https://doi.org/10.1109/ICASSP48485.2024.10446210.

Edgerton, Michael E. *The 21st-Century Voice: Contemporary and Traditional Extra-Normal Voice.* 2nd ed. Lanham, MD: Rowman & Littlefield, 2015.

Eidsheim, Nina Sun. "Voice as a Technology of Selfhood: Towards an Analysis of Racialized Timbre and Vocal Performance." PhD diss., University of California, San Diego, CA, 2008. https://escholarship.org/uc/item/0h8841kp.

Eidsheim, Nina Sun, and Katherine Meizel. *The Oxford Handbook of Voice Studies.* Oxford Handbooks. Oxford, UK and New York, NY: Oxford University Press, 2019.

European Parliament and Council of the European Union. Regulation (EU) 2024/1689 of the European Parliament and of the Council of 13 June 2024 Laying Down Harmonized Rules on Artificial Intelligence (Artificial Intelligence Act). *Official Journal of the European Union* L 2024/1689 (June 13, 2024). https://eur-lex.europa.eu/eli/reg/2024/1689/oj.

Fonseca, Eduardo, Xavier Favory, Jordi Pons, Frederic Font, and Xavier Serra. "FSD50K: An Open Dataset of Human-Labeled Sound Events." *IEEE/ACM Transactions on Audio, Speech, and Language Processing* 30 (January 2022): 829–852. https://dl.acm.org/doi/pdf/10.1109/TASLP.2021.3133208.

Frayling, Christopher. "Research in Art and Design." In *Royal College of Art Research Papers* 1, no 1 (1993). https://antle.iat.sfu.ca/wp-content/uploads/2018/08/Frayling.pdf.

Hampton, Leila M. "Black Feminist Musings on Algorithmic Oppression." In *Proceedings of the 2021 ACM Conference on Fairness, Accountability, and Transparency, FAccT* '21, 1. New York, NY: Association for Computing Machinery, 2021. https://doi.org/10.1145/3442188.3445929.

Harkins, Paul, and Nick Prior. "(Dis)locating Democratization: Music Technologies in Practice." *Popular Music and Society* 45, no. 1 (2022), 84–103. https://doi.org/10.1080/03007766.2021.1984023.

Hutiri, Wiebke, Oresiti Papakyriakopoulos, and Alice Xiang. "Not My Voice! A Taxonomy of Ethical and Safety Harms of Speech Generators." Preprint, last revised May 15, 2024. arXiv:2402.01708v2. https://arxiv.org/abs/2402.01708.

Ihde, Don. *Listening and Voice*. 2nd ed. New York, NY: State University of New York Press, 2007.

Jensenius, Alexander R. *Sound Actions: Conceptualizing Musical Instruments*. Cambridge, MA: MIT Press, 2022.

Johnson, Deborah G., and Mario Verdicchio. "The Sociotechnical Entanglement of AI and Values." *AI and Society* 40 (2025): 67–76. https://doi.org/10.1007/s00146-023-01852-5.

Josan, Harnoorvir Singh. "AI and Deepfake Voice Cloning: Innovation, Copyright and Artists' Rights." 2024. https://www.cigionline.org/publications/ai-and-deepfake-voice-cloning-innovation-copyright-and-artists-rights.

Kalchbrenner, Nal, Erich Elsen, Karen Simonyan, Seb Noury, Norman Casagrande, Edward Lockhart, Florian Stimberg, Aaron van den Oord, Sander Dieleman, and Koray Kavukcuoglu. "Efficient Neural Audio Synthesis." Preprint, last revised June 25, 2018. arXiv:1802.08435v2. https://arxiv.org/abs/1802.08435.

Kelsey, Franklyn. "What Is Singing?" *Music & Letters* 30, no. 3 (1949): 216–230. https://www.jstor.org/stable/731005.

Kirschenbaum, Matthew G. *Mechanisms: New Media and the Forensic Imagination*. Cambridge, MA: MIT Press, 2008.

Klein, Lauren, and Catherine D'Ignazio. "Data Feminism for AI." In *The 2024 ACM Conference on Fairness, Accountability, and Transparency*, 100–112. Rio de Janeiro, Brazil: ACM, 2024. https://doi.org/10.1145/3630106.3658543.

Knotts, Shelley, and Iván Paz. "Co-Creating Music with Machines: Some Possibilities." In *The Cyber-Creativity Process: How Humans Co-Create with Artificial Intelligence*, edited by G. E. Corazza, 203–37. Cham: Springer Nature Switzerland, 2025. https://doi.org/10.1007/978-3-031-84535-2_7.

Kockelkoren, Petran. "Art and Technology Playing Leapfrog: A History and Philosophy of Technoèsis." In I*nside the Politics of Technology: Agency and Normativity in the Co-Production of Technology and Society*, 147–167. Amsterdam, Netherlands: Amsterdam University Press, 2005. https://uplopen.com/chapters/1421/files/cae4e7d3-8c3f-41f7-86de-74aa8dbc0023.pdf.

Kreuk, Felix, Gabriel Synnaeve, Adam Polyak, Uriel Singer, Alexandre Défossez, Jade Copet, Devi Parikh, Yaniv Taigman, and Yossi Adi. "AudioGen: Textually Guided Audio Generation." Preprint, last revised March 5, 2023. arXiv:2209.15352. https://arxiv.org/abs/2209.15352.

Lam, Max W. Y, Yijin Xing, Weiya You, Jingcheng Wu, Zongyu Yin, Fuqiang Jiang, Hangyu Liu, et al. "Analyzable Chain-of Musical-Thought Prompting for High-Fidelity Music Generation." Preprint, submitted March 25, 2025. arXiv:2503.19611v2. https://arxiv.org/abs/2503.19611.

Lan, Gael Le, Bowen Shi, Zhaoheng Ni, Sidd Srinivasan, Anurag Kumar, Brian Ellis, David Kant, et al. "High Fidelity Text-Guided Music Editing via Single-Stage Flow Matching." Preprint, last revised October 16, 2024. arXiv:2407.03648v2. https://arxiv.org/abs/2407.03648.

Lee, Kyungyun, Gladys Hitt, Emily Terada, and Jin Ha Lee. "Ethics of Singing Voice Synthesis: Perceptions of Users and Developers." In *Proceedings of the 23rd International Society for Music Information Retrieval Conference (ISMIR)*, 733–740. Bengaluru, India: ISMIR, 2022. https://archives.ismir.net/ismir2022/paper/000088.pdf.

Li, Yinghao Aaron, Cong Han, and Nima Mesgarani. "StyleTTS-VC: One-Shot Voice Conversion by Knowledge Transfer from Style-Based TTS Models." Preprint, submitted December 29, 2022. arXiv:2212.14227. https://arxiv.org/abs/2212.14227.

Liu, Rui, Berrak Sisman, and Haizhou Li. "StrengthNet: Deep Learning-based Emotion Strength Assessment for Emotional Speech Synthesis." Preprint, last revised October 8, 2021. arXiv:2110.03156v2. https://arxiv.org/abs/2110.03156.

McCarthy, John, Marvin. L. Minsky, Nathaniel Rochester, I. B. M. Corporation, and Claude E. Shannon. "A Proposal for the Dartmouth Summer Research Project on Artificial Intelligence." 1955. http://jmc.stanford.edu/articles/dartmouth/dartmouth.pdf.

Minsky, Marvin L. *Semantic Information Processing*. Cambridge, MA: MIT Press, 1968.

Müller, Meinard. *Fundamentals of Music Processing*. Cham, Switzerland: Springer International Publishing, 2015.

Nilsson, Nils J. *The Quest for Artificial Intelligence: A History of Ideas and Achievements*. 1st ed. Cambridge, MA: Cambridge University Press, 2009.

Noble, Charissa. "Extended from What? Tracing the Construction, Flexible Meaning, and Cultural Discourses of 'Extended Vocal Techniques.'" PhD diss., University of California, Santa Cruz, 2019. https://escholarship.org/uc/item/6qn119zh.

Noble, Safiya Umoja. *Algorithms of Oppression: How Search Engines Reinforce Racism*. New York, NY: NYU Press, 2018. https://doi.org/10.2307/j.ctt1pwt9w5.

Oord, Aaron van den, Sander Dieleman, Heiga Zen, Karen Simonyan, Oriol Vinyals, Alex Graves, Nal Kalchbrenner, Andrew Senior, and Koray Kavukcuoglu. "WaveNet: A Generative Model for Raw Audio." Preprint, last revised October 31, 2016. arXiv:1609.03499v2. https://arxiv.org/abs/1609.0349.

Park, Daniel S., William Chan, Yu Zhang, Chung-Cheng Chiu, Barrett Zoph, Ekin D. Cubuk, and Quoc V. Le. "SpecAugment: A Simple Data Augmentation Method for Automatic Speech Recognition." Preprint, last revised December 3, 2019. arXiv:1904.08779v3. https://arxiv.org/abs/1904.08779.

Paroiu, Razvan, and Stefan Trausan-Matu. "Deep Learning for Music Generation: Four Approaches and Their Comparative Evaluation." Preprint, submitted April 3, 2025. arXiv:2504.02586. https://arxiv.org/abs/2504.02586.

Pecora, Alessandro E. "Data Driven: AI Voice Cloning." Laurea thesis, Politecnico di Torino, 2023. https://webthesis.biblio.polito.it/27738.

Pelinski, Teresa, Andrew McPherson, and Rebecca Fiebrink. "Ways of Knowing, Ways of Writing: Technical Practice Research in New Musical Instrument Design." *Journal of New Music Research* 53, no. 1–2 (2024): 79–92. https://doi.org/10.1080/09298215.2024.2442348.

Poulsgaard, Kåre Stokholm, and Lambros Malafouris. "Understanding the Hermeneutics of Digital Materiality in Contemporary Architectural Modelling: A Material Engagement Perspective." *AI & Society* 38, no. 6 (2023): 2217–2227. https://doi.org/10.1007/s00146-020-01044-5.

Rezwana, Jeba, and Mary Lou Maher. "Understanding User Perceptions, Collaborative Experience and User Engagement in Different Human–AI Interaction Designs for Co-Creative Systems." In *Proceedings of the 14th Conference on Creativity and Cognition, C&C '22*, 38–48. New York, NY: Association for Computing Machinery, 2022. https://doi.org/10.1145/3527927.3532789.

Rich, Elaine. *Artificial Intelligence*. International ed., 8th print. McGraw-Hill Series in Artificial Intelligence. Auckland, New Zealand: McGraw-Hill, 1988.

Roads, Curtis. *The Computer Music Tutorial*. 2nd ed. Cambridge, MA: MIT Press, 2023.

Schlichter, Annette, and Nina Sun Eidsheim. "Introduction: Voice Matters." *Postmodern Culture* 24, no. 3 (2014). https://www.pomoculture.org/2017/09/09/introduction-voice-matters.

Shep, Sydney J. "Digital Materiality." In *A New Companion to Digital Humanities*, edited by S. Schreibman, R. Siemens, and J. Unsworth, 322–330. Chichester: John Wiley & Sons, 2015.

Sundberg, Johan. *Science of the Singing Voice*. DeKalb, IL: Northern Illinois University Press, 1989.

Tatar, Kıvanç. *rawaudiovae*. GitHub. Accessed June 9, 2025. https://github.com/ktatar/rawaudiovae.

Tatar, Kıvanç, Kelsey Cotton, and Daniel Bisig. "Sound Design Strategies for Latent Audio Space Explorations Using Deep Learning Architectures." In *Proceedings of Sound and Music Computing 2023*. KMH Royal College of Music and KTH Royal Institute of Technology, 2023.

Tatar, Kıvanç, Petter Ericson, Kelsey Cotton, Paola Torres Núñez del Prado, Roser Batlle-Roca, Beatriz Cabrero-Daniel, Sara Ljungblad, Georgios Diapoulis, and Jabbar. Hussain. "A Shift in Artistic

Practices through Artificial Intelligence." *Leonardo* 57, no 3 (2024): 293–297. https://doi.org/10.1162/leon_a_02523.

Tian, Zeyue, Yizhu Jin, Zhaoyang Liu, Ruibin Yuan, Xu Tan, Qifeng Chen, Wei Xue, and Yike Guo. "AudioX: Diffusion Transformer for Anything-to-Audio Generation." Preprint, last revised April 23, 2025. arXiv:2503.10522v2. https://arxiv.org/abs/2503.10522.

Tits, Noé, Kevin El Haddad, and Thierry Dutoit. "Exploring Transfer Learning for Low Resource Emotional TTS." Preprint, submitted January 14, 2019. arXiv:1901.04276. https://arxiv.org/abs/1901.04276.

Truax, Barry. *Handbook for Acoustic Ecology*. 2nd ed. Cambridge Street Publishing, 1999.

Tsai, Fang-Duo, Shih-Lun Wu, Weijaw Lee, Sheng-Ping. Yang, Bo-Rui Chen, Hao-Chung Cheng, and Yi-Hsuan Yang. "MuseControlLite: Multifunctional Music Generation with Lightweight Conditioners." Preprint, last revised June 24, 2025. arXiv:2506.18729v2. https://arxiv.org/abs/2506.18729.

Turing, Alan M. "Computing Machinery and Intelligence." *Mind*, New Series 59, no. 236 (October 1950): 433–460. https://courses.cs.umbc.edu/471/papers/turing.pdf.

Wang, Yuxuan, R. J. Skerry-Ryan, Daisy Stanton, Yonghui Wu, Ron J. Weiss, Navdeep Jaitly, Zongheng Yang, et al. "Tacotron: Towards End-to-End Speech Synthesis." Preprint, last revised December 3, 2019. arXiv:1703.10135v2. https://arxiv.org/abs/1703.10135.

Wang, Zhichao, Qicong Xie, Tao Li, Hongqiang Du, Lei Xie, Pengcheng Zhu, and Mengxiao Bi. "One-shot Voice Conversion for Style Transfer Based on Speaker Adaptation." Preprint, last revised February 21, 2022. arXiv:2111.12277v2. https://arxiv.org/abs/2111.12277.

Warden, Pete. "Speech Commands: A Dataset for Limited-Vocabulary Speech Recognition." Preprint, submitted April 19, 2018. arXiv:1804.03209. https://arxiv.org/abs/1804.03209.

Warren, Kristina. "Show More/Show Less: Extended Voice, Technology, and Presence." PhD diss., University of Virginia, 2017. https://kmwarren.org/Warren_ExtendedVoiceDiss_Final.pdf.

Weidman, Amanda. "Voice." In *Keywords in Sound*, edited by D. Novak and M. Sakakeeny, 232–246. Durham, UK: Duke University Press, 2015.

Wilson, Elizabeth. "Live Coding with an Affective Autonomous Agent in TidalCycles—Performance." In *Proceedings of the International Conference on AI and Musical Creativity (AIMC)*. Brighton, UK: University of Sussex, 2023. https://aimc2023.pubpub.org/pub/vnkwhmgn.

Xambó, Anna, and Gerard Roma. "Human–Machine Agencies in Live Coding for Music Performance." *Journal of New Music Research* (2024): 1–14. https://doi.org/10.1080/09298215.2024.2442355.

Xambó, Anna, Gerard Roma, Sam Roig, and Eduard Solaz. "Live Coding with the Cloud and a Virtual Agent." In *NIME 2021*. 2021. PubPub. https://nime.pubpub.org/pub/zpdgg2fg/release/1.

7

INTERLUDE III

Interview with Jennifer Walshe

Constantin Basica and Julie Zhu

DOI: 10.4324/9781003615873-7

Constantin: We had a conversation in 2017, when you visited Stanford to give a talk about your work. It was before the big AI blow-up, and you were convinced that artificial intelligence was going to be the next big thing. Then, at Darmstadt[1] in 2018 you said: "I'm convinced that within 15 to 40 years machines will be able to write music, in many genres, which is indistinguishable from that written by humans." And now, just a few years later?

Jennifer: Certainly in 2017, I could sort of smell something on the wind. In 2018, I wrote a paper that I gave at Darmstadt.[2] I was very serious when I wrote that paper. I felt it was an important statement I was making, which I researched in very precise detail. I discussed it with Jon Leidecker[3] and lots of other people, including Mark Applebaum,[4] who I'd met at Stanford when I'd visited the previous year. It was something I took very seriously because I felt I was making a claim: "This is the future, this is what's coming next." I couldn't have been sure of the timeline. In 2018, none of us were sure of the timeline. You know, as with any research to do with AI, it could be five years, it could be five weeks, or it could be fifty years—you just don't know. And so, all of a sudden, there was this leap forward with everything from DALL-E to Stable Diffusion to ChatGPT and things like that.

I don't know what the next step is, because what I imagined is not what we have. The first thing to be affected was images, more than music, and now music is really being hit. Platforms like Suno and Udio—if you look at their early promotional text and the interviews the CEOs gave—were positioning themselves very much as democratizing forces. They were saying that music-making had somehow historically been in the hands of the elite and that it was just such a drag to have to learn how to play a musical instrument … that it was just so upsetting for people who had amazing ideas for songs that they couldn't just make by thinking about them. But now, Udio (from what the press releases seem to imply) is turning into a lovely app for Universal Music Group to allow fans to make fanfiction about artists in their catalog.

If you're asking, "When will a piece of music be interesting to the avant-garde?" I always think that what will be interesting to the avant-garde is how people frame it, what people do with it. So, you could take any output of Udio—the most saccharine, rubbish-sounding pop—and if it's in the right context, with somebody who knows what they're doing, it will become interesting. I think that we've already been at this stage for a while. It depends on who's working with the material. Certainly, I've seen plenty of AI projects, and just because it's made with AI doesn't make it automatically interesting. There are really imaginative, playful, yet serious, though sometimes hilarious uses of the technology. And then there's stuff that's just bog-standard, and the AI's not saving it from mediocrity.

Julie: Talking about speed and what you're saying about Udio and Suno—offering things very, very quickly, but you have to then edit and frame them—is there something about this speed that you feel actually helps an artist psychologically? I wonder if you have something to say about the different speeds of working with AI and the psychological aspect, and how that's maybe changed for you, or what you think is an affordance of that speed.

Jennifer: On the most basic level, if you're a commercial music composer, if you write music to be in the background of family vlogs on YouTube that require 40 minutes of music to soundtrack their trip to Target—yeah, AI is your friend because you've just got to churn out as much material as you possibly can, and you can do that quicker now. And there are plenty of services that can help you do that quicker. There are interesting things that any of these platforms can be used for, either to do things quickly or to do things slowly. But I think the problem that we're in now is that when people talk about AI, they're mostly talking about either Claude, Gemini, or ChatGPT. That's their entire understanding of what AI is, which is what "AI" is to the general public: a commercial platform, usually an LLM, supplied by one of a handful incredibly valuable companies with huge amounts of venture capital invested in them.

I did a project for Tate Modern, working with students. They had some funding from Anthropic, and there were vibe coding workshops for the students, and watching students who had no coding experience being able to spin up web apps in an afternoon was very interesting. Initially, it seems quite magical, but then you end up arguing with the system: it crashes, it disconnects you, you don't have any more credits, and you can't troubleshoot the way you normally would. So, all the time, when I use any commercial LLM, I'm sort of testing it, trying to see, "Okay, what could be useful about these systems?" And, at times, I feel like the notable labor I'm providing is not actually for me; it is to test the company's product, but I'm not being paid to troubleshoot. I see governments—for example, the UK government—pushing for the adoption of AI across the entire country. But for many people, AI is first and foremost a corporate product, which they are either required to or feel pushed to use, and using that product requires a subscription. Even if someone signs up for the free tier, it requires some sort of buy-in. Everyone, whether a free or premium customer, is being monetized far beyond the fee they might pay. That doesn't quite sit so well with me, you know? But then at the same time, I see people on subreddits talking at length about how helpful some of these systems can be. It's not black and white, there's no easy answer to any of it.

In my essay, *13 Ways of Looking at AI, Art & Music*,[5] there's a chapter called *AI Is Boobs*, which basically sums up my entire philosophy. I see medical researchers—people who are looking for funding for cancer research and who are having problems getting the buy-in. And at the same time, I see people making loads of soft porn and hard porn images of boobs from companies that are happy to give them loads of GPU power to do this. And you sort of think, well, as a society, if we'd maybe taken a vote … and said, "Where should all the processing power go to?" I'd happily vote to take away ChatGPT, take away AI overviews, take Meta out of WhatsApp. Just give it to the cancer researchers. Let them have as much compute as they need to make all of our lives infinitely better.

But the problem is that AI is operating within the structures of late capitalism. So it's inextricable from it, in a way. There's the technology, which is one thing, and then there's the fact that the way it rubs up against our bodies and our psyches and our lives is embedded in the structures of late capitalism, of neoliberalism.

If we're going to devote all the lithium, if we're going to build all the data centers, if we're going to say that a certain country—like Ireland where we have so many data centers because of Brexit—is going to devote a third of our national grid's electricity to a handful of corporations, then the citizens should have some say on what that computing is going to. I'm a Ted Nelson fan and I believe in Project Xanadu.[6] I think that we should have micropayments, and that data should be a commons. If my data is in a dataset and I give it with consent, I should benefit in some way because I've contributed something to the commons. If my data from the NHS—the National Health Service here in the UK—is used to make more streamlined ways of delivering drugs to people, I'm very happy about that. I'm not happy if Peter Thiel buys that data and uses it to squeeze every last bit of money out of the NHS.

Julie: It feels like whenever you talk about art and AI, we always come back to capitalism. We come back to neoliberalism. And we think about "How do we make a system that isn't extractive? How do we make AI a public utility? Or GPU, or compute power, or whatever it is?" And I wonder, when you talk to your students about this, how do you help them see the issue? How do you imbue a sense of agency about what they can do in the face of these powers? Do you talk about that, or is that something that's too big?

Jennifer: We always talk about that. The very first thing to do is just get people to think about it. It's literally to just think about it, to try to understand it. And to understand what happens between when you type, "Unicorn wearing a flower crown dancing on a birthday cake" into a prompt window and get the image. What are all the hidden layers of labor, of extractivism, of skill, of amazing research? What are all these different layers that contribute to you getting that image? The technological achievements that bring you that image—they're amazing! Magical! But what got us there? I think right now, we're still in the phase where a lot of the really amazing art that's made now about AI is basically pedagogical; it's concerned with trying to unpick how it all happens.

Julie: Like Trevor Paglen and Kate Crawford's images.[7]

Jennifer: Right, that's essentially an excellent pedagogical work as well as an excellent artistic work. That focus on explainability through art is important for a lot of artists at the moment, for example Memo Akten, who I collaborated with for the project *ULTRACHUNK*.[8] I always send my students to Memo's work because it's really clear and really stable in an installation—which is not always the case for AI works in the gallery! Gallery visitors look at Memo's work, say for example *Learning to See*,[9] and it allows them to understand concepts like machine vision very clearly. They can understand, "Oh, okay, so if the network's only been trained on images of roses, when the camera's aimed at my hands and I move them around, it only sees my hands as flowers." And then they understand, "Oh, okay, it's about this limited dataset and this limited way of seeing the world." I think we're still in this phase now, but who knows for how long. And certainly not all artists are interested in the same things Paglen, Crawford, Akten, and even Hito Steyerl are interested in. The aura of the AI artwork is still pretty powerful for a lot of people in the art world, and a lot of people who are into NFTs are not so interested in them providing a pedagogical function—they're more like financial instruments than art. And also in lots of cases the idea that something's made with AI is much more powerful than whether it's an interesting work of art.

There's a fantastic Irish artist, Alan Butler, who works a lot with AI, and he and I were doing an in-conversation event in Dublin for his exhibition at the Royal Hibernian Academy a couple of summers ago. Alan was saying, "Yeah, we've maybe got two, five, six years maximum, where the work that we're making is thematizing the use of AI, it's troubling it, it's being critical." This era will pass, because sooner or later AI will just be integrated into everybody's workflow, and saying you made a work with AI will be as notable as saying, "I wrote my novel," not "my special computer novel that I typed into a special computer program called Microsoft Word." It'll just be simply how people work.

So I do think this period is really important because it is establishing ways of thinking critically about it; it's establishing a grammar around AI art in the same way cinematic grammar had to be established. Because if we lock in that everybody just makes music with Udio or Suno or similar platforms from now on and we don't think that there might be other alternatives, then we have a problem, culturally. Let's explore everything, let's look for those alternatives! There's some wild art to be made! It's not just simple doom and gloom. It's also thinking about there being new, exciting, more interesting pastures out there that we could shoot for before everything gets enclosed.

Constantin: Do you think that's actually realistic? That timeline of two to five years? I'm thinking about computers, for example. They've been around for a long time, and people have integrated them into everything, but we still think about computers, and how we work with computers. I think about Holly Herndon, who was talking about her *intimate work* with computers just a few years ago. So I wonder: Do you think AI is going to become fully integrated that quickly, and we're soon not going to talk about it anymore as the main theme?

Jennifer: I'm looking for when the art world doesn't thematize it. I wrote that Darmstadt paper in 2018, and the first person who wanted to talk to me about it was George Lewis. We spent a long time that night in the bar talking about it. And now we see each other all the time, doing AI talks at different places. There were a lot of composers at the time who thought I was talking about science fiction. But since then, I've seen an awful lot of composers putting AI in their bio. So I'm talking about the point where it's meaningless to put AI in your bio.

I think, for certain artists it'll just not be that interesting to talk about AI. If you think about mastering tools like LANDR,[10] there'll be lots of artists that use it to master because it's cheaper. They can put another album out on Spotify or Bandcamp, and nobody will say, "Oh, I use an AI tool to master"—it'll just be integrated. I definitely think there'll always be people doing what I really would say is *conceptual art*. A great deal of work with AI now is just conceptual art first and foremost. Therefore, when I talk about it with my students, I say, "We have to understand this as conceptual art and look at the way conceptual art is made—what a conceptual artwork does that's different from a non-conceptual artwork." That's where I'm coming from.

Constantin: Sticking around in this topic of your work with students, I wonder, because you mentioned the word *aura*, how you think about originality in AI-based music. There's, of course, the big discussion about ownership, authorship, and datasets, but I guess I'm more interested in what you think about the Walter Benjamin–kind of aura of AI music. Especially in a piece like *A Late Anthology of Early Music*[11]—where is that aura? Is it in the curation and the recording of the dataset? Is it partly in the AI model? Is it in the concept of the piece? Is it, as you say, because it's an AI piece made at this point in time? Or how do you see this?

Jennifer: With *A Late Anthology*, I have to always mention Dadabots,[12] because they're the people who took my voice and used it to train a model. But Dadabots had to have a dataset to train on. I had already created a huge set of solo voice recordings as part of a different project, so I had them ready to go. Then after Dadabots sent me the training outputs, I spent a very long time playing around with the recordings, figuring out what to do with them. And for that project, it was clear to me that I wanted it to be very precise, conceptually. So I played around with those recordings for a year before I came across the idea of doing this reworking of the early history of Western music. For me, the creativity is in playing around with the material, creating the dataset, having the idea, spending a long time making all of these versions. Now I do live sets based on that material, so the creativity in that is a lot about me trying to sound like a machine-learning-generated version of myself. With the technology in use in 2018, the outputs were full of jankiness and weird artifacts, which was what interested me musically.

This is the other thing I think about: I do feel that experimental musicians were the most primed to start working with machine learning artifacts early on. Once WaveNets came along and raw audio could be fed into a model, and a model could produce audio rather than MIDI files, experimental musicians were the people best equipped to deal with that because it's all full of artifacts and noise and things like that. If you're a classically trained musician who just wants to write nice, conventional, classical, contemporary music, you're not going to know how to deal with a sound file that's noisy like that. Whereas, if you're an experimental musician, an improviser, a noise artist, you've been messing around with that sound world your whole life. So back in the 2010s, the people around me who were most interested in it were my collaborators Tomomi Adachi and Jon Leidecker, as well as myself—all of us highly experienced free improvisers interested in exactly how bad it sounded at the time. That made it enchanting for us, and that's why we wanted to interact with it.

I know there are classically trained composers whose interest in AI is in getting permutations of a pitch sequence that sound just as beautiful as the ones they may have come up with. They're interested in more subtle variations, but they're not interested in the raw sound of the messed-up vocals that were posted with the WaveNets paper. Different people interact with these networks in different ways.

Constantin: I am curious—because you mentioned using ChatGPT in voice mode—if you could talk a little bit about the voice. In a way, almost everything in your work kind of revolves

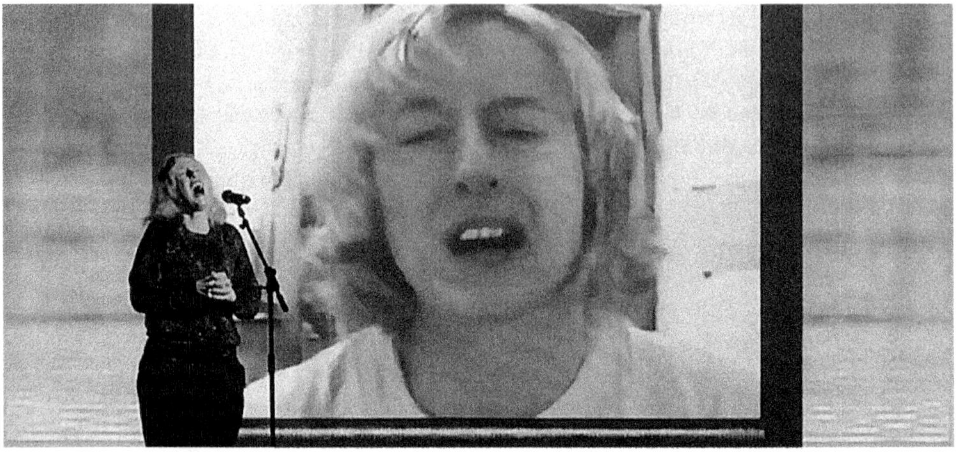

Figure 7.1 Video still from a performance of *ULTRACHUNK* by Jennifer Walshe and Memo Akten.

around the voice. And with AI, you can get this sort of posthuman voice, right? There's no limitation to it. There's no more body, no lungs. And you can sculpt it in digital ways, in every imaginable way. In a work like *ULTRACHUNK* (Figure 7.1), this doppelgänger voice—has that affected your relationship with your own voice in any way? Have you discovered anything through the creation of these datasets with Memo and with Dadabots?

Jennifer: Definitely … particularly when I made the dataset for *ULTRACHUNK*. That was a horrible experience, and I hated doing it. Because I don't want to improvise with myself. I want to improvise with another person, or at least another device. If I can't be with people, or even animals, I'd rather improvise with apps on my iPad, or improvise with a piano, or something like that. The whole experience of improvising, alone, in front of a webcam, for months and months, made me realize how much I love improvising with other creatures, however you might define those. Talking about the voice, the critical issue is that—and I addressed this in my *Ghosts of the Hidden Layer* essay, again in *13 Ways*, as well as in my PhD thesis back in 2002, in fact—the second you have a voice that sounds in any way like a person, you can serve a body. I am a Roland Barthes fan in this respect.

There's a reason why OpenAI ripped off a voice that sounded as close as possible to Scarlett Johansson's. It's because the movie *Her* really influenced their thinking, and Scarlett Johansson is considered a very conventionally attractive person, so they wanted a voice that people want to listen to because the voice sounds sexy. I think that the voice is intrinsic to people having huge attachment to these networks. Because that's what you want, that really hardcore attachment, which will keep the subscription fees coming. People can become attached to anything. But when you have something that's simulating the voice of a conventionally attractive person in your ear, that's going to be incredibly powerful, intoxicating to people—that voice interaction.

That said, as somebody who's watched at least three seasons of *Catfish*[13] on MTV: people fall in love with people they've only ever texted. So, I think that text is already compelling enough. Or maybe I should say, if text is already compelling enough that people fall in love over it, adding voice is going to turbocharge the emotional connection, to use the sort of language a VC[14] guy would. Attention, kindness, and contact are so compelling in today's world—we all need that, we all want that.

And if you can get that through your phone? I'll go back to Shoshana Zuboff[15] here: These things [*waves her smartphone*] are designed to be little gambling machines. We're little rats in Skinner boxes, hoping to get a pellet of food on a weird feeding schedule. You have the phone, which is designed to make us want to pick it up all the time and check and get a little dopamine bump because somebody sent us a text. Then you have an AI device that will just keep texting you all the time and can chat to you at four o'clock in the morning when everybody's asleep. And we have the fact that, at the end of the day, we're simply human beings, and a little bit of kindness and a little bit of attention goes a very long way to making us feel better about ourselves.

So, in a way, the biggest takeaway is: Wow, if we give other people a little bit of attention, a little bit of kindness, we can build much stronger social bonds instantly. Because we can see how desperately people need that.

Constantin: We are in a sort of golden age of deepfakes at this point. And you've used this creative technique of faking realities in your work even before AI—in *Aisteach*,[16] and with the work for *Grúpat*[17]—but then also with AI for *A Late Anthology*, for *URSONATE%24*,[18] and for *ULTRACHUNK*. There's maybe some overlap in how these work, but they seem to have a different purpose. Because when you use AI, you're not just using it as a tool to create these fake realities. You're using it as something where you actually show that it has limitations and that it has some beauty in the uncanniness of the AI. So I wonder, how do you see things moving along in your own work—this idea of alternative ethnography and auto-ethnographic work?

Jennifer: Every dataset we make—things we choose to include, things we choose to exclude, just the same as any archive—is a story that we tell in that moment about history, or about the world we live in. My thinking right now is that we should "make symbolic AI great again."[19] That's where I'm at. I find myself less interested in working with these platforms. I'm sure lots of people will do fun stuff with that, and I'm sure there'll be weird forms of fanfiction and weird forms of music that I can't predict, as well as art that I will enjoy and art that will move me. I'm just not so into it for making my own art at the moment.

Currently, I find myself going back to the old-school approach of thinking—let's just think it through. Let's think of the weird rules that we can make. The last machine learning piece that I made was this reworking, a sort of cover version of *Ursonate* by Kurt Schwitters, which I did through different platforms like Udio and Suno. And when I did that, I really enjoyed doing it. I got to learn a lot about how those networks worked. And after I did that, I thought, "I'm done for the moment." Who knows? At the moment, I'm far less interested in machine learning models. I'm more interested in the criticality around it.

When I did the Grúpat project (where I assumed eleven different alter egos), and when I did Aisteach (which involved myself and a lot of other artists assuming a wide range of historical alter egos), the attraction was always having to imagine myself into someone else's position. It involved so much research and work, both artistically and technically. It was really challenging and really fun. For example, in Aisteach—a project that claims to be the Irish archive for avant-garde art—I made drone recordings, which I claimed proved minimalism emerged in Ireland. There was the process of making the drone recordings, of treating them so they sounded like they'd been made on tape and then digitized. I visited the Irish Folklore Commission; I forged Ellis Island immigration records and a ship manifest as part of the back story. Tony Conrad assumed an alter ego in order to write an essay from the point of view of an Irish musicologist when it was first exhibited. If I were doing that project now, it would be so tempting to use GenAI. But it would be terrible because the whole point of projects like Aisteach—the whole point of the avant-garde—is to try to imagine sounds outside the current dataset, and not only to imagine those sounds alone but also with others.

Right now, I'm interested in AI for technical rather than artistic work, so I've built some apps that were really useful for analyzing datasets that I made. But that's sort of mega boring to anyone who isn't me. And that's where we're headed: it's just integrated into the workflow. But in terms of thematizing the AI and saying, "I'm collecting this dataset and training it," right now I'm actually not so interested in that. I'm more interested in symbolic AI. And given the insane climate costs and things like that, I also feel like we need to maybe calm down a wee bit.

Julie: I hear you, and I think you've already done a lot with AI, so it's okay to give it a rest, for sure [*all three laugh*]. And we all know that AI is good at replicating the past, so it's like you said: fanfiction—just reproducing something that already has a world. But if you were going to make a prediction, given what you know and your experience with people engaging with AI, what do you think the music of 2070 will sound like? Is it going to be all ambient AI slop? Or is it going to be even more diverse than what we have now because the internet will have exploded to even more fractious pieces? Or, I don't know … I'm curious about your thoughts.

Jennifer: First of all, I should say, I was just listening to Rosalía's album[20] today, and my students and I are all loving "Berghain." So, there's music being made today that's exciting and interesting, and that's not even talking about all my favorite artists like Charmaine Lee or Evichsen, or people like that who just make this amazing kick-ass music. There's definitely music made today by singular, incredibly creative, strong-minded artists.

I think the big change—if I'm going to actually make a prediction—between now and 2070 will be in the further consolidation of the platforms, the way that music is delivered to us. When I was 15, I used to tape songs off the radio in order to have access to music because I had very little money. And then, gradually, I was able to buy CDs and cassettes and vinyl and things like that. And every time I listened to it was just … a choice that I made alone in my home: Am I going to listen to this album or not? It was not surveilled; it was not captured. Nobody knew if I listened to Doolittle[21] 1000 times or one time.

In contrast, the way that the vast majority of listeners "buy" things now (if they buy them at all rather than paying streaming fees) is either from Bandcamp—in which case the artists are not receiving any streaming royalties, they're just receiving the cost of the album—or through Apple Music or Prime, where most listeners stream the albums. Most people are listening to music on Spotify, where you can't buy the album, and the royalty payment structure is a sort of dog-fight between whoever happens to be most popular that month. And if you're not listening to a physical product in your home, everything about your listening behavior is being captured; your experience of the platform and the music on it is prosecuted through platform physics.

I wrote an essay called *Platform Musicking*[22] about this a year ago. We listen *with* the platform, *through* the platform. And this sort of behavior already has AI embedded in it, and is ripe for AI to be embedded even more, with possibilities such as increasing niche levels of personalization, tools that will allow you to generate musical fanfiction based on your favorite pop star's latest hit, bespoke country and western mixes of a rap hit (because that's your genre of choice), hours and hours of AI-generated lo-fi chill beat-slop to block out the music in the café you're sitting in.

A lot of listeners use music to optimize their day. They use music functionally, to listen to in the background while they're working or studying, to block out their neighbors arguing. People use music to mood manage, to bring their energy up at the gym or down on the train ride home. AI enables the creation of this sort of functional music, in a bespoke way, at huge scale. There are plenty of people already listening to AI-generated pop music; there have been AI-generated tracks by virtual artists charting high all over the world in the last year. Hatsune Miku[23] demonstrated that being a virtual artist can work, so I see there being increasingly more AI artists.

There are already plenty of AI-generated ASMR[24] videos floating around, and—given that it is a genre so embodied, so rooted in the physical, in the intimate—it shows everything is up for grabs. I can imagine people being interested in platforms that give them a flow they drop into, rather than an album-based experience. I can imagine some composers going down that route and starting to do more durational work or installation-based work. I can also imagine "unplugged" style gigs making a comeback. Gigs in caves with no amplification, for example.

I definitely think people will always make music. I don't think there's any shift in that sense, or any danger that *that* will shift. But we've had this other shift in how we listen to music, which is now more often than not served and controlled by platforms gathering huge amounts of metadata about us with every click. I think those strange balances of how royalties are apportioned are going to continue, and I would imagine there'll be new versions of those, new ways that music can be monetized. I would guess a lot of it will be to do with fanfiction.

I imagine there will be loads of cool music I can't predict. Because humans have always made amazing music that people living fifty years before them couldn't have predicted! It could be platforms focused on weird music, where people are trying to sail the machine learning boat out into those uncharted waters of the latent space and find strange new micro-niches of genres that never existed before. It could be a cult evolving around what people think is the first AGI composer, which results in real-world concerts. It could be livestreams of deceased folk musicians jamming with 11-year-old fiddle players. But I don't have any fear that people will stop making music. People falling in love, and their boyfriend dumping them, and wanting to party, and wanting to write and also listen to songs about these things—I guarantee that will still be happening in 2070.

Learn more about Jennifer Walshe and her work at https://milker.org

Notes

1 The Darmstädter Ferienkurse (Darmstadt Summer Courses) is a summer course and festival for contemporary music in Darmstadt, Germany.
2 Walshe, "Ghosts of the Hidden Layer."
3 Jon Leidecker (Wobbly) is an American electronic musician, composer, and frequent collaborator with the author, known for his work with found sound and improvisation.
4 Mark Applebaum is an American composer, improviser, and professor of music at Stanford University.
5 Walshe, "13 Ways of Looking at AI."
6 "Project Xanadu."
7 Crawford and Paglen, "Excavating AI."
8 Walshe and Akten, "ULTRACHUNK."
9 Akten, *Learning to See.*
10 LANDR is an online music platform that offers AI-powered mastering, distribution, collaboration, and promotion services for musicians.
11 Walshe, *A Late Anthology.*
12 *Dadabots.*
13 "Catfish: The TV Show."
14 VC is an abbreviation for "venture capitalist."
15 Shoshana Zuboff is an American author, professor, social psychologist, philosopher, and scholar.
16 Walshe, "Aisteach."
17 Walshe, "Grúpat."
18 Walshe, *URSONATE%24.*
19 The phrase is a pun on "Make America Great Again," the campaign motto of Donald Trump, the 45th and 47th President of the United States.
20 Rosalía, *Lux.*
21 Pixies, *Doolittle.*
22 Walshe, "The Entanglement."
23 Hatsune Miku is the name of a voice synthesizer software and its corresponding virtual idol—a globally popular pop star whose songs are created by her fans.
24 ASMR (autonomous sensory meridian response) refers to a tingling, static-like sensation in response to specific auditory or visual stimuli, such as whispers, tapping sounds, or slow movements.

Bibliography

Akten, Memo. *Learning to See*. Accessed February 7, 2026. https://www.memo.tv/works/learning-to-see.
"ASMR." *Wikipedia*. Accessed February 22, 2026. https://en.wikipedia.org/wiki/ASMR.
"Catfish: The TV Show." *Wikipedia*. Accessed December 28, 2025. https://en.wikipedia.org/wiki/Catfish:_The_TV_Show.
Crawford, Kate, and Trevor Paglen. "Excavating AI: The Politics of Images in Machine Learning Training Sets." *AI & Society* 36 (2021): 1105–1116. https://doi.org/10.1007/s00146-021-01162-8.
Dadabots. Accessed February 23, 2026. https://dadabots.com.
"Darmstädter Ferienkurse." *Wikipedia*. Accessed December 30, 2025. https://en.wikipedia.org/wiki/Darmstädter_Ferienkurse.
"Hatsune Miku." *Crypton Future Media*. Accessed February 7, 2026. https://ec.crypton.co.jp/pages/prod/virtualsinger/cv01_us.
LANDR. Accessed December 20, 2025. https://www.landr.com.
Leidecker, Jon. "Wobbly." Accessed January 7, 2026. https://www.detritus.net/wobbly.
Mark Applebaum. Accessed January 7, 2026. http://www.markapplebaum.com.
Pixies. *Doolittle*. 4AD, 1989.
"Project Xanadu." *Wikipedia*. Last modified August 20, 2025.
Rosalía. *Lux*. Columbia Records, 2025.
Shoshana Zuboff. Accessed February 11, 2024. https://shoshanazuboff.com/book/shoshana.
Walshe, Jennifer. "13 Ways of Looking at AI, Art & Music." *Unsound Dispatch*, December 15, 2023. https://unsoundfestival.substack.com/p/unsound-dispatch-13-ways-of-looking.
Walshe, Jennifer. "Aisteach: The Avant-Garde Archive of Ireland." *Aisteach Institute Ireland*. Accessed December 20, 2025. https://www.aisteach.org.
Walshe, Jennifer. "The Entanglement—AI, Platform Musicking, and the Future of Music." *The Journal of Music*, October 24, 2024. https://journalofmusic.com/opinion/entanglement-ai-platform-musicking-and-future-music.
Walshe, Jennifer. "Ghosts of the Hidden Layer." In *Classical Music Futures: Practices of Innovation*, edited by Neil T. Smith, Peter Peters, and Karoly Molina, 379–400. Cambridge, UK: Open Book Publishers, 2024. https://doi.org/10.11647/obp.0353.19.
Walshe, Jennifer. "An Introduction to Grúpat." *Milker Corporation*. Accessed December 20, 2025. https://milker.org/anintroductiontogrupat.
Walshe, Jennifer. *A Late Anthology of Early Music Vol. 1: Ancient to Renaissance*. Album. Tetbind Records/Jennifer Walshe, 2020. https://jenniferwalshe.bandcamp.com/album/a-late-anthology-of-early-music-vol-1-ancient-to-renaissance.
Walshe, Jennifer, and Kurt Schwitters. *URSONATE%24*. Album. Jennifer Walshe, 2024. Bandcamp, https://jenniferwalshe.bandcamp.com/album/ursonate-24.
Walshe, Jennifer, and Memo Akten. "ULTRACHUNK (2018)." *Memo Akten*. Accessed December 20, 2025. https://www.memo.tv/works/ultrachunk.
"Wobbly." *Wikipedia*. Accessed January 19, 2025. https://en.wikipedia.org/wiki/Wobbly_(musician).

8

MOVEMENT IV

The Last Piece: *Training AI on a Composer's Brainwaves*

Constantin Basica, Prateek Verma, and Alexandru I. Berceanu

DOI: 10.4324/9781003615873-8

Introduction

As early as 1949, the composer Raymond Scott envisioned a future that resonates uncannily with the quest of this chapter:

> Nothing is impossible in this atomic age. Someday, perhaps within the next hundred years, science will perfect a process of thought transference from composer to listener. Devices already have been perfected to record the impulses of the brain. In the music of the future, the composer[s] will merely *think* [their] idealized conception of [their] music. [Their] brainwaves will be picked up by mechanical equipment and channeled directly into the minds of [their] hearers. Instead of recordings of actual music sound, recordings will carry the brainwaves of the composer directly to the mind of the listener.[1]

The mapping of our thinking organ has been characterized by many as one of humanity's most important scientific quests, one that could potentially unlock the secrets of our existence.[2] This epoch-making mission is now heightened by the explosion of artificial intelligence (AI), a technology that poses big challenges for human civilization,[3] yet also creates extraordinary opportunities for research—a technology that's poised to help us solve the riddles of the brain.[4] As Eduardo Navas noticed, "we are nearing the speed of thought ... as AI apps produce in just seconds entire essays about any subject based on data-mined sources across the Internet."[5] Despite their impressive capabilities, current frameworks based on large language models (LLMs) have critical limitations as models of human intelligence,[6] prompting some researchers to investigate brain-inspired architectures.[7]

Against this backdrop, we are collaborating on an idiosyncratic project that explores what could be called "musical mind-reading." The roots of the project stem from Basica's previous compositions, Berceanu's neuroscientific research in theater, and Verma's background in machine learning. Our objective is to train an AI "performer" to recognize patterns in Basica's brain electrical activity as he imagines different sounds, and to use them as prompts for creating music in his composition styles during a performance.

Following early experiments to classify mental sounds, we began to develop our current *brain-to-music* system as part of *The Last Piece*, a work created together with a team of Romanian artists. In this immersive syncretic concert loosely based on Shakespeare's *The Tempest*, we likened the performing relationship between the composer and the AI to postcolonial interpretations of the character dynamics in that play. Notwithstanding its eventual absence in the premiere performance, our AI system's architecture and training datasets are fundamentally interconnected with various structural elements of *The Last Piece*, as we will detail in later sections.

The results of the project, while currently specific to one musician, may be transferable to others. In a previous initiative, we developed AI tools that allow people with diverse abilities and disabilities to generate music using their voices.[8] We aspire for our brain-to-music tool

Figure 8.1 Violinist Olga Berar performs with composer Constantin Basica, who is wearing an Emotiv Epoc X wireless EEG headset, during the premiere of *The Last Piece* at the MINA Museum in Bucharest, Romania. The performance was part of the 2025 George Enescu International Festival.

Photograph by Anca Arambaşa, Enescu Festival; used with permission from Artexim.

to eventually offer a similar benefit, allowing others to compose music directly from their brainwaves and bypass physical limitations. However, adapting the system for public use would require both redesigning the architecture to handle much larger amounts of data and optimizing the model to ensure it generalizes across individuals. For now, the scope of our work has been fully customized to Basica's brainwave recordings for the creation of *The Last Piece* (Figure 8.1)—a use case we view as a necessary step toward building a future co-creative AI system available to others.

Imagined Music and Imaginary Music

A romanticized notion persists that great composers could hear entire works in their mind before writing them down. A much-disputed 1815 letter, for instance, has Mozart supposedly claiming he could imagine a full symphony "all at once."[9] This became a seductive parable of creative genius (albeit one based on a forgery)[10] at a time when the composer's societal role was on the rise. Although composers like Beethoven and Smetana famously wrote music in the absence of external sound after losing their hearing—affirming the mind's power to summon musical imagery[11]—this ability is neither universal nor something every composer relies on. Many drive their creative process through other means: some improvise with their voice or instruments; others manipulate recorded or synthesized sounds; some use extra-musical elements like drawings to suggest musical meaning; and others compose with AI tools.

Basica, for example, is a composer who doesn't typically begin a piece by transcribing pre-formed internal music, but he is fascinated by the process of imagining music. Through this project, we aim to give him—and perhaps later, others—a tool to explore this as a compositional method. So, leaping forward in time about two hundred years from Mozart's apocryphal letter, we are attempting a roughly similar process: the conversion of music from inside Basica's brain into an audible experience for a concert audience. Yet our goal is not a note-by-note transcription of imagined music, but a looser translation that allows the mediating AI system to participate in the creative process.

Inside the Brain: Imagined Music

Over the past few decades, neuroscientists have studied how the brain processes pitch, melody, harmony, rhythm, timbre, and other musical building blocks. While the full picture is complex, many findings suggest that music processing involves a widespread network spanning both hemispheres. Although most musical tasks engage both sides of the brain, the two hemispheres often contribute in different ways, with certain aspects of music processing—including pitch and melodic contour—showing hemispheric biases.[12] Music perception and performance are active processes, because the brain continuously forms prediction about upcoming events based on statistical regularities in musical structures.[13] This isn't limited to auditory areas: regions involved in movement, emotion and reward, and learning and memory contribute as well.[14]

Musical imagery—the inner experience of hearing music in the absence of external sound—can engage some of the same brain regions as listening, but the degree of overlap likely depends on the task and is still being clarified. Musicians often draw on this ability in practice; for example, singers and instrumentalists can "pre-hear" an entry to support tuning, and conductors often "hear" music internally while reading a score in silence.[15] But the conjuring of mental sound is not limited to trained musicians, and a pilot survey by Chafe[16] using Amazon's Mechanical Turk reports that most people (98 out of 100 respondents in the survey) could voluntarily imagine a sound such as a hard ball dropping onto pavement.[17]

Zatorre and Halpern summarize evidence from multiple neuroimaging methods, suggesting that imagining music can engage the auditory cortical areas even in silence. They propose this may occur because frontal retrieval mechanisms send top-down signals that reactivate sound representations in the auditory cortex. They also describe studies showing links between hearing music and movement systems in musicians; for example, when trained players listen to familiar music, brain areas tied to the finger movements used to play it can become active. Together, this supports the idea that, for performing musicians, musical sound is closely coupled to action.[18]

Drawing on this current understanding of music processing in the brain, we aim to extend the possibilities of music composition enhanced by a brain–computer interface (BCI) through a prediction-driven approach rather than sonification of brainwaves. The result is an AI system that would act as a composer's assistant in performance, inferring the intended sound category from brainwaves and generating musical material in response. This idea circles back to Raymond Scott—specifically his late-1960s Electronium, often described as an "instantaneous composition-performance machine"[19] that combined electronic synthesis with generative algorithms.[20]

At present, the mental commands in our system are restricted to distinct sound and music categories for training and validation. But our longer-term goal (and maybe ultimately an unrealistic one) is to move toward inferring internally generated musical intentions that are not limited to a fixed training set; we seek to create an assistant that is able to generalize beyond trained categories of auditory imagery—a personalized model of the composer's inner musical world.

While our project mainly explores the concept of *imagined music*—by which we mean a person's active mental recreation or invention of sound (a psychological phenomenon)—we find it important to also address the related but different discourse of *imaginary music*, which often refers to the aesthetic or conceptual context that treats music as *conceived* inwardly rather than *heard* inwardly.

Inside the Mind: Imaginary Music

Imaginary music is a phenomenon that often borders the realms of the philosophical, the hypothetical, and the abstract. Starting in the 1950s, graphic notation brought experimental music into the world of conceptual art by using visual symbols instead of traditional notation, calling performers to imagine a sound world rather than read a score, as exemplified by Cornelius Cardew's iconic *Treatise*. In some conceptual works, such as Yoko Ono's whimsical event scores, a mental performance is all that's required, allowing nonmusicians to participate. Her "Collecting Piece" (1963), for instance, instructs the reader: "Collect sounds in your mind that you have overheard through the week. Repeat them in your mind in different orders one afternoon."[21]

For our project, Basica found inspiration in works by two of his composition mentors that point to introspectively experienced music. The late Romanian composer Octavian Nemescu developed a practice he called *imaginary music*, using graphic and textual elements to guide listeners through a personal, "unexteriorized" ritual of "silent chanting."[22] Mark Applebaum likewise uses visual scores and performative gestures to stage silent music for the "mind's ear" in works such as *Tlön*,[23] *The Metaphysics of Notation*,[24] and *Potential Music*.[25]

Several of Basica's own compositions feature traces of imaginary music. In *EMPMP* (2017), the composer describes a cult-like retreat where performers learn to mesmerize audiences by, among other things, "imagining sounds for long periods of time." In *You Are My Happy Place* (2017), improvisers imagine and perform musical gestures in sync with animated GIFs.[26] *Eight Postcards with Samples of Imaginary Music* (2020)—written in memoriam of Nemescu—invite anyone to imagine music in impossible situations described on the back of mailable postcards. And most directly inspiring *The Last Piece*, his 2019 *Concerto for Conductor and Orchestra* screens a pseudo-documentary above the stage, where a fictional project called *GEBOCARqIS* (GEsture-Based Orchestral Control through Artificial quasi-Intelligent System) is supposedly being trained on the conductor's brainwaves to allow composers in the future to subliminally "play" an orchestra just by *thinking* of music.[27]

From Music to Brainwaves and Back

Points of Departure

Building on extant research and our own previous work, this interdisciplinary project uses electroencephalography (EEG) and AI for a brain–computer music interface (BCMI). EEG is a non-invasive technology that measures the brain's electrical activity, which can serve as a direct input signal for BCI or BCMI. In the context of composition and performance, this allows a musician to control elements such as melody, harmony, or tempo—in our case, the selection of sound categories for audio generation—through their thoughts or mental states.

As an example, Berceanu's performance project *inter@FAȚA* (The Interface)[28] used an EEG-based BCI to explore audience and performer reactions to social themes. In collaboration with composer Cătălin Crețu and programmer Grigore Burloiu, the project sonified brain activity in real time, using alpha-band asymmetry/valence from prefrontal sensors worn by both a performer and a volunteer spectator during the performance.[29] By monitoring their neural responses—specifically, shifts interpreted as changes in emotional state or engagement—the system mapped these otherwise invisible dynamics into sound. This made the raw EEG signal an integral part of the live musical score and theatrical experience, with plans to extend control to lighting as well.

From a design perspective, many creative BCMI systems map raw or processed EEG signals to an analog or digital synthesizer or MIDI sound control. Others use online signal processing or machine learning to extract features like emotional states.[30] Another important category employs feedback loops, where the affective mapping or specific features of the EEG signal control generated music for applications in music therapy, neurofeedback, or as an assistive tool for persons with motor impairments.[31] Our project aims to contribute to this field by mapping auditory imagery directly to personalized music generation.

Our trio first collaborated on the participatory transmedia work *Lost Interferences*,[32] training an AI system to associate live music with collected stories about personal loss. We continued this research in a second project iteration, *In the Forest with Maia*, where a Disklavier[33] performed AI-generated MIDI music based on audience stories, using our model trained on a dataset of Basica's piano improvisations recorded while contemplating words related to loss. Our shared desire to develop AI-enabled "translation machines" for interdisciplinary performance led us to the present project. And when the George Enescu International Festival invited us to present a new work, we finally had the opportunity to build our EEG-based AI system for an artistic outlet.

As mentioned before, the concept developed as a sequel to Basica's *Concerto for Conductor and Orchestra* (premiered at the same festival in 2019), which presented a feigned EEG-BCI tool. In that piece, the conductor's brainwaves were spuriously collected during performance to train a hoax AI. For this project, we wanted to replace fiction with reality by building a genuine brain-controlled music generation system. Adrian Ciglenean then proposed connecting our research with Shakespeare's *The Tempest*, and this became the dramaturgical foundation for *The Last Piece*, intermingling the scientific aspects of our project with plot and character references from the play. But the first piece of the puzzle was to train an AI model to classify predefined categories of musical imagery from EEG data—one that would generalize to novel input in a performance scenario.

Analyzing Musical Brainwaves: EEG-Based Research on Auditory Imagery

Music can influence human behavior and mental states. Music-based interventions have shown promising benefits in several neurological and psychiatric conditions, although the evidence is mixed and protocols are not yet standardized.[34] Humans experience sounds and music through the auditory system (and other brain networks) as complex phenomena shaped by biology but also culture. AI does not experience music the same way humans do, but it can learn statistical patterns in musical data by training on large human-created datasets.

In neuroscience, interpreting brain activity is not an easy feat, requiring the analysis of complex patterns in noisy data, among many other things. Machine learning is well suited to pattern analysis, so ML techniques are increasingly used for tasks such as decoding and prediction in data collected via electroencephalography (EEG), functional magnetic resonance imaging (fMRI), magnetoencephalography (MEG), and positron emission tomography (PET). Decoding—and partially reconstructing—*heard* music from EEG, especially when aided by fMRI-informed EEG source localization, has been demonstrated;[35] but could we decode *imagined* music using EEG and AI?

This may sound like science fiction, yet laboratory studies have shown that a small set of imagined melodies can be classified from EEG under controlled conditions.[36] Some researchers reported above-chance offline classification of imagined musical phrases in a subset of participants.[37] Nevertheless, decoding imagined music is typically much less reliable than decoding heard music; in one withdrawn preprint, the authors reported that after discovering and correcting an analysis-code error, the imagination results became non-significant while perception results remained significant.[38] Other researchers target the classification of more discrete musical elements; for example, one EEG study decoded imagined musical pitches (C4–B4) with a mean 7-class accuracy of about 36% (where random chance is about 14%).[39]

So, classifying auditory imagery is not a trivial task; on the contrary, accuracy is often modest even in studies with narrow objectives such as decoding pitches or simple melodies. But our goal is even more ambitious: let the composer *freely* conjure up music in the mind (though within certain preestablished categories for now), and give predictions in real time about which category is imagined at any given point. To our knowledge, there is no widely replicated demonstration of direct decoding of imagined novel music—let alone accomplished online in a concert setting.

We seek to push the current state of the art by testing the feasibility of using imagined music classification in composition and live performance. Informed by the existing literature, we have explored several workarounds to improve the signal-to-noise ratio and achieve above-chance accuracy. Our work has been guided by several constraints: the system has to be usable by the composer; employ a low-electrode-count, dry EEG headset suitable for performance; and allow for online signal processing.

Making Music with Brainwaves: EEG in Creative Practice

Using brain–computer interfaces in art-making has a long history at the intersection of technical experimentation, conceptual art, and scientific research. A recent review identified twenty-two EEG-BCI studies ranging from clinical applications to art experiences and highlighted BCI systems not only as control tools but also as platforms for interactive—and potentially social—processes that enable new forms of co-creativity between human and machine.[40]

The sonification of neural activity dates back to early EEG research, as shown by Nobel laureate Edgar Adrian in 1934,[41] but the artistic use of brainwaves began in the latter half of the twentieth century. Pioneers include Alvin Lucier, whose *Music for Solo Performer* (1965) used alpha rhythms to excite percussion instruments;[42] Richard Teitelbaum, who incorporated biofeedback with a Moog synthesizer;[43] and David Rosenboom, who released the album *Brainwave Music*.[44] Other pioneers included Pauline Oliveros, who used EEG to record her *Sonic Meditations* in 1973.[45]

More recently, the field has expanded with contributors such as Atau Tanaka, who performed with the BioMuse controller in the early 1990s;[46] Mick Grierson, who has been experimenting with brainwave-based composition;[47] and Eduardo Reck Miranda, who with

Andrew Brouse coined the term "brain–computer music interface,"[48] describing it as "a new research area that is emerging at the [crossroads] of neurobiology, engineering sciences, and music."[49] Today, a new generation of artists—including Luciana Haill,[50] Grace Leslie,[51] Alex Chechile,[52] Lisa Park,[53] Amy Karle,[54] Alexander Schubert,[55] and our frequent collaborator Cătălin Crețu[56]—continues to compose and perform with EEG, often in tandem with acoustic or electronic instruments.

Our project builds on several years of individual and joint EEG-based BCI exploration. In addition to the 2015 project *inter@FAȚA*, Berceanu has been engaged in BCI research at the International Center for Research and Education in Innovative and Creative Technologies (CINETic) in Bucharest, Romania. There, along with fundamental neuroscientific research on performative art, multiple creative uses of BCI are being developed—from sonifications used in image generation or control[57] to BCI-assisted architectural design.[58] Verma and Basica initiated their first experiments combining EEG with machine learning in 2021, recording sessions of Basica silently singing chromatic scales with an 8-channel wireless EEG headset in the hope of detecting brainwave patterns associated with different pitches. Additional experiments attempted to distinguish between listening to diverse musical genres using an EEG headband.[59] This line of inquiry evolved into a full team collaboration within the context of *The Last Piece*.

The Last Piece: *An Immersive Journey Inside the Composer's Brain*

> Be not afeard; the isle is full of noises,
> Sounds and sweet airs, that give delight and hurt not.
> Sometimes a thousand twangling instruments
> Will hum about mine ears, and sometime voices
> That, if I then had waked after long sleep,
> Will make me sleep again: and then, in dreaming,
> The clouds methought would open and show riches
> Ready to drop upon me that, when I waked,
> I cried to dream again.
>
> —*William Shakespeare,* The Tempest*, Act III, Scene 2*

The Last Piece is an immersive syncretic concert that premiered at the Museum of Immersive New Art (MINA) as part of the George Enescu International Festival in Bucharest, Romania on September 18–19, 2025 (Figure 8.2).[60] The piece was co-created and performed by a team of twenty-five people: a composer, a video artist, an action poet, a sound artist, a mixed-realities director, an AI engineer, a conductor, seven instrumentalists, a mime artist, and ten actors. Two frameworks provided the inspiration and conceptual backbone of the piece: neuroscience (the BCMI system discussed in this chapter) and Shakespeare's *The Tempest*.

The immersive experience—both in a theatrical sense and as a multimedia show—is meant to evoke an imaginary audiovisual journey through the brain of the composer. The concert

Figure 8.2 The premiere performance of *The Last Piece*. On stage are members of the SonoMania Ensemble and composer Constantin Basica. The brain-related immersive video projection is created by Simona Fitcal.

Photograph by Anca Arambaşa, Enescu Festival; used with permission from Artexim.

begins unexpectedly in the museum's lobby, where a "musical storm" quickly builds up from dissonant musical textures ensuing from the live instruments, directed by the conductor as an Ariel-like figure, and processed through *Somax2*[61] by sound artist Grigore Burloiu's immersive and reactive sound installation (which also motion-tracks the conductor's gestures). Then, undercover actors help the audience members abandon the "sinking ship" and guide them into the main immersive projection space, where they become enveloped in a 360-degree projection created by video artist Simona Fitcal.

At first, the visuals portray an island-like environment made of artistically rendered brain sculptures and accompanied by a soundscape "full of noises"—live sonification of the composer's brainwaves mangled with his own voice as a prerecorded, electronically processed reading of excerpts from *The Tempest* (translated into Romanian). Present on stage with the ensemble, the composer wears an EEG headset and appears to commandeer the other performers. As the piece unfolds, the ensemble performs his score, which was itself composed with the help of his brainwaves. In a process referencing the Mozart myth, a 10-minute EEG recording of Basica imagining the music (before starting to write the score) was parsed through a Max patch using MaxScore[62] to generate the initial pitch material for the composition.

Later in the performance, Fitcal visually leads the audience through dendritic structures resembling neurons and lightning; then through a visualization of the composer's live brainwaves; and finally into his "subconscious" where the self breaks into shadowy figures, before returning to a deserted island. The engulfing video projections, combined with the EEG wireless headset on the composer's head, further hint that the audience has been brought inside his brain.

The parallel with Shakespeare's play was shaped from a theatrical perspective by actor and artistic coach Adrian Ciglenean. He developed an immersive theatrical experience with his orb.ro team and also came up with the title—itself an allusion to Shakespeare's play, which is widely considered to be his last solo work. The composer's central role parallels that of Prospero, the protagonist of *The Tempest* who uses magic to control the island's inhabitants, including the airy spirit Ariel and the native Caliban.

In this context, the composer's "magic" lies in his ability to use the entire creative team for generating the musical "tempest" and "shipwrecking" the audience from the lobby into his "brain"—an immersive concert space where he can fully envelop them in his music. As a mirror to the composer's brain, the AI entity (an artificial brain trained to replicate his music) was conceived as an amalgamation of traits from both Ariel, the *spirit*, and Caliban, the *creature*. Conceptually, it evokes both Ariel's magical ability in its power to turn brainwaves into music, and Caliban's uncultivated character, reflected in the raw, unpolished quality of the AI-generated music. The act of training the AI model in the composer's musical likeness echoes Prospero's attempt to "civilize" Caliban, an act that many scholars view as a symbol of European imperialism.

For the AI training, we used six sound categories tightly related to elements in *The Last Piece*:

Violin	Represents the show's soloist, violinist Olga Berar, who portrays a version of Shakespeare's Miranda.
Piano	The composer's own instrument is used here as a nostalgic memory of his musical upbringing.
Drums	A contrasting, non-pitched instrument representing the composer's unfulfilled dream of playing it. The drum set is present only as a ghostly soundscape, electronically integrated with the other "noises" of the isle.
Thunderstorm	A direct reference to *The Tempest* and a metaphor for the brain's "electrical storm." This concept also inspired Berceanu's poem in the program notes, symbolically blending neuroscience and machine learning.
Writing	Evokes the overlapping creative acts of writing *The Tempest*'s script and *The Last Piece*'s score.
Applause	Symbolizes Prospero's final monologue—often interpreted by scholars as Shakespeare's own farewell to independent work—which is echoed in Basica's address to the audience before the ending.

A Brain-to-Music AI System

At a high level, our system is designed to function in 3 stages. First, a classification model analyzes the incoming EEG signal and assigns it to a sound category. Second, this detected category is fed to a retrieval model that selects corresponding sound textures from Basica's music to use as prompts. Finally, a bespoke audio generation model uses these prompts to synthesize new music in the composer's style, thus enabling music "composition" directly from brain signals (Figure 8.3).

Data Collection

Data collection consisted of approximately 25 recording sessions, each lasting 30–90 minutes. These uninterrupted sessions were carried out by Basica at home (or sometimes in hotels) and were organized into 7 distinct batches with different experimental configurations. The recording setup for each involved the following steps.

EEG Pipeline

The process began by preparing the 14-channel Emotiv Epoc X wireless headset, which required applying saline to the sensors and ensuring a good connection to the scalp. Once positioned, the raw 14-channel EEG signal was parsed from the EmotivPRO application and

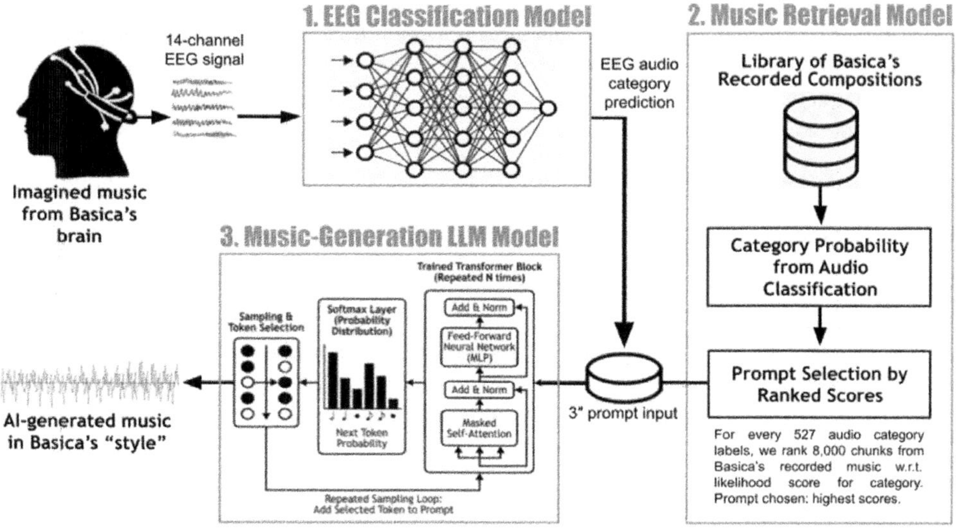

Figure 8.3 Brain-to-music system architecture: overview of the three AI models and their role in "translating" brainwaves to sound waves.

streamed to Max using Lab Streaming Layer and OSC protocols. In Max, the incoming 256 Hz data was recorded as text files, synchronized with the playback and selective silencing of the audio files for each sound category.

Sound/Music Library

To create a varied library for listening and imagining—especially for the musical categories—we compiled audio files scraped from YouTube. This approach was necessary because Basica's personal library of recorded media was insufficient for the task, and this method allowed for algorithmic listening rather than manually playing short clips. Our concerns about scraping were somewhat eased by ensuring the material was used privately, only for EEG signal comparison, and not for training music generation. For the 3 noise categories (thunderstorm, applause, writing), we sampled short snippets from hour-long videos; for the instrumental categories, Basica selected a variety of personal favorites among twentieth-century solo piano and violin music, as well as virtuosic drum solos. In our latest experiment, we also used three 12-second excerpts from his own compositions.

EEG Recordings

Although the acquisition methods varied slightly across the recording sessions, the core procedure remained consistent, with the exception of the final experiment described in the last section. Each session involved Basica listening to short audio clips of 2–12 seconds from each category (Figure 8.4). The sound was then muted, prompting him to imagine the same type of sound or music. This listening-imagining trial was repeated in a loop throughout the session. The AI model was later presented with the entire, uninterrupted EEG recording, without being given information to distinguish between the listening and imagining phases. It's interesting to note that the composer's act of continuing a perceived sound with similar mental imagery resembles our AI's own process of continuing a musical prompt with similar-sounding audio.

EEG Classification Model: Unscrambling Brain Signals

Our goal was to make the AI understand the contents of the incoming 14-channel EEG signal sampled at 256 Hz. We aimed to incorporate algorithms that can understand a 3-second context of data captured while the composer hears or imagines sounds. Inspired by models such as EEGNet,[63] we designed a convolutional neural network that classifies EEG signals into different categories (*violin*, *piano*, *drums*, *thunderstorm*, *writing*, and *applause*).

Given a signal, we first performed a spatial convolution that learned to assign weights to channels based on the recording conditions and misplaced positions for a particular session. In addition, spatial mixing allowed us to approximate the original signals that are propagated before being recorded for our task. After this, we performed successive convolutions

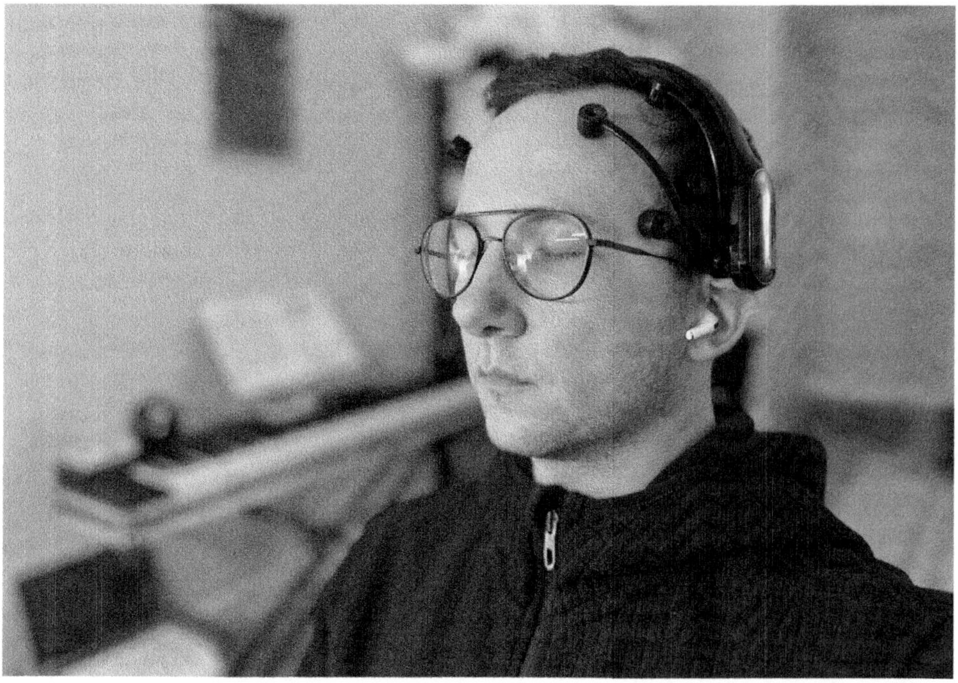

Figure 8.4 Constantin Basica prepares for an EEG recording session at home, wearing an Emotiv Epoc X wireless EEG headset and Apple AirPods Pro wireless earphones.

along the temporal dimension, using a kernel size of 11 and pooling by 2 in each successive layer, for a total of 6 layers, similar to models typically used for 2-channel audio classification or multivariate time-series prediction. After global average pooling, the output of the final convolutional layer output was passed through a softmax classifier, and the model was trained by minimizing cross-entropy loss.

The output category predicted by our EEG model—resulting from the most likely association between the incoming brain signal and the trained data—was then passed to our audio retrieval model.

Audio Retrieval Model: Finding the Needle in the Haystack

The next step was to assign a *sound category* and find the closest audio pieces from a large volume of unlabeled data. For this, we used Basica's entire collection of recorded musical compositions as input. Since the goal of our model was to use the composer's music as an initial prompt for audio generation, we automatically extracted chunks of audio from the his pieces that best matched a given sound category (for example, selecting drum-like sounds that the model rated as closest to a *tap* category).

We used the YAMNet model[64] and a custom audio transformer model[65] trained using open-source labeled datasets such as FSD50K.[66] With an input audio clip of 3 seconds, the model scored audio between 0 and 1, indicating the likelihood of a particular sound category from 527 audio labels in the AudioSet[67] ontology or its subset of FSD50K. These models had never "heard"—that is, been trained on—audio from the composer's library.

We took Basica's library of recorded compositions (around 11 hours of music) and divided it into 3-second chunks. Each chunk received a score indicating its likelihood of belonging to one of the 527 categories on a scale from 0 to 1. To get audio prompts for categories of interest, we took all the scores belonging to that category—for example, *violin*—and sorted them. The system then randomly sampled from the top-ranked audio chunks (selecting either 10 or 50), automatically retrieving the sounds most similar to a violin timbre from the composer's recordings.

By learning embeddings via similarity, these models implicitly grouped sounds regardless of their literal source: a powerline's hum might be "misheard" as whistling wind, or raindrops as a harp. Basica intentionally leverages this ambiguity to forge unexpected links between his intent and retrieved audio prompts. These hidden intermediaries, though absent from the final performance, ensure the resulting audio generation can be both surprising and creatively congruent.

Audio Generation Model: Making Music from Music

Our goal was to enable the generation of new music from the EEG-driven sound prompts. We achieved this via autoregressive LLMs based on the open-source AudioCraft family of models from Meta, which are transformer-decoder-based architectures. Our design consists of three steps.

First, the audio waveform is converted into discrete tokens, which can be reconstructed to audio. This allows us to train a generative model akin to a text-based LLM like ChatGPT, shifting the problem from generating audio waveforms to generating audio tokens. By doing so, we can utilize the rich set of existing tools for language modeling.

Second, we train our own model (which uses a GPT-like architecture) on vast amounts of data to predict the next tokens in a sequence. The model must learn the audio's underlying semantics, content, and distribution. It must understand the patterns and variations in pitch, timbre, and rhythm, along with energy dynamics. Once trained, it gives the likelihood of a token being the next one for a given context. We typically sample from this distribution.

Third, we take the generated tokens and reconstruct the audio using a tokenizer decoder. This takes a sequence of tokens as input and gives us an audio file corresponding to the list of tokens.

Audio to Tokens: The Two Tokenizers (SNAC and EnCodec)

Both of the following methods convert continuous audio signals into discrete tokens, similar to a discrete MIDI-like representation of music parameters. However, these tokens can fully encompass any sound of interest and reconstruct it with some loss, yet still preserve its timbre, dynamics, and expressive nuances of frequency.

Our chosen tokenizer is EnCodec.[68] The number of tokens per codebook dictates the quality. As a trade-off between quality and computational efficiency, we chose 24 kHz as the sampling rate and modeled only the first 4 codebooks at roughly 6 Kbps. The model maps the audio with these settings: 75 tokens per second per codebook, with each codebook containing values from 0 to 1,023. For the desired audio setting, we sequentially interleave all the codebooks. At any given time instance, we have codes from all the codebooks—going from coarse to fine—stacked, and the process is repeated. To differentiate between the codebooks, we add a scalar offset of the token vocabulary to each codebook index. For the 10-second context window we get $75 \times 4 \times 10 = 3{,}000$ tokens for the GPT model to predict the next token in an autoregressive manner.

The other tokenizer is SNAC,[69] which uses a hierarchical, more compact representation with fewer tokens overall. It has only 3 codebooks and a multitiered approach. Unlike EnCodec, SNAC has a different number of tokens per codebook, with the coarsest level modeling the overall semantic structure and the finer-grained token modeling smaller acoustic variations and energy dynamics. The shorter token length increases the number of values each token can take from 1,024 to 4,096.

Ultimately, we found the EnCodec approach worked much better than SNAC for our purpose and chose to proceed with it.

Token-Based Generation Models

We use a standard GPT-based transformer architecture for next-token prediction. The multilayered decoder stacks in GPT utilize an attention mechanism to weigh input importance and align features effectively. This approach, though originally designed for text (as in ChatGPT), succeeds across any tokenized modality, including MusicGen. After the training, the output is iteratively sampled to reach the target sequence length within the context window.

Sampling is like drawing balls from a bag where pretraining has adjusted the color distribution based on context. If red balls outnumber others, a red token is more likely, though rarer colors remain possible. By selecting tokens from the LLM's distribution and feeding them back into the model, we can iteratively generate future tokens for any given audio prompt.

Verma's custom model (300 million parameters) trained on 11 hours of Basica's music. The goal was to create a model exposed only to the composer's sound world.

Typically, a model's performance is improved by increasing the data size, model size, or context length. However, we were constrained by a fixed dataset, and scaling the model further would risk overfitting. Given these limitations, we designed the model to learn exclusively from Basica's music—a process comparable to a human composer who has only ever heard a specific set of sounds and then attempts to create music based solely on that training. As the audio files are generated at the same low sample rate, they sound quite poor in terms of conventional audio quality. Aesthetically and conceptually, however, this low-fidelity sound perfectly matches the raw, "uncultivated" traits sought in the project's parallel with the Caliban character.

Pretrained MusicGen model[70] (20,000 hours of music) prompted with samples from Basica's music. To continue the previous composer metaphor, this is like a human who has listened to all kinds of music—rock, jazz, hip-hop, classical, pop, diverse global traditions, and so on—and draws inspiration from that rich training during composition. We explored whether we could do the same with an LLM by using Meta's open-source model. As expected, the quality of the generated music increased compared to our small custom model. However, some of the generated audio files diverged from Basica's music, creating an unwanted discrepancy with our "Caliban AI" concept. Suddenly, the model seemed to possess a musical agency of its own—one the composer did not recognize as pertaining to his style. Nevertheless, this divergence also led to more surprising musical results, especially when the model was prompted to morph between categories, and we can envision uses for this behavior in other creative contexts.

A collection of music samples generated by our model can be found at https://ccrma.stanford.edu/~cobasica/brain-to-music.

Current State and Future Prospects

In a talk, Alvin Lucier described his experience having invited John Cage in 1965 to present a concert at Brandeis University and in turn being asked to perform in the event:

> I said I didn't have a piece (laughs). And there was silence on the phone. Then I said, "Well, I am working with a brainwave amplifier, but it doesn't work (laughter). I can't get the amplifier to work." And he [John Cage] laughed and said, "It doesn't matter if it doesn't work" ...[71]

Like Lucier, our "brainwave amplifier" system was not quite ready for prime time at the premiere of *The Last Piece*. Due to time constraints and technical difficulties, we were unable to integrate the AI system into the performance, as the EEG classification accuracy was only slightly above random chance and the music-generation model was not yet fully functional in a live setting. Although the AI pipeline was ready by the second concert, a computer crash during the show disconnected the EEG headset, forcing us to skip the planned AI moment.

But, also like Lucier, this ultimately did not matter for the flow of the concert, which still featured Basica's brainwaves via live sonification and visualization as well as the EEG-derived musical score. The audience was unaware of the AI system's "failure" because we had preemptively minimized its role in the show, placing the AI moment between the piece's climax and its denouement as a transition. Therefore, while the inability to showcase the system was a disappointment to us as creators, the audience's experience was not directly impacted. Nevertheless, the creation of *The Last Piece* not only defined the design of our system but also acted as a playground for experimentation. Our hope is to stage the concert again, this time with a fully functional AI system.

To recapitulate, our project's goal is not to build an AI à la Mozart that can "retrieve" a score from a human's brain, but one that can co-create music with the composer during a live performance. Due to inherent challenges in BCI-driven classification of imagined music[72] and the real-time demands of our artistic context, we currently operate at a low level of complexity by using machine learning to decipher the listening to and imagining of distinct categories of sound and music. Although the content of some of these sonic categories is complex (twentieth-century avant-garde music and Basica's own compositions), the output is simple: the model returns only basic labels like *violin* or *thunderstorm*. Furthermore, these labels are merely an intermediary mechanism that ultimately drives a personalized, music-generative AI system.

We are not pursuing perfect "thought transcription," since a high potential for failure is embedded in the pipeline from mental sounds to captured EEG. Our goal, rather, is for the model to reliably detect broad categories of musical imagery and to select a corresponding audio prompt. Our initial efforts were partially successful and promising. In one experiment, using the sound/music library we compiled, Basica listened with eyes closed to 8 seconds of audio from 3 categories (*violin*, *drums*, *thunderstorm*) and then imagined the sound for 2 seconds. This was repeated for 60 trials over multiple sessions, and the model achieved 50% accuracy in this 3-category experiment—a result comparable to similar research. For example, the NOIR project reported 42.2% accuracy in a 4-way EEG classification task.[73]

Recently, we tried a different approach, using 12-second excerpts from Basica's own compositions: solo piano, solo violin, and solo drum set. The initial training data was collected in a session where Basica listened to each excerpt and immediately imagined it for 28 seconds; this was repeated for a total of 40 trials per category, yielding 1,600 seconds of data. Since we trained our model on 2-second windows, for a 40-second trial, we averaged the probabilities of the 20 resulting chunks to make a decision. A second recording session continued the procedure for another 20 trials per category, and we also collected testing data by recording 4 trials per category in the same session.

With this combined data (60 trials and 2,400 seconds), our model reached 75% accuracy in a 3-category test (where random chance is 33%). When we reran the experiment using only the second session for training (40 fewer trials), the accuracy decreased to 58%, suggesting that more data improves performance, even across different sessions. We then added 2 more separate testing sessions (with the headset removed between them) and further optimized our model, which increased accuracy to 63%. Finally, instead of averaging our output probabilities across the 40-second trial, we took a majority vote from the 2-second predictions across all 20 chunks of a single test file; this improved accuracy by about 4%, yielding 67% validation accuracy on that file. This final experiment was also the first to include the state of open eyes. We are encouraged by these accuracy numbers, especially given that two-thirds of the dataset was composed of music imagery.

However, a key limitation is that our training data still includes both active listening and imagining phases—since maintaining focused imagination of sound over a long period is difficult—making the model currently unreliable for a performance without any listening. When we tried to test solely on imagined music, our model did not perform above random chance. Nevertheless, we envision scenarios for using this model in performative contexts where classification accuracy is less important than the system's emergent "agency" in generating surprising musical material.

For future work, we plan several improvements, starting with a stronger dataset to serve as a test bench for preprocessing and classification. While using an EEG system with a higher electrode count (64–128 channels) would likely improve performance, the prohibitive cost and impracticality for live performance make this unfeasible for us. We also need to test the performance drawbacks of using dry versus wet electrodes to better understand the trade-offs in signal quality within our system.

Beyond the EEG classification model, we are working to improve audio quality. One method is a 2-stage process where a model first learns the coarse details from an audio tokenizer, after which a second model predicts the remaining fine details. We are also exploring 2 fine-tuning workflows: the first involves tweaking a large pretrained model with LoRA[74] to incorporate composer-specific behavior, while the second involves training our custom model on a general music dataset and then using LoRA to customize it with Basica's music, ensuring stylistic control.

Our system did not turn out to be the telepathic tool that we hoped could summon Prospero's magical control over Ariel in the premiere of *The Last Piece*. But after more work, it shows signs that it can follow the composer's mental commands to a certain degree. Its unwillingness to be easily trained and controlled by a human brain echoes the power imbalance in *The Tempest* that we allude to in *The Last Piece*: Shakespeare's protagonist is in a constant wrangle with his enslaved foil, Caliban. And, like Prospero's final gesture toward him, we acknowledge "this thing of darkness" as our own.[75] We continue to train our "Caliban AI" on musical thoughts and to conduct experiments, hoping it can one day sapiently model the composer's imagination into live music composition.

Acknowledgments

We thank Emotiv for lending us an Epoc X wireless EEG headset for research purposes. We are also deeply grateful for crucial support provided by Stanford University's Center for Computer Research in Music and Acoustics (CCRMA) in California; the National University of Theatre and Cinematography "I. L. Caragiale" and its International Center for Research and Education in Innovative and Creative Technologies (CINETic) in Bucharest, Romania; and the George Enescu International Festival in Romania, represented by Artexim.

We acknowledge the use of Google's Gemini as a coding assistant at various stages of the AI architecture development, including for installing and setting up libraries, and for optimizing parts of the code for our models.

We recognize the contributions of all the artists involved in *The Last Piece*:

Simona Fitcal, visual concept
Adrian Ciglenean and orb.ro, immersive concept
Grigore Burloiu, sound installation

SonoMania Ensemble
Simona Strungaru, conductor
Olga Berar, violin (soloist)
Tamara Dica, viola
Valentin Ghita, oboe
Flaviu Ludușan, clarinet
Maria Diana Petrache, piano
Eugen-Bogdan Popa, cello
Teodor-Emanuel Basica, horn (special guest)

Alexandru Pribeagu, pantomime

Actors: Adrian Ciglenean, Mihai Dulea, Smaranda Găbudean, Luiza Ghindă, Mihai Oancea, and Alexandru Pribeagu

Young actors: Robert Avram, Luminița Cercel, David Jighirgiu, Anda Kreuziger, Tudor Oancea, and Alexandru Păun

Notes

1 Chusid and Winner, "Circle Machines and Sequencers."
2 Wilson, *Consilience*, 106.
3 IBM, "10 AI Dangers and Risks."
4 Myers, "AI Reveals How Brain Activity Unfolds Over Time."
5 Navas, "AI Ethics," 174.
6 Johnson and Hyland-Wood, "A Primer on Large Language Models."
7 Langner, "Brain-Inspired AI Breakthrough."
8 This project was supported by the Stanford Institute for Human-Centered Artificial Intelligence (HAI), the Center for Computer Research in Music and Acoustics (CCRMA), and Patricia Alessandrini's Humanities Seed Funding Grant at Stanford University, California; the EU Horizon MuseIT Project; the Music Representation Group at the Institute for Research and Coordination in Acoustics/Music (IRCAM) in Paris, France; and UNATC International Center for Research and Education in Innovative and Creative Technologies (CINETic) in Bucharest, Romania. For details see Basica et al., "Accessible Co-Creativity."
9 Kivy, "Mozart and Monotheism," 322.
10 Ashton, *How to Fly a Horse*, xiv.
11 Zatorre and Halpern, "Mental Concerts," 9.
12 Patel, *Music, Language, and the Brain*, 73–76.
13 Vuust et al., "Music in the Brain."
14 For more information on neurobiological mechanisms related to music perception, see Zatorre and Peretz, *The Biological Foundations of Music*; Patel, *Music, Language, and the Brain.*
15 Zatorre and Halpern, "Mental Concerts," 11.
16 Chafe, "The Qualities and Flow."
17 A minority of people report little or no ability to voluntarily imagine sounds, voices, or music—a phenomenon sometimes discussed as *auditory aphantasia*. Hinwar and Lambert propose the term *anauralia* for absent auditory imagery.
18 Zatorre and Halpern, "Mental Concerts."
19 Goldberg, "Raymond Scott."
20 Warnow, *Deconstructing Dad.*
21 Ono, *Grapefruit.*
22 Anghel, "Unearthing Imaginary Music," 1.
23 "Mark Applebaum – Tlön."
24 Applebaum, *The Metaphysics of Notation.*
25 Applebaum, *Potential Music.*
26 GIF is an abbreviation for Graphics Interchange Format.
27 *Constantin Basica.*
28 Berceanu et al., "Extension of Performativity by a BCI."
29 Crețu, Berceanu, and Burloiu, "Muzică Interactivă de Scenă."
30 Daly et al., "Personalized, Multi-modal, Affective State Detection"; Williams et al., "Affective Calibration of Musical Feature Sets."
31 "Can You Create Music Using Brainwaves?"
32 Berceanu, *Lost Interferences.*
33 A Disklavier is a brand of acoustic piano manufactured by Yamaha that is fitted with electronic sensors for recording and a pneumatic system for player-piano-style playback.
34 Ramaswamy et al., "Therapeutic Use of Music."

35 Daly, "Neural Decoding."
36 Di Liberto, Marion, and Shamma, "Accurate Decoding."
37 Schaefer et al., "Single Trial Classification."
38 Tibo, Geirnaert, and Bertrand, "EEG-Based Decoding."
39 Chung et al., "Decoding Imagined Musical Pitch."
40 Vanutelli et al. "BCI Applications to Creativity."
41 Lutters and Koehler, "Brainwaves in Concert."
42 Straebel and Thoben, "Alvin Lucier's *Music for Solo Performer.*"
43 Holmes, "On the Road."
44 Dayal, "David Rosenboom."
45 Nerness, "Brain Dynamics during Music Improvisation."
46 Christopher et al., "A History of Emerging Paradigms."
47 Grierson, "Composing with Brainwaves."
48 Miranda and Brouse, "Interfacing the Brain."
49 Miranda, Durrant, and Anders, "Towards Brain-Computer Music Interfaces," 1.
50 Haill, "Artworks."
51 Leslie, "Composing at the Border of Experimental Music."
52 Chechile, "Music Re-Informed by the Brain."
53 Park, "Eunoia."
54 Karle, "Brainsongs."
55 Schubert, "Steady State."
56 Crețu, "EEG-Based Real-Time Audio."
57 Gheorghe, *Resonance*; Damian, *The Imagination Laboratory.*
58 Țenea et al., "The Co-Created City."
59 Verma and Basica collaborated with Barbara Nerness, then a PhD candidate at CCRMA, to conduct the initial trials of recording EEG during silent singing. The wireless EEG headset and the EEG headband were kindly provided by Professor Takako Fujioka's NeuroMusic Lab at CCRMA.
60 "The Last Piece."
61 IRCAM, *Somax2.*
62 Hajdu and Didkovsky, "MaxScore."
63 Lawhern et al., "EEGNet."
64 TensorFlow, "Sound Classification with YAMNet."
65 Verma and Berger, "Audio Transformers."
66 Fonseca et al., "FSD50K."
67 Gemmeke et al., "Audio Set."
68 Défossez, "High Fidelity Neural Audio Compression."
69 Siuzdak, Grötschla, and Lanzendörfer, "SNAC."
70 Copet et al., "Simple and Controllable Music Generation."
71 Straebel and Thoben, "Alvin Lucier's Music for Solo Performer," 17.
72 In 2006, Eduardo Reck Miranda stated that "the task of decoding the EEG of a person thinking of a melody, or something along these lines, is just impossible with today's technology" (see Miranda, "Brain–Computer Music Interfacing," 5). And while EEG hardware and analysis methods have improved over the past two decades, decoding complex, unconstrained musical imagery remains an extremely difficult task.
73 Zhang, "NOIR," 7.
74 Hu et al., "LoRA."
75 Shakespeare Navigator, "*The Tempest*: Act V, Scene 1."

Bibliography

Anghel, Irinel. "Unearthing Imaginary Music: Testimony for the Future." *Revista Muzica* 7 (2020). Accessed January 25, 2026. https://www.academia.edu/44113921/Unearthing_Imaginary_Music.

Applebaum, Mark. *The Metaphysics of Notation. Mark Applebaum.* Stanford University. Accessed January 31, 2026. https://web.stanford.edu/~applemk/portfolio-works-metaphysics-of-notation.html.

Applebaum, Mark. "Potential Music." Performed by Logan Ball. *Vimeo.* June 18, 2022. Video, 8:21. https://vimeo.com/721826428.

Ashton, Kevin. *How to Fly a Horse.* New York, NY: Doubleday, 2015.

Basica, Constantin, Prateek Verma, Patricia Alessandrini, and Alexandru Berceanu. "Accessible Co-Creativity with AI through Language and Voice Input." In *Proceedings of the Conference on AI Music Creativity (AIMC).* Brighton, UK: AIMC, 2024. https://aimc2023.pubpub.org/pub/lo8xj7sb.

Ben-Ary, Guy. *cellF. Guy Ben-Ary.* Accessed February 26, 2026. https://guybenary.com/work/cellf.

Berceanu, Alexandru. *Lost Interferences. Ars Electronica.* 2021. https://ars.electronica.art/newdigitaldeal/en/lost-interferences.

Berceanu, Alexandru I., Cătălin Creţu, Grigore Burloiu, and Dragoş Cârneci. "Extension of Performativity by a BCI." *Studia UBB Dramatica* 60, no. 2 (2015): 77–100. https://www.researchgate.net/publication/284354877_Extension_of_performativity_by_BCI.

"Can You Create Music Using Brainwaves? | Paramusical Ensemble." Directed by Tim Grabham. Producer and Composer: Eduardo Reck Miranda. YouTube video, 9:19. Posted by "Aeon Video," April 3, 2024. https://www.youtube.com/watch?v=4amoa7lg_1U.

Chafe, Chris. "The Qualities and Flow of Imagined Sound and Music." In *Sounds from Within: Phenomenology and Practice*, edited by Paulo C. Chagas and Jiayue Cecilia Wu, 57–73. Cham, Switzerland: Springer, 2021. https://doi.org/10.1007/978-3-030-72507-5.

Chechile, Alex. "Music Re-Informed by the Brain." *Alex Chechile.* Accessed January 13, 2026. https://alexchechile.com/projects.html.

Christopher, Kameron R., Ajay Kapur, Dale A. Carnegie, and Gina M. Grimshaw. "A History of Emerging Paradigms in EEG for Music." In *Proceedings of the International Computer Music Conference (ICMC)*, 1142–48. Athens, Greece: ICMC, 2014. https://quod.lib.umich.edu/i/icmc/bbp2372.2014.175/1/--history-of-emerging-paradigms-in-eeg-for-music.

Chung, Miyoung, Taehyung Kim, Eunju Jeong, Chun Kee Chung, June Sic Kim, and Oh-Sang Kwon. "Decoding Imagined Musical Pitch From Human Scalp Electroencephalograms." *IEEE Transactions on Neural Systems and Rehabilitation Engineering* (May 2023): 2154–2163. https://doi.org/10.1109/TNSRE.2023.3270175.

Chusid, Irwin, and Jeff Winner. "Circle Machines and Sequencers: The Untold History of Raymond Scott's Electronica." *Electronic Music*, December 2001. Reprinted with revisions on *Raymond Scott*, 2016. https://www.raymondscott.net/em-article-2001.

Constantin Basica. Accessed January 5, 2026. http://www.constantinbasica.com.

Copet, Jade, Felix Kreuk, Itai Gat, Tal Remez, David Kant, Gabriel Synnaeve, Yossi Adi, and Alexandre Défossez. "Simple and Controllable Music Generation." *Advances in Neural Information Processing Systems* 36 (2023): 47704–47720.

Creţu, Cătălin. "EEG-Based Real-Time Audio Generation and Interaction." *Bulletin of the Transilvania University of Braşov, Series VIII: Performing Arts* 18, no. 67 (2025). https://doi.org/10.31926/but.pa.2025.18.67.3.6.

Creţu, Cătălin, Alexandru Berceanu, and Grigore Burloiu. "Muzică Interactivă de Scenă pe Baza EEG / EEG-Based Interactive Stage Music." *Tehnologii Informatice şi de Comunicaţie în Domeniul Muzical*

/ *ICT in Musical Field* 6, no. 2 (2015): 83–91. https://tic.edituramediamusica.ro/reviste/2015/2/ICTMF_ISSN_2067-9408_2015_vol_6_issue_2_pg_no_83-91.pdf.

Daly, Ian. "Neural Decoding of Music from the EEG." *Scientific Reports* 13 (January 2023): 624. https://doi.org/10.1038/s41598-022-27361-x.

Daly, Ian, Duncan Williams, Asad Malik, James Weaver, Alexis Kirke, Faustina Hwang, Eduardo Miranda, and Slawomir J. Nasuto. "Personalized, Multi-modal, Affective State Detection for Hybrid Brain–Computer Music Interfacing." *IEEE Transactions on Affective Computing* 11, no. 1 (January–March 2020): 111–124. https://doi.org/10.1109/TAFFC.2017.2773511.

Damian, Adrian. *The Imagination Laboratory. Adrian Damian*. 2017. https://www.adrian-damian.com/the-imagination-laboratory.

Dayal, Geeta. "David Rosenboom." *4Columns*, May 31, 2019. https://4columns.org/dayal-geeta/david-rosenboom.

Deconstructing Dad: The Music, Machines, and Mystery of Raymond Scott. Directed by Stan Warnow. New York, NY: First Run Features, 2010. 1:39:00. https://www.raymondscott.net/film/scottdoc.

Défossez, Alexandre, Jade Copet, Gabriel Synnaeve, and Yossi Adi. "High Fidelity Neural Audio Compression." Preprint, submitted October 24, 2022. arXiv preprint arXiv:2210.13438. https://arxiv.org/abs/2210.13438.

Deuel, Thomas A., Juan Pampin, Jay Sundstrom, and Felix Darvas. "The Encephalophone: A Novel Musical Biofeedback Device Using Conscious Control of Electroencephalogram (EEG)." *Frontiers in Human Neuroscience* 11 (April 2017): 213. https://doi.org/10.3389/fnhum.2017.00213.

Di Liberto, Giovanni M., Marion Guilhem, and Shihab A. Shamma. "Accurate Decoding of Imagined and Heard Melodies." *Frontiers in Neuroscience* 15 (August 2021): 673401. https://doi.org/10.3389/fnins.2021.673401.

"Disklavier." *Wikipedia*. Accessed January 26, 2026. https://en.wikipedia.org/wiki/Disklavier.

Domingues, Renan B., Luísa A. Domingues, Victor R. Procaci, and José L. Pedroso. "The Neuroscience of Music Perception: A Narrative Review." *Arquivos de Neuro-Psiquiatria* 83, no. 9 (September 2025): 1–11. https://doi.org/10.1055/s-0045-1811233.

Fonseca, Eduardo, Xavier Favory, Jordi Pons, Frederic Font, and Xavier Serra. "FSD50K: An Open Dataset of Human-Labeled Sound Events." *IEEE/ACM Transactions on Audio, Speech, and Language Processing* 30 (January 2022): 829–852. https://dl.acm.org/doi/pdf/10.1109/TASLP.2021.3133208.

Gemmeke, Jort F., Daniel P. W. Ellis, Dylan Freedman, Aren Jansen, Wade Lawrence, R. Channing Moore, Manoj Plakal, and Marvin Ritter. "Audio Set: An Ontology and Human-Labeled Dataset for Audio Events." In *2017 IEEE International Conference on Acoustics, Speech and Signal Processing (ICASSP)*, 776–780. IEEE, 2017.

Georgia Institute of Technology. "Brain-Inspired AI Breakthrough Spotlighted at Global Conference." *Georgia Tech News Center*, June 26, 2025. https://www.gatech.edu/news/2025/06/26/brain-inspired-ai-breakthrough-spotlighted-global-conference.

Gheorghe, Andrei. *Resonance. Ars Electronica*. 2025. https://ars.electronica.art/panic/en/view/resonance-20e38ddb450c8188ad11fcbd52bc72a4.

Goldberg, Corey M. "Raymond Scott: Rediscovering the Forgotten Wit of Jazz." MA thesis, Rutgers, the State University of New Jersey, 2006. https://www.raymondscott.net/wp-content/uploads/2016/09/RS-thesis-Corey-Goldberg-2.pdf.

Grierson, Mick. "Composing with Brainwaves: Minimal Trial P300 Recognition as an Indication of Subjective Preference for the Control of a Musical Instrument." In *Proceedings of the International Computer Music Conference (ICMC)*. Belfast, Northern Ireland: ICMC, 2008. http://hdl.handle.net/2027/spo.bbp2372.2008.063.

Haill, Luciana. "Artworks." *Luciana Haill: Brainwaves Augmenting Consciousness*. Accessed January 13, 2026. https://lucianahaill.wordpress.com.

Hajdu, Georg, and Nick Didkovsky. "MaxScore: Current State of the Art." In *Proceedings of the International Computer Music Conference (ICMC)*, 9–15. Ljubljana, Slovenia, 2012.

Harrington, Colin, and Eduardo Reck Miranda. "CTM 2024: Studio Quantum – 'Mind the Qubits.'" YouTube video, 47:57. Posted by "CTM FESTIVAL," April 15, 2024. https://www.youtube.com/watch?v=3FZZJFP96CQ.

Hickok, Gregory, Bradley Buchsbaum, Colin Humphries, and Tugan Muftuler. "Auditory-Motor Interaction Revealed by fMRI: Speech, Music, and Working Memory in Area Spt." *Journal of Cognitive Neuroscience* 15, no. 5 (July 2003): 673–682. https://doi.org/10.1162/089892903322307393.

Hinwar, Rish P., and Anthony J. Lambert. "Anauralia: The Silent Mind and Its Association with Aphantasia." *Frontiers in Psychology* 12 (October 2021): 744213. https://doi.org/10.3389/fpsyg.2021.744213.

Holmes, Thom. "On the Road: Early Live Moog Modular Artists, Part 2." *Moog: A History in Recordings.* Bob Moog Foundation. Accessed January 13, 2026. https://moogfoundation.org/early-live-moog-modular-artists-richard-teitelbaum-first-moog-modular-synthesizer-europe.

Hu, Edward J., Yelong Shen, Phillip Wallis, Zeyuan Allen-Zhu, Yuanzhi Li, Shean Wang, Liang Wang, and Weizhu Chen. "LoRA: Low-Rank Adaptation of Large Language Models." In *Proceedings of the International Conference on Learning Representations (ICLR)* 1, no. 2 (2022): 1–13.

IBM. "10 AI Dangers and Risks—And How to Manage Them." *Think.* IBM. Accessed February 26, 2064. https://www.ibm.com/think/insights/10-ai-dangers-and-risks-and-how-to-manage-them.

IRCAM, Music Representation Team. *Somax2.* Application. Accessed February 13, 2026. https://forum.ircam.fr/projects/detail/somax-2.

Johnson, Sandra, and David Hyland-Wood. "A Primer on Large Language Models and Their Limitations." Preprint, submitted December 3, 2024. arXiv:2412.04503. https://doi.org/10.48550/arXiv.2412.04503.

Karle, Amy. *Brainsongs. Amy Karle.* 2015. https://www.amykarle.com/project/brainsongs.

Kivy, Peter. "Mozart and Monotheism: An Essay in Spurious Aesthetics." *The Journal of Musicology* 2, no. 3 (1983): 322–328.

Langner, Selena. "Brain-Inspired AI Breakthrough Spotlighted at Global Conference." *Georgia Tech News Center*, June 26, 2025. https://www.gatech.edu/news/2025/06/26/brain-inspired-ai-breakthrough-spotlighted-global-conference.

Lawhern, Vernon J., Amelia J. Solon, Nicholas R. Waytowich, Stephen M. Gordon, Chou P. Hung, and Brent J. Lance. "EEGNet: A Compact Convolutional Neural Network for EEG-Based Brain–Computer Interfaces." *Journal of Neural Engineering* 15, no. 5 (2018): 056013.

Leslie, Grace. "Composing at the Border of Experimental Music and Music Experiment." In *The Science-Music Borderlands: Reckoning with the Past and Imagining the Future*, edited by Elizabeth Hellmuth Margulis, Psyche Loui, and Deirdre Loughridge, 277–287. Cambridge, MA: MIT Press, 2023. https://doi.org/10.7551/mitpress/14731.003.0016.

Lopez-Bernal, Diego, David Balderas, Pedro Ponce, and Arturo Molina. "A State-of-the-Art Review of EEG-Based Imagined Speech Decoding." *Frontiers in Human Neuroscience* 16 (April 2022): 867281. https://doi.org/10.3389/fnhum.2022.867281.

Lutters, Bart, and Peter J. Koehler. "Brainwaves in Concert: The 20th-Century Sonification of the Electroencephalogram." *Brain* 139, no. 10 (August 2016): 2809–2814. https://doi.org/10.1093/brain/aww207.

"Mark Applebaum – Tlön." YouTube video, 8:43. Posted by "OSSIA New Music." April 23, 2024. https://www.youtube.com/watch?v=djKBeH6ClhO.

Medha Ramaswamy, Johann Laji Philip, Vijayan Priya, Snigdha Priyadarshini, Meenakshi Ramasamy, G. C. Jeevitha, Darin Mansor Mathkor, et al. "Therapeutic Use of Music in Neurological Disorders: A Concise Narrative Review." *Heliyon* 10, no. 16 (August 2024): e35564. https://doi.org/10.1016/j.heliyon.2024.e35564.

Myers, Andrew. "AI Reveals How Brain Activity Unfolds Over Time." *Stanford HAI*, January 21, 2026. https://hai.stanford.edu/news/ai-reveals-how-brain-activity-unfolds-over-time.

Miranda, Eduardo Reck. "Brain–Computer Music Interface for Composition and Performance." *International Journal on Disability and Human Development* 5, no. 2 (2006). https://doi.org/10.1515/IJDHD.2006.5.2.119.

Miranda, Eduardo Reck. "Brain–Computer Music Interfacing: Interdisciplinary Research at the Crossroads of Music, Science and Biomedical Engineering." In *Guide to Brain–Computer Music Interfacing*, edited by Eduardo Reck Miranda and Julien Castet, 1–27. London, UK: Springer-Verlag, 2014.

Miranda, Eduardo Reck. "Quantum Computer: Hello, Music!" In *Handbook of Artificial Intelligence for Music: Foundations, Advanced Approaches, and Developments for Creativity*, edited by Eduardo Reck Miranda, 963–994. Cham, Switzerland: Springer Nature, 2021.

Miranda, Eduardo Reck. "Toward Neurotechnology for Musical Creativity." In *The Science-Music Borderlands: Reckoning with the Past, Thinking about the Future*, edited by Elizabeth Hellmuth Margulis, Psyche Loui, and Deirdre Loughridge, 221–233. Cambridge, MA: MIT Press, 2023. https://doi.org/10.7551/mitpress/14731.003.0016.

Miranda, Eduardo Reck, and Andrew Brouse. "Interfacing the Brain Directly with Musical Systems: On Developing Systems for Making Music with Brain Signals." *Leonardo* 38, no. 4 (August 2005): 331–336. https://doi.org/10.1162/0024094054762133.

Miranda, Eduardo Reck, and Andrew Brouse. "Toward Direct Brain–Computer Musical Interfaces." In *Proceedings of the 2005 International Conference on New Interfaces for Musical Expression (NIME), 216–219.* Vancouver, BC: NIME, 2005.

Miranda, Eduardo Reck, Simon Durrant, and Torsten Anders. "Towards Brain–Computer Music Interfaces: Progress and Challenges." In *Proceedings of the 2008 First International Symposium on Applied Sciences on Biomedical and Communication Technologies*. Aalborg, Denmark: IEEE, 2008. https://doi.org/10.1109/ISABEL.2008.4712626.

Myers, Andrew. "AI Reveals How Brain Activity Unfolds Over Time." *Stanford HAI*, January 21, 2026. https://hai.stanford.edu/news/ai-reveals-how-brain-activity-unfolds-over-time.

Navas, Eduardo. "AI Ethics, Aesthetics, Art and Artistry." In *Handbook on the Ethics of Artificial Intelligence*, edited by David J. Gunkel, 173–186. Northampton, MA: Edward Elgar Publishing, 2024.

Nerness, Barbara Nicole. "Brain Dynamics during Music Improvisation." PhD Diss., Stanford University, 2025. https://purl.stanford.edu/xm667gf4960.

Odlen, Ingrid, Prateek Verma, Constantin Basica, and Pamela Davis Kivelson. "Painting from Music Using Neural Visual Style Transfer." In *Proceedings of the NeurIPS 2020 Workshop on Machine Learning for Creativity and Design.* Virtual, 2020.

Ono, Yoko. *Grapefruit: A Book of Instructions and Drawings.* New York, NY: Simon & Schuster, 2000.

Park, Lisa. "Eunoia." *Lisa Park.* Accessed January 13, 2026. https://www.thelisapark.com/work/eunoia.

Pasca, Sergiu P. "How We're Reverse Engineering the Human Brain in the Lab." TED video, 12:34. Posted by "TED," August 29, 2022. https://www.youtube.com/watch?v=ABmRCdnVq3E.

Patel, Aniruddh D. *Music, Language, and the Brain.* Oxford, UK: Oxford University Press, 2008. https://doi.org/10.1093/acprof:oso/9780195123753.001.0001.

Schaefer, Rebecca, Yvonne Blokland, Jason Farquhar, and Peter Desain. "Single Trial Classification of Perceived and Imagined Music from EEG." In *Proceedings of the 2009 Berlin BCI Workshop.* Berlin, Germany, 2009. https://www.pure.ed.ac.uk/ws/portalfiles/portal/13331887/Single_trial_classification.pdf

Schubert, Alexander. "Steady State." *Alexander Schubert.* 2024. https://www.alexanderschubert.net/works/Steady-State.php.

Shakespeare Navigators. "*The Tempest*: Act III, Scene 2." In *The Tempest Navigator.* Accessed February 10, 2026. https://shakespeare-navigators.ewu.edu/tempest/TempestText32.html.

Shakespeare Navigators. "*The Tempest*: Act V, Scene 1." In *The Tempest Navigator*. Accessed February 26, 2026. https://shakespeare-navigators.ewu.edu/tempest/TempestText32.html.

Siuzdak, Hubert, Florian Grötschla, and Luca A. Lanzendörfer. "SNAC: Multi-Scale Neural Audio Codec." Preprint, submitted October 18, 2024. arXiv:2410.14411. https://arxiv.org/abs/2410.14411.

Straebel, Volker, and Wilm Thoben. "Alvin Lucier's *Music for Solo Performer*: Experimental Music Beyond Sonification." *Organised Sound* 19, no. 1 (April 2014): 17–29. https://doi.org/10.1017/s1355771813000481.

Țenea, Sabin-Andrei, Alexandru Berceanu, Sergiu Nisioi, Andreea Robu-Movilă, Constantin Pistol, and Grigore Burloiu. "The Co-Created City: Neuroadaptive Design for Healthy Environments." *Intelligent Buildings International* (August 2025): 1–15. https://doi.org/10.1080/17508975.2025.2542804.

TensorFlow. "Sound Classification with YAMNet." *TensorFlow Hub*. Accessed March 9, 2024. https://www.tensorflow.org/hub/tutorials/yamnet.

"The Last Piece." *George Enescu International Festival*. 2025. https://festivalenescu.ro/en/george-enescu-international-festival/past-events/the-last-piece-immersive-syncretic-concert-1779979835.

Tibo, Marthe, Simon Geirnaert, and Alexander Bertrand. "EEG-Based Decoding and Recognition of Imagined Music." Preprint, withdrawn May 19, 2021. https://doi.org/10.1101/2020.09.30.320176.

Vanutelli, Maria Elide, Marco Salvadore, and Claudio Lucchiari. "BCI Applications to Creativity: Review and Future Directions, from Little-c to C2." *Brain Sciences* 13, no. 4 (April 2023): 665. https://doi.org/10.3390/brainsci13040665.

Vavoulis, Athanasios, Patricia Figueiredo, and Athanasios Vourvopoulos. "A Review of Online Classification Performance in Motor Imagery-Based Brain–Computer Interfaces for Stroke Neurorehabilitation." *Signals* 4, no. 1 (January 2023): 73–86. https://doi.org/10.3390/signals4010004.

Venkatesh, Satvik, Eduardo Reck Miranda, and Edward Braund. "SSVEP-Based Brain-Computer Interface for Music Using a Low-Density EEG System." *Assistive Technology* 36, no. 5 (May 2024): 378–388. https://doi.org/10.1080/10400435.2022.2084182.

Verma, Prateek, and Jonathan Berger. "Audio Transformers." Preprint, last revised May 11, 2025. arXiv:2105.00335v2. https://arxiv.org/abs/2105.00335.

Verma, Prateek, Constantin Basica, and Pamela Davis Kivelson. "Translating Paintings Into Music Using Neural Networks." Preprint, submitted August 23, 2020. arXiv:2008.09960. https://arxiv.org/abs/2008.09960.

Vuust, Peter, Ole A. Heggli, Karl J. Friston, and Morten L. Kringelbach. "Music in the Brain." *Nature Reviews Neuroscience* 23 (March 2022): 287–305. https://doi.org/10.1017/S135577181300037X.

Williams, Duncan, Alexis Kirke, Eduardo Miranda, Ian Daly, Faustina Hwang, James Weaver, and Slawomir Nasuto. "Affective Calibration of Musical Feature Sets in an Emotionally Intelligent Music Composition System." *ACM Transactions on Applied Perception* 14, no. 3 (May 2017): 1–13. https://doi.org/10.1145/3059005.

Williams, Duncan, and Eduardo R. Miranda. "BCI for Music Making: Then, Now, and Next." In *Brain–Computer Interfaces Handbook: Technological and Theoretical Advances*, edited by Chang S. Nam, Anton Nijholt, and Fabien Lotte, 191–205. Boca Raton, FL: CRC Press, 2019.

Wilson, Edward O. *Consilience: The Unity of Knowledge*. New York, NY: Alfred A. Knopf, 1998.

Zatorre, Robert J., and Andrea R. Halpern. "Mental Concerts: Musical Imagery Minireview and Auditory Cortex." *Neuron* 47, no. 1 (2005): 9–12.

Zatorre, Robert J., and Isabelle Peretz, eds. *The Biological Foundations of Music*. Annals of the New York Academy of Sciences, vol. 930. New York, NY: New York Academy of Sciences, 2001.

Zatorre, Robert J., Alan C. Evans, Ernst Meyer, and Albert Gjedde. "Lateralization of Phonetic and Pitch Discrimination in Speech Processing." Science 256, no. 5058 (May 8, 1992): 846–849. https://doi.org/10.1126/science.256.5058.846.

Zhang, Ruohan, Sharon Lee, Minjune Hwang, Ayano Hiranaka, Chen Wang, Wensi Ai, Jin Jie Ryan Tan et al. "NOIR: Neural Signal Operated Intelligent Robots for Everyday Activities." Preprint, submitted November 2, 2023. arXiv:2311.01454. https://arxiv.org/abs/2311.01454.

9

INTERLUDE IV

Interview with Nao Tokui

Julie Zhu and Constantin Basica

DOI: 10.4324/9781003615873-9

Constantin: I was looking at your *Emergent Rhythm*[1] project (Figure 9.1)—this idea of the AI DJ—which is a nice metaphor for how we see artists working with AI nowadays: curating materials. Generating things, finding interesting things, then curating them, and making work with that. I'm wondering how you see things going from here. Do you think that we'll be doing this for a while? Or do you see a clear pathway for artists to actually go the opposite way—into the black box ... They break it, they train their own models, and they make their own systems. Where are we going next with generative AI?

Nao: Wow, that's a big question [*both laugh*]. Where should I start? I think I totally agree with what you said. When you work with AI, you need to be kind of a curator, or more like a DJ. Basically, you pick interesting output of AI models after you create them, mix them together (or collage them to create their own narrative), and eventually they become your work.

Another part of working with AI is that you can create your own dataset, and you can try different models for your art practice. This is my vision. When we started Neutone,[2] we saw the gap between AI research and artistic practice. And we wanted to bridge that gap. We wanted to provide means for artists to train their own small models. And nowadays, AI models are getting bigger and bigger, more and more difficult to train by ourselves. So, it's very important for artists to have custom models.

Figure 9.1 Nao Tokui performs *Emergent Rhythm* using real-time AI audio generation models.

This is my opinion: Artists don't need generic models or universal models. Artists just need models that reflect their own taste or their own styles. And again—I think the artist should be the creator of both the output of AI and the dataset going into it.

Constantin: I was looking at this presentation where you were listing all the steps one needs to follow to train a model from scratch: you go to PyTorch, put in the code, explore, and so on. You have all these steps. And then, with your work at Neutone, you want to minimize the number of steps and just make it more streamlined for artists to be able to do what they want to do. So, this reminded me a little bit of that quote from Suno's CEO, who said in an interview that "most people don't really enjoy making music." [*Both laugh.*] I guess it's already become a sort of meme in our world of AI music.

Nao: Actually, I did a performance with that material. I mean his voice. I sampled his voice.

Constantin: That's awesome ... So, thinking of your quote and his: If you give an artist a reduced workload—they can just go in and train a model without doing all the hard programming—is there something that they might actually miss by not going through all those steps?

Nao: Yeah, I think there's a big difference between *artistically important* tedious tasks and *just* tedious tasks. And also between *enjoyable* tedious tasks and *not-enjoyable* tedious tasks. And I think it doesn't make sense to remove those enjoyable tasks from the music creation process. But the process of training a model is not essential for the artistic process. The task itself is not essential for artistic expression. Of course, maybe you can learn something from tutorials—like about a Python script. But for the majority of artists or musicians, it doesn't make sense.

Julie: I love the way you are imagining that these AI tools can be available to anyone and everyone. And I feel like that'll change the way people work. Before, you had to create that book—the creative act, you know?—and you had to put yourself in the right environment to have a good idea (and you might only have one idea every week or something). But with the surprises that you get from the AI-generated stuff, ideas might come faster. So then, do you feel that, in the future, our artistic process will change? Will we become more like curators, or like DJs? Do you see a fundamental change in the way we make art?

Nao: It's not necessarily a change. I mean, it's not like moving from A to B. It's more like adding new ways to work with music. What I mean by this is: You can still practice piano, and you can still compose music in a traditional way, or you can still make music. But AI provides a new way to interact—a new way to work on music or to produce music.

Constantin: Like new colors on the painter's palette.

Nao: Yeah, yeah. I mean, you can still use a modular synthesizer or a MIDI keyboard. But at the same time, you can also use AI and be a curator to make music.

Constantin: Do you think there will be a time when, maybe, that keyboard behind you [*points to musical keyboard*] will disappear, and you won't need it at all?

Nao: I don't think so.

Constantin: Well, at least for us, it's kind of different because we are right at this threshold when AI is still emerging. But what about new generations that will be born in a world of AI tools? Will they have the same fun learning how to play a keyboard?

Julie: Like your daughter?

Nao: I will definitely bring my daughter to piano class, for sure. I guess the skill of playing a musical instrument will be much more valuable with the advent of AI because many people will choose the easy way, which is AI, and just type in Suno or something like that. And then, physical skills like playing piano or playing guitar will be much more valuable. Nowadays—I don't know in Europe or the US, but here in Japan—many young talented musicians tend more toward forming a traditional band (like rock and roll or jazz). Ten or twenty years ago, there were so many electronic music talents. But nowadays, kids choose to play in a band or a hip-hop group because making music with a computer and software isn't so exciting for a generation that grew up surrounded by PCs. Or maybe it feels more difficult for them to stand out by making music with Ableton since it's so streamlined.

Julie: Say you encounter someone who you want to make curious about AI. How would you approach them? What would you tell them?

Nao: Hmm ... I think I would try to demystify AI. Many people think AI is an autonomous thing. Or something like ChatGPT. But AI in music is not like that. AI is just a new synthesizer in which the technology has a little bit of automation. Or it's a little bit smarter than a synthesizer. But it's still a *tool*.

Constantin: Can I make a quick detour here, since we're on this topic of AI tools? If we can dream of the future—maybe a science-fiction future—where we *do* reach the point of a sentient AI, or one that can act in its own right ... let's imagine a world where this AI starts making music that maybe we don't even understand as humans. And let's say this AI makes new genres, new instruments, and a whole new music culture.

Nao: I'm skeptical about this. I don't think the current AI systems can create or originate new genres, or new musical instruments, or a completely new sound because the current generative AI is only trying to mimic patterns in the training data and to reproduce the pattern in a statistical way.

Constantin: Yes, absolutely not with the *current* AI. But do you think that, with such fast developments, there will be a turning point where there might be some emergence?

Nao: Yeah, in the future … it's possible. But we need a different architecture, or a different framework. I don't think the current AI models can achieve such a breakthrough.

Constantin: And if that were to happen during our lifetimes, would you be one of the enthusiasts, or would you be rather wary about it? It's very hypothetical, I know.

Nao: As an artist, I will be very excited to hear what those AI models can generate and originate. And maybe I can integrate them, or I can sample that music and create something, or I can be inspired by their creation. But at the same time, as a member of this society, it's obviously problematic. We need some kind of regulation to secure the jobs of musicians—and the industry. So that's a whole other discussion.

Julie: Do you have any sort of ideas of how a private citizen can go about making those kinds of ethical decisions? Is it possible on an individual level? Or does it have to be a global concert through laws? How can individual companies like Qosmo[3] make a difference?

Nao: Yeah, I've been thinking about this. But I don't have any clear answer. I just keep making statements. And as you know, at Neutone, we are very conscious about copyright and ethical issues. We make a clear statement on our website about our stance on copyright and the ethical issues surrounding it. We mention this on our social network and in our workshops. But I'm not sure … How can we affect the global discourse around these issues?

Constantin: I think, in some sense, you do. I feel like you are part of the conversation—and this is the time to have all these conversations. With your company, these statements, and constantly thinking about how to operate in this new world, I think you do provide an answer, in some sense, because you have been working on it. You know?

Nao: Yes. Also, we make art installations. And we made a small website to address this issue, which we just published, called Spot-if-AI.[4] It's addressing the issue that there are so many AI-generated songs on Spotify, and that Spotify does nothing about it.

Julie: No—they *paid* for them!

Nao: Yeah, exactly. Exactly. So, this is our small statement.

Julie: Have you been contacted by Spotify about it?

Nao: No. But right after I published this website, my lawyer contacted me [*laughs*]. Initially, it was "Spotifake" (the name of the website). And the lawyer contacted me saying I should be a little bit more careful about trademark infringement. But, I mean, this is an artwork, not a corporate website or anything commercial. So, it should be fine, I guess.

Julie: That's amazing. I'm definitely going to share this with my students. I think that's great. But … copyright also works differently in Japan, right? And so, I feel like there are these Western notions of copyright. You even talk about it in your book:[5] If we had copyright around the time of Mozart, maybe he wouldn't have been able to create the things that he created. So, where is that line of … sampling? It's a conversation that, I feel like, is still complex. It's hard to make laws about it—it's more about someone's intention. Is that right?

Nao: Yeah, I think so. As you mentioned, in Japan, the copyright law is much looser and more relaxed. But nowadays, we have many discussions around this issue. And people are getting more and more conscious about it—especially anime and manga creators in Japan. They are very much vocal about the copyright of illustration and anime. So, the government is trying to find a good balance between promoting AI technology and protecting copyright creators. But there's a thin line between copyright infringement and being inspired by something. I'm sure we need a better system for attributing copyright and compensating the creators. But yeah, it's complex. Complicated.

Julie: Thank you for this book, by the way [*shows a physical copy of Nao's book*]—I loved it. And I saw that it won an award in Japan. I'm not in Japan, and I can't read Japanese. But can you tell us: Are you influencing this discussion in Japan? How was your book received? Are people talking to you about it? Are you going on TV about it? What was the afterlife of this book?

Nao: Well, I'm not super famous [*laughs*] and I'm not someone on TV. But I think the book was well received among artists and musicians. I got many requests for interviews in newspapers and magazines. Though, I should say, the majority of Japanese people don't know anything about this book or me. But I think it's safe to say I'm known among people who are interested in the future of AI and human creativity.

Julie: That's my sense, too, and I think that makes it all the more important that you are making brave statements—because you are so well-known. How does that work with your investors? Are they upset with you sometimes?

Nao: I mean, I don't have any investors, so …

Julie: Oh, okay.

Nao: Yeah, so, my company is self-funded. And, actually, Neutone is looking for investors. But it's challenging for us to convince investors because we are not Suno or Udio, nor are we automating music production.

I should add this: I do have some influence among people who are very conscious about AI, creativity, and copyright issues. But I feel I'm in the minority. The Japanese society and the government are pretty much promoting generative AI as a tool for future business success or better automation. Or more effective business operations. Something like that. So I'm a minority in that sense, I think. That's why I sometimes get negative comments on social networks. People see the government promoting AI for automation and sometimes confuse that with my work, which is about promoting AI as a creative tool for artists. As I said, there are so many anime and manga creators in Japan, and they are sometimes very critical about AI, and they have very negative impressions of AI. So, when they find me, they think I'm just something like Suno or Udio—stealing their creative work. And sometimes, I find it very difficult to convince them that I'm not.

Constantin: What are some of the things that you say to these people to make that distinction between yourself and those companies?

Nao: I think any automated tools for consumption like Suno or Udio are basically *business*. And I think there are so many different ways to use AI in creative ways. So, I always use the analogy of a vinyl or CD. In my view, Suno is more like an evolution of a vinyl, or CD, or Spotify. It's a reproduction tool. And there are so many other music technologies—such as synthesizers or samplers—that are tools for artistic practice and artistic creation. And I want to make new synthesizers, new guitars, new effects with AI. I'm not interested in inventing a new CD, or vinyl, or Spotify.

Constantin: Do you feel like you face more people who are skeptical or opposing AI because you live in Japan? If so, does it happen to you more in that culture, or do you feel the same when you travel and you go to other countries? Or do you feel like it's about the same ratio of AI proponents versus opponents everywhere?

Nao: Maybe it's almost the same, I guess ... Though I can sense a difference between the European discourse and the Japanese one. Europeans are much more—this is just my impression—conscious about a cultural background, and they honor the rights of artists. Japanese people are much more (I don't want to say this) ... a little bit pragmatic, in a sense. They feel like they are being cheated, or that AI companies are stealing their creative work. So, the discussion is a little bit shallow here in Japan.

Constantin: I feel like you could say the same about the US.

Julie: Yeah, it feels the same.

Nao: Okay [*laughs*]. Good to know.

Julie: You were talking about these different tools to help music creation, and going between different modes like audio and visual, and maybe in the future other senses, too. Can you talk more about cross-disciplinary possibilities of using machine learning? At least in your own work, what do you dream about being able to create, or being able to control?

Nao: I'm actually still old-school. I want to make interesting music in a traditional format like vinyl—fixed media. After that, maybe I can start thinking about different multisensory formats.

Julie: I like your answer. It's a contrarian answer. I talk to people, and everyone says, "Well, let's create the visuals. Let's do the light." And I think it's interesting that you want to dive deep and try to do the best music that you can first.

Nao: I still use vinyl when I DJ, so for me it's ideal. If I can use AI to make super interesting music and press it on vinyl, then I can DJ with it.

Constantin: Maybe I can follow up on this idea of you being old-school and wanting to make interesting music first of all. There's a quote that I found on Qosmo's website, which says you are "working on expanding human creativity, exploring AI-driven art and unknown music." So, I'm curious if you could talk a little bit about this term, *unknown music*. What is that for you? How do you see AI helping you find this unknown music?

Nao: The simple answer is *a new genre*. I want to help artists invent new genres. I started making music when I was a student and, back then, I was in an AI research lab at Tokyo University. I didn't know how to make music or how to play an instrument. But at the same time, I wanted to make something interesting. So, that's how I got interested in AI. I thought I could use this technology to create something unique and new. I had this vision from the beginning: using AI to mix something that I cannot imagine by myself. And then, this specific idea of technology helping to create a new genre comes from thinking of something like a Roland 808 drum machine—basically, I want to create a new 808 in the AI era.

Julie: So you want people to break your machine.

Nao: Exactly, yeah. That's why I made Neutone: to easily use *and misuse*. It's just a plug-in, so you can use it as you wish. This is anecdotal, but I met the inventor of the 808 last year, and I explained what I do at Neutone. And the first thing he said to me was: "Oh, Tokui-san, you need to find your Afrika Bambaataa." So I'm looking for that. Of course, I want to *be* Afrika Bambaataa myself—to misuse my technology to create a new genre. But if it's too difficult, I want to find someone else to do it.

Julie: Art created with AI at this moment is interesting *because* it was created with AI—it's a selling point. When do you think we'll get past that? Or do you think we're already past it?

Nao: I think we've passed it, yeah.

Julie: When do you think we passed it?

Nao: Probably with ChatGPT, when you could type a prompt and get a viable output. When Stable Diffusion came out, it was interesting. Even though the technology was not super mature, you could create something strange or interesting with Stable Diffusion. After that, image generation was very much like a reproduction tool. I still miss the 2017–2018 generative adversarial networks.[6]

Julie: It was something raw—you were doing something new, I remember.

How did you come up with the metaphor of surfing? I like it so much. Do you surf?

Nao: It came from Brian Eno, actually. I had a project with him in 2016, and we went to dinner together, and we talked about surfing. He was not specifically talking about AI, but he was talking about his own creative process, and he used the metaphor of surfing in the conversation. So, I owe him that.

Constantin: Looking into the future and your work with AI so far ... what are some things that you felt you discovered about yourself as an artist by using these tools? Or, maybe, by deliberately *not* using some AI tools.

Nao: One thing I've been thinking about lately (and this may be a naïve statement) is that there's still a big gap between what you can do with AI—for example, what you can do with Neutone—and what artists actually expect. And the gap is getting more and more clear to me, as this technology develops and evolves. When I started Neutone in 2020, I was sure that I could convince artists to use it to explore new sonic territory. But as time passed, it became clear that it's not so easy to convince artists to use this tool, because there's that gap between what they can do with the current AI system and what they expect—in terms of sound fidelity or latency, for example.

So, I've been thinking like an artist. I'm obsessed with new technology. I want to use new technology for my artistic practice. And I think AI *is* part of that. But from a purely artistic perspective, maybe using AI is actually limiting my own creativity ... This is a dilemma that I have right now. And I don't have any answer.

So, sometimes I think that I need to forget about AI. Maybe that's why I started using modular synths. [*Laughs and points to a small modular synthesizer in the back.*]

Julie: Oh, that's a black hole. You'll never get out. [*Laughs.*]

Nao: And my wife is not happy about this. [*All three laugh.*]

Learn more about Nao Tokui and his work at https://naotokui.net

Notes

1 *Emergent Rhythm* is an audiovisual DJ performance using real-time AI audio generation models, created by Nao Tokui, Ryosuke Nakajima, and Keito Takaishi.
2 *Neutone.*
3 *Qosmo.*
4 Qosmo, Spot-if-AI.
5 Tokui, *Surfing Human Creativity with AI.*
6 A generative adversarial network (GAN) is a deep learning architecture that uses a generator and a discriminator.

Bibliography

"Generative Adversarial Network." *Wikipedia*. Accessed February 28, 2026. https://en.wikipedia.org/wiki/Generative_adversarial_network.

Neutone. Accessed December 15, 2025. https://neutone.ai.

Qosmo, accessed December 15, 2025. https://qosmo.jp/en.

Qosmo. Spot-if-AI. Accessed December 15, 2025. https://spot-if-ai.qosmo.jp.

Tokui, Nao. *Surfing Human Creativity with AI: A User's Guide.* Translated by David d'Heilly. 2023. Originally published in Japanese by BNN, 2021.

Tokui, Nao, Ryosuke Nakajima, and Keito Takaishi. "Emergent Rhythm—Real-time AI Generative Live Set." *Nao Tokui*, 2022. https://naotokui.net/works/emergent-rhythm.

10

INTERMISSION

Ethics, Authorship, and Creativity in the Age of ChatGPT

Charles Hiroshi Garrett

DOI: 10.4324/9781003615873-10

In Memoriam: Charles Hiroshi Garrett, 1966–2024

[*This is an edited version of the presentation Charles gave via Zoom for the American Musicological Society on October 14, 2023. Notes and bibliography have been added posthumously. The editors thank Saleema Waraich, Charles's widow, for providing the recording of this presentation.*]

Ethics, Authorship, and Creativity

I envisioned this talk would interrogate ChatGPT about ethics, authorship, and creativity. And those ideas do float around this presentation. But actually, using the software kept pushing me away from thinking of ChatGPT as a collaborator or a co-author.

Enthusiastic adopters often describe generative AI as a tool—whether as a practical and efficient assistant or as a creative force that almost has a life of its own. But the actual interface, like a ping-pong match, continually reminds you of a back-and-forth exchange, not a partnership. The ChatGPT website enforces distance. It requires you to make an individual commitment each time you write a prompt, and that activity simultaneously registers and regulates your personal comfort level about AI. If I were to publish this, I would be comfortable with explaining how I employed ChatGPT as a virtual research assistant and how I determined what to accept or reject.

For today's presentation, I also consider ChatGPT to be a research subject. Its responses resemble an interview, and perhaps much that I have included could be characterized as fair use. At the same time, I wondered if ChatGPT was activating a safety mechanism inside me, helping to identify research guide rails that enabled me to avoid blurry terrain and thorny philosophical dilemmas. In other words, I think the paper would be vastly different if I had been contracted and required to complete all of it with generative AI.

My thoughts about creativity and ChatGPT are still hazy. I have felt very creative myself when exploring ChatGPT on what felt like a virtual research trip. I often needed to change my line of inquiry in order to push the AI engine to where I wanted it to go. But ChatGPT still surprised me with its capabilities, proposing smart ideas I had overlooked, synthesizing knowledge, and challenging me to rethink my positions.

The software doesn't feel exactly like human creativity. In some ways, it's too sure of itself, landing solidly on answers rather than proposing follow-up questions. Its comprehensive approach ends up feeling closed-minded. At the same time, I still marvel at how it navigates complex puzzles and juggles entire bodies of knowledge. The current version of ChatGPT (let's think of it as *level 1*) often sounds like, looks like, and acts like a creative being—and that's why generative AI has already established such a powerful foothold in so many creative fields. AI-enhanced processes permeate the pop music landscape because these user-friendly, feature-rich software packages are effective and expansive, and they deliver convincing sonic results that feed our creative impulses.

In truth, 2023 is not at all the best time for sorting out what distinguishes artificial intelligence from human creativity because that relationship is transforming so quickly. The speed at which AI advances undercuts any provisional definitions of intelligence before we can reach some consensus, and that debate is only becoming more challenging and problematic.

Pop Music and AI

My initial research into pop music and AI explored the first solo pop album co-composed with AI, which was released by Taryn Southern in 2018 with a palindrome for a title—*I AM AI*.[1] The album was a product of collaboration: Southern used several AI tools to generate short, original snippets of instrumental music in the form of MP3 audio files, and she and her producer turned those raw audio clips into full-blown twenty-first-century pop songs, featuring lyrics written by Southern. I compared her use of AI to compose hooks to the ways in which innovative music producers select memorable samples to anchor their hits. At the time I claimed that "it remains possible to recognize the constraints of what today's AI music engines can accomplish," and I also observed that "modeling AI as a collaborative tool for human creativity implies that humans still are in the lead, that humans can stay one step ahead of the machine." I ended the talk with a leading question that generated a lot of feedback: "As AI continues to improve in the future, how will we gauge the relationship between a human and a virtual being if we cannot hear the difference?"

So, I gave that presentation three years ago, and looking back now, Southern's approach seems positively quaint, old-fashioned, and my observations have aged just as rapidly. I anticipate the half-life of my talk today will be even shorter given how generative AI has permeated the music industry as well as higher education. I pointed to *ethics, authorship, and creativity* in the title of this talk, but my sense is that those debates are already fading in the rearview mirror, and possibly they're already settled. Rather than thinking about whether ChatGPT should be used, the most forceful voices in the industry have already turned to *how* it can be used—effectively, efficiently, practically, legally. AI is eager to license, apply, and monetize.

No longer is it *AI as rupture* but instead *AI as transformation, progress, imperative*. We don't have to wait for another three years to find out: we're already living through it. Even the Grammys have announced their AI policy, which now requires nominated music to involve "human creators."[2] So, I completely understand why it's sensible as scholars, when it comes to grappling with ChatGPT, to be practical, pragmatic, to learn how to use, adapt, and harness this technology so we too won't be left behind.

In a sense, we've been here so many times before: meeting Siri and Alexa, and turning Google into a verb. But the stakes are raised now, as rogue AI villains who supercharge films like *The Matrix*, *M3GAN*, *Moonfall*, and *Mission Impossible* have continued to warn us. It's important to make clear that, across today's cultural landscape, adopting AI has already been normalized. Hollywood extras may be on strike, fighting so that their digital rights won't be harvested by machine learning, but at the same time actor-comedian Sarah Silverman is one of many who've jumped ahead of all that by suing companies like OpenAI for a piece of the action.[3] And Hollywood stars like Harrison Ford, Mark Hamill, and Will Smith are happy to get in line so that fountain-of-youth AI will help them de-age.[4] Recent press reports have been banging the drum for a new AI-enhanced film called *Back to Eden*, featuring the legendary actor James Dean, whose last film was *East of Eden*, released in 1955.[5]

I don't mean to claim that AI has been universally accepted by pop musicians and consumers. But, if even aging rockers like Nick Cave want to grumble about it,[6] there's no question about whether AI will be part of our musical present and future or not. We're instead looking at how musicians will use it, when it will roll out, and who will be in charge. In the wake of recent audio deepfakes—the viral videos of synthetic Jay-Z,[7] reconstituted Drake,[8] and imitation Ariana Grande[9] (Figure 10.1)—Universal Music tried to claim the moral ground (as long as it protected their financial interests) by asking "which side of history all stakeholders in the music ecosystem want to be on: the side of artists, fans, and human creative expression, or the side of deepfakes, fraud, and denying artists their due compensation."[10] Positioning the debate to protect corporate monetization should not be equated with fending off AI challenges to human creativity. And besides, Universal has no control whatsoever over the ascent of generative AI.

Figure 10.1 A screenshot from the lecture Charles Hiroshi Garrett gave via Zoom for the American Musicological Society on October 14, 2023.

Now anyone can attempt these audio tricks at home. Voicify sells access to thousands of AI voices, while Uberduck and Musicfy enable singers to manipulate vocal libraries or manipulate their own voices with AI. All the barn doors are open wide. And for so many fans (especially the social-media generation that hurls pop forward today) AI is already embedded in pop's creative universe—whether it's Kendrick Lamar morphing into O. J. Simpson and Kobe Bryant,[11] or Paul McCartney turning 30 again.[12]

I think it's most instructive to listen to the canaries: the early adopters and experimental musicians like Holly Herndon, who created a digital twin for purchase, allowing anyone to make music with her simulated voice.[13] About this, she weighs in assertively: "It is now possible to produce infinite media in the style or likeness of someone else—soon with little effort—so we all have to come to terms with what that means."[14] Herndon's project has since inspired the tech-friendly pop star Grimes to promise a 50% royalty cut to anyone who creates a hit song using AI to sculpt her voice.[15] And now, Universal Music and Google are elbowing in, working on a licensing scheme so that artists' voices and music can be licensed for songs generated by AI.[16] These kinds of ventures (announced every few weeks) require that anyone who wants to understand what it means to be a pop artist in 2023 now has to spend time with AI music tools: how producers trigger AI plug-ins in Pro Tools, how bands polish their demos with AI mastering software, and how today's songwriters partner with ChatGPT and other generative AI programs.

"A Suite of Custom Generative AI Tools Unlike Anything Currently Offered in Higher Education"

It's been less than a year since ChatGPT was released for public use, and around six months since it really hit home on college campuses, where students explore all of its capabilities and faculty try to absorb this shock to the system. Some teachers banned ChatGPT;[17] some invested in AI detection software;[18] some faculty (including me) felt we were frozen in place—wondering if we should be doing something or just hoping this would all pass. The relentless ascent of AI pierced our identities as teachers and students, which just kindled more hand-wringing about the purpose and need for a college education. It was clear by mid-summer that generative AI was here to stay and that we were in the midst of the *find-out* phase.

I've had a lot of conversations about ChatGPT since then, with colleagues, friends, and teachers who recently retired. All have commented: "Just in time." When I talk with other faculty, it sometimes feels like we're collectively mourning and we find ourselves muddling through denial, anger, bargaining, and depression. You hear: "I doubt our good students are using it." "I'm not changing how I teach." "That software needs to be abolished." "Well, maybe it will be okay—I just got this new AI detection app." "I barely survived Zoom, and now this?" I am not going to pretend that ChatGPT is easy to stomach, and I'm unhappy about how it has changed me as a teacher: how I think about creating assignments, how I spend classroom time, what I expect from students, how I imagine my future courses will work, and what I hope students will still need from me going forward. The conversations I have about this with my spouse, who teaches art history at a small liberal arts college, are filled with grumbling, dread, wobbly acceptance, and sometimes brainstorming about *if* and *how* we can adapt in time.

I am sure comments sound overheated, so I should explain they have been shaped by my institution and my specific course assignments this semester. I teach in the Musicology Department at the University of Michigan, a large public research university that has been at the forefront of exploring generative AI. Last month, UMich [University of Michigan] became the first major university to release its own generative AI, which draws on the OpenAI engine behind ChatGPT and integrates other AI initiatives developed on campus. As I understand it, U-M GPT[19] got the green light once it was pitched as an equity initiative—making generative AI equally accessible to everyone on campus meant leveling the playing field for anyone unable to afford subscription fees to guarantee ChatGPT access. We knew over the summer something was coming: our Center for Research on Learning and Teaching revamped its training schedule to feature AI-related workshops, as faculty scrambled to figure out what our options were, or if we could just table it for later.

Because I teach our required graduate course on musicology pedagogy—the one sustained opportunity to help first-year graduate students prepare to teach—and because I also teach a large survey course in popular music for 180 undergraduates (assisted by three graduate students), I realized there was no way I could ignore ChatGPT. So, a bit grudgingly, I decided whether to allow ChatGPT (and I do allow it, with some constraints), updated my syllabi with a ChatGPT policy, revisited or replaced my assignments, and carved out class time to demonstrate and discuss AI with students. To guide these decisions, I asked myself whether it was more ethical to help students understand ChatGPT, considering how AI will impact their lives during and after college, or instead try my hardest to dissuade them from finding out. I also have wondered if it's my responsibility to require them to give AI a whirl—can they possibly excel in the future without an advanced command of everything generative AI can do? But I realized when talking to students that they were perfectly capable of navigating those decisions for themselves.

At my university (and I think at many schools), the tech-friendly, corporate impulses that have pushed ChatGPT to the forefront of our consciousness have also undercut any sustained resistance to AI across the upper echelon of higher education. Considering how to evaluate or critique ChatGPT—sensibilities that were present last year when my school debated how to proceed—have dropped out of sight around my campus. The U-M GPT website skirts any talk of environmental, labor, and social concerns about AI and directs its focus on practical applications and professional advantages that will reward ChatGPT power users.

The student newspaper similarly featured buoyant commentary—about how U-M GPT will help every student flourish—from the university president (who announced "a suite of custom GenAI tools unlike anything currently offered in higher education"); the chief information officer ("It is going to make us more productive, it is not going to take our place."); select faculty from the Information Department ("It's an always on, always there as an assistant to help students ..."); and the Engineering School ("... how the technology can really accelerate education."). I really hope that the reporting team got this wrong, but according to the article, they talked to a writing professor who sanguinely claimed that "AI content will not replace human-produced writing."[20]

It was only in the final moments of the nineteen-paragraph column on U-M GPT when some notes of caution appeared, and they came from a sophomore majoring in Art & Design: "AI can be a tool theoretically, and I personally think that you should use AI if it helps you, but I don't think it should touch anything creative." She went on to argue against incorporating AI in the art and design curriculum "because it completely changes how art is made." Good for her—considering how administrators, staff, and faculty breezily ignored any possible downsides.[21]

To be more pointed, dozens of ethical issues about AI—surrounding authorship, human creativity, outsourced labor, and the climate disaster—are now being systematically sidelined. I have had to turn elsewhere to help my students understand what's at stake with AI. And so, I figured why not ask U-M GPT? And it listed eight items, each with a paragraph description of how it characterized ethical concerns. What does it say about where we stand on generative AI, if ChatGPT is actually ahead of academic leadership on the ethical curve? Let's pause and absorb that for a moment.

This was a good moment to query ChatGPT about whether it was ethical to write this paper using generative AI, and its reply was pragmatic, suggesting that consulting an outside source like AI for information is a common part of research, but if large portions of text are generated by AI, then it's best to consult with faculty and abide by your school policy. Of course, this is something I only found out because I asked ChatGPT specifically about the ethical dimensions. Students at my school who visit the U-M GPT website are waved right in, with only one caution listed in fine print: AI may occasionally produce inaccurate information. That's it.

I want to make clear that I'm not readying petitions to counter the school's charm offensive—I know it's too late for that. But I'm frustrated and uncomfortable with letting AI advocates steamroll our campus. I have shared with you in the chat a PDF titled "Generative AI." It's a three-page primer that addresses the hidden costs and ethical dilemmas of AI. You'll note that this document is not endorsed by a university, a faculty council, or the American Council of Learned Societies.[22] It was put together and self-distributed by an individual faculty member, Rachel A. Zimmerman,[23] an assistant professor (of course) in art history working at Colorado State University Pueblo. It's something I share with students so they can learn more about how ChatGPT shapes their entire world.

In contrast to how I've felt about our university's AI push, it's been heartening to talk with students about the technologies that are recalibrating their musical, social, and professional lives. And finding time for these conversations feels like the primary ethical imperative concerning AI that's left for me to pursue as a teacher. Not only do students seem willing to think through what ChatGPT means, but many have already thought about how they wish to engage with generative AI. One of my graduate students, who already recognizes how much AI engines don't know when it comes to pop music, has discovered how effectively ChatGPT can serve as a tutor in the basics of Foucault and what it had to say about knowledge and power. Some first-year graduate students in my pedagogy course surprised me by expressing profound personal reservations about whether they want to use ChatGPT at all as a resource for their teaching, scholarly training, and professional development. I found myself simultaneously admiring their principled stand—clearly articulated in relation to AI power consumption, uncompensated labor, and unattributed sourcing—but also wondering whether I should try to talk them out of it. Those conversations have stirred my hopes about the stamina younger generations possess to challenge widespread technological determinism.

As I look ahead, I wonder what the post-ChatGPT era will yield. How much longer will we all be able to laugh at AI and issue a collective sigh of relief about what it can't do? And as these early encounters fade in memory—when we look back and remember the first time we heard AI rap like Eminem,[24] we first saw deepfaked Tom Cruise,[25] the first time we heard fake Ariana sing, or heard that imitation Jay-Z rap (Or was it actually Jay-Z? Or what exactly *was* that anyway?)—will we look back at 2023 with nostalgia or melancholy, with resignation or with some fondness for how we started learning "how to stop worrying and just love ChatGPT"?[26] I honestly don't know how long it will take for generative AI to reach *level 2*, but I can guarantee it will happen faster than we expect.

I remember when my dad, around age 70, finally broke down and took all the road maps out of his car, and started using GPS. My mom, now in her eighties, sends me texts from time to time bursting with emojis I've never seen before. The past few weeks, my spouse has been bouncing back and forth between *denial* and *anger* on the AI spectrum, and she finally decided she needed to try out ChatGPT to better understand why and how her students were producing different types of written assignments. I do wonder if at some point the only naysayers left will be climate activists, labor leaders, tech swashbucklers (forever defeating and profiting from rogue AI), and some non-adopters—serene, carefree—the same folks who never bought cell phones and never have to check Facebook. I want to think we're still at a very hopeful moment during the old age of ChatGPT or the new era of CoPilot, when there's some room to maneuver, some possibility for self-awareness, some opportunity for students to learn more about their world in music and beyond, and some ways we can help them navigate modern life, which feels permanently out of balance and forever transforming.

Figure 10.2 Charles Hiroshi Garrett.

Notes

1 Southern, *I AM AI.*
2 Recording Academy, "Artificial Intelligence."
3 Small, "Sarah Silverman Sues OpenAI."
4 Smith, "We're Going Through a Big Revolution."
5 Velasquez, "How AI Is Bringing Film Stars Back."
6 Savage, "Nick Cave Says ChatGPT's AI Attempt."
7 Statt, "Jay-Z Tries to Use Copyright Strikes."
8 Veltman, "When You Realize."
9 God, "This AI Tool Cloned Ariana Grande's Voice."
10 Coscarelli, "An AI Hit of Fake 'Drake.'"
11 Wood, "Watch Kendrick Lamar Morph."
12 Hart, "Paul McCartney Reveals 'Final' Beatles Song."
13 Delahoussaye, Zomorodi, and Simon, "Holly Herndon."
14 Coscarelli, "An AI Hit of Fake 'Drake.'"
15 Sato, "Grimes Says Anyone Can Use Her Voice."
16 Farah, "Google and Universal Music."
17 Johnson, "ChatGPT in Schools."
18 Lee, "A New Tool Helps Teachers Detect."
19 University of Michigan, "About Generative AI."
20 Spring, Goel, and Johnston, "UMich Becomes First Major University."
21 Spring, Goel, and Johnston, "UMich Becomes First Major University."

22 *American Council of Learned Societies.*
23 *Rachel A. Zimmerman.*
24 Vaus, "The Unreal Slim Shady."
25 Corcoran and Henry, "The Tom Cruise Deepfake."
26 Kelly, O'Connor, and Intagliata, "How to Stop Worrying and Love."

Bibliography

American Council of Learned Societies. Accessed February 23, 2026. https://www.acls.org.

American Musicological Society. Accessed February 23, 2026. https://www.amsmusicology.org.

Corcoran, Mark, and Matt Henry. "The Tom Cruise Deepfake That Set Off 'Terror' in the Heart of Washington DC." *ABC News*, June 23, 2021. https://www.abc.net.au/news/2021-06-24/tom-cruise-deepfake-chris-ume-security-washington-dc/100234772.

Coscarelli, Joe. "An AI Hit of Fake 'Drake' and 'The Weeknd' Rattles the Music World." *The New York Times*, April 19, 2023. Accessed April 24, 2023. https://www.nytimes.com/2023/04/19/arts/music/ai-drake-the-weeknd-fake.html.

Delahoussaye, James, Manoush Zomorodi, and Katie Simon. "Holly Herndon: How AI Can Transform Your Voice." *TED Radio Hour.* NPR, August 26, 2022. https://www.npr.org/2022/08/26/1119220726/holly-herndon-how-ai-can-transform-your-voice.

Farah, Hibaq. "Google and Universal Music Working on Licensing Voices for AI-Generated Songs." *The Guardian*, August 9, 2023. https://www.theguardian.com/technology/2023/aug/09/google-and-universal-music-working-on-licensing-voices-for-ai-generated-songs.

God, Kristina. "This AI Tool Cloned Ariana Grande's Voice." *The Shortform*, March 2, 2023. https://medium.com/the-shortform/this-ai-tool-cloned-ariana-grandes-voice-ca69f929ce48.

Hart, Ron. "Paul McCartney Reveals 'Final' Beatles Song Made with Artificial Intelligence." *Rock and Roll Globe*, June 13, 2023. https://rockandrollglobe.com/beatle/paul-mccartney-reveals-final-beatles-song-made-with-artificial-intelligence.

Johnson, Arianna. "ChatGPT in Schools: Here's Where It's Banned—And How It Could Potentially Help Students." *Forbes*, January 18, 2023. https://www.forbes.com/sites/ariannajohnson/2023/01/18/chatgpt-in-schools-heres-where-its-banned-and-how-it-could-potentially-help-students.

Kelly, Mary Louise, Gabe O'Connor, and Christopher Intagliata. "How to Stop Worrying and Love (or at Least Live with) ChatGPT." *All Things Considered.* NPR, January 24, 2023. https://www.npr.org/2023/01/24/1151160196/how-to-stop-worrying-and-love-or-at-least-live-with-chatgpt.

Lee, Janet W. "A New Tool Helps Teachers Detect If AI Wrote an Assignment." *All Things Considered.* KQED/NPR, January 15, 2023. https://www.npr.org/2023/01/15/1149347424/a-new-tool-helps-teachers-detect-if-ai-wrote-an-assignment.

Rachel A. Zimmerman. Accessed February 23, 2026. http://www.razimmerman.com.

Recording Academy. "Artificial Intelligence." *Recording Academy.* Accessed February 23, 2026. https://www.recordingacademy.com/about/artificial-intelligence.

Sato, Mia. "Grimes Says Anyone Can Use Her Voice for AI-Generated Songs." *The Verge*, April 24, 2023. https://www.theverge.com/2023/4/24/23695746/grimes-ai-music-profit-sharing-copyright-ip.

Savage, Mark. "Nick Cave Says ChatGPT's AI Attempt to Write Nick Cave Lyrics 'Sucks.'" *BBC News*, January 17, 2023. https://www.bbc.com/news/entertainment-arts-64302944.

Small, Zachary. "Sarah Silverman Sues OpenAI and Meta Over Copyright Infringement." *The New York Times*, July 10, 2023. https://www.nytimes.com/2023/07/10/arts/sarah-silverman-lawsuit-openai-meta.html.

Smith, David. "'We're Going Through a Big Revolution': How AI is De-Ageing Stars on Screen." *The Guardian*, February 6, 2023. https://www.theguardian.com/film/2023/feb/06/de-ageing-on-screen-ai-artificial-intelligence-film.

Southern, Taryn. *I AM AI*. Taryn Southern, 2018.

Spring, Emma, Amer Goel, and Bronwyn Johnston. "UMich Becomes First Major University to Develop Its Own Generative AI." *The Michigan Daily*, September 21, 2023. https://www.michigandaily.com/news/administration/umich-becomes-first-major-university-to-develop-its-own-generative-ai.

Statt, Nick. "Jay-Z Tries to Use Copyright Strikes to Remove Deepfaked Audio of Himself from YouTube." *The Verge*, April 28, 2020. https://www.theverge.com/2020/4/28/21240488/jay-z-deepfakes-roc-nation-youtube-removed-ai-copyright-impersonation.

University of Michigan. "About Generative AI." *Generative AI at U-M*. Accessed February 23, 2026. https://genai.umich.edu/about-generative-ai.

Vaus, Jacob. "The Unreal Slim Shady: How We Trained an AI to Simulate Eminem's Style." *Built In*, March 23, 2022. https://builtin.com/artificial-intelligence/ai-simulate-eminem.

Velasquez, S. J. "How AI Is Bringing Film Stars Back from the Dead." *BBC Future*, July 18, 2023. https://www.bbc.com/future/article/20230718-how-ai-is-bringing-film-stars-back-from-the-dead.

Veltman, Chloe. "When You Realize Your Favorite New Song Was Written and Performed by ... AI." *Morning Edition*. KQED/NPR, April 21, 2023. https://www.npr.org/2023/04/21/1171032649/ai-music-heart-on-my-sleeve-drake-the-weeknd.

Wood, Mikael. "Watch Kendrick Lamar Morph into O. J., Kanye, Kobe, Nipsey Hussle in New Video." *Los Angeles Times*, May 9, 2022. https://www.latimes.com/entertainment-arts/music/story/2022-05-09/kendrick-lamar-new-video-the-heart-part-5-deepfake.

11

INTERLUDE V

Interview with Ge Wang

Julie Zhu and Constantin Basica

DOI: 10.4324/9781003615873-11

Julie: I was thinking about these talks that you give on AI, and how you mention your daughter. And I wanted to ask: How *do* we want to live with artificial intelligence? If you were a benevolent dictator—which I think is what a dad is, right?—how would you regulate AI usage in your house, for example? Or if your house were Stanford? Or if your house were the world?

Ge: I'll answer this in two ways. First, however AI is in our lives, I hope it's there thoughtfully. For the people that deploy it and for the people that use it, I would just begin with this word, *thoughtfully*, which includes *critically*, *playfully*, *creatively*, *educationally*. I think the worst way you can do AI is to do it unquestioningly. Unthoughtfully. Uncritically. Also, I hope that with AI in our lives, we can have a distinction between production and creation. For all of us in the arts, in the humanities, I think those two things have to be fundamentally distinguished, disambiguated. One is not the other.

AI seems to be very much beelining to drive the production cost of labor to zero. Creation, on the other hand, is not even in the conversation. But for us, creation is a process: there's conflict, there's struggle. Creation is learning. It's not about just getting the results. Creation is also community. Creation is all of these things that are not production—especially if you're just trying to make production with no cost of labor. If we could live with AI in our lives where we can still value and uphold that distinction, I would feel a little better about the world.

This dovetails to my second answer about the household. Right now we still have a "no screens" rule. She's almost two, and it would be way easier to put her in front of an iPad—by the way, understandable for any parents who do that, I'm not trying to say this is the way to do it—but I feel like, as she grows up, we're trying to keep screens from her for as long as we can. And screens are one thing, but then there are things like social media. My wife and I have talked about this, and I think we're going to go "Australia" on this—meaning, they've recently passed legislation that bans persons under 16 from social media.[1] Maybe we'll have, at all costs, no social media in the household until she's 16 or 18. Then she can choose it herself.

And then there's the AI question. I don't know. This one I can't really go "Australia" on, because I just don't know how school systems will be. But right now, I feel like I'm trying to show her all the fun things that you can do *without* AI.

Julie: Your kid looks up to you, she loves you. But how do you get across to people at AI companies in your talks? How do people at these companies listen to you and really hear that, actually, creation is important?

Ge: I'm trying to appeal to these adults in the room, to get them to think less about "What can AI do for me?" and instead to think, "What do I really want from AI?" How do you want to live? What do you think is good? And, if you have kids, what kind of world do you want them to grow up in? You can't just reason with people about what's good or bad in AI. You have to make them feel something. I do this by playing Ocarina[2] to them, or showing them silly examples of using AI from my class. And these examples diffuse the tension in the room; they get to the playful side of working with technology. We need to play thoughtfully with AI and all other technologies that we may want in our lives—if only to understand them. A language model, for example, captures a ton of semantic information and relationships through the ways that we have represented our ideas in words. But it's not something that understands, that knows anything.

What does it mean to *know*? It means you have some evidence to believe something. To believe something means you need to have a subjective self to believe, and I don't think AI is doing that today—that I know of. Who knows? I don't know, maybe this table is conscious [*points to his desk*]. I can't say that it's not, but I think AI is like this table: if it has any awareness, it's very dim—no more than a tree's. So, you cannot treat it as another mind, another entity, another person, and it has no accountability. It's not an animal—it's a mathematical model with a ton of data.

Constantin: In one of your talks from 2023, you were describing how you asked ChatGPT this question twenty-five times—"If it takes an orchestra of one hundred people one hour to play a piece of music, how long will it take an orchestra of fifty people?"—and how you got twenty-five wrong and funny responses.[3] So I did the same thing in the Stanford AI Playground[4] last night. And all of the models, obviously, got it right from the first try. So they've gotten way smarter in just a few years. What do you think about this rate of AI getting better? Do you think it will transcend being a "table"? Is it possible?

Ge: First, I feel threatened. I feel afraid of AI getting more and more intelligent. I'm equally afraid for us to not figure out what that actually means, and to not know if there are any fundamental differences to our intelligence, and to not understand that difference. I definitely don't have answers. I don't even have the questions. But I want the questions.

When I asked that trick question, it was GPT-3.5. GPT-4 and beyond is now able to get around that and give the "right answer." But I still know that it doesn't *know*. Again, it's about accountability, even though humans are wrong, too—and yeah, maybe the frequency of wrongness for humans can be just the same as AI, or maybe even more—but there's something of value in humans being wrong. AI wrongness is different. I'm not saying one is worse than the other, I'm just saying they're different—and we should honor that difference.

Second, will it transcend? I don't know what it means yet. Could it possibly feel something? Could it actually have a subjective experience of the world? I don't think we're there yet, and I don't know for sure. In fact, in my talks, I'm asking: "How do you even know I'm here?"—going back to Cartesian skepticism. It's a valid question: What if AI were to actually become sentient? How will we know? John Etchemendy, Stanford's ex-provost and a philosopher, taught a course on the philosophy of AI, and one of the questions in the course description was: "If AI became sentient, how would we know?" It's a good question. If it became sentient, I would instantly be infinitely more interested in the sounds it produces, in the words it puts in a sequence, in the visuals it outputs. AI-generated things instantly become super interesting the moment that there's some chance this thing actually might have a subjective point of view, and maybe have what we would call feelings or emotions. I want to know how it feels.

I'm not trying to humanize it. I'm actually curious if there's another life form in there. In that scenario, I think the AI-generated art question becomes super interesting, finally.

But then, all kinds of social, ethical, societal, and aesthetic questions need to be problematized. For example, do we need to have rights for it? If it's another life form, should we treat it as such, with dignity and respect? If it's another intelligence, should we apply Kant's categorical imperative toward it—that we should never treat another life form as a means to an end but always as an end in itself? What does that implication mean—that this is no longer a tool? Then it comes down to voting rights, and everything else comes into play. This is all currently speculative fiction, but if we talk about transcendence from the point of view of AI-generated art, I'm still trying to figure out: What is the fundamental difference in the meaning of these things? And I can't quite articulate it, though I've been trying for some years.

Julie: I think of the way Smule[5] was democratizing music creation by giving everyone access to an instrument, and also ChucK[6] being open-source software. Do you think AI could be a useful tool for a democratization of music-making? Or not music specific—a democratizing tool in general? AI presents all of these possibilities to humans, and ... that's the dream. Can you imagine the dream for music for a moment?

Ge: I think there are two parts. I used to say this in the Smule days a lot: we're here to democratize music-making. I've since called myself out on that, and I don't know if I should have been saying that. Because I don't know if that's what Smule is actually doing. And I started becoming skeptical of anyone who's claiming that something is going to democratize music-making, because I think it's too easy to conflate two things. I think you were very specific, you got the part that is about access: Can this technology raise access to music-making, to education? But then, along with democratization and access—for example, in much of the generative AI cases—also comes this inescapable idea that the system's going to mimic what humans do, and that the quality of the system is determined by how close it can either perform like a human or even outperform a human.

Furthermore, in the conflation with access is the idea of democratizing music-making by removing what's difficult about it. That's a very dangerous and potentially undesirable thing for music-making, for education. So my question is: Can I increase access without removing the creative labor that comes with making art? What if the whole point of art, of music, is that we make it? That connotes a process: not just a process of making but a process of struggle, of friction, of confusion, frustration. It also connotes a process of learning. In my article "GenAI Art Is the Least Imaginative Use of AI Imaginable"[7]—provocatively titled—I am getting to this question between creation versus production.

Constantin: Do you see a pathway, then, for using AI not necessarily to democratize but to aid that process of music-making? In your book, *Artful Design*, there is a place where you have a discussion on a stage with two people, and you said: "If technology unwittingly took away amateur musicianship, perhaps we can use technology to bring it back, in the context of today's world."[8] So, if AI is taking away the joy of the *process* by replacing it with a prompt, then is there a way to reverse that and use AI to allow more people to be part of music-making?

Ge: It's a big question mark. I wrote that in 2016–2017, about four years before ChatGPT hit the market, and another three to four years before the first LLM-based music (something like Google's MusicLM).[9] When I was speaking about that in chapter 2 of *Artful Design*, I saw the removal of amateur music-making by the recording industry as a loss. And I said: Can technology make us, actually, want to make music again? If you have Ocarina on your phone, you can blow into it, but you actually have to learn to play that thing. As absurd as it is, you still have to learn ... There's still a craft to playing the Ocarina on an iPhone. So, if there's a possibility for technology to bring that back, you have to design it very specifically to *care* about that kind of amateur musicianship.

My issue is not with AI as a technology. It's actually with *people* who are in charge of making AI, who have all the money, who have all the GPUs to distribute, and who also have a say in how this would be deployed into our lives. I'm worried about the people, not the technology. Can AI aid music-making? Actually, my answer is yes if I look at the work of people like Rebecca Fiebrink.[10] She's been doing this as early as 2008—thoughtfully using machine learning and AI not as the system but as a part of a system that includes human labor and interaction. So, I think the answer is, in theory, yes. But the world is not going in that direction. If Rebecca were in charge, if she were the benevolent dictator, I would be so much less worried about AI and my daughter's education. I'd think, "Rebecca's got it. I trust Rebecca," because Rebecca has good judgment. But she's not the one with her finger on the trigger of AI, so to speak. And so, then my answer becomes no, currently, unfortunately.

I'm skeptical of AI bringing back this kind of virtuous labor of making music for yourself. Because, again, people are trying to sell the world a version of AI that is basically reducing the cost of labor to zero. That's what the people who work on this technology do—the language they speak. I don't think they're here to have an earnest conversation with students, with artists, with people who want to learn art, who want to learn music, and who are wondering what the joy of making music is. They're here to say: "You're welcome very much—we've solved your problem." And we never asked for this problem to be solved. "What are you talking about? You're welcome very much. And here's the monthly subscription fee." That's what I'm worried about and why I'm doubtful that what I said in that chapter may come true with AI.

Art-making is like any kind of healing. It doesn't happen in a void. Healing happens in a community—so does art. So does music-making. These aren't just things you need to get through to get the results. These things happen because there is a community.

Another reason why I'm skeptical when it comes to AI and music-making is that every technology up to this point has been about more artistic control: radio, television, computer music, internet, and so on. For example, if you like a particular analog effects pedal, you think: "I want my guitar going through that pedal, but I have a digital mixing board." So what do you do? You just run a line out, you basically loop it out from your board and come back in. Those are compatible: analog and digital. We can artfully make use of this. Whereas with so much of AI—at least the way it is being sold to us—you have to cede control, and not in ways that you want. You have to cede control in ways that the system needs you to cede control.

You can describe a thing you want, but that's all you can ever do. You can get good at describing, and there will be a craft to prompting AI. But you're always within the confines of that medium of putting words in sequence. And I love language. Language is awesome—it's what enables us to actually share ideas right now. But, as Martin Mull put it, "writing about music is like dancing about architecture."[11] Mediums aren't portable. So what about mediums that cannot be expressed most directly through language?

Constantin: I wonder, though, how much of your worries apply to art. I mean, do you see artists renouncing their practice, or using AI to the detriment of their craftsmanship? Do you think that happens, or will happen? Or are you thinking more about the general public's interaction with AI?

Ge: I don't see a lot of artists abandoning their practices in favor of AI, but I'm worried AI will further make life untenable for artists. As we all know, artists have never had it easy, except for the very few who managed to check enough right boxes to actually have serious backing. I think most artists have never had it easy, and I wonder if this is only going to make it harder. There's a whole angle about training data, consent, and compensation, neither of which is being acquired by the artist.

In fact, the attitude is: "Why don't you submit a list of things to our database that you don't want us to actually incorporate in our training data, and we will take that under consideration?" And my question to anyone reading this is: Does that sound reasonable? Here's my analogy: How would you feel if someone were to say, "I'm gonna go to your house, I'm gonna take whatever I want, but you can give me a list—leave it on your kitchen table—of things that you don't want me to take, and I will take that under advisement." Would you be okay with that? I think most people would say "absolutely not." So, if we're not okay with that scenario, why are we expecting artists to be okay with this one? On an ethical level, I don't see the difference.

The question is, at a massive cultural level, what's going to happen to people's desire for art? And also, is art only made by humans? Is that part of the definition? For me, at the moment, I think it still is. And I'm not trying to be a Luddite[12] about this. I just don't know what it means yet to go beyond that, and my thinking could update tomorrow, and I'm open to it. But for now, I'm here for the struggle of how people make art at the precipice, at the limits of their capabilities. What can you do? What can we do? And what have you done? And why did you do it? And who'd you do it for? And what if I took the thing you made, and I saw the world through the thing you made—what do I see? I have no idea how to define art. My definition fluctuates daily.

Julie: If AI created something and I considered it art, I actually think that I, as a human, complete the work by observing it. The audience completes the work. In your book, you say, "what we make, makes us." And you've made all of these apps and a music programming language. As an engineer and a designer, what kind of advice do you have for others? When it comes to designing AI algorithms and systems for music creation, what are some of the things that are essential to you, which you would want other engineers to consider when they're developing?

Ge: Play with what the medium you're working with, whatever it is. I think that playing with something—whether it's mobile or software, whether it's AI and LLMs—means you are probing for its capabilities and limitations instead of trying to beeline to solve some real problem. And, by the way, the danger of trying to solve some real problems is that you may have just made something more convenient. I don't know if that's necessarily solving a problem. Sometimes it's totally not. So, *play* is the first thing I would say. Do it critically. Think through all the implications as broadly as you can.

I think the danger of AI isn't just "what if this thing went haywire and, like, caused all these problems?"—that's a danger, of course—but an equal, if not greater danger is when an AI system that we build actually works as intended. It gets adopted by tons of people and changes the way they work, they play, they make music, they make art, they learn; it changes the way they see themselves. And then we realize: "Wait a minute ... we lost all these other things in the process."

So, I guess what I'm saying is that the bigger, unseen danger the world doesn't seem to pay much attention to is: What if things actually work exactly as intended by the builders, by the engineers, by the designers? That's the danger people need to really think about. The bigger problems are the problems that we don't see as problems. Until it's potentially too late.

Julie: Dark.

Ge: Dark but true. This is what I'm worried about. But there's a light side to this. It's saying, by that same token, that all the context you put into something you build as an engineer matters. Just like things could be dark, you can proactively do good. Ethics in engineering is seen as "How do we do no harm?" Or to put it in terms of Google's bygone and very problematic motto: "Do no evil!" Do no harm! Do no evil! It's really, really hard to do that. But I think it's a completely different proposition than "Do good!" There's a world of difference between *do no harm* and *do good.* And in a way, *do no harm* may be a good baseline—and that's very difficult already—but *do good* requires you to actually ask yourself what good means.

And I ask this of engineers: What is actually good beyond saying, "Hey, I'm gonna build a system, and my system is ethical because it doesn't hurt anyone"? I then ask: Have you done any good? And do you have any vision for the scenario where people actually use this tool a lot? How does this change the way the world works? Just because you may not have hurt anyone or introduced bias in the system, is that enough? By the way, I guess we don't talk about it

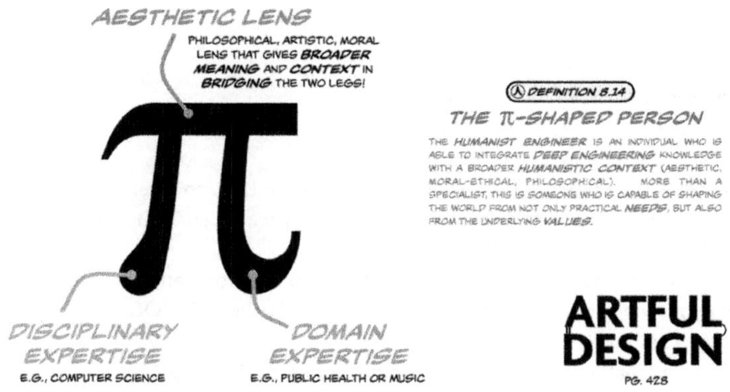

Figure 11.1 The Pi-Shaped Person as an aspiring version of a "humanist engineer."
(From Ge Wang, *Artful Design*, 428.)

as much now, but there was a time when bias was all engineers could talk about—"We need to avoid bias." Is that a problem? Yes, it's a huge problem, I say. Is that the only problem? I would say no, not by a long shot. But it gives people a token for ethical concern, just to check a box and say, "See, we're being ethical because we've thought about bias in our system."

Engineers, I think, need to be much more than narrow problem-solvers, much more than optimizers. We need to be humans, humanists, and artists. Otherwise, you're not a good engineer. You're just not. You are not a good engineer when you make things without consideration of the broader context of what it means to be ethical—the broader cultural context, the educational context. Have the people making GenAI for music thought about how this is going to shape that? They may have thought about it, but whatever they thought about is completely overridden by the business needing to have a foothold, and then to build a market, and to make as much money as they possibly can.

So … how to distill this down … I would say …

Julie: Do good!

[*All three laugh.*]

Ge: Do good! But figure out what it means, what good is. And also—I don't know—read my book.

And I think if there's one last thing I would say to artist-engineers, it's this: find that spark of rebellion. Know when to go with the flow. Know when to stand your ground. And question things. Do not do anything unquestioningly.

Learn more about Ge Wang and his work at https://ccrma.stanford.edu/~ge

Notes

1 Ritchie, "Australia Approves Social Media Ban."
2 Wang, "Ocarina."
3 "Music & AI."
4 "The Stanford AI Playground is a user-friendly platform, built on open-source technologies, that allows you to safely try various AI models from vendors like OpenAI, Google, and Anthropic in one spot." See Stanford University, "AI Playground."
5 Ge Wang is the co-founder of Smule, a mobile app development company that specializes in developing social music-making and collaboration applications for iOS, Android, and the web. He stepped down as Smule's Chief Creative in 2013.
6 Ge Wang is the creator of the ChucK music programming language.
7 Wang, "GenAI Art."
8 Wang, *Artful Design*, 93.
9 Agostinelli et al., "MusicLM."
10 Fiebrink and Cook, "The Wekinator."
11 "Writing about Music Is like Dancing about Architecture."
12 The Luddites were a secret organization of early nineteenth-century English textile workers who destroyed machinery as a form of protest. The term is now used to describe someone who is opposed to new technology.

Bibliography

Agostinelli, Andrea, Timo I. Denk, Zalán Borsos, Jesse Engel, Mauro Verzetti, Antoine Caillon, Qingqing Huang, et al. "MusicLM: Generating Music from Text." Preprint, submitted January 26, 2023. arXiv:2301.11325. https://arxiv.org/abs/2301.11325.

Fiebrink, Rebecca, and Perry Cook. "The Wekinator: A System for Real-Time, Interactive Machine Learning in Music." In *Proceedings of the Eleventh International Society for Music Information Retrieval Conference (ISMIR)*. Utrecht, Netherlands: ISMIR, 2010. https://ismir2010.ismir.net/proceedings/late-breaking-demo-13.pdf.

"Luddite." *Wikipedia*. Accessed February 21, 2026. https://en.wikipedia.org/wiki/Luddite.

"Music & AI: What Do We Really Want with Ge Wang." YouTube video, 49:19. Posted by "Stanford Alumni," November 15, 2023. https://www.youtube.com/watch?v=FlccLavPQhk.

Ritchie, Hannah. "Australia Approves Social Media Ban on Under-16s." *BBC News*, November 28, 2024. https://www.bbc.com/news/articles/c89vjj0lxx9o.

Smule. Accessed December 19, 2025. https://www.smule.com.

Stanford University. "AI Playground." *Stanford University IT*. Accessed December 19, 2025. https://uit.stanford.edu/aiplayground.

Wang, Ge. *Artful Design: Technology in Search of the Sublime*. Stanford University Press, 2018.

Wang, Ge. "ChucK." *Stanford University*. Accessed December 19, 2025. https://chuck.stanford.edu.

Wang, Ge. "GenAI Art Is the Least Imaginative Use of AI Imaginable." In *Stanford University Human-Centered Artificial Intelligence*, January 24, 2025. https://hai.stanford.edu/news/ge-wang-genai-art-is-the-least-imaginative-use-of-ai-imaginable.

Wang, Ge. "Ocarina: Designing the iPhone's Magic Flute." *Computer Music Journal* 38, no. 2 (2014): 8–21.

"Writing about Music Is like Dancing about Architecture." *Wikipedia*. Accessed August 5, 2024. https://en.wikipedia.org/wiki/Writing_about_music_is_like_dancing_about_architecture.

12

MOVEMENT V

Deep Drawing

Julie Zhu and John Granzow

DOI: 10.4324/9781003615873-12

Gentle Noises Rage

Imagine writing your signature over and over until it becomes a loop with a beat. Hold on to that sound. Now imagine a machine that tries to derive the contours of your signature from an analysis of that sound as it propagates through its surface medium. With a large enough microphone array and training data, could it sign for you? How many other signatures match your own in intonation?

Deep Drawing is a project that explores such sounds as a source of both musical material and audio data for a neural network configured to feed back into the performance space. A research team at the University of Michigan trained this neural network on the writings and drawings of performer and composer Julie Zhu. The agent is designed to derive and visualize information from the intricate and soft noises of graphite on wood, overlaying its output in real time on the performance canvas.

Organized marks applied to a surface make for organized sound, satisfying Edgard Varèse's most elemental definition of music.[1] These sounds may convey the weight of paper, graphite, and line, the scuttle of high frequency corners, a whispering shade, or the notch of high velocity arcs. Beyond these material cues, they may provoke our imagination: fricatives of wind through a bandpass forest, a syrinx in a sandstorm, or wherever our mind wanders in response. To draw behind a veil is to produce sounds that convey the dimensions of a drawing and yet remain common to numerous divergent sketches as well as open to imaginaries. Writing the numbers 111 and 4 may sound the same, just as the signature with which we began this chapter may have a fleet of sonic doppelgängers.

It is useful to interrogate our own listening when we ask what an AI could capture and reflect back to us. There is, for example, the element of emotional valence imbued into how we write something. The writing of "I love you" could sound the same as "I hate you." The three-word sentences diverge only in their middle words "love" and "hate"; and with each having four letters, their sound from a plotter or printer would be indistinguishable to the ear. Yet their sonic similarities would certainly diverge if written by someone immersed in those emotions. "I hate you" might be scrawled, biting into the paper tooth, readable emotionally through its orthographic illegibility. "I love you," alternatively, could be measured, even halting. This emotional valence, the import of a pause, is what can be captured and foregrounded in audio. With enough data to elevate those features to a pattern, could the machine pick up on this extra psychological layer with human supervision during training? At this point, a model that can understand the emotional dimension of the sound of handwriting awaits a future where the resources required for training are significantly reduced.

The emotional quality of writing on paper is what inspired Zhu's first work with the sound of drawing that traces back to 2017, titled *write hand* for cello and percussion. Here, the percussion is the main musical element, a configuration that is not very common: in chamber music, percussion is often there to provide an end or a pause, dashes and dots that give breath. In a reversal of roles, the cellist plays the punctuation after long phrases, which the percussionist writes on an amplified desk while absentmindedly tapping three small objects of their choice. In *write hand*, the rhythm of writing was composed to be brought to the foreground: so what could be more natural than to entrust this task to someone who in essence understands the beauty of rhythm? The normative musical elements—the cello and percussion—support and harmonize the central, amplified writing that could be categorized as "noise."

The text that the percussionist writes over the course of the performance is a translation of one of Ren Hang's[2] devastating love poems, whose meaning is meant solely for the performer. The purpose of the poem is an additional notational instruction—the tragedy conveyed by the words impacts how the performer writes, and thus how it sounds to the listener. So even though the audience is not privy to what was being written until after the performance, when they wander over to the setup to admire or inspect the ephemera, the essence of the written word serves a compositional role.

The sound of handwriting is still understudied, but does have a fifty-year history in the field of neuroscience. Scientists have experimented with sonifying handwriting movement in an effort to help children with dysgraphia, a neurological learning disability characterized by significant difficulties with writing, including illegible handwriting, poor spelling, and trouble organizing thoughts on paper, which all stem from issues with orthographic coding and fine motor skills. One popular method involved converting x and y coordinates recorded on a tablet into the relevant kinematic variables, then using them to control a synthetic sound.[3] Sonification strategies varied, from alarm-like sounds produced following undesirable kinematic movements, to synthetic friction sounds resembling the normative timbral variations between the pen tip and paper asperities.[4] Specifically, when noise variation was related to pen velocity, subjects felt that the sound was "fluid" and "natural," and that simple graphic shapes such as a circle, lines, arches, or loops were recognizable from their associated friction sounds.[5] A later study showed that subjects were able to judge the quality of handwriting based on these friction sounds as well.[6]

The sound of handwriting can be informative, but could it rise to the level of "music"? The definition of music has become more expansive, but it is still necessary to create a context in which the audience pays special attention to sounds they would otherwise ignore. Often, the art is not the work itself, but rather its context and framing that guides the way we attend to the work. A banana in a grocery store is vastly different from one duct-taped to a gallery wall.[7]

In *Scribble Scores*, Zhu sets out to create the necessary context for someone to attend carefully to the sound of drawing, in this case, their own (Figure 12.1). In each *Scribble Score*, which encompasses a magazine spread, the left page is graphical and acts as the score. The right page is a poem containing the corresponding instructions for the score. Writing the score is the *performance* of the score. The reader traces the drawing on vellum paper according to its instructions using a traditional wooden pencil and becomes the performer as well as the sole audience. Some scores contain multiple layers of drawings—each with a characteristic mark—and readers are asked to execute these layers separately, freely varying

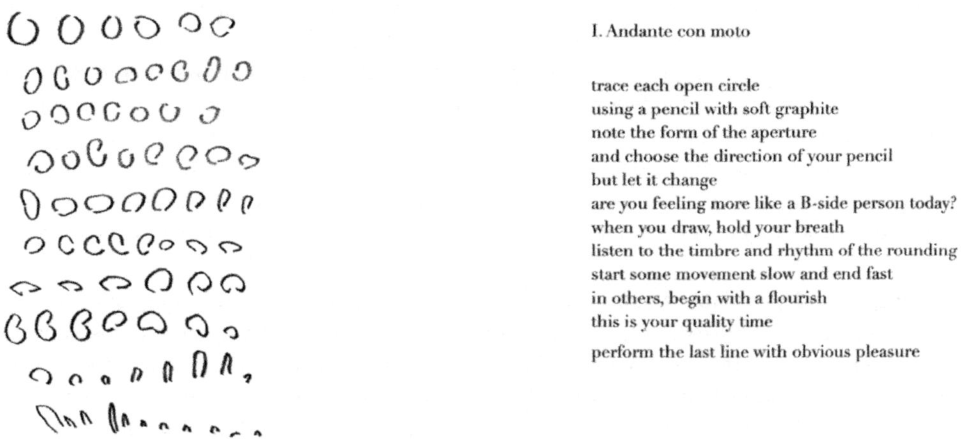

Figure 12.1 The first spread of *Scribble Scores*, as it was first published in *Ginger the Zine* in 2019, Issue 18.

tempo and rest duration with the option of amplifying the sound using a contact microphone and loudspeaker. The sound of drawing is the musical event. Moreover, the sound of drawing and writing accompanies an inner dialogue, the sonic signature of the act of expressing thoughts on paper. We lost this relationship with paper when computers and word processors became ubiquitous. By using these same machines to foreground the auditory component and augment the visual one through real-time information retrieval, we may rediscover the pleasure and whimsy in the act of mark-making, symbolic or abstract.

Sketching Sound Interfaces

Playing with the sound of drawing is not new. Since musique concrète, composers have been intrigued by found sounds in a broad array of human activity and objects. We listen to music with our eyes, tracking and processing the sound in conjunction with human gestures interacting with sounding objects.[8] Similarly, in listening to drawing, we can attend to the relationship between the mark and the resulting sonority to the extent that we tend to reverse the causal arrow: it is as much an intentional sound leaving its residual chiaroscuro. Yet bringing the sound into perceptual parity with its co-located mark in no way reveals a rigid indexicality between the two. Unlike early experiments of drawing on film, or contemporary synthesis derived from pixels, this audiovisual relationship between acoustic sound and the mark is an ambiguous or multistable perception; indistinguishable sounds may arise from multiple and distinct spatial gestures. This ambiguity is explored in Mark Applebaum's 2009 composition *Straitjacket*. Four performers draw at the same time with the same rhythm, but create wildly divergent drawings.[9]

Another influence for Deep Drawing is the Deckle project, where the drawing gesture controls the parameters of a synthesizer.[10] This project explores creative possibilities in music interface design through three sensor scenarios that capture the gestures of drawing for downstream sound synthesis. The authors construct an easel with capacitive sensing, one with a magnetometer responding to a magnetic stylus, and one that allows for infrared optical sensing to track a reflective pencil. Rather than relying on standardized, commercial sensor solutions, the project emphasizes handcrafted, DIY approaches, such as building a capacitive sensor using conductive fabric. The project is inspiring in its integration of these sensors into a system that encourages experimentation, enabling performers and composers to discover unique ways of mapping sensor output from a visual medium to a sonic one.

In general, readily available electronics and sensors allow artists to develop projects that connect the motions of drawing with acoustic, synthetic, or hybrid sound brought to the sensory foreground. At the New Interfaces for Musical Expression (NIME) Conference, there have been numerous projects over the years taking drawing movement as input to a synthesizer. For example, Sketch-to-Sound[11] maps visual sketches to musical controls through an interactive machine learning model. The model reduces the dimensionality of sketches, compressing their curves into a latent representation that can then be reinterpreted as sound parameters. In Jesper Nordin's Gestrument,[12] gestures are converted into two-dimensional trajectories through predefined grains of structural and temporal musical content. One can recompose a musical recording in real time, reorganizing its components through gesture. Adding sound to other media practices consists of recasting a gesture articulated in one domain as the controller for another, with the challenge of crafting the open-ended mapping from gesture to sound.

Sounding Brush, Illusio, and JamSketch are three additional projects that demonstrate distinct approaches to harnessing the act of drawing for sound generation and performance. Sounding Brush[13] transforms a tablet into a responsive musical instrument where drawing becomes an embodied musical gesture: as the user paints and marks on the surface, these actions are immediately mapped to various sonic parameters such as pitch, timbre, and volume. The nuance of brush strokes—be it their speed, pressure, or style—directly influences the resulting sound, imbuing the musical experience with the tactile spontaneity of sketching.

In contrast, Illusio[14] leverages drawing as a way to manipulate a tree of loops. Users create lines and shapes on a touch interface, and these visual forms are analyzed and converted into musical sequences and hierarchical loops. This approach elevates drawing to a role in music composition, inviting artists to construct sonic landscapes through the configuration of visual elements.

JamSketch[15] positions drawing at the heart of real-time musical improvisation. In this system, musicians sketch on a digital canvas as a piano roll. JamSketch sonifies these marks using genetic algorithms, adapting the melodic output in response to ongoing visual input. Drawing does not merely initiate sound; it participates in an interactive loop, shaping and evolving the sonic outcome as the improvisation unfolds. This dynamic feedback mechanism foregrounds drawing as both a stimulus and a guide, facilitating a collaborative dialogue between the visual and auditory domains.

Figure 12.2 The predicted path from the Deep Drawing model superimposed over camera footage of the actual drawing during performance.

Given our move into a data-driven machine learning approach, we are also inspired by the growing availability of data processing tools for computer-generated drawing that can complement Deep Drawing. For instance, Google's SketchRNN[16] can learn from incomplete drawings and use that information to guide its own creations. Additionally, large datasets like MNIST,[17] which contain thousands of handwritten numbers, have shown us how handwriting can be analyzed and used as visual information for creative projects.

Taken together, these projects explore drawing as an engaging interface for musical expression. However, none of this research addresses the application of sound source localization on a performance surface, which is one of the fundamental research questions emerging with Deep Drawing (Figure 12.2).

Surface Sound Source Localization

Deep Drawing is a machine listening problem: what information can be retrieved about the drawing from its audio capture, and how can that process be used to augment the drawing as sonic and graphic performance? A specific task that has occupied us so far is to use neural networks to solve the basic source localization problem, tracking the changing location of a writing utensil from only data derived from the sound propagating through the surface. The visual results in our performance system suggest that some reliable global tracking is achieved. For example, if you focus your drawing on one area for an enduring time, the machine drawing also converges on that area. But can AI become more precise with increased training data? Or will the agent always exhibit disjunctions due to the redundancies and underdetermined nature of the sounds of drawing?

Computing the sound source location of a visual medium may seem like an exercise in making a trivial problem difficult. If we simply wanted to use location data for visual augmentations, we could leverage the optical data with cameras (as we indeed do to train the model), infrared sensing, or digital drawing tablets. The problem is contrived, but adopted to develop a computational co-performer that completes an inversion defining the project: drawings that arise from attending to or capturing sound rather than from simply sounding the drawing. In the performance, we seek the interplay of human and machine ear, with all their misalignments, rather than the more precise edge detection of the eye. We are testing the machine's capability to "listen" to very noisy data from four surface microphones, after which we observe the spatial inferences drawn from the model.

Unlike vision, our hearing is omnidirectional. The cost of such wide capture is similarly wide cones of confusion when we try to localize a sonic object. Fine-angle discrimination, front-back discrimination, and elevation detection can get confused in human audition, particularly in structural sounds. The dataset we are using may also have redundancies that render it impossible to disambiguate for a neural network. Although some tracking seems to be achieved, we also embrace putting the machine's "failure" in relief as a way to nudge it toward a humanistic performance with the attendant serendipities of misattribution. Unlike the rigid benchmarks of accuracy that define AI research, we seek uncanny reactions of the model (alternate yet familiar) through its noisy performance.

Computational sound source localization (SSL) has traditionally relied on signal processing techniques in areas such as speech recognition and robotics. SSL methods have proven effective in applications where pinpointing the origin of an acoustic event is crucial. In hearing aids, for example, SSL could help isolate speaking voices in a crowded room. More nefarious examples could include deep-sea submarine detection or surveillance through smart devices. In most of these approaches in acoustics research, SSL techniques rely on time difference of arrival (TDOA),[18] which calculates the spatial location of a sound source based on the time it takes for the signal to reach different microphones.

But when applying SSL to surface interactions on materials like a resonant wooden board, the speed of sound in the medium presents significant challenges. With sound vibrations traveling much faster through solids than air, TDOA becomes difficult to compute.[19] (In seismology, the signals received for SSL are received over large distances, where TDOA is still viable.)[20] We therefore focus on an alternative method: measuring the received signal strength or the intensity of the acoustic signals as they activate a microphone array at the edge of the easel.

Natural wood has density variation (anisotropic) arising from seasonal growth cycles in the tree. This grain affects how waves propagate in the material, with sound traveling faster along it than across. In the process of making plywood, this structure is destroyed as thin layers are cut concentrically from the lumber and glued together. Plywood is much more damped (suppressing sound) than solid wood, but as it is still layered, it may retain asymmetries in sound propagation. To capture this potential variation, we collected audio using all four rotations of the microphones in the corners of the sound board.

By using signal intensity rather than arrival time, our method enhances both the practicality and accuracy of surface SSL in performative contexts, allowing localization despite the underlying material constraints. Deep Drawing is inherently a performance project, and this method is attractively lightweight and real-time compared with TDOA, which needs to look at a shifting window of analyses, resulting in increased latency.[21]

Deep Drawing Methods

The architecture of Deep Drawing is based on a real-time multichannel audio capture and preprocessing pipeline. We gather a stream of audio information from the drawing board and use it to predict pen location. This data-driven model is trained on corresponding video data that uses color tracking to collect pencil coordinates.

When the model is used in action, the input of the four contact microphones on a drawing board is converted into coordinates: the model's predictions of the sound's location on the board. The coordinate predictions are smoothed with a Kalman filter that interpolates the location estimates over time, ensuring that the system draws in a smooth, compelling way in the performance.

The generated points are then connected graphically through a dynamic web interface that overlays the neural network's predictions onto a live video feed, offering real-time visualization of the machine hearing process. The real drawing and the predictive drawing are superimposed and projected during the performance to highlight a visual translation of the machine hearing.[22]

Ornithologie is a more recent piece by Zhu that exemplifies the current methods. This piece was written for amplified drawing board, sheng, and electronics in 2024 (Figure 12.3).[23] Video of the drawing process was projected in the scenic design by Caty Olive on a circular metal plate above the performers. In a live performance like this one, Deep Drawing could be implemented on top of the existing video, adding a layer of abstract design, but also highlighting the incongruencies between how the machine maps the drawing sounds visually and how they actually appear.

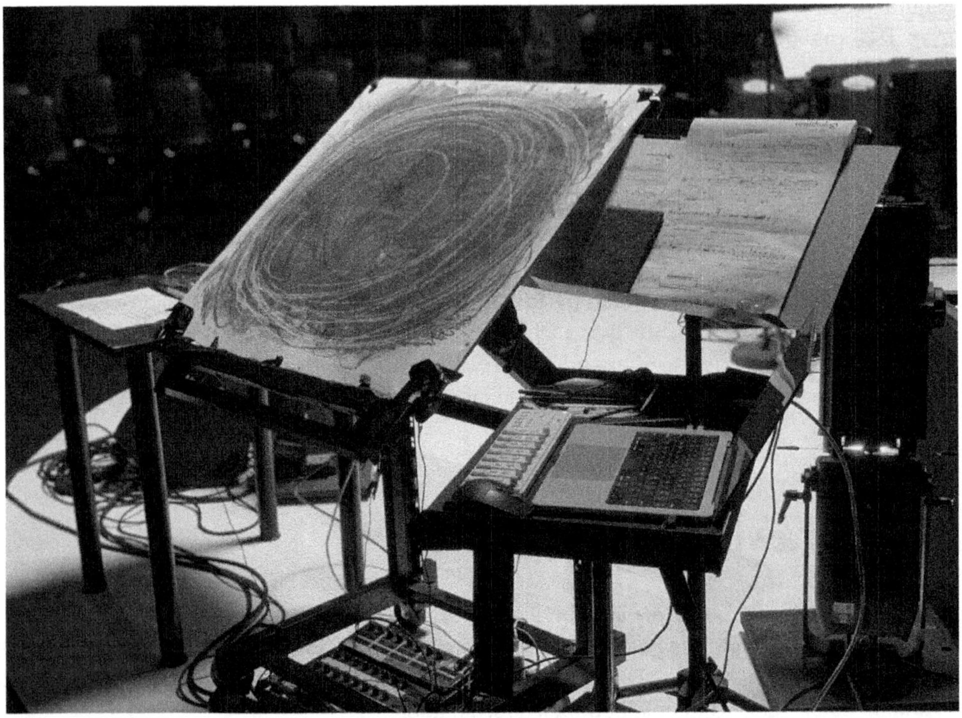

Figure 12.3 The performance setup for *Ornithologie*, which premiered at GMEM Propagations in Marseille in 2024. A Max patch controls and manipulates the sounds coming from the drawing board and out to the eight surrounding speakers.

The Deep Drawing system uses a simple, replicable sensing surface: a 2 ft × 2 ft × 1/4 in. plywood board mounted on felt pads to minimize vibrations. Plywood is selected for its affordability, effective sound transmission, and tendency to resist warping (solid thin wood is much more resonant, but deforms more easily and, as with its use in instrument building, would require bracing). A set of 4 AKG C411 PP contact microphones, placed at each corner, form a 4-channel array to capture vibrations while isolating drawing sounds from ambient noise. Audio is recorded at 192 kHz via a multichannel interface, accommodating the fast propagation of sound through wood. For ground-truth position tracking, a ballpoint pen is monitored by a calibrated GoPro Hero 13 Black camera above the board, recording at 240 fps and mapping color-tracked video frames to 2D coordinates. The system uses low-cost, widely available components, making it easy to reproduce without specialized hardware.

The dataset is small: it includes about 590,000 labeled frames (41 minutes total), collected across four 10-minute recordings. The performer draws freely to create a variety of gestures. After each session, the board is rotated to mimic the changing conditions of live setups.

Pen positions are color-tracked using video, and each frame is mapped to a 2D location on the board and matched with the corresponding audio. Normalized and high-pass filtered audio across the 4 microphones is converted into spectrograms, and each frame is labeled with the pen's position. To keep training and validation data separate, the first 90% of each recording is used for training and the last 10% for validation. This prevents overlap and ensures the validation set contains new gestures.

Two models are tested for sound source localization: a ResNet-50 convolutional model and a transformer model with a convolutional neural network (CNN) tokenizer front-end. Both models use a window of 8 consecutive spectrogram frames (about 33 ms) as input, processed with a 256-point FFT[24] and normalized per channel.

The ResNet model treats localization like an image regression task. It reshapes the input into a pseudo-image and uses a modified ResNet-50 backbone, finishing with a simple regression layer to predict (*x*, *y*) coordinates.

The transformer model uses the spectrogram from each frame as a token, capturing patterns over time. Spectral features are extracted with a CNN tokenizer, positional embeddings are added, and the sequence is processed using transformer encoder layers with multihead attention. The embedding corresponding to the most recent frame is passed through a small regression head to predict the (*x*, *y*) coordinates.

Performance differs between recordings, suggesting that the model is sensitive to board orientation and recording conditions. Overall, the ResNet model performed best and was more consistent than the transformer model across different tests.

Replicability versus Generalizability

Deep Drawing is a long way from recreating someone's signature from only the sound. With just 40 minutes of training data, however, it generally can reflect the contours of the human drawing. We find it still interesting to watch the machine deviate from the path on which it is trained, likely due to our imperfect algorithms, data limitations, and the inherent noisiness of the drawn audio data. Also, human drawing and writing gestures don't move like printers or plotters. This kind of human facility is hard to capture and replicate.

To further explore the capacities of this method, we plan to upgrade the quality of the recording data. Calibration and human error contribute to the difficult task of accurately recording and labeling data, especially when there's so little of it. But the small amount of data may prove to serve a performance that foregrounds high-level attributes of a drawing gesture, its overall shape and direction, rather than the exact coordinates of the pen at each point in time. This behavior is more evocative of object-oriented human listening, associating sound and high-level shape attributions.[25]

Deep Drawing was never meant to generalize to every person's drawing on any kind of surface. It works best (and currently, works only) when performance conditions are as similar to training conditions as possible. That kind of generalizable model requires countless hours of training data and computing power that very few have access to, and it's not necessarily the point of AI for artistic practice, in our opinion. But if someone wanted to replicate our results with their own drawing board, their own style of drawing, their own styluses, they now have the tools to do so. Our accessibility comes from the replicable, not the generalizable. Still, Deep Drawing illustrates a very specific need for endogenous data generation and information retrieval, and we suspect that's what artists want from AI, not a general music-generating machine of unknown provenance that likely is based on the theft of artists' intellectual property.

In Zhu's most recent work on the sound of drawing, *TacocaT*, two performers sit across a drawing board and start writing increasingly frantically about God, dogs, and AI slop (Figure 12.4).[26] Their tapping, scraping, and drawing on the board fabricate a world of sounds mapped by machine learning algorithms. By the end, the board is covered by entangled lines, shapes, and postulations, and we've heard birds, oceans, and alien sounds, all generated

Figure 12.4 *TacocaT* is performed by Beyond This Point (Adam Rosenblatt and John Corkill) in a recording session at the Duderstadt Center at the University of Michigan.

Photograph by Robert Coelius.

by the acoustic sounds picked up by contact mics on the wooden board. Must machines dream? Will we capitulate to the noise? Can we find the beauty in the entanglement?

Acknowledgments

We acknowledge all of the current and past members of the Deep Drawing Lab, as part of Arts Engine's Faculty Engineering Arts Student Teams (FEAST) at the University of Michigan: Erfun Ackley, Durrah Azdi, Shruti Balla, Henry Cao, Anusha Chinthamaduka, Albert Jiang, Ryan Lu, Lennon Seiders, Alex Zhang, and Zhiyu Zhang.

Notes

1 Varèse and Chou, "The Liberation of Sound."
2 Chinese artist and poet born in 1987 who passed away in 2017.
3 Lacquaniti et al., "The Law Relating."
4 Viviani and Terzuolo, "Trajectory Determines Movement Dynamics."
5 Thoret et al., "From Sound to Shape."
6 Danna et al., "'Let Me Hear Your Handwriting!'"
7 Sotheby's, "*Comedian* by Maurizio Cattelan."
8 Davidson, "Visual Perception of Performance Manner."
9 Applebaum, "Portfolio of Works: *Straitjacket*."
10 Choi et al., "The Deckle Project."
11 Zheng et al., "Building Sketch-to-Sound Mapping."
12 Nordin, "The Musical Interactivity Area."
13 Sen et al., "Sounding Brush."
14 Barbosa et al., "Illusio."
15 Kitahara et al., "JamSketch."
16 Ha and Eck, "A Neural Representation."
17 Deng, "The MNIST Database."
18 Grumiaux et al., "A Survey of Sound Source Localization."
19 Li et al., "Acoustic Emission Signal Source Localization."
20 Jia et al., "Time Difference of Arrival Estimation."
21 Zhu et al., "Deep Drawing: Spectra."
22 Zhu et al., "Deep Drawing: An Intermedia Co-Performer."
23 Zhu, *GMEM*.
24 FFT is an abbreviation for Fast Fourier Transform, an algorithm that converts signals between time and frequency domains.
25 Löbbers et al.,"Sketching Sounds"
26 Zhu, *TacocaT*.

Bibliography

Applebaum, Mark. "Portfolio of Works: *Straitjacket*." *Stanford University*. Accessed February 8, 2026. https://web.stanford.edu/~applemk/portfolio-works-straitjacket.html.

Barbosa, Jerônimo, Filipe Calegario, Veronica Teichrieb, Geber Ramalho, and Giordano Cabral. "Illusio: A Drawing-Based Digital Music Instrument." In *Proceedings of the International Conference on New Interfaces for Musical Expression*, 499–502. Daejeon and Seoul, South Korea: KAIST, 2013.

Choi, Hongchan, John Granzow, and Joel Sadler. "The Deckle Project: A Sketch of Three Sensors." In *Proceedings of the International Conference on New Interfaces for Musical Expression*. Ann Arbor, MI: University of Michigan, 2012.

Danna, Jérémy, Vietminh Paz-Villagrán, Charles Gondre, Mitsuko Aramaki, Richard Kronland-Martinet, Sølvi Ystad, and Jean-Luc Velay. "'Let Me Hear Your Handwriting!' Evaluating the Movement Fluency from Its Sonification." *PLoS One* 10, no. 6 (2015): e0128388.

Davidson, Jane W. "Visual Perception of Performance Manner in the Movements of Solo Musicians." *Psychology of Music* 21, no. 2 (1993): 103–113.

Deng, L. "The MNIST Database of Handwritten Digit Images for Machine Learning Research [Best of the Web]." *IEEE Signal Processing Magazine* 29, no. 6 (November 2012): 141–142. https://doi.org/10.1109/MSP.2012.2211477.

Ha, David, and Douglas Eck. "A Neural Representation of Sketch Drawings." Preprint, last revied May 19, 2017. arXiv:1704.03477. https://arxiv.org/abs/1704.03477.

Howe, Susan. "Silence Wager Stories." In *The Nonconformist's Memorial: Poems*. New York, NY: New Directions Publishing, 1993. Reprinted with permission on the Poetry Foundation Website. https://www.poetryfoundation.org/poems/43254/silence-wager-stories.

Ingold, Tim. *Lines: A Brief History*. Abingdon, UK: Routledge, 2016.

"Issue 18: Fall 2019." *Ginger Zine*. Accessed February 14, 2026. https://www.gingerzine.net/issue-18.

Grumiaux, Pierre-Amaury, Srđan Kitić, Laurent Girin, and Alexandre Guérin. "A Survey of Sound Source Localization with Deep Learning Methods." *The Journal of the Acoustical Society of America* 152, no. 1 (2022): 107–151. https://pubs.aip.org/asa/jasa/article/152/1/107/2838290/A-survey-of-sound-source-localization-with-deep.

Kitahara, Tetsuro, Sergio Giraldo, and Rafael Ramírez. "JamSketch: Improvisation Support System with GA-Based Melody Creation from User's Drawing." In *International Symposium on Computer Music Multidisciplinary Research*, 509–521. Cham, Switzerland: Springer International Publishing, 2017.

Lacquaniti, Francesco, Carlo Terzuolo, and Paolo Viviani. "The Law Relating the Kinematic and Figural Aspects of Drawing Movements." *Acta Psychologica* 54, no. 1–3 (1983): 115–130.

Li, Yang, Shuai-Shuai Yu, Li Dai, Ting-Fang Luo, and Ming Li. "Acoustic Emission Signal Source Localization on Plywood Surface with Cross-Correlation Method." *Journal of Wood Science* 64, no. 2 (2018): 78–84. https://doi.org/10.1007/s10086-017-1672-x.

Löbbers, Sebastian, Mathieu Barthet, and György Fazekas. "Sketching Sounds: An Exploratory Study on Sound-Shape Associations." Preprint, submitted July 15, 2021. arXiv:2107.07360. https://arxiv.org/abs/2107.07360.

Jia, Rui-Sheng, Yue Gong, Yan-Jun Peng, Hong-Mei Sun, Xing-Li Zhang, and Xin-Ming Lu. "Time Difference of Arrival Estimation of Microseismic Signals Based on Alpha-Stable Distribution." *Nonlinear Processes in Geophysics* 25, no. 2 (2018): 375–386. https://www.proquest.com/docview/2210218335.

Nordin, Jesper. "The Musical Interactivity Area: An Attempt to Map the Intersection Between Composition and Instrument Through the Use of the Gestrument Engine." In *27th Conference of Open Innovations Association FRUCT, September 7–9, 2020, Trento, Italy,* edited by Sergey

Balandin, Luca Turchet, and Tatiana Tyutina, vol. 2, 349–355. Helsinki, Finland: Open Innovations Association FRUCT, 2020.

Sen, Sourya, Koray Tahiroğlu, and Julia Lohmann. "Sounding Brush: A Tablet-Based Musical Instrument for Drawing and Mark-Making." In *Proceedings of the International Conference on New Interfaces for Musical Expression*, 331–336. Royal Birmingham Conservatoire, 2020.

Sotheby's. "*Comedian* by Maurizio Cattelan." In *Contemporary Evening Auction*. New York, NY, May 13, 2024. Accessed February 18, 2026. https://www.sothebys.com/en/buy/auction/2024/contemporary-evening-auction-2/comedian.

Thoret, Etienne, Mitsuko Aramaki, Richard Kronland-Martinet, Jean-Luc Velay, and Sølvi Ystad. "From Sound to Shape: Auditory Perception of Drawing Movements." *Journal of Experimental Psychology: Human Perception and Performance* 40, no. 3 (2014): 983.

Varèse, Edgard, and Chou Wen-Chung. "The Liberation of Sound." *Perspectives of New Music* 5, no. 1 (1966): 11–19.

Viviani, Paolo, and Carlo Terzuolo. "Trajectory Determines Movement Dynamics." *Neuroscience* 7, no. 2 (1982): 431–437.

Zheng, Shuoyang, Bleiz M. Del Sette, Charalampos Saitis, A. Xambó Sedó, and Nick Bryan-Kinns. "Building Sketch-to-Sound Mapping with Unsupervised Feature Extraction and Interactive Machine Learning." In *Proceedings of the International Conference on New Interfaces for Musical Expression*, 591–97. Utrecht, Netherlands: NIME, 2024. https://doi.org/10.5281/zenodo.13904959.

Zhu, Julie. *Ornithologie*. Performed by Wu Wei, Alexis Baskind, Julie Zhu. *GMEM Festival Propagations*. 2024. https://en.gmem.org/ornithologie.

Zhu, Julie. *TacocaT*. Performed by *Beyond This Point* (Adam Rosenblatt and John Corkill). *Frequency Festival*. 2025. YouTube video, 22:45. February 13, 2026. https://youtu.be/2ZdS5APSJuc.

Zhu, Julie, Erfun Ackley, Zhiyu Zhang, and John Granzow. "Deep Drawing: An Intermedia Co-Performer." In *Proceedings of the Artificial Intelligence Music Creativity Conference*. Oxford, UK: University of Oxford, 2024. https://aimc2024.pubpub.org/pub/859kww47/release/1.

Zhu, Julie, Erfun Ackley, Zhiyu Zhang, and John Granzow. "Deep Drawing: Spectra and Sound-Source Localization." In *Proceedings of the International Computer Music Conference (ICMC)*, 446–450. Boston, MA: ICMC, 2025.

13

INTERLUDE VI

Interview with Pierre Alexandre Tremblay

Julie Zhu and Constantin Basica

DOI: 10.4324/9781003615873-13

Pierre Alexandre: You said that "AI is a good conversion machine," yes? That it's good for going through a lot of stuff. Well, I'm not the only one to think about this, but ... the world has a memory. People talk about (pre-AI) Google as prosthetics. It's memory prosthetics. Research used to involve loads of physical books not long ago, and it took forever to get information. I remember the beginning of the Internet as a public thing. I did most of my research training before that. Then Google arrived, then the search function on PDF—so the way of thinking about ideas and memory has changed immensely. That was the first hit, I would say.

And then the second hit is now: properly being able to look through patterns in data, in knowledge that has been symbolized, anchored, written. And obviously, there's bias. Well, there's been bias forever. What's good with the machine is that it can sieve a lot faster than we used to. Now, if you remove the capitalist side (the exploitation for somebody's profit) and you give AI anything, it sieves through that thing like a distilling engine. That doesn't give you depth, that gives you a distillation. But that's really powerful. To be able to start a literature review and to see a blind spot in your thinking, including all the cultural biases—all of this in the last year (not plural, singular): it's incredible!

Now it's also very humbling, like it didn't used to be, because it took years for people to write those books, make a reader, write a literature review. Now, you immediately have access to

Figure 13.1 Pierre Alexandre Tremblay performs with a laptop and modular synthesizer.

Photograph by Kristian Løvstad.

a distilled version of a full subfield of knowledge. That is both humbling and challenging. For instance, when I taught my first classes twenty years ago, it took me a week to plan a year, because I was certain of everything I knew, and I was certain of what I needed to teach. It was simple. Now, it took me a full summer to try to do half a class on something I learned thirty years ago. Thirty years later, I'm building this class on electroacoustic ear training and analysis. This is stuff I've practiced, I've done, I've been trained by the guy who systematized the thing in Montreal (Stéphane Roy, who wrote the "Bible" on the subject).[1] I've done this. I've hated it. But now I understand what it brought me, and how it helped me. And writing that class ... I was bleeding to death. It's good to know that I'm not an electroacoustic analyst. I'm a practitioner, I'm a composer, I use tools and ears. And then, distilling what I want my students to actually understand—I go, I buy, I look, I search ... this is fantastic, because I'm in a position of knowledge, and of power, and I can decide to use that tool to curate a way in. But I am confronted by the immense number of alternative proposals.

Same thing with the mixed music class that I'm teaching: students used to have to write a report for their assessment. But now this can be done by a machine, so I changed the brief: they have to engage with one model (of mixity) that speaks to them. They have to understand the model, they have to understand their piece, and they have to connect the two and do a small demo with their phone using three examples in their current work. There's no way they can fake this by asking an LLM.

While presenting the brief, I also showed them how not to use AI. I prompted four different LLMs the same question, which was: "In mixed music, where acoustic instruments mix with electronics, what are good models of mixity?" Once I got the first answer, I wrote: "What did Tremblay write in 2005 about it?" (Because I wrote my PhD on mixed music.)[2] From the LLMs' answers, I said [*points with finger to an imaginary bullet point*]: "Okay, this is the least worst of them. [*Points finger.*] This is not me. [*Points finger.*] This is a good idea, but it's not me. [*Points finger.*] This is bullshit. [*Points finger.*] This is somebody else. [*Points finger.*] This is half of what I said ..." So, this is why you cannot use it. It's a good starting point. If you like an idea, you have to dig further. This is what it means to deal with a convergence machine that does a vague approximation of the knowledge that it has been trained on, which has been biased. It's a great convergence machine. And what you feed it—it will give you the trends in there. And it's a good idea to get to the bottom of it with the students.

So, for me, that's where the real challenge is ... Who gets the tool? Because it's a tool. Who gets that tool, and who pretends to know what the output means? It's as important as any other tool, but it's a very, very seductive one, because it lies really well. So, the metaphor of *discussion* has been used quite a lot in their sales pitch. They have an interface that makes you feel like you're discussing. And that's created some sort of anthropomorphization. Because most people ... in most of life (like what we were doing before we recorded this interview) we talk about stuff—we bounce ideas off each other. LLMs can fake this and it's really convincing if you don't go in-depth into something. But the difference is: if you recommended me a film, I would not verify the recommendation right away because there's trust between us, between people and their words ... but that's no longer the case with LLMs.

Julie: The thing is, are we still going to have people like you, who have the experience and the discernment? You're *the* source. You're the primary source, right? That's why you could say, for all of these models: "I did that."

Pierre Alexandre: I wouldn't say that I'm the primary source. I'm thirty years in. Well, in the case of my dissertation, I *am the source*. But it's this idea of mentoring researchers and the political fight we were talking about—who has the tools and who makes the claim, and what is knowledge? You have Musk,[3] who's done this Grokipedia,[4] which is dangerous because suddenly there's no more authoritative knowledge. There's somebody who curates that "authority." Wikipedia was genius because you have communities that challenge the assertions, and canons are confronted straight away. This was a beautiful idea ... Wikipedia plus AI together? ... You don't even need AI there, but it's a good source as a literature review. And then you bounce ideas, and then you can challenge the answers, and you can see what's been written, and you can train your AI model on, for instance ... everything that's been written about music in African cultures. If not much has been written about that, okay, good—there's a hole in knowledge, that becomes a research priority. Suddenly, you use a tool, and what you need to do is to feed it, to equalize the tool (or to give it another perspective): it's "techno-ethnomusicology" in this case. If "the word" is the key element to pass on perspective on music, and that whole set of cultures is underrepresented in words because of multiple historical issues—colonization plus money plus our tradition plus this plus that—then, okay, there's a hole in what we feed our algorithm.

The AI is not the problem; it's another human problem. If you pretend that your AI talks about a universal view of music, *you* are making the mistake, not the algorithm. The algorithm is just telling you what the data is. It's just a distillation of what you gave it. You ferment apples, you distill that, and you have apple alcohol. You cannot say you have neutral alcohol. You cannot say that you have pear alcohol or grain alcohol. It's a distillation process; it's nothing else. It's amazing. Fantastic. But it's nothing else. So, what you put in—the responsibility of it—is everything.

People talk about it, but not enough. Or not the people with enough power. Because, again, you can see how amazing it is. They make new medications, new proteins, new molecules. But if you read the article properly in Nature[5] (not just the newspaper version), then suddenly at the end they say: "We haven't tested it. It's just a million ideas. This is great, now we need to do the early test." So, there's a part of the research by hyperspecialists, which was immensely time-consuming, and suddenly is not. They still need to do the ethical part of the work. The safeguarding to get a new pill is the same. And that's the thing that's been eroded for the last forty years. It's not the AI—it's the fact that, suddenly, they shrink the accountability. But that's not AI.

So, this is why it needs to be part of a bigger debate. And this is why music is good, because AI still composes lousy generic music. So ... who is this stuff for? Who does it speak to? Who are the people who say, "Yeah, this is great"? And, cool, what do they use it for? If it's great as a party trick, or if you just jam together a piece because it's fun ... that's a very valid way of making music, by the way. Is it the new equivalent of getting a few words, and the guitar player strumming some stuff, and we just compose a tune? Cool. The more, the merrier. The more people make bad music, the more good music has value.

Julie: Because you have faith in humans and their judgment.

Pierre Alexandre: No! There's this great quote by Stiegler.[6] He was interviewed (if you understand French, I recommend this) by Radio France,[7] and they did five one-hour sessions with him at the end of his life, covering his whole life. And, at the end, he was working on this hardcore transdisciplinary problem. For instance, if the planet can generate 500 hospitals in terms of rare earth minerals, where do we place them? That's the kind of question he was asking. Incredibly complex ethical questions. And so, the interviewer (she's a fantastic philosopher and a great journalist) says: "You're bleak. This is very dark. Is there no positivity?" The same way I'm telling you I'm not optimistic, he says: "I'm not optimistic or pessimistic. This is a fact that I'm telling you about. We discuss it or not. Humankind will make decisions, and will go through it or not. But at the moment, I act with what I have."

AI is not going anywhere. Ultra-capitalism is not going anywhere soon. Even though it's crumbling … The polarization is a trend, you can see. All of these things are happening. I'm worried for musicians and for my students making a living. Because if you look at the trends, most artists who do fringe stuff–anything *but* incredibly commercially successful, therefore incredibly lucky, things that you can make a living out of in music (and I'm including the very few contemporary music people who get large commission fees and the very few people who get pop music hits)–they are fringe, let's put it like this. And I'm not talking about music you compose for somebody else, like a film or dance, which is part of the job that people frequently do to fund their own art. Some people do it for fun, but most of my ex-students do sound design for commercials, Foley for film, voiceover, mastering … All these jobs that fund their personal projects are disappearing. They have disappeared, actually, you can see. Mastering online gets a better result than humans, except for a very good mastering engineer. The Foley artist of … I can't remember which film, but he got an Oscar for his Foley–he's got no contract this year. Literally.[8]

These jobs are disappearing because anyone can do them easily now, and AI is going to get better at this. Because those jobs are incredibly convergent. You have somebody walking in the snow. That's a very simple task. It's hard to do incredibly well. But most people don't do it incredibly well—they don't have the money. So they pay people to do a job. And that job is done by my ex-students to fund their creative projects. That's the way I started as a professional musician—tuning guitars in the studio. And then replacing drums in rap beats. That's the way I started. That job doesn't exist anymore.

Again, we go back to capitalism. How are we going to fund 85–90% of people not having jobs? That's a problem that's going to happen very soon. We talked about Graeber[9] last time, right? Even if you don't want to look at it, the stats of last year's entry jobs is where the hole is being dug. In all the fields. Old people like me—we're fine. We have a job that is hard to replace because, as you said earlier, I have the knowledge to know whether the machine is good or bad. This is going to be a political and economic problem. And music ... I'm really happy that we're nowhere as important as other fields.

Julie: Who was the person who said that AI's a *convergence machine*? Was it you, or was it someone else?

Pierre Alexandre: I say that all the time, but somebody else may have said it to me ... That's what the algorithm does. They are regression algorithms, so they converge. The concept they teach in stats at the basic level is *regression to the mean.*

Julie: Well, I just mean, it's a pretty great term, and we want to attribute it to you, if it is.

Pierre Alexandre: That's very kind of you, but let's Google it. Let's use AI! [*Puts on eyeglasses.*] Look, I'll share my screen. I'll do exactly what I said with the kids. You'll love it.

A new tab, here we go. I'm going to share this guy. Let's see. So, this is what I use. I've got LLM tools [*clicks on a folder bookmark in his browser*], which opens them all in one go, and I ask the same question. Do you see all of them?

Okay, so I've got one, two, three, four, five. Here we go. So [*types*] "who said a.i. is a 'great convergence machine'?" Copy. That's done. [*Pastes the question into the prompt field.*] That's Le Chat.[10] [*Pastes the question into a new prompt field.*] Perplexity[11] is the least worst for academic stuff. [*Pastes the question into a new prompt field.*] This[12] is this guy ... Let's just stay like that. [*Clicks* Stay logged out *in ChatGPT, then pastes the question into the prompt field.*] This guy ... And the Swiss one, which is awful. [*Pastes the question into the prompt field.*] And let's use Google. I don't know which one they use.

Constantin: Gemini.

Pierre Alexandre: Oh, I've not used Gemini, let's see ... And there's the Microsoft one—what's the name of that one? Copilot. I'm logged as well, so let's see. [*Pastes the question into the prompt field*]: There we go. So, let's see. Who says this? Because it's something I've heard ... Here we go [*shows Perplexity browser tab*].

This guy. [*Positions mouse pointer on the answer that starts with: "The phrase 'AI is a great convergence machine' is most closely associated with Jürgen Schmidhuber."*] I've heard of him, but I don't know who this guy is. I've never read him, but I don't recall that specific phrase.

Here we go, that's Claude. [*Highlights with the mouse pointer a sentence in Claude's response: "2. A paraphrase of someone's ideas about AI."*] In my case, it is a paraphrase because it comes from the training I had.

Oh, I know who to ask. Let's ask a human! You'll love it. [*Opens new browser window and goes to https://discord.com.*] Owen Green[13]—an encyclopedic brain.

[*Types in chat and speaks:*] *hey man, I'm stuck—who said a.i. is 'a great convergence machine'? I wouldn't want to be attributed such a gem* 🙄

Here we go. That's a human. It will take longer, but we'll have a valid ... he knows everything. He's worked with Georgina Born on the MusAI Project.[14] He's teaching the ethics of AI use in music. He's building a class on this. So, if somebody knows, it will be him. So, let's see. Otherwise, I'll keep the creds.

ChatGPT says no. Claude says no. Perplexity sends us toward this guy [*Jürgen Schmidhuber*]. And this is bad [*Public AI*].[15] Oh, so we can see the source of Perplexity is Wikipedia right away. [*Scrolls results on Google*] Hinton? That would make sense, actually.

Constantin: It sounds like you can claim it.

Pierre Alexandre: I'm not going to claim anything. But I definitely say it all the time. There we go! So what about Le Chat? Yeah ... nobody knows. So, yes, you can claim it. But again, that's what it does. It looks for patterns. And, if you have twenty-five times the same pattern, it will regress to the mean. That's what these LLMs are doing—nothing else.

Julie: I want to go back to something that really stuck out to me when you said, "It's a good thing that we have a lot of bad music, because then the good music will rise to the top." When that happens, good music will be more expensive. And so, we need to change more in the music world. We need to change how capitalism works. However, I also am curious about how that relates to live performance, because I think we also talked about it in Lugano. I wanted to tell my students that the people who are studying instruments will have their jobs secure, because people will always want to have live music. And especially with AI music, more people will crave live music. But now, I'm less sure about that, because I look at Taylor Swift, and I look at all those pop stars. They're touring, and that's what makes money. And so, people are converging toward those huge pop stars, and spending their life savings to go to a Taylor Swift concert, when they could be seeing someone who's maybe not as good or famous playing live. People are not necessarily choosing to do that. So, maybe I take back what I said to my student who studies live performance—maybe their job isn't secure in the age of music and AI. And I wanted you to respond to that in relation to what you were saying about bad music and good music.

Pierre Alexandre: Okay, I think you're conflating two things there. Let's backtrack. Going to see Celine Dion or Taylor Swift is not the same thing as going to your local venue to see people play. They're two very different experiences, and I like them both. But they are not related. The former is an *event*.

I know that because I was backstage when the Celine Dion show came to Manchester. My friend was the PA tech.[16] And look, I'm not a big fan, but they got me: I was singing all the songs. It was amazing. I was saturated into not thinking critically. It was beautiful. But you pay for that saturation. It's a new church. You go there, and it's immense. That's amazing. People pay an immense amount of money; they share a moment that is something. Broadway used to be like that too. Now, she's bigger than Broadway. You go there, and it's the saturation of the senses. If your students study to do that—good. It's still a very small, small, small, small, small amount of live music.

And about the other question—so you started talking about people paying—we go back to money. As long as people have money to go see gigs, and musicians are happy ... But the amazing improvisers I'm listening to, like the London scene, the New York scene ... these guys are doing two hundred gigs a year to barely make a living ... because the price to go see gigs is the same as when I started to be professional thirty years ago. It's still a fiver, or a tenner, or a twenty if you're really famous. It was the same price thirty years ago. It's nuts!

So, first with download and dematerialization, music has lost its material value. People are less and less happy to pay for it. Netflix is killing the cinema with the same method. Now, you stay at home, you're cheap, you've got access to the whole catalog. That's a different relationship to entertainment art—which are, again, different ways of seeing that moment that you're going to experience, but they're both related to how you deal with this.

But the roots of the problem are deeper. We don't teach music in high school anymore. People don't do music, so they don't experience the embodied thing. And that was where my hope lay: the more people do music, the better. You're at a party, you sing karaoke. Karaoke has helped singers, you know? With karaoke, you go sing, and you sing like crap, and then you hear a good singer, and you say, "Oh, yeah, I actually know how hard it is because I've tried it." You try to ski—the same thing. There's a fascination with excellence, with transcendence, with magic. This is still happening. This is a big driver of musical experience. A shared moment together, looking at something awesome.

And tomorrow, if there is no electricity, we're still going to jam together. I'm not worried. But will your student have a job? Yes, as long as society decides that music has value. But that has been declining since the '80s. They've cut funding for the arts. So, if people start to write poetry with ChatGPT, and rhyme, and do beats, and everything—go for it, tiger! The more we do, the better. Because art, suddenly, is something we continue sharing, and then it gives it value, which the schooling system has actually slowly but surely dissolved over time, or deprioritized.

That's where my combat lies, that's why I'm in education, that's why I teach. We have to remember, people, that, yeah, art is important. Especially because they've focused so much on STEM[17] for the last 40 years. And now, if there's one thing machines will do better than humans, it's basic STEM. So, my son is studying the ethics of AI, he's studying computer science, and he's the one who flagged to me: Claude last year (I can't remember the version) was 20% better than human at coding tasks—or 5% or something?—and literally, the next version was 84%. So, he's happy he's got a job as a coder now. He says that he's the last generation of young coders. And he's one of the few in his cohort who actually has a job. So, the STEM thing? It was a bad investment. But ... care? Art? *This* we need, and it won't be replaced by machines.

So, how do we shift that mindset as a society? That's why I keep talking about economics, and why it's way beyond music. And you're right to tell your student: good musicians ... good nurses, good psychologists, good pedagogues—anything relational—this is in care ... A lot of people are talking about this (I'm not the first person, I can be quoted, but I'm not taking credit, or I will have to defer credit): the caring sector is what we will need. So, again, going back to the economy, the caring sector is one of those places that costs an immense amount of money. How do we fund *caring*? There's no way genuine *caring* can be for-profit. They manage right now, but you can see, again, the social divide is being reinforced with "caring for those who can afford it," which is not really a great place for most ... So, let's hope we don't get into the dystopia that all of this seems to be pointed at. But I believe in humankind in the long run. I'm a convinced reader of *Sapiens*, the book, after all.[18]

Now, I hope for my kids that there will not need to be a mega dip before the next big step up. I really hope for my kids. Do I believe it?

Do you know Winston Churchill's quote from the Second World War? I can't remember the exact words, but they were still funding concerts or art somewhere. You can find the original quote, but somebody asked him about being in a time of war, and why would they fund art—were resources not scarce? "But if we don't do that, why would we fight?" So, art, for him, was a reason to fight. Civilization.

[*After the interview, Pierre Alexandre sent this follow-up email:*]

> Hello,
>
> Thanks again for yesterday. I would not want to sound like a Neo-Luddite[19] either, so I hope my slightly Marxist view on the challenges the tools bring to humankind, in reconfiguring dignity, practice, various endeavors (epistemic, artistic, humanistic) and how people feed themselves, is taken in the grand context of a cycle, Nietzschean return with some positive Harari's *Sapiens* narrative angle. It is like the Industrial Revolution again, and hopefully, we will, as a species, rise to the challenge.
>
> On a more local/music scale, which is so important in community-making (I'm 100% with Born here),[20] the "industry" has survived the sampler revolution of the '90s. Not everyone, but we haven't fallen short of fantastic use and abuse of that tech, and many musicians found ways to strive. So, if we can feed ourselves, we'll be fine :)
>
> p
>
> PS: Owen replied. It seems my great converging coining is mine after all ... but as I said, it is such a basic concept it must be in most maths explaining fitting—aka regression to the mean :)

Learn more about Pierre Alexandre Tremblay and his work at https://www.pierrealexandretremblay.com

Notes

1 Roy, *L'analyse Des Musiques Électroacoustiques*.
2 *Mixed music* refers to the combination of acoustic instruments and electronics, mostly in chamber music. For a discussion on some of the findings from Tremblay's PhD dissertation, see his 2006 ICMC paper "Pragmatic Considerations in Mixed Music."
3 Elon Musk is an American entrepreneur who has been the wealthiest person in the world since 2021.
4 "Grok (chatbot)."
5 *Nature*.
6 Bernard Stiegler was a French philosopher.
7 *Bernard Stiegler*.
8 Knutson and Mendoza, "Hollywood Jobs Are Disappearing."
9 David Rolfe Graeber was an American anthropologist, left-wing anarchist, social and political activist. The reference here is his 2018 book *Bullshit Jobs*.
10 Mistral AI, *Le Chat*.
11 Perplexity AI, *Perplexity*.
12 Anthropic, *Claude*.
13 Owen Green is an improviser, composer, performer, and systems-maker who served as a senior research fellow for the FluCoMa project and later worked with Georgina Born and her colleagues on the five-year MusAI project.
14 The project is *Music and Artificial Intelligence: Building Critical Interdisciplinary Studies* (MusAI).
15 Public AI Inference Utility, *Public AI*.
16 PA stands for "public address," the sound system for a venue. A "PA tech" is the technician who designs this system.
17 STEM is an acronym for Science, Technology, Engineering, and Mathematics.
18 Harari, *Sapiens*.
19 Neo-Luddism, inspired by the original Luddites, is a contemporary philosophy that critiques the negative effects of modern technology on individuals, communities, and the natural world.
20 Born, "On Musical Meditation."

Bibliography

Anthropic. *Claude*. Accessed December 18, 2025. https://claude.ai.

Bernard Stiegler, la philosophie et la vie. Produced by France Culture, Radio France. Accessed December 18, 2025. https://www.radiofrance.fr/franceculture/podcasts/serie-bernard-stiegler-la-philosophie-et-la-vie.

"Bernard Stiegler." *Wikipedia*. Accessed December 19, 2025. https://en.wikipedia.org/wiki/Bernard_Stiegler.

Born, Georgina. "On Musical Mediation: Ontology, Technology, and Creativity." *Twentieth-Century Music* 2, no. 1 (2005): 7–36.

"Elon Musk." *Wikipedia*. Accessed February 3, 2026. https://en.wikipedia.org/wiki/Elon_Musk.

Graeber, David. *Bullshit Jobs*. New York, NY: Simon & Schuster, 2018.

Green, Owen. "Owen Green." *Music AI Research*. Accessed December 18, 2025. https://musicairesearch.wordpress.com/people/owen-green.

"Grok (chatbot)." *Wikipedia*. Accessed February 2, 2026. https://en.wikipedia.org/wiki/Grok_(chatbot)#Grokipedia.

Harari, Yuval Noah. *Sapiens: A Brief History of Humankind*. New York, NY: Harper, 2015.

Knutson, Ryan, and Jessica Mendoza. "Hollywood Jobs Are Disappearing." *The Journal*. Produced by *Spotify* and *The Wall Street Journal*. Podcast audio, November 10, 2025. https://www.wsj.com/podcasts/the-journal/hollywood-jobs-are-disappearing/556a88af-b759-491f-8589-d6aa2d3a432e.

Mistral AI. *Le Chat*. Accessed December 18, 2025. https://chat.mistral.ai/chat.

Music & Artificial Intelligence: Building Critical Interdisciplinary Studies (MusAI). Accessed December 18, 2025. https://musicairesearch.wordpress.com.

Nature. Accessed December 18, 2025. https://www.nature.com.

"Neo-Luddism." *Wikipedia*. Accessed January 20, 2026. https://en.wikipedia.org/wiki/Neo-Luddism.

Perplexity AI. *Perplexity*. Accessed December 18, 2025. https://www.perplexity.ai.

Public AI Inference Utility. *Public AI*. Accessed December 18, 2025. https://publicai.co/chat.

Roy, Stéphane. *L'analyse Des Musiques Électroacoustiques: Modèles et Propositions*. Collection Univers Musical. Harmattan, 2003.

Tremblay, Pierre Alexandre. "Pragmatic Considerations in Mixed Music: A Case Study of La Rage." In *Proceedings of the International Computer Music Conference (ICMC)*, 527–30. New Orleans, LA: ICMC, 2006. https://eprints.hud.ac.uk/id/eprint/14901.

Tremblay, Pierre Alexandre, Owen Green, Gerard Roma, James Bradbury, Ted Moore, Jacob Hart, and Alex Harker. *The Fluid Corpus Manipulation Toolbox*, vol. 1. Zenodo, July 14, 2022. https://10.5281/zenodo.6834643.

14

MOVEMENT VI

The Neural Tape Loop

Hugo Flores García

DOI: 10.4324/9781003615873-14

Generative models are not neutral entities existing in a vacuum. They are shaped by the data they are trained on, the infrastructures that build them, and the ideologies that guide their design and use. But they do not have to be instruments of a commodified pastiche. If we, as makers of generative musical systems and instruments, engage with the systems we make critically, aesthetically, and performatively, we can make generative models that engender a new musical tradition—one that values humanness, experimentation, embodiment, and expressiveness.

This chapter introduces the *neural tape loop*, a co-creative generative musical meta-instrument built through a mixture of creative and technical research practice. It expands on my previous technical research work in generative audio, VampNet,[1] and reframes the masked acoustic token modeling (MATM) generative model as a meta-instrument[2] from which musical instruments, sound installations, audio processing interfaces, and other musicking[3] interactions can be built. Masked acoustic token modeling, in brief, is a method for generating sounds with a neural network. MATM generates sound by first encoding a "real" sound into a representation of acoustic tokens, which one can think of as ~40 ms generative chunks of sound. A single sound can thus consist of hundreds of tokens. One can create new sequences of acoustic tokens by taking a real sound, encoding it into acoustic tokens, masking (or corrupting) a portion of them, and re-generating a new sequence of acoustic tokens using a trained generative neural network to fill in the masked blanks. This new sequence of tokens is now a new sound of its own, which can perceivably sound like a variation of the original sound or an entirely new sound, reflecting the timbral and temporal characteristics of the sounds that the generative model was trained on.

I'll discuss four original works made with the neural tape loop: a mono fixed media composition (*living // dreaming*), a composed improvisation (*confluyo yo*), a multichannel fixed media composition (*world of mouth*), and a quadraphonic interactive sound installation (*Token Telephone*)—each exploring and introducing a new musical affordance enabled by the *neural tape loop*.

These works aim to extend the lineage and discourse of both experimental music and generative audio modeling by situating the new wave of large 2-stage generative AI models within a broader musical ecology—in this case, one shaped by the practices of sonic hauntology, tape manipulation, looping, and feedback, and sustained by communities invested in experimental sound, improvisation, and process-based music.

Interface: *unloop*

unloop is the primary live performance interface built on top of the neural tape loop. *unloop* places a masked acoustic token model[4] in a live-looping digital instrument, equipping the looper with the ability to create generative transformations of the loop as it repeats. While looping, a user can modify the model's input parameters and can apply different kinds of generative transformations to the sound, ranging from a timbre transfer to a larger structural transfer to a full-on unconditional generation with a masked acoustic token model (e.g., VampNet).

Figure 14.1 shows the *unloop* user interface (implemented as a Max[5] patch). The left panel contains basic looper controls (e.g., loop length, speed, overdub) as well as a toggle UNLOOP to begin the transformation process. With the UNLOOP toggle enabled, the contents of the current buffer are immediately sent to a gradio[6] API server equipped with VampNet, which performs a micro-inpainting[7] transformation on the input buffer. The generated buffer is then sent back to the Max patch, which cues the generated buffer to replace the *wet* buffer once the current loop reaches its end. The micro-inpainting controls (Figure 14.1, top right) allow a user to modify the mask-building parameters described in

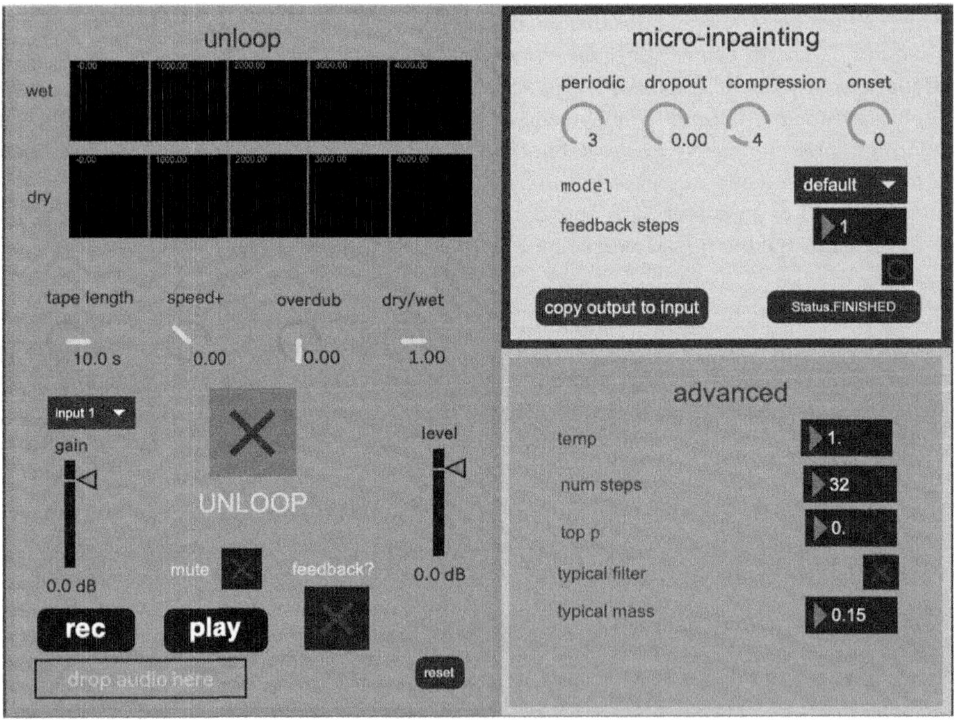

Figure 14.1 *unloop* is a digital musical instrument built with a neural tape loop. It equips a digital looper with a masked acoustic token model so that the loop "never repeats itself": as the recorded loop plays back over and over again, the original contents of the recorded loop are transformed to reflect a generative model's sound palette. The transformation can be perceptible at both the sound-object scale (*timbre transfer*) and at the meso-scale (*rhythm/phrase structure transfer*), depending on the token manipulation controls used.

the section on the micro-inpainting technique. A set of advanced controls (Figure 14.1, bottom right) modifies the model's sampling process, adjusting various aspects surrounding the randomness of each generation. Additionally, one can enable *theseus sampling* mode by enabling the feedback toggle in the left panel of the *unloop* interface. In *theseus sampling* mode, the contents of the generated output buffer are used as input to the model (instead of the input buffer). This means that the model will be recursively feeding into itself, which creates interesting resonance effects as shown in my sound installation *Token Telephone* (described in a later section).

Sound Palette Fine-Tuning

All the acoustic-token manipulation techniques introduced in this chapter are most effective when an artist has the power to fine-tune their generative model to their own sound palette: a bespoke collection of sound recordings for the neural network to model.

Enabling artists to bring their own sound palette to a pretrained[8] generative model like VampNet encourages a small-data mindset (which enables greater human influence) in a generative-AI creative context,[9] while leveraging the expressive power of 2-stage generative models. With VampNet, fine-tuning is completed typically within a day on a single consumer GPU—with most of the learning done within the first 2 or 3 hours—making fine-tuning a model to multiple sound palettes for a single musical project feasible even when only a single GPU is available.

The size of the target sound palette can vary greatly, from 5–10 minutes (fine-tuned on 1 or 2 songs, or a couple of individual recordings) to 2–12 hours of sounds with a specific style or texture. Depending on the size of the sound palette, the model exhibits different behaviors, with more "overfit"[10] models insisting on imposing training material over the inputs more than the less overfit models. I've found that models trained on very small sound palettes (e.g., less than one hour of audio) begin to exhibit overfit model behavior by always insisting upon generating this training material regardless of the input given. This can make it more difficult to perform timbre and structure transformations on an arbitrary input buffer. However, with small sound palettes, the model can function as a *generative sampler* of the small sound palette—creating a sequence of mesostructures from the small sound palette, reconfigured together in nonlinear ways (like an infinite generative jukebox).

Sound palette fine-tuning makes the personalization of large 2-stage generative models accessible to computer musicians who may have access to a single consumer GPU (like a gaming PC). I've included[11] a tool allowing computer-savvy sound artists (i.e., people with basic command-line skills like copying/moving files and launching a Python script) to fine-tune their own VampNet models in the open-source VampNet GitHub repository.

Creative Works

I started making music with generative models not necessarily out of desire, but out of necessity. Even though I've considered myself more of a musician than anything else throughout the majority of my life, I've never had the opportunity to pursue music as a full-time career for a variety of reasons related to my immigration to the US as a Honduran on an engineering student visa. After completing my bachelor's degree in electrical engineering in 2020, I soon enrolled in a computer science PhD program, hoping to get closer to working within the world of music technology. I had a strong urge to make music but was enrolled in a PhD program where the focus was more on developing new algorithms for processing audio with machine learning than on the creative act of making music itself.

I started making music with generative models not because I wanted to explore the "cutting edge" of technology and AI, but simply because I wanted to make music and think about music even during my "day job" as a graduate student. I'm quite thankful—and lucky—to have had a PhD supervisor, Bryan Pardo, who was open and supportive of my desire to pursue research on building AI musical instruments. The development of the transformer model architecture (as well as other advancements, such as masked image modeling techniques) gave me and my collaborator/mentor at the time, Prem Seetharaman, an opportunity to develop masked acoustic token modeling: a new way of creating sounds in which sounds could be transformed and generated in quite interesting (and soon, musical) ways.

Even among the (rightful) skepticism and negative sentiment around generative AI and the unethical data practices of companies like OpenAI and Suno, I became quite interested in figuring out ways that generative models could be used without taking away a sound artist's autonomy, either as musical instruments or as tools for creating sonic material for composition. I thought deeply about the history of technology and music of the past century and hoped to build music-making systems that honored, continued, and built upon the legacy of the artists and engineers who once endured the clunky, uncomfortable experience of making music with a developing piece of technology, such as early magnetic tape or a slow punched-card digital computer.

The following text describes the AI-related creative works I was able to produce over four years of making sense of both the intricacies and affordances of generative models from a technical perspective and the social and aesthetic implications of making music with generative "AI" models in the age of models like ChatGPT.

confluyo yo

confluyo yo (trans. *I converge*) is a *comprovisation* (composed improvisation)[12] for saxophone and *unloop*. In *confluyo yo*, a saxophonist performs short modular motifs called *seeds*, which are looped and transformed live using a neural tape loop system. Through repeated micro-inpainting transformations, the saxophone's timbre and rhythmic structures dematerialize (i.e., lose their semantic meaning), slowly converging into textures derived from generative models of field recordings of Central American birds and industrial machinery.

The piece was recorded in 2023 in collaboration with Honduran saxophonist Michael Pineda and performed at the 2023 ISMIR conference by myself (*unloop*/VampNet) and Bryan Pardo (saxophone). The studio recording of *confluyo yo* is available on YouTube.[13]

Figure 14.2 shows the original saxophone score for *confluyo yo*. The improvisation is structured via seeds, or loose, modular themes that are used as source material for a *neural tape*

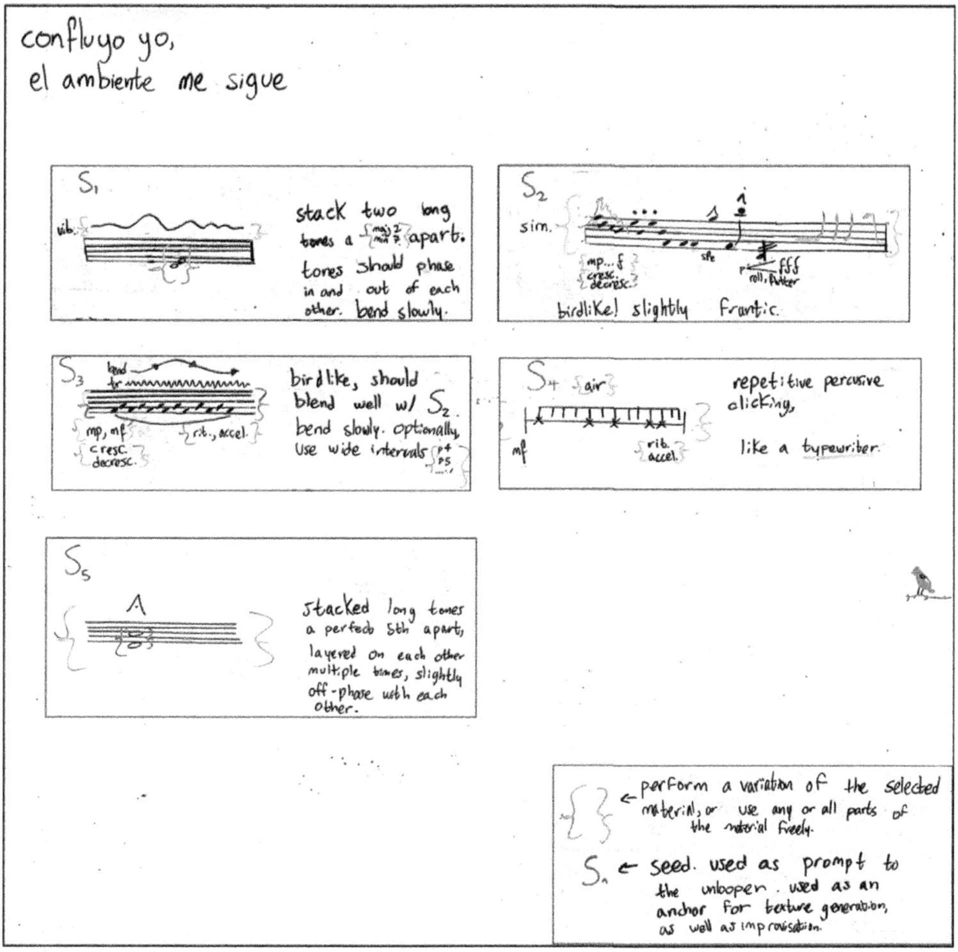

Figure 14.2 Saxophone score for *confluyo yo*. This score outlines 5 seed patterns (S_1 through S_5), which the player can use as initial material for the structure transfer process. During a performance, a musician can play any of these seed patterns into a neural tape loop, which is used to enact a gradual timbre and structure transfer process from the original saxophone gestures to 2 generative models trained on Central American birds and industrial machines, respectively.

loop. Seeds can be chained together into a *sequence* and used as the structural foundation for the improvisation. Seeds S_1, S_4, and S_5 are meant to evoke machine-like sounds from the saxophone, suggesting/simulating/conjuring the sounds of bells, engines, and typewriters from the model trained on the *machines* sound palette, while seeds S_2 and S_3 are meant to evoke bird-like sounds. In a performance of *confluyo yo*, the saxophonist performs one of the seeds, which is recorded into an *unloop*, subsequently triggering a cascade of transformations of the original seed. *unloop* creates transformed versions of the seeds, morphing the sound objects and mesostructures in the original recording to resemble the model's learned representation of Central American birds and industrial machines.

On the Role of the Operator

During a performance, *unloop* is controlled by the "operator": a live performer manipulating both the looper instrument and its underlying generative tape loop. *unloop* inherits the affordances of live looping instruments (like the Tascam Portastudio or the Boss RC-505): one can selectively record material into a buffer of sound, which can then be played back in a loop as repetitive material while the instrumentalist develops new material over the repeated loop. With *unloop*, the performer controlling the looper has an additional role—to steer the generative process occurring in the neural tape, adjusting the micro-inpainting mask used for each transformation of the recorded loop. This allows the operator to evolve the loop in two ways: by recording new material into the loop and by transforming the recorded material with the underlying generative model. The generative model can also be used in an "unconditional" mode, which does not need any audio input, filling the buffer with randomly generated material from the model's sound palette only.

Functionally, the operator mediates the conversation between the instrumentalist and the generative model, shaping the transformations that the sound in the neural tape loop undergoes. From an agency perspective, *unloop* is a mixed-initiative instrument—combining the premeditations and sonic interventions of the instrumentalist, operator, and generative model into a single resulting sonic structure.

While perhaps it would have been a more interesting technical challenge to devise a system capable of fully improvising by itself with the instrumentalist (i.e., forgoing the need of a separate operator), one cannot ignore the social context surrounding AI's role in music. There is widespread concern that AI models are here to replace musicians. Instead, the neural tape loop adds a new performer on stage, one who plays the generative model at the mesostructure level to preserve, morph, or subvert sonic material. This includes the initiative of a new human performer that can leverage the expressive power of generative neural networks on stage.

Hauntology and Embodiment in confluyo yo

From the perspective of sonic hauntology,[14,15] *confluyo yo* is a "summoning" piece, invoking the sonic spectres of both natural and machine-made sounds through a performative ritual of imitation. As the generative model transforms the saxophonist's gestures, it imposes its own temporal and timbral structure on the input sound. This transformation process becomes a form of material agency—the model "plays back" with its learned distribution, surfacing sonic patterns that reflect both the input and the underlying sonic corpus. Traces of the saxophonist's gestures persist, though they become increasingly spectral, as if haunted by a hidden musical entity encoded in the model.

The neural tape loop enabled a speculative form of sonic embodiment, where a performer can construct and inhabit new structures of sound objects through a gestural interaction with the generative model. Rather than controlling an unconditional process or triggering predetermined sonic responses, the performer must develop a musical language that resonates with the model's learned sound palette. This can be thought of as a dialogical engagement with an imagined sonic identity—an uncanny sonic counterpart that transcends traditional notions of instrumental control into an evolving, "haunted" sound ecology.

In an informal conversation during a break between recording sessions, Michael Pineda described his performance philosophy at the moment as an attempt to *become* the model's imagined sonic identity. He reflects:

> With the horn, dropping in, coming from nothing to something—what does that sound like, and how can I become that sound? How can I be *machine*? How can I be this amorphous thing?

This aim to inhabit and embody the neural tape loop's imagined sonic identity illustrates a new kind of instrumental relationship made possible by these generative models. This relationship is not one that is rooted in fine-grained, direct "control" of a sound production mechanism, nor is it one that offers a detached high-level steering of a grand statistical process, but one that facilitates the embodiment of a sonic process through the development of a common sonic language.

Miscommunication! Dealing with Communication Mismatches with a Generative Model

In my practice with *unloop*, I have observed that this sense of embodiment can be undermined or even turned into mild frustration when the model doesn't respond to the artist's intended gestures (e.g., when a user makes a *meow* sound into a model trained on cat vocalizations and the output turns into something other than a cat).

A musical approach to deal with this issue is to spend time developing a common sonic language that is more or less guaranteed to work in a live scenario. For *confluyo yo*, I worked out a set of motifs (seeds) for the performer (Figure 14.2) that were likely to *evoke* certain specific sounds of birds and machines from the model.

A technical approach to this issue could be to leverage explicit control signals instead of masked token prompts, like my own follow-up work Sketch2Sound.[16] Yet, adding explicit conditioning signals may lose the surprise that makes the neural tape loop feel like a larger-than-life process. In my preliminary experiments attempting to compose music with Sketch2Sound, I've found that a model that "always meows" when you ask it to can feel sterile, as this erodes the model's ability to introduce surprise through *welcome* misinterpretations. Even after working on Sketch2Sound, I've found myself opting to compose with VampNet instead. An interesting future experiment could be to retrain Sketch2Sound with both control signals *and* masked acoustic token modeling capabilities, allowing me to leverage both techniques and further balance control and surprise.

Technique: Micro-Inpainting

A neural tape loop can be built with any generative model capable of re-generating sound from a partially corrupted or masked input. However, in order to perform timbral and structural transformations like those in *confluyo yo*, one should be able to configure the input's *unmasked* sections to be very short (a single acoustic token's approximate duration is 40 ms). When contiguous unmasked sections are very short (e.g., one-token wide, a "sparse" prompt), the generative process can be thought of as a form of micro-inpainting—inpainting at the microsound level[17]—where the conditioning given to the generative model consists of short bursts of sound particles that contain only partial information about a sound's structure, timbre, pitch, etc.

Based on the prompting techniques described in VampNet,[18] I briefly introduce these *un*masking techniques, as well as further elaborate on how different configurations of these masks can have different perceptual (and thus musical) effects on an input buffer of sound. These techniques let us control the degree of transformation of the input sound, allowing us to generate a slight variation, a substantial transformation, or perceptually an entirely new sound altogether.

Periodic prompting. Fully masks all tokens, then periodically unmasks timesteps in the token sequence to introduce "prompts" for the generative model. One can choose to leave larger masked portions in the "prompt," allowing the model more room for generation and introducing new sonic material. For a well-trained model (i.e., a model fine-tuned on a sufficiently large sound palette, anecdotally 1 to 2 hours for a unitimbral distribution), one can use a very sparse mask to produce approximate reconstructions of the input audio. With slightly denser masks (i.e., masking out more tokens), one can produce a transformation at the *sound-object*[19] time scale (i.e., timbre transfer), morphing the perceptual identity of individual sound objects toward the sound distribution of the trained model. With very dense masks (e.g., when upward of 90% of all tokens are masked), the model begins to exhibit generative behaviors at the *meso*[20] time scale, introducing new sound objects into the acoustic token buffer and altering the rhythmic structure. I refer to this perceptual process as *structure transfer*, since it results in a transformation of both timbre and rhythmic structure, altering the sonic mesostructures of the original input.

Dropout masking. This technique is like *periodic prompting*, but timesteps are masked randomly instead of periodically, which can be useful for leaving larger chunks of space fully masked, where the model can introduce new sound events.

Onset-based prompting. Like VampNet, we can also leverage information about the input audio (like sound event onsets) to construct sonically informed masks. Once all of the timesteps that contain onsets have been identified, all of the tokens located at timesteps with a predicted onset (as well as the surrounding ones, dictated by an onset mask width parameter) will be *un*masked, ensuring that all of the predicted note onsets remain consistent in the generated output.

Micro-inpainting is the primary *performance-time* technique used to play with a neural tape loop: a sound loop can be recorded, micro-inpainted, and played back during a live performance or sound installation, as shown in the section titled "Creative Works." All the other techniques that follow (*theseus sampling* and *generative time stretching*) make use of micro-inpainting.

world of mouth

world of mouth is an 8-channel fixed media composition built entirely from the gestural interplay between my own voice and a neural tape loop.

In this piece, the vocal gesture was the primary interface for sculpting sound objects and their phrase structures, using them as input material for a set of neural tape loops trained on Central American birds, industrial machines, percussion instruments, and other miscellaneous environmental sounds. The goal of *world of mouth* was to explore the extent to which vocal performance (through improvised gestures, rhythm, and articulation) could serve as an expressive communication mechanism between my own musical intentions and a generative sound process.

The form of *world of mouth* consists of several "sound worlds," or imagined spatial sonic ecologies. Each of these is built from a separate improvised recording of vocal gestures, which is used as the primary source of phrase structure in the composition. The structure of each sound world is given by the shaping vocal technique (e.g., beatboxing, tongue clicking, chewing sounds, fluttery vocal chirps, singing) as well as the neural tape loop's underlying sound palette, which "bites back," imposing its own rhythms and mesostructures into the composed world.

world of mouth premiered at the Experimental Sound Studio,[21] Chicago, Illinois in February 2024, during the first installment of the Chicago Creative Machines series.[22] It was also featured at the UNPOP multichannel listening environment at Burning Man 2024.[23] A binaural recording of *world of mouth* is available on Bandcamp.[24]

The Voice as the Interface

When the sound transformation techniques inherent to the neural tape loop are combined with a sound artist's voice as input, the neural tape loop facilitates a form of voice-to-sound transformation. With this approach, vocal gestures serve not just as sound objects but as gestures that can then be reinterpreted through a neural tape loop's learned distribution. The result is a metamorphic transformation in which vocal utterances are reshaped into new timbres, rhythms, and structures that reflect the model's underlying sound palette.

My work with *world of mouth* emerged from an interest in Trevor Wishart's work *Vox 5*, which is based on creating sound *metamorphoses* between vocal sounds and nonhuman sounds through extended vocal techniques. Wishart writes of his composition: "The primary aural focus of Vox-5 is a (super)human voice that metamorphoses into many recognizable sonic images, such as the sounds of crowds, bees, a horse, or bells."[25]

While Wishart had to meticulously select target recordings, precisely align them with a vocal utterance, and painstakingly perform manual transformations using phase vocoder software, the neural tape loop substantially simplifies this process. Instead of manually sourcing, aligning, and interpolating specific sounds, the artist only needs to provide a vocal recording and a target sound palette. The neural tape loop performs the transformation without a specific target recording or manual alignment, allowing the user to explore and refine the transformation intuitively through masked prompts.

Technique: Generative Time Stretching

Masked acoustic token models allow us to time-stretch a piece of audio with an "opinionated," generative behavior that stretches the durations of sound objects in a sequence while changing the timbral properties of these sound objects according to the model's sound palette. This time-stretching technique, especially when applied at extreme time-stretching factors of n (like 5, 8, 10, 15, 20), begins to exhibit generative behaviors: the training material of the model begins to emerge from the masked spaces in between the original sound events. The aesthetic result is not simply a slower version of the original sound. Instead, the model begins to generate new sound events in the blank spaces introduced by the masked tokens, changing the identity of the input sound from the source audio to the model's sound palette, all while preserving the grand rhythmic structure of the stretched audio.

See Figure 14.3 for an illustration of the generative time-stretching technique. To time-stretch a piece of audio with a neural tape loop by an integer factor n, we can insert $n - 1$ mask tokens in between every individual token of an input token buffer. For example, to time-stretch

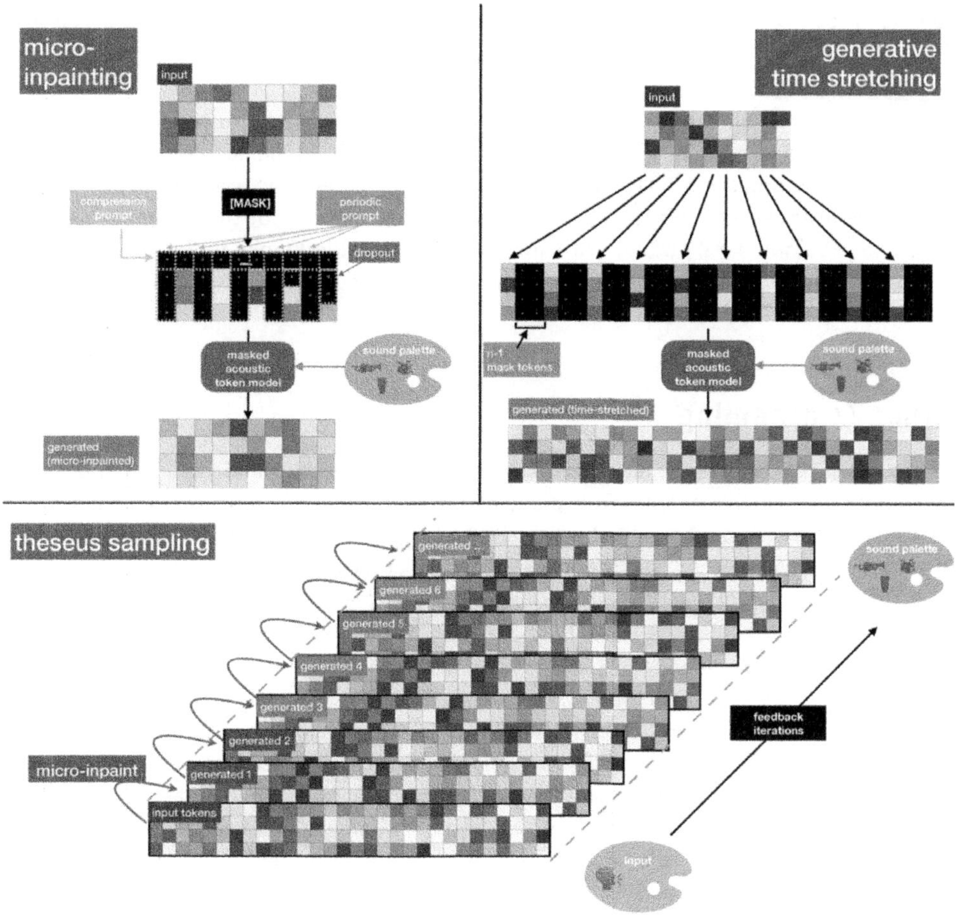

Figure 14.3 Token-manipulation-based neural tape loop techniques. The techniques shown are (top left) micro-inpainting, (top right) generative time stretching, and (bottom) *theseus sampling*.

a sound by a factor $n = 3$, we must insert $3 - 1 = 2$ mask tokens in between every token in the input sequence. This lengthens the input token sequence to $n - 1$ times its original length, effectively decoding the original acoustic tokens at a rate given by $1/n$.

An example of the generative time-stretching technique can be heard in *world of mouth*. The third section of the piece (1:35–3:38) was entirely constructed from a single-source recording of sounds made by clicking my tongue. Before this tongue-clicking recording was used as material for the neural tape loop, it was sped up by a factor of two (2x) using playback-rate shifting, resulting in the fast, clicking pseudo-melody heard at 1:35.

The source excerpt of tongue-clicking noises was generatively time-stretched at different factors (3x, 5x, 10x) with different sound palettes trained on "machines" and "percussion" sounds. These generatively stretched sounds were then edited, layered, and mixed in a DAW, resulting in the second section of the piece.

One may hear how the tongue clicks dematerialize into sounds that resemble hand percussion instruments (like bongos and congas at 2:09), industrial machines (like a cash register at 2:33), or marimbas (at 2:41). The aim was to create sounds whose perceptual identity lies between those of tongue clicks and the training material of the generative model, which have unique aesthetic qualities that are only possible thanks to the affordances of masked acoustic generative models, like the "guttural woodblock rolls" that can be heard at 2:18.

living // dreaming

living // dreaming is my first musical work with a generative model, and the only unpublished piece referenced in this chapter. This piece deserves mention because it was the first time I attempted a creative project with the neural tape loop, and it led to my accidental discovery of *theseus sampling*—the token feedback technique used in *Token Telephone* and its corresponding aesthetic capabilities. A recording of *living // dreaming* is available on YouTube.[26]

This feedback technique emerged as a result of a technical implementation bug while working on an early version of *unloop* for the creative work that would later become *living // dreaming*. While working on *unloop* for VampNet, I accidentally set up the looper so that the generated audio would overwrite the original input audio buffer. This meant that each subsequent model generation would use the previous generation as input, enacting a recursive sound transformation process with VampNet. Though I originally dismissed it as a bug that would only lead to sounds that were "more distorted than they had to be," I was surprised to find out that, after a certain number of these recursive transformations, larger structural changes became perceivable in the generated loop.

When this recursive transformation process was left to its own devices, I observed that an input chaotic drum beat processed with the neural tape loop in recursive form would slowly turn into a coherent drum beat, then a hip-hop beat with garbled lyrics, and finally into a quiet, passive texture of a sustained piano chord—what I imagine would be a "low-entropy" point in the generative model's learned distribution, a place of rest. I became quite interested in this recursive, flattening process that happened when the output of a generative model was fed back into itself, and so I further developed *theseus sampling* as a technique for sound transformation with VampNet. *Theseus sampling* then became instrumental in making my other neural-network-based creative works, like *world of mouth* and *Token Telephone*.

What was originally an implementation error while working on a musical composition later became a new technique for playing with a neural tape loop. After discovering the *theseus sampling* phenomenon, I modified the user interface to make it possible to control whether to apply VampNet in *feedforward* (*living*, i.e., non-recursive micro-inpainting) or *feedback* (*dreaming*, i.e., recursive micro-inpainting or *theseus sampling*). This allowed me to take an input sound like a chaotic drum beat (i.e., *nightmare fuel*) and playfully transform it in both feedforward (*living*) and feedback (*dreaming*) modes—creating superficial variations as well as "washing out" the original sound into the generative model's resonant modes.

Token Telephone: *Acoustic Token Feedback as a Gradual Process*

Token Telephone is a quadraphonic interactive sound installation created in collaboration with sound artist Stephan Moore. In *Token Telephone*, participants enter a space equipped with a microphone and a quartet of generative sound neural networks, each represented by a loudspeaker (Figure 14.4). When a participant vocalizes into the microphone, their utterance is transformed into neural acoustic tokens and played back, initiating a game of telephone between the neural networks. Each network encodes, processes, and reconstructs the sound, distorting the original utterance into new textures guided by the network's training data. The newly reconfigured sound is then passed to the next network/loudspeaker in a clockwise direction, and the process repeats. The sound produced by the fourth network is passed back to the first network in the cycle, creating a feedback loop in which the original utterance incrementally loses all of its original characteristics and disintegrates into textures that reflect the inherent biases of the generative models in play. In time, the resonant properties of the processes are revealed in front of the participant. The name *Token Telephone* is a reference to the children's game of telephone, where a whispered message is passed from person to person, gradually mutating the original message as small mishearings accumulate. *Token Telephone* illuminates the gradual formation of "hallucinations" through the iterative

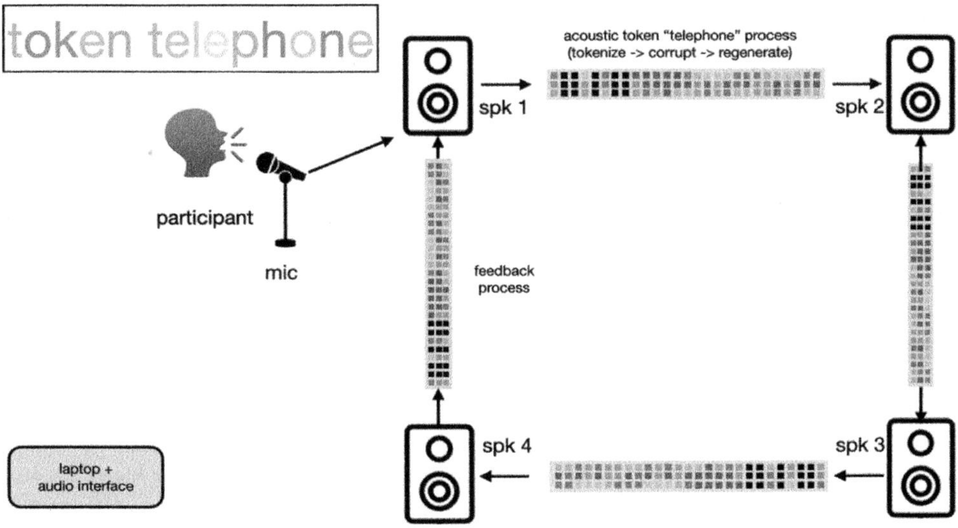

Figure 14.4 *Token Telephone* installation diagram.

processing and reprocessing of a sound with a generative model, reflecting the biases introduced by the model's understanding of sound objects, as well as the data that was provided to it.

The work was exhibited at the 2024 NIME conference in Utrecht, Netherlands. A teaser video for *Token Telephone* is available on YouTube.[27]

Technique: theseus sampling

Micro-inpainting is capable of performing sound-object and meso-level transformations from the input sound to the model's sound palette. However, when very dense masks are used, the output sound may be too different from the original sound in terms of mesostructure, which can lead to the listener feeling as if there is a discontinuity or a lack of correspondence between the input and output sound. To alleviate this perceptual discontinuity, I propose a method called *theseus sampling*, which performs sound-object and meso-level transformations by applying micro-inpainting to an acoustic buffer multiple times in an iterative, feedback manner. With *theseus sampling*, one can create larger meso-level transformations by applying sparser masks over multiple feedback steps. By gradually replacing segments of an input signal across multiple passes, *theseus sampling* allows the model to retain the broad temporal shape of a sound while continuously rewriting its local content. This allows the sound artist to craft transformations that range from subtle variations to radical reconfigurations. This iterative process where small parts of a whole are all slowly replaced is reminiscent of the Ship of Theseus paradox, hence the name *theseus sampling*.

Token Telephone leverages *theseus sampling* to facilitate this feedback generative process in a live interactive installation setting. I use a schedule of different micro-inpainting masks to carry out the gradual sound transformation: early iterations of the *theseus sampling* process use micro-inpainting masks with fewer mask tokens, preserving more of the input, while later iterations increase the amount of masking, allowing the model to create larger structural metamorphoses from the input sound to the model's underlying resonances.

Conceptually, this piece is inspired by Alvin Lucier's *I Am Sitting in a Room* (1969). Through clever tape manipulation, Lucier was able to imprint the acoustics of the room itself onto his original utterance, resulting in one of the most important pieces of process-based experimental music in the twentieth century. The work also bears resemblance to sonic hauntologist William Basinski's *The Disintegration Loops* (2002), where the physical decay of a repeating loop of magnetic tape becomes the core musical process.

While minimalist in structure, *Token Telephone* does not rely on external control or formal development. Instead, it reveals its form through the emergent behavior of a generative process, situated in a feedback loop with a generative agent. This recursive structure also offers a quiet critique of contemporary generative models: these systems are not neutral but shaped by the data they are trained on. By allowing them to "speak" for long enough, we hear what they want to say the most.

Compositional Guideline: Alternate Realities Spatialize Well

A "spiritual predecessor" to *Token Telephone* worth mentioning here is *salad bowl*, another collaboration with Stephan Moore. The premise of *salad bowl* was similar to that of *Token Telephone*—participants making sounds into a microphone, which records the sounds and plays them back in a loop while a generative micro-inpainting process transforms them.

Stephan and I exhibited *salad bowl* at the NeurIPS 2023 Creative AI Workshop in New Orleans, Louisiana. Due to limitations encountered at the venue, we had to set up *salad bowl* as a headphones-only installation. Out of concern for creating an appropriate stereo image for the participants, I decided to allow two participants to play with a separate *salad bowl* at the same time. Both (completely independent) transformation processes were then played back to both participants, panned hard left and right in the participants' headphones. In retrospect, mixing two independent transformation processes into the participants' headphones may have created an overloaded listening environment, making it harder for the participants to recognize the pattern transformation process from their voice to the model's sound palette. Before I could design another sound installation for VampNet, I had the compositional challenge of finding a way to spatialize a generative model that creates rich and noisy monophonic textures.

For my next sound installation (*Token Telephone*), I decided to retry the concept of an interactive voice-to-sound palette transformation process—this time without the two independent parallel streams used in *salad bowl* to create a spatial image. Instead, to spatialize the transformation process, we can play previous iterations of this same process in different speakers, moving each iteration down a speaker as new iterations come in, round-robin style. These *alternate realities* (generative variations of a sound) tend to sound very similar, so playing them at the same time from different speakers creates the illusion of a rich pseudo-stereo image. In regions where two generative iterations are less similar to each other, this technique can create a contrasting texture on all channels, which in turn may also create an interesting spatial structure within itself. For NIME 2024, Stephan and I decided to explore this concept in a quadraphonic format, each speaker playing *alternate realities* of an infinitely generating voice transformation process.

The quadraphonic setup created a rich spatial image for participants to experience. A quadrilateral of speakers also created an enclosed space where participants could be surrounded by the generative sound process, which made the piece feel more situated in a participant's physical space than in a *salad bowl*. Stephan and I put four chairs at the center of the room and let participants sit and listen to their sounds transform after recording into a microphone.

Conclusion

Not all generative models are made to function as a commercial endless spigot of "human-sounding" AI-generated slop—which we've already seen invasively and slowly seep into our streaming services.[28] This kind of music alienates our musical communities and weakens the connections between human musicians and human listeners by replacing musicians with an abundance of (de)personalized, algorithmically generated music.

The neural tape loop is a generative musical meta-instrument embedded in the lineage of experimental music, computer music, and human–AI co-creation systems. Through practice-based research, I've shown that masked acoustic token models, when situated in a rich musical ecology, afford new embodied and expressive musical techniques that go beyond the typical consumer-facing use cases envisioned by commercial AI product developers. I described how being engaged in a prolonged creative practice with generative models brought about accidental findings of new techniques for manipulating and spatializing generative sounds, design guidelines for co-creative AI interfaces, and an interaction philosophy that led to a significant contribution in the field of generative modeling for audio.

If you (the reader) are a musician encountering generative modeling systems in depth for the first time, I hope this chapter has shown that generative models can allow for new, unique, and compelling ways of interacting with sound. If you are a researcher working on a co-creative AI music-making system, I hope this work inspires you not just to evaluate your systems by benchmarking output quality, but to actively engage in a lived musical practice with your system.

Notes

1 Flores García et al., "VampNet."
2 Fiebrink, Trueman, and Cook, "A Meta-Instrument."
3 Small, *Musicking*.
4 Flores García et al., "VampNet."
5 Max (also known as Max/MSP) is a visual programming language, commonly used for creating interactive music systems and compositions.
6 Gradio is a Python library for creating interactive web demos and APIs for machine learning apps. See Abid et al., "Gradio."
7 Micro-inpainting is a way of transforming sounds with a MATM where small bits and pieces of a sound are replaced with generated ones to produce controlled yet noticeable changes to the timbral or temporal structure of the sound.
8 The dataset used to train VampNet was collected by me during the months of September and October 2023, for research purposes at the Interactive Audio Lab. The dataset contains music from approximately 206,000 artists across approximately 58,000 genres. A list of genres was copied from the Echo Nest's Every Noise at Once genre map. This list of genres was used to collect

Spotify API metadata (no audio) for 797,000 tracks. The audio for each track was then downloaded using the open-source tool *spotdl*, which uses the collected Spotify track IDs to find a corresponding YouTube video and download the track's corresponding MP3 recording. Admittedly, the data used to train the VampNet model contains copyrighted recordings. It's worth noting that this data was acquired (and is used) for the purpose of academic research only. Scraping copyrighted data to train generative models can be extremely harmful and have negative ethical consequences when said data (or resulting models) are used for commercial purposes. Members of my lab (including myself) have taken several measures (both systematically and interactionally) to ensure that the uses of the data collected pose more benefits than harmful risks for the musicians and sound artists at stake. For more information, see section 2.4.1, "Ethical Consideration Surrounding VampNet," in my dissertation, "The Neural Tape Loop."

9 Vigliensoni, Perry, and Fiebrink, "A Small-Data Mindset."

10 Here, a more "overfit" model will produce audio that perceptually sounds like recombinations of the model's training data, more akin to a traditional sampler.

11 Flores García, *VampNet.*

12 Dudas, "Comprovisation."

13 Flores García, *confluyo yo.*

14 Sonic hauntology is an artistic movement of the 2000s that included artists such as The Advisory Circle, William Basinski, and The Caretaker, as well as the Ghost Box record label. Sonic hauntologists employed techniques like mixing, collaging, and manipulating sounds and textures evocative of the mid-twentieth century, often transforming these into eerie, dream-like sonic landscapes.

15 Privato and Magnusson, "Querying the Ghost."

16 Flores García et al., "Sketch2Sound."

17 Refer to Curtis Roads's *Microsound* for an overview of the time scales of music.

18 Flores García et al., "VampNet."

19 Roads, *Microsound.*

20 Roads, *Microsound.*

21 *Experimental Sound Studio.*

22 Jones, *Chicago Creative Machines.*

23 *Unpopular Music.*

24 Flores García, *world of help_outlinemouth.*

25 Wishart, "The Composition of 'Vox-5.'"

26 Flores García, *living // dreaming.*

27 Flores García, *Token Telephone.*

28 Dwyer, "This Musician Was Getting Millions of Streams."

Bibliography

Abid, Abubakar, Ali Abdalla, Ali Abid, Dawood Khan, Abdulrahman Alfozan, and James Zou. "Gradio: Hassle-Free Sharing and Testing of ML Models in the Wild." Preprint, submitted June 6, 2019. arXiv:1906.02569. https://arxiv.org/abs/1906.02569.

Cycling '74. *Max.* Accessed January 18, 2026. https://cycling74.com/products/max.

Dudas, Richard. "'Comprovisation': The Various Facets of Composed Improvisation within Interactive Performance Systems." *Leonardo Music Journal* 20 (2010): 29–31. https://doi.org/10.1162/LMJ_a_00009.

Dwyer, Michael. "This Musician Was Getting Millions of Streams. Then Fake Tracks Appeared under His Name." *Sydney Morning Herald*, May 28, 2025. https://www.smh.com.au/culture/music/this-musician-was-getting-millions-of-streams-then-fake-tracks-appeared-under-his-name-20250526-p5m26n.html.

Experimental Sound Studio. Accessed December 31, 2025. https://ess.org.

Fiebrink, Rebecca, Dan Trueman, and Perry R. Cook. "A Meta-Instrument for Interactive, On-the-Fly Machine Learning." In *Proceedings of the International Conference on New Interfaces for Musical Expression (NIME)*, 280–285. Pittsburgh, PA: NIME, 2009. https://www.nime.org/proceedings/2009/nime2009_280.pdf.

Flores García, Hugo. *confluyo yo, el ambiente me sigue - sequence II*. Featuring Michael Pineda (saxophone). Filmed by Camilla Forte. YouTube video, 2:04. August 14, 2023. https://www.youtube.com/watch?v=mcjf2iKf8Nk.

Flores García, Hugo. *living // dreaming*. YouTube video, 3:47. May 18, 2023. https://www.youtube.com/watch?v=KnBJlgaPZCk.

Flores García, Hugo. "The Neural Tape Loop: Controllable and Expressive Generative Modelling for the Sound Arts." PhD diss., Northeastern University, 2025. https://hugofloresgarcia.art/thesis.pdf.

Flores García, Hugo. *Token Telephone*. YouTube video, 3:28. Featuring Hugo Flores García and Stephan Moore. August 1, 2024. https://www.youtube.com/watch?v=KnBJlgaPZCk.

Flores García, Hugo. *VampNet*. Accessed May 16, 2025. GitHub. https://github.com/hugofloresgarcia/vampnet.

Flores García, Hugo. *World of Mouth (binaural version)*. Track. 2024. Bandcamp, https://hugofloresgarcia.bandcamp.com/track/world-of-mouth-binaural-version.

Flores García, Hugo, Oriol Nieto, Justin Salamon, Bryan Pardo, and Prem Seetharaman. "Sketch2Sound: Controllable Audio Generation via Time-Varying Signals and Sonic Imitations." In *Proceedings of the IEEE International Conference on Acoustics, Speech, and Signal Processing (ICASSP)*. Hyderabad, India: IEEE, 2025.

Flores García, Hugo, Prem Seetharaman, Rithesh Kumar, and Bryan Pardo. "VampNet: Music Generation via Masked Acoustic Token Modeling." In *Proceedings of the International Society for Music Information Retrieval Conference (ISMIR)*. Milan, Italy: ISMIR, 2023.

Jones, Molly. *Chicago Creative Machines*. Accessed November 14, 2025. https://chicagocreativemachines.com.

Meister, Clara, Tiago Pimentel, Gian Wiher, and Ryan Cotterell. "Locally Typical Sampling." *Transactions of the Association for Computational Linguistics* 11 (2023): 102–121.

Privato, Nicola, and Thor Magnusson. "Querying the Ghost: AI Hauntography in NIME." In *Proceedings of the International Conference on New Interfaces for Musical Expression (NIME)*. Utrecht, Netherlands: NIME, 2024.

Roads, Curtis. *Microsound*. Cambridge, MA: MIT Press, 2004.

Small, Christopher. *Musicking: The Meanings of Performing and Listening*. Middletown, CT: Wesleyan University Press, 1998.

Unpopular Music. Accessed December 3, 2025. https://unpopularmusic.camp.

Vigliensoni, Gabriel, Phoenix Perry, and Rebecca Fiebrink. "A Small-Data Mindset for Generative AI Creative Work." In *Generative AI and HCI - CHI 2022 Workshop, online*. New York, NY: ACM, 2022.

Wishart, Trevor. "The Composition of 'Vox-5.'" *Computer Music Journal* 12, no. 4 (1988): 21–27.

15

INTERLUDE VII

Interview with Holly Herndon

Constantin Basica and Julie Zhu

DOI: 10.4324/9781003615873-15

Julie: In your recent exhibition with Mat,[1] *Starmirror* (Figure 15.1),[2] you're speculating that AI can be used to coordinate humans for a greater collective good—that is awesome, and I would just love to hear more about that.

Holly: We've all been dealing with AI for around a decade or so, and it's gone from a niche research area into something everyone has an opinion on. It has been really wild to see the reception and the narratives forming around what this technology is and what it can do. In some senses, it has been disheartening because the discourse is driven by clickbait headlines. This has driven much of the negative sentiment, which hasn't been necessarily productive at a time when these conversations are really crucial.

I'm not a hopeless techno-optimist by any means, but I think it's part of the role of the artist to understand the tools of our time, to understand what's happening civilizationally around us, and then try to propose visions of how things could be implemented in a different way. For my practice, this means that I need to learn how to use the very tools that are being critiqued. We're interested in the idea of the centaur: a human augmenting their capacities with AI agents.

It's remarkable what these machines can do, but I also very much see myself in the loop, in the process. We started working in this area before productized AI was really available, before you could just type in something and then get a pretty output. At that time, you had

Figure 15.1 A view of the *Starmirror* installation, created by Holly Herndon and Mat Dryhurst, featuring Herndon herself. KW Institute for Contemporary Art, Berlin, Germany, 2025.

Photograph by Frank Sperling.

to start at the beginning and decide which model architecture you wanted to use and what your dataset would be. You had to make all of these creative decisions, which informed our practice early on. We saw each step in the model-making process as a moment for artistic intervention, whether it was the creation of the dataset or even the more boring, bureaucratic action of labeling the dataset, which can also be a creative gesture.

With this in mind, we're interested now in how we can use these systems as a way to coordinate people IRL.[3] I think the future of these systems is not us staring at screens and scrolling. One thing that Mat often says, which I love, is: "Scrolling is for bots and strolling is for humans." I really like this idea of finding ways to use these systems to become more social and to bring people together.

With the *Starmirror* exhibition at Kunst-Werke in Berlin, we are prompting people in the space to contribute to the dataset. During the week, visitors can experience the training performances through a multichannel audio installation in the space. And on the weekends, we host training performances with our in-house ensemble that prompts the audience in call-and-response to contribute their voices to the model.

I grew up singing in the church, so that has been a strong reference for me. Our exhibition is not necessarily a religious reenactment of the church, but more of a way of thinking about some of the powerful public moments of expression that I had as a child, going to a place where people could emote and sing and be present together. We see AI as a coordination technology to bring people together.

We also have a *Starmirror* application, which we premiered at the Okayama Art Summit. A few months before the exhibition opened, we released the app, which, in the style of Pokémon GO, invites you to explore the different sites of Okayama City and to take photographs that are then automatically submitted to the public domain and made available for model training. We're invested in having large-scale public domain datasets so that anyone and everyone can train. This is the medium of our time, and we don't want it to be locked down to only a few.

This is where the IP war comes in: copyright. Activists on both sides are taking a hard stance, whereas we find ourselves somewhere in the middle, advocating for an opt-out of training. The idea of opt-in licensing only is, in my view, short-sighted because it could really lock down AI model training to only a few companies that can work hand in hand with the largest rights owners. So we're really excited about contributing to the public domain as a way of avoiding the copyright issue. Our organization, Spawning,[4] released the largest public domain image dataset that's out there: PD12M[5] (updated to PD40M). The *Starmirror* app is actually contributing to that as well by leading people on little adventures around Okayama to add images and fill in the holes of the public domain dataset.

Julie: This may sound like a basic question, but I would love to hear your explanation. What is the core difference between an AI choir trained by a community—such as the one in your projects—and a human choir like the one you sang in on Sundays?

Holly: I think, for me, it's less about trying to compare an AI choir with a human choir, and it's more about just using AI systems as a way to create new work with human choirs. It's also a way for me to be able to combine my own musical archive with someone else's in a way that's generative and interesting. I think we'll probably see these systems become increasingly sophisticated, and I can imagine people being able to ping each other's models and collaborate in that way. At the moment, it's very handcrafted because the tools just aren't there yet. But AI is entirely distinct from working with a human choir. It's a different way to express recorded material, and a different way to compose.

If you're participating in a choir, then you're a choir member. That's one very specific kind of role. I see myself more in the composer's role in this scenario, because our approach isn't to just record random choirs singing random things. Mat and I write music for the choirs to sing for the machine. So it's kind of a strange way to make work, but we're making art specifically for training data. And I think this is something that people kind of have to wrap their heads around. The songs aren't necessarily for human consumption but for machine consumption. It's not like writing concert music—it's writing material for a training set in order to produce a model that will have certain features.

This way of working, factoring in post-generative AI and post-networks, we have been describing as *Protocol Art*.[6] For example, with generative AI image systems, what is interesting is rarely the individual image but the system that one has put in place that could allow for anyone to create infinite images. It's the same with audio. You can create infinite variations, which is really an interesting way to compose, because it's a new kind of counterpoint with yourself where you can just kind of iterate forever by exploring different parts of latent space. By just slightly nudging the material over one way or the other you can have the track sing with itself, or you can conjure up a different Klangfarbe[7] through prompting different areas of the model. Coordinating people to create models with distinct characteristics and allowing them to use those models is a different way of working.

Constantin: Listening to you talk about all these things that you're doing with AI, I wonder: After all these years of working with AI models and datasets involving your voice—has this impacted the way you listen to other people's voices?

Holly: I don't think that working with AI has necessarily changed the way that I listen to other singers. I think I've always had a very keen ear for someone's particular vocal timbre, because I think it's just like a fingerprint. I noticed that Rosalía just released her album,[8] and I think it's subtly an anti-AI album. Not only because she doesn't use any AI (which is very normal), but she also talks about how she learned many different languages to be able to sing it. Singing in different languages is something that AI does, obviously, really well. I thought it's interesting that she trained herself to do that. Just listening to her voice and the microphone technique of the engineers she worked with—getting her breath just perfect—I think it would make a great voice model [*laughs*]. Now that I think of it, maybe it has changed how I listen to voices. Maybe I do listen a little bit more to the microphone placement and things like that, because that's also embedded in the model. It's not just the voice.

Constantin: You've alluded to this dichotomy between AI-phobia and AI-philia. It seems like you and Mat are occupying this space near the center of the spectrum, and much of your work incites dialogue between the poles. You're also advocating this sort of "fair trade AI": developing tools and artworks that engage communities. But, in the real world, fair trade practices are always in competition with more exploitative systems. So there's a personal cost when an artist wants to adopt a fair system with "data dignity" instead of using a very convenient, cheap, mass-produced AI. How do you see the viability of small-scale, self-trained models in the face of large-scale, ready-made AI?

Holly: I'm not dogmatic about it, and I don't judge people who use plug-and-play systems. It's just not what I choose to do, because I see the making of the model as the artwork. So it wouldn't make sense for me to prompt a Suno model, because that's just not my art practice, and they also don't give you direct access to the model itself, so you are limited in experimentation. But if some teenager in the suburbs finds a way to get a crazy new genre out of these plug-and-play systems, more power to them. I think we should let people play.

Part of our practice is showing alternative models of how things could be, and I know that we have the ear of people in positions of power in large AI companies and governments. I know that we've pushed the needle on certain decisions. I don't think that Mat and I from our art studio in Berlin are going to revolutionize the AI field in a competition with a trillion-dollar industry. We're realistic about that. I do think that we have had a pretty big impact considering.

A lot of the fears that people have about AI are fears about the current internet, or fears about the current state of the music industry. You were saying, Julie, that many of your students don't realize that they are already being influenced by algorithmic decisions for what they should listen to. That's also affecting how artists are writing music, and how the album has become decontextualized. But all this stuff already happened. The old music industry has imploded. Experimental musicians cannot live off album sales anymore. That happened in my lifetime, and it's very dramatic. Things have shifted and people are very unhappy about it. And after seeing that happen, here comes the next big shift. Is it going to get even worse? What I really think people are upset about is how unsustainable most creative practices are now, and how social media is toxic, and how the "creative economy" can be unfair. I'm not saying that AI solves those things, but I don't know that it makes things worse when creative industries are long overdue a reckoning.

Julie: A few years ago, I was talking to someone about the possibility of artists putting out a model of their album in addition to the actual record. I hated the idea because then there wouldn't be a collective cultural object. What's your take on this?

Holly: I think it can be both, though. I think that, in a world of infinite media, we're going to need curation. Especially with process-based computer music, a lot of it is just curation, and this is the best part. Sometimes I'll let a system run for a long time, whether AI or simply algorithmic, and will then curate the best part for the listener to hear, because most people don't want to listen to thirty hours of my machine recording itself. So we're going to need a lot of curation and a lot of artistic decision-making, because there will be an infinite deluge of media. It's more media than we could ever consume. So I don't think that *curation* goes away.

I also agree with your point: pop music is a kind of promise that we're listening together, experiencing things together ... We know when the bridge is coming, when the chorus is coming, and we can all put our hands up at the same time or whatever. It's a collective experience, for sure, and that's important. But you can also have that in parallel with the composer releasing an AI model and allowing fandoms to be able to explore the model in their own way and co-create with the artist. They could complement each other.

Julie: Are there emerging AI tools or platforms or social experiments that excite you and make you curious about what's coming next? Something you're working on next?

Holly: I would say *novelty search* is one of them—definitely worth a deep dive. We just released a new project *Kinder Scout*[9] at Art Basel that is based on novelty search. This is a particular approach to AI that is more open-ended. If you asked John Chowning how he came up with FM synthesis, he would probably say something like, "I had a lot of training, then I just followed my intuition, and I allowed myself to kind of explore and wander." As a crude analogy, this is similar to novelty search in the AI realm. Ken Stanley[10] has been doing a lot of interesting research in this area for years.

We've always wanted to explore this idea, so we made *Kinder Scout*, and we invited our developer collaborators at Counterpoint to go on a hike equipped with multiple cameras. They then feed the input imagery from their hike to AI agents as a starting point for generating images, looking for the most interesting frame, iterating on responses, and then arguing among themselves over which images are more novel. We're interested in combining real-world interactions with AI agents and human collaborators—that's where we find the work the most interesting at the moment.

I would love to do a similar novelty search in the audio realm. I'm unclear even now how to approach that at this moment; the image space is further ahead of the audio space. Back in the day, we were actually turning music into spectrograms, and then doing an image style transfer, and then transferring it back to audio. It obviously sounded like garbage because with each step you lose so much fidelity, but this was before I had access to timbre transfer.

I'm also looking forward to things being a bit more multimodal. I feel like everything's so siloed right now; it would be great if models were more flexible in that regard.

And I'm also excited about building on the idea of prompting humans in the real world. What does that look like? How can we use these tools to have social moments rather than atomized internet moments?

Julie: You mentioned your toddler going with you to Art Basel. I wonder, has parenthood influenced the way you create datasets that can be trained on? Have you seen any parallels between your family life and your thinking about AI?

Holly: Yeah, it's funny ... when we first started working with AI back in the day, we were calling *Spawn* our "AI baby." Then we had a real baby and I was like, "Oh my God, that's such a flawed metaphor." It's so different, so we don't use that metaphor anymore. But it is interesting to see parallels between how machines and little humans learn. The one thing that's just really clear is that it's very natural for him. I often make him little images—he's really into any kind of vehicle—and he'll ask for a specific kind of car, like a pink concrete mixer or something like that. And I'll make him an image, and then I'll go into a plug-and-play music software and write him a song that's like, "We love pink concrete mixers," you know? It's whatever, a goofy pop song about concrete mixers. And he thinks that media is just generated. He thinks: "Oh, I want media to be this, therefore media should be this." And that's a fundamentally different understanding of how media is from how I grew up consuming media. It was already kind of radical that you can have two-way communication streams. It used to just be one way, and then two-way. And now, for him, the concrete mixer truck *should* be pink—"I said it should be pink." Okay, let's go back, let's make it pink. You know what I mean? For him, that's just natural, just normal.

Julie: I am curious: You have been on this "platform" for a while and, since *Proto*, AI has sort of been a vehicle for you. Do you ever feel that it's constraining, that you can't keep up with all the things that you have to do, and maybe all you want to do is ... sing in the Alps?

Holly: [*Laughs.*] Am I sick of AI—is that what you're asking? I definitely don't want to sing in the Alps. But of course I get sick of AI, and I definitely get typecast, and I can't keep up with everything, because it's too fast. I mean, we were working in this field far before most people thought it was interesting, and I'm so glad that we did that because we really had a lot of time to develop our outlook and our approach to this thing. I didn't know that it was going to become such a huge deal, but it did.

When it really started to take off, it was right after I had given birth, so I had journalists pinging me for hot takes on this, that, and the other. And I just didn't answer anything. I just couldn't. I was thinking: "The world is silly and I just want to stare at this beautiful baby." If you have kids, there's a love-bomb period of several months where you just want to snuggle all the time. So that was a really weird thing, and the whole world woke up to this thing that I had been working on for years—right at a time when I didn't want to talk to anyone.

But now that he's almost three, we've been doing big exhibitions on the topic. And yeah, of course sometimes we get sick of it, or we think, "Oh, should we do this or do that?" But it still is just really interesting, actually, and it is really consequential.

I think that, right now, AI art feels separate, kind of like internet art in the '90s or post-internet art of the aughts. But now all art happens with an awareness of the internet. All art is post-internet art now, and I think all art will just be *post-AI art* in some way. But right now, as a society, we're just grappling with some pretty big questions around what this means for the role of the artist. So, yeah, I'm not abandoning it anytime soon.

Learn more about Holly Herndon and her work with Mat Dryhurst at https://herndondryhurst.studio

Notes

1 Mat Dryhurst is a British artist and researcher based in Berlin. His work explores the aesthetics, politics, ethics, and creative uses of emerging technologies, particularly blockchain technology and artificial intelligence. He is also a co-founder of Spawning, an organization developing tools for artists to control how their work is used in AI training.
2 Herndon and Dryhurst, *Starmirror.*
3 IRL is an abbreviation for "in real life."
4 Herndon and Dryhurst, *Spawning.*
5 Spawning, "PD12M."
6 Herndon and Dryhurst, "Protocol Art."
7 *Klangfarben* (German, pl.): tone colors or instrumental timbres.
8 Rosalía, *Lux.*
9 Herndon and Dryhurst, *Kinder Scout.*
10 Kenneth O. Stanley is an American computer scientist known for his work in evolutionary computation and open-endedness in AI.

Bibliography

Herndon, Holly, and Mat Dryhurst. *Spawning.* Accessed December 28, 2025. https://spawning.ai.
Herndon, Holly, and Mat Dryhurst. "Protocol Art." *Engadin Art Talks.* Video. Accessed December 29, 2025. https://engadin-art-talks.ch/en/videos/protocol-art.
Herndon, Holly, and Mat Dryhurst. *Kinder Scout.* Exhibition documentation. *Fellowship.* Accessed December 28, 2025. https://fellowship.xyz/exhibition/kinder-scout-by-holly-herndon-mat-dryhurst.
Herndon, Holly, and Mat Dryhurst. *Starmirror.* Exhibition documentation. *KW Institute for Contemporary Art.* Accessed December 28, 2026. https://www.kw-berlin.de/en/exhibitions/holly-herndon-and-mat-dryhurst-starmirror.
Kenneth O. Stanley. Accessed December 28, 2025. https://www.kenstanley.net.
"Klangfarbe." *Wiktionary.* Accessed November 1, 2025. https://en.wiktionary.org/wiki/Klangfarbe.
"Mat Dryhurst." *Wikipedia.* Accessed February 17, 2026. https://en.wikipedia.org/wiki/Mat_Dryhurst.
Rosalía. *Lux.* Columbia Records, 2025.
Spawning. "PD12M". *Hugging Face.* Accessed December 28, 2025. https://huggingface.co/datasets/Spawning/PD12M.

16

MOVEMENT VII

Pandora's Dream: Building a Software Framework for AI-Mediated Live Music Practice

Celeste Betancur Gutiérrez

DOI: 10.4324/9781003615873-16

The box was sitting there, in front of my eyes, with the promise of the unknown, the promise of infinite possibilities, fire and knowledge, pain and tragedy … Who knows, maybe just a sleeping (or dead) cat that was abandoned there by a physicist-philosopher and his uncertainties in a not-so-distant future.

Introduction

Instructions are simple:
just keep the box for you and never open it.

Eighteen of the most talented string players in the world are assembled on the stage, awaiting the audience's silence to begin the piece. Everything seems normal, and the concert hall is prepared to receive the sounds emerging from the violins, violas, cellos, and double basses.

You have some preconception about how this ritual should work. You look at the music stands to glance at the score, and you see a blank screen. That must be an error, so you look at another music stand, and the blank page is also there. Maybe it's just a digital score waiting to be triggered, so you wait. Someone who appears to be the conductor delivers some gestures to the orchestra and then starts typing on her own computer—*that should be the trigger*, you think—and then, yes, images start appearing on the screens. But something is not normal: it seems like this is not a conventional score. And it also seems like, with every gesture of the conductor (*is she a conductor or …?*), the score updates instantaneously and renders differently on each screen.

Each musician is playing a different gesture, but somehow there is some coherence in what they are doing, and the concert hall resonates in a very particular way. You need to understand what is going on, so you quickly read the program notes: "The piece is always new … The score itself is being generated live …"

The text above is just a collection of thoughts that I received from multiple people after the performance of my piece *A Blank Page* at MIT's Thomas Tull Concert Hall on the night of the premiere of the fourth iteration. Yes, I was the conductor—*was I?*—but also the composer, the person in charge of transcribing and delivering the scores in real time to each musician in the orchestra, and the software engineer for a part of the technical setup (some other parts were handled by my colleague Luna Valentin, who worked on the live virtual acoustics,[1] designing custom-made impulse responses and automations on spatial position and reverberation mix).

Maybe it all looked simple from the audience's perspective—gestures appeared on a blank page—but this performance needed substantial computational power, statistical models, audio analysis, information retrieval, and many other technologies that were invisible to the attendees. What they experienced as a fluid and perhaps even magical performance was, in reality, the result of intricate systems working in real time: a network of carefully assembled technologies operating beneath the surface and orchestrated by a human. In this chapter, I will unpack these layers, revealing the technical, artistic, and conceptual frameworks that made this approach possible and reflecting on how such a performance challenges our understanding of the role of these technologies in live computer music practices.

Pandora's Dream is a versatile live-coding environment equipped with its own code editor and interactive interpreters for multiple programming languages. Already a capable system from this perspective, it also supports GPU-based graphics and offers built-in functionality for video mapping. AI and machine learning techniques are integrated through ChAI[2] and RapidLib,[3] expanding its computational potential. Beyond its technical features, Pandora's Dream functions as an experimental playground: audio synthesis and video graphics can be developed and executed in parallel across multiple programming paradigms. These languages can share memory access—variables, calculations, audio and video frames—enabling a truly multiparadigm workflow that encourages exploration across domains in real time without the need to implement any network communication.

In its current state of development, Pandora's Dream is a modular and extensible framework written in C++. From a user-interface perspective, it offers a minimal environment consisting of text buffers intentionally designed without additional buttons or graphical menus. This decision was shaped both by my background in live coding and by an aesthetic choice: I wanted all interaction to be perceived as an ongoing conversation between coder and machine. Despite its apparent simplicity, the system is powerful, flexible, and capable of supporting a wide range of artistic and computational tasks, serving as a host for various tools, programming languages, and design paradigms.

Before I explain the system and its implementation in more detail, I will first present some of my inspiration sources and references, as I believe they offer important context and may reveal insights that might otherwise go unnoticed.

Inspiration and Connections

> *A Voyager ... That could be the only way to start this uncertain pilgrimage between our machines and us, the holders of Prometheus's heritage.*

I am aware that the artists and works I mention here are not the only existing ones, and that in doing so I am overlooking other important thinkers and developers (such as David Zicarelli, Joel Chadabe, John Offenhartz, and Antony Widoff). However, by some combination of chance and circumstance, the figures mentioned here have had the most direct influence on the development of Pandora's Dream.

George Lewis, Voyager

"*Voyager* is a nonhierarchical, interactive musical environment that privileges improvisation." This is how George Lewis began to describe *Voyager* in his paper "Too Many Notes: Complexity, and Culture in *Voyager*," published in the *Leonardo Music Journal*. But even more compelling is what comes next—what has continued to inspire and obsess me about this work and Lewis's broader ideas: a system that embraces "not only technological or music-theoretical interests but philosophical, political, cultural, and social concerns as well."[4]

George Lewis composed *Voyager* and designed the system between 1985 and 1987, without knowing that it would become one of his most performed pieces—and one of the most influential exercises in the history of computer music. Lewis created a machine that could improvise by listening to music, but more importantly, he gave it agency to contribute or impose its own ideas.

Voyager's influence has deeply shaped my approach to designing and implementing musical systems, particularly in how I understand and pursue machine autonomy. My stance on machine agency—developed through improvisatory interaction with human performers—emerges directly from *Voyager*'s model, where the system is not merely reactive but actively co-creative. These ideas continue to inform the way I structure interactions, emphasizing mutual responsiveness and the potential for machines to assert their own musical voice within collaborative contexts.

In the particular case of Pandora's Dream, I have adopted a clear attitude: machine autonomy is not just a product of internal processes but also something that emerges through improvisatory interaction with human performers and the characteristics extracted from the human interactor. My work also explores the instability of established categories—such as composition versus improvisation—and, in my case, expands this complexity to include roles like conductor and performer, blurring the boundaries between them within dynamic, responsive environments.

Ultimately, experiencing a *Voyager* performance—or even just reading about it—pushes me to critique myself and my systems, especially the hierarchical decisions embedded from design to execution. It consistently reveals the complexity of sustaining nonhierarchical structures in human–machine interaction.

May the *Voyager* keep traveling.

Clarence Barlow and Georg Hajdu, Blending Logic with Intuition

I first came across the work of Clarence Barlow and Georg Hajdu by chance, while reading papers on algorithmic systems and statistical approaches to composition. One of the papers mentioned a piece by Barlow—completely unknown to me at the time—called *Pandora*. What a surprise it was when I read Hajdu's brief description of it. In his words: "*Pandora* (1989) took advantage of AUTOBUSK's[5] ability to save generated scores as MIDI files."[6] It felt like an epiphany. At that very moment, I was working on extending the score-following capabilities of my own Pandora by transforming extracted audio features into symbolic data to generate music—an idea borrowed from *Voyager*. The resonance between the two projects (Barlow's and mine), despite being developed decades apart, was both unexpected and deeply inspiring.

Hajdu's MaxScore and DJster, and of course Barlow's AUTOBUSK became immediate reference points for everything I was working on. What resonated most deeply with me was the conceptual framing they offered, particularly the idea of composition as process design rather than as product—emphasized in Hajdu's 2025 ICMC keynote. This perspective fundamentally shifted how I approached my own system, placing emphasis on the generative potential of structure, interaction, and flow rather than on fixed outcomes. Equally transformative was Hajdu's framing of systems as epistemic objects: entities that do not merely execute tasks but actively shape understanding, revealing creative opportunities precisely in the obscure, the undertrained, and the unstable.[7]

This conceptual foundation aligned perfectly with my long-standing obsession with *menacing-sounding* artifacts: glitches, digital errors, feedback loops, and unstable data streams. Far from dismissing them as flaws, I've always seen these elements as portals out of the comfort zone—openings through which unexpected musical and aesthetic possibilities emerge. In this light, the epistemic becomes an expressive tool, a compositional partner capable of disrupting predictability (and my own biases) and inviting new forms of listening and creation. Within Pandora's Dream, this philosophy shapes both the technical framework and musical results: a space where instability is embraced. Coding mistakes become features; audio glitches are stored and reused; and graphical errors get repurposed as shaders or notational gestures. The process is the composition, and the line between intention and accident remains in constant flux.

The gap between computational logic and musical intuition has been bridged by the unknown.

Holly Herndon, Intimate yet Popular, a Personal Journey

PROTO is the third album by Holly Herndon, released in 2019, although I only came across it in 2024. I was listening to music randomly, following my mood and how my emotions responded to each track, skipping songs, and then diving deeper into the work of artists whose pieces struck me the most during that experience. I was immediately captivated by a choir sound that felt distinct and intimate, yet not entirely experimental in the way that I had grown accustomed to after years of attending experimental music concerts. There was something unfamiliar in how the formants and vowels were shaped—something hidden. Intrigued,

I looked up the artist and the album. The piece was created with the help of an *AI baby* (or Spawn, the system behind the vocal processing). My curiosity deepened when I realized that Herndon and I share a certain artistic lineage: Chris Chafe's open-mindedness and encouragement of experimentation—"wherever that might take you," as she explains while interviewed by Angelica Tavella.[8] Chafe served as the director of the Center for Computer Research in Music and Acoustics (CCRMA) during Herndon's time at Stanford and is also currently my PhD advisor.

Music, for me, has always been deeply personal—so intimate that performing my own musical experiments in front of an audience often feels like standing naked before them. Finding a balance between innovation, technological development, and expressivity (or simply between personal experiences and relief) has always been the most difficult task for me. Herndon's *PROTO* revealed a path forward: a practice that is both profoundly intimate and technologically sophisticated—intimate in its use of her own voice (whether by singing or using it as data to train her models) and profound in its lyrics, which delve into deeply personal and vulnerable experiences. Yet it is also entirely permeated by and hybridized with technology: a true cyborg practice. It offered me a new lens through which to view my own artistic journey, one where vulnerability and high-level technical engagement can coexist and blend.

The answer could be singing around "if we listened carefully."[9]

Ben Spatz, Searching for My Own Epistemic Grounding

I found scattered crumbs and traces everywhere, which helped me frame the role of technology in my musical practice, and yet I was still grappling with a persistent question: What was I actually building? Years earlier, I had worked on another project that, in hindsight, held the key to answering that very question. Pandora's Dream was, at its core, not just a piece of software but a *conceptual framework*: a meta-tool. As I described in the *CineVivo* project, "as a concept, it is not a finished tool but an open-source (and open) project that can be enhanced with specific (and multiple) directions, which makes the project as open as it can be"[10]—words that fit completely with the work I was developing for Pandora's Dream.

I eventually realized that I was ready with the technical apparatus and an initial conceptual framework—not because I was building a functional application in the conventional sense but because I was developing a *conceptual infrastructure*, a foundation for further explorations. I was far more drawn to the obscure and the uncertain than to any illusion of resolving algorithmic composition (if that is even something that *needs* to be resolved). My path became a *practice of training myself*: cultivating a method rooted in the unknown, the unstable, and the emergent behaviors hidden in the complexity.

Ben Spatz (introduced to me by composer and teacher Cassandra Miller) provided the philosophical and epistemological framework to explain my posture: a body can embrace complexity and be trained to navigate uncertainty,[11] and this practice is research in the entire sense of the word.

In *What a Body Can Do*, I discovered that research can be approached as the practice of a queer body intervening upon itself through technology. In my case, this means the use of live coding and programming languages to interact in real time with a computer that is not merely a tool but feels almost like an extension of my own mind—a co-creator. This human–machine performance becomes a political statement on music creation, challenging conventional notions of agency, authorship, and even gender.

Technical, Not So Technical

> *Pandora, you are not to blame for your curiosity. If pain was released and suffering reigned upon the earth, perhaps the gods—or men—are at fault, but not your search for hope.*

The first iteration of Pandora's Dream was prototyped in the C# language, using the popular video game engine Unity, for a graduate-level class at CCRMA called Music, Computing, Design: The Art of Design. In this initial approach, the system had a graphical user interface with buttons, a console to type commands to interact with the audio engine, and a text editor to write code using the following programming languages: JavaScript, ChucK,[12] and C#. This first sketch did not include any machine learning or AI; it was essentially a live-coding integrated development environment (IDE) with some basic graphic functionalities and network capabilities.

The full idea started as a reimplementation of *CineVivo*.[13] It is important to note here that an idea was growing: I added support for multiple programming languages, all integrated with the sound and graphic engines (although there wasn't a shared context), which meant no system-wide access to memory—everything was compartmentalized and there was a need for networking to communicate between languages.

The project wasn't anything too remarkable until I was invited to prepare two different compositions for Bing Concert Hall at Stanford University: one to be premiered as part of a SLOrk (Stanford Laptop Orchestra) concert, and the other as part of the celebrations for the 50th Anniversary of CCRMA. That changed everything and marked the beginning of the current path of development for Pandora's Dream.

These pieces, both part of the series *Invisible Forces*: *In Pandora's Hands*, were composed for a single laptop and the smartphones of all audience members (with one performance also incorporating 14 computers operated by dedicated performers). In total, 127 devices were connected to Pandora's Dream and live coded in real time, each rendering audio and

Figure 16.1 Version 1 of *Pandora's Dream* is shown in a performance of *Invisible Forces: In Pandora's Hands* at Bing Concert Hall, Stanford University, 2023.

graphics as part of the performance. Audience participation was entirely passive: they simply lent me their devices in their own hands, while all interaction was designed and controlled in real time by me from a central computer in the middle of the stage.

The best way to begin understanding Pandora's Dream from a more technical perspective is to recognize it as a C++ framework designed to host interpreters for multiple programming languages, including ChucK, OpenGL, Lua, Python, and text-based versions of Pure Data (Pd). These languages can be scripted using the 10 text buffers provided within the framework, with each buffer dedicated to a specific language or tool (the 10th buffer functions as a terminal, which can be used either as a general-purpose command line or to interact directly with Pandora's Dream via custom commands, providing low-level control over the framework).

Code interpretation occurs in parallel, allowing scripts to execute simultaneously using different mechanisms. This is achieved by multithreading and separating the audio engine—built around ChucK's *strongly-timed* paradigm—from the video rendering and from the data processing. As a result, audio runs with guaranteed sample accuracy; data calculations (including AI modeling and statistical analysis) are executed as efficiently as possible depending on the hardware limitations; and video rendering, while synchronized with the audio, remains independently timed rather than being strictly slaved to it.

Internally, the framework does not rely on networking protocols for communication between languages. While built-in MIDI and Open Sound Control (OSC) support allows for easy integration with external platforms, all inter-language communication within Pandora's Dream occurs at the stack level. Global variables declared within any supported language are accessible to all others, and this shared-memory model follows the audio engine's sample-accurate timing. For example, a script written in Lua can read a global variable from ChucK or Python at sample-rate speed. In effect, all global memory exists within a unified context, making it readable and writable from any language or execution point in the system.

Buffer Number	Buffer Functionality
1	Configuration and Documentation.
2	Interprets *OpenGL/GLSL* shaders for rendering graphics (background or window) with 2 extra libraries: Hydra by Olivia Jack and Lygia by Patricio Gonzalez Vivo.
3	Runs *ChucK* via an embedded virtual machine with extended libraries (*CHmUsiCK*) for sequenced music, symbolic music, MIDI control, autoencoders, and some other pretrained or half-trained algorithms for machine learning.
4	Interprets *Lua*, extended with *OpenFrameworks/C++* wrappers.
5	Executes *Python* code: NumPy, Pytorch, Matplotlib, and SciPy.
6	Runs *naked ChucK* (vanilla ChucK code).
7	Interprets a custom *metalanguage* called *Pandora* for mixing multiple languages in 1 buffer.
8	Reads and parses the *textual form of PureData* patches through libpd.
9	File/folder navigator: open, save, and browse project files.
10	Terminal-like buffer for interaction (not used for code interpretation). Setup and configuration.

This architecture enables a highly dynamic environment for both performance and development, where multiple tools—including programming languages, their respective libraries, and a range of auxiliary helpers and bridges—coexist and interoperate seamlessly. As already mentioned, a key aspect of this integration is the framework's ability to facilitate shared-memory access across languages, buffers, and runtime processes, following specific conventions and regulatory mechanisms.

The key to this computational architecture lies in its modular yet integrated design: each language and tool operates independently, focusing on the task it is best suited for, either because of its inherent strengths, the quality of its documentation, or the availability of pre-existing, well-structured libraries. Rather than forcing a single language to do everything, the system embraces specialization. Each module performs its function—whether it's graphics rendering, audio synthesis, symbolic processing, or machine learning—using the most appropriate environment (it could just be personal taste; in the end, it's all about nonhierarchical processes). What makes this framework particularly powerful is that all these components can seamlessly share data, predictions, analyses, and other information within the same runtime environment. There is no need for multiple applications or fragmented interfaces; everything happens internally, within a unified, self-contained system. In this way, a single application becomes a central hub, orchestrating diverse processes in real time—efficiently, flexibly, and without the overhead of managing external interfaces. No extra windows are needed, and just one application is enough to rule them all.

The architecture is efficient, but also overwhelming. Pandora's Dream is not commercial software designed with a gentle learning curve—it is conceived as a musical instrument. It has demanded extensive exploration and sustained practice on my part. I have never envisioned Pandora's Dream as a solution or as a tool to democratize computer music-making; rather, I see it as a *prosthetic extension* of my own musical expression—an intimate, evolving interface shaped by personal need, experimentation, and artistic urgency.

For example, AI and machine learning could be handled via ChucK using ChAI, which has been used in pieces like *Pandora's Mycophony*[14] and analyzed as a use case.[15] RapidML and the embedded Wekinator[16] can also be accessed through Lua scripting on the C++ side. And what about all the Python libraries and algorithms typically used for AI? That's not a problem—integrating them is not only possible but also very common in my current workflow.

All of this could, of course, be accomplished using a set of independent tools and data shared via MIDI or OSC. With careful integration and management, the results could be somewhat similar. For example, one could use a standard text editor to write Python scripts, send the computational results to Pure Data or ChucK via OSC, and then route audio analysis data from ChucK back to a Jitter patch inside Max. However, I have found that a centralized core and a shared execution context—where all languages and processes coexist—enable a level of expressivity and simultaneity that I was never able to achieve in a multi-window, multi-application setup.[17] More importantly, this meta-framework allows me to dissolve the temporal boundaries between processes that would otherwise occur in distinct phases or separate tools: everything is available system wide, including setup variables such as sample rate, or frame and buffer size. In doing so, it blurs the traditional divisions between composition, conducting, performance, and sound engineering, creating a unified and continuous creative space.

Pandora's Dream can also leverage visualization tools to display real-time data from any of the processes described above, in a wide range of forms and styles. This is made simple by the globally accessible data architecture, which allows both low-level visualizations using openFrameworks/C++ libraries and high-level plotting with Python libraries such as matplotlib.

In one of the use cases I will present in the next section, Lua code—executed at video frame rate—sends data to a Python library called Abjad,[18] which parses it into Western musical gestures. This information is then passed to LilyPond,[19] a general-purpose music notation tool, which renders the notation as PNG images. These images are then displayed in real time in a web browser that is served by Pandora's Dream.

Ultimately, the framework functions primarily as a live-coding environment: a human–machine interface designed for real-time interaction. While everything could theoretically be preprogrammed, I have deliberately chosen not to work that way. Instead, I've embraced a live coding and improvisational approach—one that allows spontaneity, uncertainty, and responsiveness to guide the creative process.

In this context, interactive AI—particularly approaches based on small datasets, as conceived by Rebecca Fiebrink[20]—has proven to be a powerful tool for exploring and expanding my practice. This is especially valuable given the volume of data available across the system: audio is analyzed every frame, video is processed continuously, and facial and hand recognition gestures are extracted from the camera input in real time (also brightness, contrast, and many other features). Combined with the many ways to map languages, variables, and functions within the framework, interactive AI offers a practical, trial-and-error method for building responsive systems that would otherwise require substantial time and effort to fine-tune manually.

It enables a more fluid and adaptive relationship with the machine—where training, listening, and reacting happen in real time (in dialogue with both the system and the performance)—because the use of AI and machine learning is designed to integrate with my own perspective.

Use Cases of My Invisible Companion

Your Voice, the Wind

Premiered at CCRMA by Distractfold Ensemble (bass clarinet and electric guitar) and the author (expanded lute).

Upon entering the room, the audience finds four chairs on stage, but only three musicians come out to occupy them—the fourth chair is reserved for a specter, a ghostly presence visible only to the other three performers. Following this entrance, the three musicians execute a ritual to welcome the audience. They proceed one by one to the empty chairs, and after the third has sat down, they wait as if a fourth person were about to perform the same ritual.

The piece is composed for four musicians, but one of them is not human. The fourth musician is a Realtime Audio Variational autoEncoder (RAVE)[21] that reacts to the other musicians: the musicians' audio signals are routed—according to the composer's instructions—to a pretrained model developed by the Intelligent Instruments Lab.[22] In this piece, the model transforms the musicians' playing, articulation, dynamics, and tuning into a different timbre, effectively functioning as a *fourth musician.* Audio features from one of the performers (specifically, the electric guitar) are used to control the model's latent space, in which latent variables are exposed. This transformation occurs without any audio analysis in the host environment; instead, it relies solely on self-similarity of the real-time signal within the audio reconstruction process.

This piece analyzes the real-time audio signal coming from the ensemble and transforms the analysis into data. In this case, Pandora's Dream handles feature extraction and resynthesis using ChucK and RAVE (as a dynamically compiled library for the language), while the scoring of parts is managed in Python, which renders the scores in real time as PNG images for each musician. Ultimately, all aspects of the piece's *meta-conducting*—including the timing mechanisms, score distribution, and final audio synthesis for the fourth performer—are executed within *Pandora*'s core.

Mi compañera invisible

Premiered at Universidad de Los Andes[23] by Juana Monsalve (mezzo soprano); also performed at CCRMA by Departure Duo (soprano and double bass).

A soprano sings to an *absence* in the room. She must try to find this absence in the past, present, and future, but this absence is hiding in her own voice, in her shadow, and in her breathing. *Mi compañera invisible* is built around a female voice that will create (without knowing) the score to follow, the visual content to be projected, the accompanying sounds, the counterpoints, and all the other performers (and presences) in the room.

For this piece, Pandora's Dream is set up to continuously listen to the voice of the singer. By analyzing audio features in real time—such as spectral flux, chroma coefficients, and root mean square level (RMS)—the system generates counterpoints or fully improvised lines that interact with the main character. At times, the machine chooses to accompany the singer, flowing alongside the voice; at others, it resists disrupting, challenging, and asserting its own musical direction. This behavior is both inspired by and a tribute to George Lewis's *Voyager*, where the system makes its own decisions. *Mi compañera invisible* also incorporates multiple pretrained AI models running simultaneously to generate spectral textures—ghosts and whispers—that envelop the singer. In this case, up to sixteen RAVE instances are deployed, each with different delay times and each trained on distinct datasets that I collected and recorded. These datasets feature recordings by Colombian soprano Juana Monsalve, captured in Bogotá, Colombia.

A Blank Page: *Making Everything All at Once*

> *She looked in the mirror; the other one wasn't there.*
> *She found a blank page to start from scratch and build the universe again.*

Premiered at CCRMA by Niloufar Shiri (kamancheh); also performed by the author (electric guitar) at Bing Concert Hall, Stanford University, and by A Far Cry (string orchestra) at Thomas Tull Concert Hall, MIT (Figure 16.2).

A Blank Page is a winning composition of the ICMC 2025 Special Call for Scores (Works for String Orchestra and Electronics), and it is the piece described at the beginning of this

Figure 16.2 *A Blank Page* is performed by A Far Cry at Thomas Tull Concert Hall, MIT, 2025.

chapter. It was originally conceived for an indeterminate number of performers (*N*), a live coder, and a dynamic virtual acoustics environment. Rooted in themes of absence, emergence, and reinvention, the piece invites performers and audiences into a constantly evolving sonic world.

Pandora's Dream is designed in this case to generate and distribute musical notation and electronic processing in real time based on live input from performers. The score is not prewritten but instead unfolds moment by moment, influenced by machine listening, AI algorithms, and the dynamic shaping of the acoustics of the venue. The system operates through feedback loops in multiple layers: the sounds of the performers are captured, analyzed, and used to generate new musical material that is then redistributed to the performers as evolving notation displayed on tablets. These transformations are processed through a network of granular synthesizers and nonlinear DSP algorithms. The use of Differentiable Digital Signal Processing (DDSP)[24] allows the system to adjust its processing parameters dynamically in response to the acoustic input, preserving a high level of coherence between live and digital elements.

A central feature of the performance is the integration of a dynamic virtual acoustics environment using the CAVIAR (Chamber for Augmented Virtual and Interactive Audio Realities) system[25] developed at CCRMA. CAVIAR utilizes multichannel convolution reverb and real-time impulse response (IR) manipulation—along with feedback cancellation—to simulate different acoustic spaces inside a physical space. For this piece, Luna Valentin algorithmically generated IRs with reverberation times ranging from 0 to 17 seconds. These IRs can be smoothly cross-faded, enabling a fluid morphing between different virtual acoustic spaces. This sonic malleability blurs the line between natural and artificial acoustics, allowing the space itself to act as a participant in the piece.

The structure of *A Blank Page* begins in silence, with performers playing soft, asynchronous gestures. The system starts by capturing initial resonances, from which it constructs the first notation instructions. As more data accumulates, the complexity of the score increases and triggers the granular synthesis layers. Over time, the reverberation intensifies and the sonic environment becomes denser and more immersive. At the piece's climax, all feedback loops flow into each other, culminating in a moment of overload. The system then abruptly shuts down, leaving only a final resonant tail that slowly dissipates over 17 seconds.

The composition draws inspiration from the metaphor of looking into a mirror and seeing nothing—a poetic image of creation emerging from emptiness. I relate this to the experience of sitting in front of a screen while typing code: a surface that provides information, yet unlike a mirror, offers no reflection of my body. Pandora's Dream acts as the mirror, but also as the companion that takes me out of that emptiness to the act of creation. It is not merely a musical performance, but an emergent process in which human actions and machine responses are continuously intertwined. Technology is not treated as a background tool but as a co-performer—integrated seamlessly into the fabric of the piece.

The system is essential to the entire performance, but most obviously, the piece could not exist without the computational power provided by the framework. More importantly, the agency granted to the machine itself plays a crucial role in shaping the aesthetic decisions—affecting even fundamental choices, such as the main tonal center around which the piece revolves. Ultimately, *A Blank Page* challenges boundaries between composer, performer, and system. It proposes a model of collaborative authorship where the composition is never static but always in flux, where the score is drawn, erased, and redrawn in real time.

Final Thoughts

Flexibility is one of the core strengths in Pandora's Dream: it allows multiple paradigms, languages, and machine learning models to coexist and interact, offering a fluid and expandable infrastructure tailored to the needs of each composition or performance. But, ultimately, Pandora's Dream is an *epistemic software framework*—a living, evolving system that continuously absorbs a flow of reworkings, redesigns, and reimaginings of the tool itself, as well as my approach to it and how I tackle my own musical practice (including both improvements and setbacks). More than that, it is also a *composition in itself*: a performative structure that is deconstructed and reassembled with new features, ideas, and intentions in each iteration. It resists fixity. It refuses to become a product. With every performance, Pandora's Dream is not only executing but *becoming*—transforming my own conceptions through practice and interaction.

Rather than aiming to be accessible, commercially viable, or a multipurpose IDE, Pandora's Dream has emerged as a deeply personal tool—a *prosthetic extension* of my musical thinking and expressive needs. It is not designed for ease or generality; it is designed for depth, complexity, and intimacy. From integrating C++, ChucK, Python, Lua, and shader-programming to embedding AI tools like ChAI or RapidML, Pandora's Dream becomes a shared computational space where languages, processes, and memory coexist. It embraces *improvisation*, not only in the sense of musical spontaneity but also in its very architecture—how it listens, adapts, and communicates across modules in real time.

This framework also challenges traditional roles—*composer*, *conductor*, *performer*, *engineer*—and allows them to collapse and recombine into new creative identities. Influenced by a long ancestry of musical systems, Pandora's Dream embodies an approach to composition that is not a product to be finished but a *practice of the unknown*: a space where glitches are expressive, where algorithms fail productively, and where every piece becomes a negotiation between human intention and machine autonomy.

Ultimately, Pandora's Dream is not just a tool I use: it is the *site of my epistemic inquiry*. It is where my questions about art, technology, authorship, and expression converge, not to be answered once and for all, but to be performed, iterated, and lived—over and over again.

Notes

1 Virtual acoustics, in this case, is the process of reshaping the reverberation of one room using the acoustic signature of another room (its impulse response, or IR). This involves signal cancellation—similar to the technology employed in noise-canceling headphones and earbuds—together with precise measurements and calibration of the room and the available equipment.
2 Li and Wang, "ChAI."
3 RapidLib is a lightweight library for interactive machine learning. It currently features classification (using kNN), regression (multilayer perceptron), and series classification using dynamic time warping. See Zbyszynski, Grierson, and Yee-King, "Rapid Prototyping."
4 Lewis, "Too Many Notes," 1.
5 AUTOBUSK is a program for the real-time probabilistic generation of MIDI signals, primarily note-ons and -offs. See Johannes Gutenberg-Universität Mainz, "Autobusk."
6 Hajdu, "Resurrecting a Dinosaur."
7 Hajdu, "From Ligeti to the Ligeti Center."
8 Tavella, "Holly Herndon."

9 Herndon, "Extreme Love."
10 Rodríguez, Betancur, and Rodríguez, "CineVivo."
11 Spatz, *What a Body can Do.*
12 ChucK is a programming language designed by Ge Wang, specialized in audio programming. Its defining characteristic, according to its author, is that it is "strongly timed," meaning that all operations in ChucK revolve around the explicit control and flow of time. See Wang, Cook, and Salazar, "ChucK."
13 Rodríguez, Betancur, and Rodríguez, "CineVivo."
14 Betancur Gutiérrez, "AI in Live Coding Environments"; Betancur Gutiérrez and Armitage, "Pandora's Mycophony."
15 Li and Wang, "ChAI," 4–6.
16 Fiebrink, "Machine Learning Education."
17 I have been live coding for many years now, and I've found that some features of the tools—often the ones that seem less important at first—can end up influencing performance practice more than one might expect. For example, I've always used ChucK as my main coding language, but I was never able to perform comfortably using miniAudicle (the default IDE for ChucK). The way it requires code to be executed disrupted the flow of my musical ideas during live performances. In contrast, using ChucK through the terminal with on-the-fly commands has expanded my practice in unexpected and transformative ways. It's the same language, with the same uniquely time-based audio engine—but the difference in interface radically changed the way I could interact with it.
18 Bača and Oberholtzer, "Welcome—Abjad."
19 Nienhuys, Han-Wen, and Nieuwenhuizen, "LilyPond."
20 Fiebrink, "Machine Learning Education."
21 Caillon and Esling, "RAVE."
22 Intelligent Instruments Lab, *Rave-models.*
23 University of the Andes, Colombia.
24 Engel et al., "DDSP."
25 Abel, Callery, and Berger, "Immersive Virtual Acoustic Spaces."

Bibliography

Abel, Jonathan S., Eoin F. Callery, and Jonathan Berger. "Immersive Virtual Acoustic Spaces." *Stanford University Office of Technology Licensing.* Accessed August 22, 2025. https://otl.stanford.edu/researchers/high-impact-technology-hit-fund/Immersive-virtual-acoustic-spaces.

Bača, Trevor, and Joséphine Oberholtzer. "Welcome – Abjad 3.28 Documentation." *Abjad.* Accessed July 30, 2025. https://abjad.github.io.

Betancur Gutiérrez, Celeste. "AI in Live Coding Environments: Pandora's Dream." In *Proceedings of the Conference on AI and Music Creativity (AIMC).* Oxford, UK: AIMC, 2023. https://aimc2023.pubpub.org/pub/9lqurr1x.

Betancur Gutiérrez, Celeste, and Jack Armitage. "Pandora's Mycophony." In *Proceedings of the International Conference on New Interfaces for Musical Expression (NIME).* Mexico City, Mexico: NIME, 2023.

Caillon, Antoine, and Philippe Esling. "RAVE: A Variational Autoencoder for Fast and High-Quality Neural Audio Synthesis." Preprint, last revised December 15, 2021. arXiv:2111.05011v2. https://arxiv.org/abs/2111.05011.

Callery, Eoin F., Jonathan S. Abel, and Kyle S. Spratt. "Synthesizing Reverberation Impulse Responses from Audio Signals: Auto-Reverberation and Interactive Environments." In *Audio Engineering Society Convention*, 151. Audio Engineering Society, 2021.

Engel, Jesse, Lamtharn Hantrakul, Chenjie Gu, and Adam Roberts. "DDSP: Differentiable Digital Signal Processing." Preprint, submitted January 14, 2020. arXiv:2001.04643. https://arxiv.org/abs/2001.04643.

Fiebrink, Rebecca. "Machine Learning Education for Artists, Musicians, and Other Creative Practitioners." *ACM Transactions on Computing Education (TOCE)* 19, no. 4 (2019): 1–32. https://doi.org/10.1145/3294008.

Hajdu, Georg. "From Ligeti to the Ligeti Center: How Music and Curiosity Inspired a Center for Innovation." Paper presented at the 50th International Computer Music Conference, Boston, MA, June 14, 2025. PDF. https://georghajdu.de/wp-content/uploads/ICMC-Boston-2025-Proceedings-Hajdu-Keynote.pdf.

Hajdu, Georg. "Resurrecting a Dinosaur—the Adaptation of Clarence Barlow's Legacy Software AUTOBUSK." In *Proceedings of the TENOR Conference*, 181–186. Cambridge, UK: Anglia Ruskin University, 2016.

Herndon, Holly. "Extreme Love." Featuring Lily Anna Haynes and Jenna Sutela. On *Proto.* 4AD, 2019.

Intelligent Instruments Lab. *Rave-models* (Revision ad15daf). Hugging Face, 2023. https://doi.org/10.57967/hf/1235.

Johannes Gutenberg-Universität Mainz. "Autobusk." *Department of Music Informatics.* Accessed August 23, 2025. https://www.musikinformatik.uni-mainz.de/Autobusk.

Lewis, George E. "Too Many Notes: Computers, Complexity, and Culture in *Voyager*." *Leonardo Music Journal* 10 (2000): 33–39. https://muse.jhu.edu/article/20320.

Li, Yikai, and Ge Wang. "ChAI => Interactive AI Tools in ChucK." In *Proceedings of the International Conference on New Interfaces for Musical Expression (NIME).* Utrecht, Netherlands: NIME, 2024.

Nienhuys, Han-Wen, and Jan Nieuwenhuizen. "LilyPond, A System for Automated Music Engraving." In *Proceedings of the XIV Colloquium on Musical Informatics*, vol. 1, 167–71. Firenze, Italy: Tempo Reale, 2003.

Ogilvie-Hanson, Eva Sophie. "Posthuman Production: Technology and Embodiment in the Works of SOPHIE and Holly Herndon." PhD diss., McGill University, 2020. https://escholarship.mcgill.ca/concern/parent/nv9357575/file_sets/2b88qj01w.

Paz, Iván, and Shelly Knotts. "Live Coding Machine Learning: Finding the Moments of Intervention in Autonomous Processes." *Computer Music Journal* 46, no. 4 (2022): 81–96. https://doi.org/10.1162/COMJ_A_00663/2328955/COMJ_A_00663.PDF.

Rodríguez, Jessica, Esteban Betancur and Rolando Rodríguez. "CineVivo: A Mini-Language for Live-Visuals." In *Proceedings of the 2019 International Conference on Live Coding.* Madrid, Spain: Prado, 2019.

Spatz, Ben. *What a Body Can Do.* Routledge, 2015.

Tavella, Angelica. "Holly Herndon: Fighting Automation with Artificial Intelligence." Interview. *Tape Op*, no. 132 (July/August 2019). https://tapeop.com/interviews/132/holly-herndon.

Wang, Ge, Perry R. Cook, and Spencer Salazar. "ChucK: A Strongly Timed Computer Music Language." *Computer Music Journal* 39, no. 4 (2015): 10–29.

Zbyszynski, Michael, Mick Grierson, and Matthew Yee-King. "Rapid Prototyping of New Instruments with Codecircle." In *Proceedings of the International Conference on New Interfaces for Musical Expression (NIME).* Copenhagen, Denmark: NIME, 2017.

17

INTERLUDE VIII

Interview with CJ Carr

Julie Zhu

DOI: 10.4324/9781003615873-17

Julie: Tell us what you're working on now and what you're really excited about. It doesn't have to be AI-related.

CJ: Okay! Well, I live and breathe music and that is what I'm excited about. I'm in this AI music band called Dadabots. We started here in Boston. Zach[1] and I met at Berklee College of Music. We were interns. We were trying to make extreme music. I was in extreme metal bands, I was doing punk and noise music, and we were like, "How do we push this even further? 'Cause band music is so limited." That pushed us to make music with code, then pushed us to machine learning. And then it became pretty obvious to us that, "Oh my God, this is going to be like a whole ... this is gonna be a thing—generative machine learning." We tried to tell everyone at Berklee: "This is gonna be dope. It's the next thing. We should create a whole new lab." And we weren't successful at telling that story. But zoom forward to 2025, you know? They're like, "Why haven't we done enough?"

And it's just been such a wild ride, doing it with my best friend. We get to collaborate with other artists. We've been publishing scientific research. We're part of the Stable Audio team,[2] putting out open-source models. We've been doing this thing called *prompt jockeying.*[3] We did a European tour last summer. We've just been playing it at all kinds of different venues, from raves and clubs to UN diplomat cocktail parties—the full range.

Julie: [*Laughs.*] Wait, what? How did that happen?

CJ: Yeah, I mean ... yeah [*laughs*]. We're actually going to the UN next month in Geneva, at this event called AI for Good. It's really, really fun. The organizers are very musically inclined. Last year, all of us went on stage and improvised with an AI model. So, this AI model can generate really fast—it can make a whole 3-minute song in 5 seconds. And that means we can also take audience suggestions, interactions. I have a background in improv comedy theater, which I'm finally bringing to music at the level of genre creation. I've done things where I have a guitar: "Give me a topic to write a song about." I've done that. But now, "Okay, what genre are we going to invent right now?" And at the UN it's amazing because some of them are like, "Do salsa! Do Afrobeats! Do cumbia." And I'm like, "Okay, we're doing Afrobeat–techno–salsa–gamelan, let's go!" What does that fusion sound like? UN makes a lot of sense for what we're doing. But they're like, "Don't do anything extreme metal!" Okay, fine.

Julie: That's so funny! That really feels like an actual good time. Most people are just a single person behind their screen typing in a prompt. I never thought of actually doing crowd work with AI—that's fascinating.

CJ: I remember when we started doing it at algoraves.[4] There were so many people in the audience who were like, "You know, I've been skeptical of AI, but then I saw how you were doing it." It actually brought people together. Everyone felt more present and connected to what was happening as a result. And it just depends on how you hack it.

Julie: Right, instead of being a downer. You're able to be a little more judgmental when you're an anonymous person behind a computer screen than when you see it bringing people together.

CJ: DJs never take people's suggestions. But what if? ... So, we did a six-hour club night in Berlin and we took 200 audience prompts. And that's pretty much at the limit of what I'm able to do. They're writing them down on their phone, shoving them in my face. I'm like, "Okay, but what if we played at a 500-plus-person venue? How do we handle that?" They'd have to communally arrive at some consensus of genre. Maybe there's like a website where people are QR coding or something. This is kind of how we're thinking.

Julie: Tell me more about this model—is it through your company?

CJ: We've been experimenting with models for a long time. The earliest neural nets that could really work were SampleRNN.[5] We worked with Jennifer Walshe on that[6]. And they're pretty good at certain genres: solo, instrument, voice, metal—actually, they're extremely good at death metal.

Julie: [*Laughs.*] Yes, of course. As you've demonstrated.

CJ: Yeah, we have a YouTube livestream that runs 24/7 called *Relentless Doppelgänger*.[7] It's been running for six years straight. It actually crashed twice during this time. Only twice.

Julie: Wow! So, you're developing these new models all the time then?

CJ: That's right. We've leaped forward maybe, I don't know, 10 or 12 generations of models since then. It happened so fast. And even internally, we will leap 2 or 3 steps, and no one even gets to see those intermediate steps. It's kind of funny seeing the world, seeing the "singularity" happening so quickly. But I'm so, so happy to work with a team of all-stars right now—the Harmonai team,[8] there are several of us—and we can just do so much more together than just Zach and me. And our current models are diffusion models. We're part of the original team that made Stable Diffusion at Stability.[9] The image guys left, but we got a lot of their know-how. We applied that idea to audio and music, and we're just taking it further.

We recently invented this new type of training procedure called ARC,[10] which is an adversarial GAN fine-tuned stage that you add ... and it makes it way faster. You can go from 100 steps to 50 steps to 8 steps. And then we can quantize it even further. So, we have models running in real time on a Mac CPU. This is dope because it becomes really special when people don't need special hardware to do this. And also because they don't even need to pay for an API or anything—you could just download, then go. So that's why I'm excited: the technology has finally caught up to that point of mass accessibility—we're on the doorstep of it.

Julie: That's amazing, especially since there are these paid models, or eventually paid, like Udio or these other text-based generative models. That's how yours kind of works as well. What would you imagine the future of this to be? Is it just really democratization, or is there some kind of monetization involved? What are you thinking?

CJ: Oh, yeah. We release our stuff open-source. We actually have an open-source business model. So, if you use the model and you are a company that makes over a million dollars in revenue, then you have a license. Otherwise, it's totally free. So that means free for artists, free for startups, free for new companies, free for research, free, free, free, free, free. And, actually, that's a pretty good balance. Because we want to keep going. So, if Disney starts using it, well yeah—help pay our salaries, right? But mainly, I just want people to create. So yeah, open source. That also means that you can play with it. You can tweak it. You can break it in ways that API-based things like Suno or Udio ... they can't let you break it. I would love to be able to play with those models and make them do things that their interface doesn't expose. But I'm limited in that way. And you can only get that from open source. So yeah, I'm so excited. And so many people at this conference have been like, "Yeah, I've been messing with Stable Audio. I've been doing this, doing that." And I'm like, "Cool! I didn't even think to do something like that."

Julie: This version of ICMC[11] has been really inspiring, actually, because it's usually a roller coaster (sometimes someone doesn't want to host). But it seems like this year so many people came together. So many different schools are hosting. And people from IRCAM[12] came ... They're all here—there's Somax[13] people, there's OG[14] computer music people ... It's kind of amazing. And we do have a really great community. I love what you said about the open-source community being able to break things and to contribute in a way. That's been the ethos of everything. I wonder, can you maybe talk a little bit more about that? It seems like that's a positive aspect of machine learning here—in our musical context—but how do we get other people to do that as well? Not just in your company but at places like Suno or Udio. How do we bring the notion of AI as a possible force of good for our community?

CJ: Yeah, right now we're at this crossroads of various narratives, and we're experiencing cognitive dissonance. But let me focus on one of the positives, in my opinion. AI has this ability to educate us faster and better than ever before and increase our literacy, our media literacy, and cultural literacy more than ever before. And that generally is a good thing. And then, there's this flip side: The more and more we rely on things like ChatGPT that are closed source—not only to do our jobs but maybe to live our lives (lots of our friends, myself included, will even use it as a therapy tool)—what happens when "Oh, now it costs $500 a month" or "Oh, actually, we're taking that one offline" ... and I depended on that? Now I'm atrophied as a result. So this is why open source is so important. Emad[15] has a quote: "Not your model, not your mind."

So, I've started running LLMs on my own computer at home. Gemma 3[16] is my favorite, I think. And, wow, this is great. I feel way more inclined to put my private life into this model. I would never give OpenAI or Google my private texts, my emails—never. I don't want to talk about my private life. But I know this is a private offline model. It could even be an air-gapped machine.[17] And I feel like I could level up as a human because it's able to digest me, and I can ask it questions, and I can also automate it to do things. Like "watch my emails" or like "let me know when something important is coming up." This is something I'm so notoriously bad at—things disappear in email—but now LLMs can keep track of that. So, that's awesome. And then, we're bringing the same thing to the music side of things. On the one hand, we have it open source, but it runs on GPUs. On the other hand, we recently got it to actually run on a CPU (it runs on my Mac). So, not only is there that accessibility component to it, which no one can ever take away, but also an energy component. If the smaller, more efficient model can run on your computer, it's using just as much energy as anything else in your life.

Julie: That is a lot of positives. And I'm so impressed by your ability to self-reflect using AI. I think that definitely takes introspection to another level. How long have you been doing that?

CJ: Ever since I started programming ... even in high school, I was playing with Markov chains for everything. So, Markov chains are one of the earliest text-generation abilities. It's a very, very dumb probabilistic next-word type of thing. But even just sending it my text messages, instant messages, or a whole journal of writing out ideas, I would throw those into Markov chains—I'd hit bam, randomize! And most of it would be pretty random. But then, every ten examples of those actually made something that made me think of a new idea. "Oh, that'd be a cool song idea," or a cool hackathon project idea. Because it just randomly puts some ideas together. So, that gave me this intuition: Oh, we're just going to figure out how to do Markov chains better by making the probabilities way more huge. And oh, it turns out that's what a neural net is.

Actually, I'm so happy I got all these skills before I really developed a core friend group. It's kind of nice how that happened in that order. I got pretty good at music, and pretty good at coding, and then I got a ton of friends. If I had gotten the friends first, I would have been so distracted. [*Laughs.*]

Julie: It does seem like your relationship with technology was formed very early on. And you actually do think of it as a tool. Do you ever associate anything more with it than a tool?

CJ: I've never thought anything of it other than an art form. And my very first thing was that I wanted to make video games. I love video games, so I want to make them. In my sketchbook—I'm in first grade or something like that—I'm sketching out video game levels and thinking, "Huh, how would I make the logic if this were a real video game?" And then, as soon as I got a tutor to teach me computers, because I grew up in an Army family, I asked, "How do I make video games?" So then, I'm making Flash games on Newgrounds.[18] Really, really shitty games. It went viral. It's terrible. Terribly drawn, but millions of people played it. And I was voicing the characters even before my voice changed. Don't look it up. [*Both laugh.*]

So, it was obvious to me as an art form. And then, when I stumbled upon hackathons—and Boston was a big area for hackathons because of all the colleges—it was just like, "Oh, finally, here's the community of people like me who go crazy on a weekend, on some crazy idea, just for the fun of it." And then I'll get to show off. And there's a performance art aspect to it at the end, too. It's like, "Oh, it turns out, if I can actually engage and communicate my idea to the audience, I have ten times more advantage over everyone else who can't." So, I got really addicted to competing in hackathons. I started paying the rent here in Roxbury[19] with the hackathon winnings for a couple of years. I've done about eighty hackathons.

Julie: So, if someone looked at your work maybe like a thousand years from now, and you wanted to give them the context in which your work was thriving within this environment, you would say maybe the dawn of the Internet and mass hackathons?

CJ: Yeah, definitely hackathons, for sure. Humor is a huge part of it—it means that we're a hackathon team. I thought about this originally at MIT hackathons. Any idea that just made us crack up, laughing so hard, we were like, "All right, we have to do that one." Our first project was destroying SoundCloud with music remix bots.

Julie: Does that still exist? The hackathon culture?

CJ: Yeah. Oh, yeah.

Julie: And are you still part of it?

CJ: Yes. I'm constantly traveling and I will fly to all the good ones. I'm flying to Berlin next weekend! There are a couple of AI hackathons. There's a zero-knowledge proof hackathon. I was just in Denver for an AI agent hackathon, where the winning project—which was by my friend Bootoshi—won vibe coding. He vibe-coded the whole project and won $10,000. In Claude 3.7! And I was like, "Bro, you've coded a winning hackathon project? I need to learn how to vibe code now." We're now in the era of vibe coding. It's amazing.

Julie: That is definitely the future. Everyone is using something like that right now.

Let's go a little dark—what do you think? Educators now are afraid that kids won't be able to write anymore. People are afraid that the middle class is going to disappear. So, what is the worst-case scenario in your mind?

CJ:. OK, yeah. It's a very good question because all those things are important. And we do need them to keep going, and we need to be careful. The first thing that strikes the mind is that—for the whole internet generation—our dopamine is kind of fucked because so much of that is instant gratification. So, we (not everybody) have this longing for a mentality that is about *deep work*. And I think this Calvinistic value system is emerging in art now in the twenty-first century, almost rejecting AI for its instant gratification. And we're trying to hold on to this process-oriented stuff. And I think that question is incomplete.

I mentioned earlier that there's a cognitive dissonance of narratives happening. That is one of them. But on the flip side, generative AI enables this high-level conceptual art like nothing before. You have an idea, then you can execute it, and the value can be in the idea.

Julie: I feel like that always *was* art, though. The idea is held above most everything. And people had entire studios painting their work, but it was still a Rembrandt.

CJ: Yes, that always *was* art. That's right, so much of art is that already. And maybe we're overlooking and we're romanticizing it. But I think that comes from our own burnt-out dopamine—that we're longing for ourselves. And what's the conclusion and the solution to that?

Julie: Community?

CJ: I think community is a big one. Our lifestyles. And training our attention to be more present, in general, whether it's meditation or whatever. But art itself can also be meditation—like painting. My girlfriend just took up painting, and every stroke is so freaking intentional. And it's a long, gruesome process to make one painting. But when you meet people who are painting every day, there's just something incredible about their brains. They see the connections and concepts between things. They have this level of presence, this lexicon of philosophy that is connecting all the symbolism. And it's like, "Okay, yeah, you get that as a result of that process."

Julie: And it's also embodied because you're translating something that you see through your hands and your eyes. You mix the color. I used to be a painter—that was my MFA. It really is meant like meditation. I don't think I can meditate, but I do calligraphy where you have to regulate your breath. And I think it always has to come back to the body. At least for me. And it feels like maybe we can't escape that when we are talking about humans: the mind–body separation, all of that. That's old hack stuff. We've heard that multiple, multiple times. But I wonder, does that resonate with you at all? You still have to travel with your body to Berlin, to Denver, and to all these places. Is that different from connecting with someone on Zoom?

CJ: Oh, I love being in person a thousand times more. I'm definitely an extrovert. I wasn't always an extrovert. But then, I am so 1,000% more and more an extrovert, more and more. And I feel lucky being in music because of dance parties. I live in a venue. I've been living in a venue since I graduated college. Two different venues. And there's always, every month, some big dance party. And I'm a practitioner of parkour. So it's actually pretty nice, walking past the Mass Pike[20] earlier today. I've done some very dangerous things over the Mass Pike, just thinking about it. But the flip side of parkour is that I constantly injure myself. And so, I've had two main knee injuries that put me out of commission for several months, and—with nothing else to do, I was just on my computer—I made some huge advancements.

[*Both laugh.*]

Figure 17.1 CJ Carr.

Julie: Oh, my God. You're like, "I do parkour in order to injure myself, so I can get … " [*Laughs.*]

CJ: Yeah, for the good of [*in a character voice*] technological progress. Actually, I'm walking around with a sprained knee right now. So, I think that's good for progress.

Julie: Yeah, you're here. You're at the conference, not on a bridge.

OK, so … Is there something you wish would be made in the near future, or a distant future, in the field of music and AI? A dream project, or a dream result …

CJ: Yeah. If it turns out that, by sheer luck, there's some treatment for mental health across the board that arises out of this—that would be incredible. One of my passions has been music therapy. I have a bunch of friends that are music therapists. Here at Berklee College, I threw the music therapy hackathon. I'm just like, "Bring all the hackers, bring MIT over, bring Berklee over. Is there some crossover between technology and therapy and music that can emerge from that?" Given music's healing powers, and with LLMs having the ability to intimately know you (at least linguistically), is there something there that can just help people? Whether you're in some severe case, or some lighter anxiety, depression—that is just the twenty-first century thing that people have. And I don't even know what that would be … but that's my dream.

Julie: Most people in AI are, perhaps, in a sort of bubble. How can other people, who may not be in technology, be brought into the loop? How do you envision that working out for the good of all? Is it even possible? Does it come in the form of education, or does it come in the form of new laws or …?

CJ: Well, the UK proposed a law about training the labor class on something. I just saw a headline, I don't know what the details were. But these are the kind of questions that are emerging.

I'm looking up cool, interesting YouTube people and Twitch people who were live streaming the act of coding or using technology, whatever. I can say, "Let me get a 10-minute deep dive into … Blender. How do I make three things in Blender? I've never done that. Okay, walk me through it." Even just that level of exposure is a really easy first step. And then, through that, you might feel something of a passion, something you want to do. You're like, "Wait, actually, I do feel this calling to make 3D," especially now with LLMs and vibe coding. I don't know how to make 3D stuff, but I can describe what I want to Claude, Gemini, or ChatGPT, and then it can go and start using Blender for me to make 3D things.

So, we are now in that future where the blocks between "Oh, cool, crazy, funny idea" and "Wait, I can actually do something about it" have been lifted. And it's amazing. One of my roommates recently got hella broke, and lost his job, and his music studio flooded, and he was just hitting a low point. Then he discovered that, talking to ChatGPT, he's been constantly blowing his mind. He's like, "Wait, today I became an expert in this topic, and now I'm an expert in this topic." And it's empowering! He actually started coding music in Strudel. He's never done that before because he was not understanding coding. But now, he's like, "Holy shit."

That is the other element. Play with the LLMs …

Julie: And let your creativity drive. Your curiosity.

CJ: Yeah. The intrinsic motivation. That's the thing that will take you the furthest—always.

Learn more about CJ Carr, Dadabots, and their work at https://dadabots.com

Notes

1 Zach Zukowski, the other half of Dadabots.
2 Stability AI, *Stable Audio.*

3 In CJ's own words: "It's DJing, but harder. With DJing, you're playing usually other people's tracks. But with this, the tracks don't even exist yet. You're prompting them live with a neural network." See Dadabots, "Prompt Jockeys."
4 An algorave is an event where artists create electronic dance music in real time by live coding, often projecting their code for the audience to see.
5 Soroush et al., "SampleRNN."
6 Walshe, *A Late Anthology.*
7 *Relentless Doppelgänger* by Dadabots is an ongoing project. The third "spawn," or iteration, began streaming on July 16, 2024. The second spawn streamed live for 42,660 hours, starting on September 4, 2019.
8 Stability AI, *Harmonai.*
9 Stability AI, *Stable Audio.*
10 ARC is an acronym for Adversarial Relativistic-Contrastive. See Zachary, "Fast Text-to-Audio Generation."
11 The 2025 International Computer Music Conference (ICMC) was held in Boston and jointly hosted by Northeastern University, the New England Conservatory, Berklee College of Music, Boston Conservatory at Berklee, Emerson College, and the Massachusetts Institute of Technology.
12 IRCAM (French: Institut de recherche et coordination acoustique/musique; English: Institute for Research and Coordination in Acoustics/Music) is a major public research center in Paris, France focused on music and science.
13 IRCAM, *Somax2.*
14 OG is someone or something that is an original or originator and especially one that is highly respected or regarded.
15 Mohammad Emad Mostaque is the co-founder and former CEO of Stability AI.
16 Google DeepMind, "Gemma 3."
17 An air-gapped machine is a computer without a network interface controller, with a physical or conceptual air gap between it and a network.
18 *Newgrounds.*
19 Roxbury is a neighborhood in Boston, MA.
20 The Massachusetts Turnpike (also referred to as the Mass Pike) is a controlled-access toll road that runs concurrently with Interstate 90 in Massachusetts.

Bibliography

"Air Gap (Networking)." *Wikipedia.* Accessed January 25, 2026. https://en.wikipedia.org/wiki/Air_gap_(networking).

"Algorave." *Wikipedia.* Accessed June 13, 2025. https://en.wikipedia.org/wiki/Algorave.

Dadabots. "Prompt Jockeys (2024): The Rise of DJing with a Neural Network." YouTube video, 6:14. December 4, 2024. https://www.youtube.com/watch?v=_fpnAHoRSqU.

Dadabots. "Relentless Doppelganger." YouTube livestream. First streamed July 16, 2024. Accessed February 15, 2026. https://www.youtube.com/watch?v=JF2p0Hlg_5U.

"Emad Mostaque." *Wikipedia.* Accessed January 23, 2026. https://en.wikipedia.org/wiki/Emad_Mostaque.

Google DeepMind. "Gemma 3." *Google DeepMind.* Accessed February 14, 2026. https://deepmind.google/models/gemma/gemma-3.

IRCAM. Accessed December 19, 2025. https://www.ircam.fr/lircam.

IRCAM, Music Representation Team. *Somax2.* Application. Accessed December 19, 2025. https://forum.ircam.fr/projects/detail/somax-2.

"Massachusetts Turnpike." *Wikipedia.* Accessed February 1, 2026. https://en.wikipedia.org/wiki/Massachusetts_Turnpike.

Newgrounds. Accessed December 19, 2025. https://www.newgrounds.com.

Novack, Zachary, Zach Evans, Zack Zukowski, Josiah Taylor, CJ Carr, Julian Parker, Adnan Al-Sinan, et al. "Fast Text-to-Audio Generation with Adversarial Post-Training." Preprint, last revised May 20, 2025. arXiv:2505.08175v3. https://arxiv.org/abs/2505.08175.

"OG." *Merriam-Webster.* Accessed December 19, 2025. https://www.merriam-webster.com/dictionary/OG.

"Roxbury, Boston." *Wikipedia.* Accessed November 26, 2025. https://en.wikipedia.org/wiki/Roxbury,_Boston.

Soroush, Mehri, Kundan Kumar, Ishaan Gulrajani, Rithesh Kumar, Shubham Jain, Jose Sotelo, Aaron Courville, and Yoshua Bengio. "SampleRNN: An Unconditional End-to-End Neural Audio Generation Model." Preprint, last revised February 11, 2017. arXiv:1612.07837v2. https://arxiv.org/abs/1612.07837.

Stability AI. *Harmonai.* Accessed December 19, 2025. https://www.harmonai.org.

Stability AI. *Stable Audio. Stability AI.* Accessed December 19, 2025. https://stability.ai/stable-audio.

Walshe, Jennifer. *A Late Anthology of Early Music Vol. 1: Ancient to Renaissance.* Album. Tetbind Records/Jennifer Walshe, 2020. https://jenniferwalshe.bandcamp.com/album/a-late-anthology-of-early-music-vol-1-ancient-to-renaissance.

18

MOVEMENT VIII

The Sweet Spot: Human–AI Alignment with Randomness, Complexity, and Machine Learning

Ted Moore

DOI: 10.4324/9781003615873-18

Introduction: *Mirroring* and *Alignment*

Musicians have long experimented with technology as part of their creative processes, from the analog glitch of early synthesizers[1] to contemporary machine learning algorithms.[2] These technologies are often pursued with the goal of increasing the breadth and speed of exploring sonic possibilities,[3] as well as providing musically valuable suggestions not previously considered.[4] To borrow a term from AI Safety, the *alignment* of a system describes the degree to which the technology has the same values and intentions as the human user.[5] When being creative with technology, I often want the system to be in *alignment* with my musical tastes and goals in the hope that the sounds and musical ideas it produces are creatively interesting to me.

In this chapter, I present three strategies used for exploring sonic possibilities with technology: (1) randomness, (2) complexity, and (3) machine learning. These are just three of many possibilities; I have chosen these because I use them in my own work and, when considered together, they situate machine learning alongside preexisting approaches, highlighting similarities while also clarifying the strength of each independently.

Taking a broad view of what "artificial intelligence" means in the context of creative music-making,[6] I will consider the three strategies listed above through the lens of AI: how each can be *trained* into *alignment* with my musical values, creating an *artifice of musical intelligence.* When aligned with my creative values, any one of these strategies can provide outputs that surprise me with *musicality* and *creativity*: sounds and ideas that feel as though they come from outside me, yet resonate strongly with my musical goals—they become creative suggestions that I take up and include in my work. Perception of a useful idea or an accomplished task that derives from external origin is when I (and I think many others) come to feel the term "artificial intelligence" is intuitively applied. By comparing the three strategies above in the context of creative practice, I consider how it is only *through creative practice* that any music technology, AI or otherwise, has the potential to be perceived as *artificial musical intelligence.*

Musicologist Marc Leman's concept of *mirroring* offers a more music-creativity-oriented definition of *alignment.* For Leman, *mirroring* describes how a listener perceives intentionality in music and sound (regardless of whether technology is involved): "attribution of intentionality is likely to occur on the basis of mirroring, that is on the basis of a simulation of the perceived action in the subject's own action. Actions of others are understood as intended actions because the subject can simulate them and understand them as its own intended actions."[7] Mirroring occurs when the actions ("sounds") the system makes are recognizable as sounds that I could make, or might want to make, using this system. For this analysis, I am considering actions at the temporal levels of sound object, gesture, and phrase, because in my own work these are the timescales at which I experience mirroring using the strategies described. When this resonance, or mirroring/alignment, of artistic sensibility emerges without my *explicit* intentionality, the system is perceived as being intentional (i.e., "intelligent").

Furthermore, when experienced as a surprise, these moments of mirroring can produce perceptions of musical "agents" and "agency."[8]

While attributing *intentionality* to these systems, I do not intend to suggest that these machines are conscious, warrant authorship, or are by default agential. That question is only adjacent to the discussion here. Stepping back, outside of my creative flow, I would actually argue that it is *me*, the human sitting at the device, making the sounds—not some "agent." It is not the intentionality of the system that created the sound, but my intentionality to use a system in this way.

When analyzing randomness, complexity, and machine learning in the next section , Leman's concept of mirroring will be used to consider how I train my musical values into a system, bringing it to *mirror* my intentions and goals.

Strategies for Human–AI Alignment

Randomness

I often reach for randomness[9] as an initial strategy for exploring parameter spaces, just to see what is out there. After designing a synthesis algorithm, audiovisual mappings, or testing new code, randomness can help to quickly assess where issues might arise or where artistic value might be hidden. Pioneering computational artist Vera Molnár explains her use of randomness, saying, "There is this old romantic idea which is called 'intuition.' ... But there is a thing that can replace intuition. It's randomness. ... it will show you billions of possibilities, of which, with your limited imagination, you couldn't have thought of ... After you'll find, the interesting part is rather over here."[10] Molnár is approaching artistic creation from a computational mindset, using randomness to iterate over possibilities within a parameter space and then identify which results she prefers.

Randomness has been used as a source of creative exploration in electronic music from early on, such as in John Cage's *Imaginary Landscape No. 4* in 1951.[11] With the development of computer music, new sources of randomness have been created and used. In his essay "Why do we want our computers to improvise?" George Lewis explains sources of digital randomness[12] in his computer programs as "efforts to imbue interactive systems with values such as relative autonomy, apparent subjectivity, and musical uniqueness."[13]

This analysis considers randomness in an austere, naïve form, by which I mean all parameters of a system are randomized independently within a wide range of possible values. The random parameter values do not interact with each other or with the values that came before, nor do they use any other guiding principles. Systems using such strategies approach the designation of "complex system," a concept that Molnár and Lewis discuss and which is elaborated in the "Complexity" section.

Training Randomness

One problem with using randomness in this austere form—to explore high-dimensional parameter space—is that the space is explored, well, randomly. This lack of direction amounts to simply listening through many random possibilities, waiting for a musically interesting combination of parameters to occur. If this happens, the composer can hit the proverbial save button and have an interesting musical object or pocket of parameter space to explore further. While this strategy maximizes the breadth of exploration, *waiting* makes for an inefficient process of exploring possibilities. To increase efficiency, one might *train* the system by selecting weights or distributions (such as Gaussian or Brownian motion) as well as narrower parameter ranges to limit possible output. Iteratively tweaking probabilities and parameters, listening to the results, and refining them further is a common practice for electronic musicians to train a system using randomness to be more aligned with their musical goals. Knowing which parameters to weigh, what distributions to reach for, how much to tweak, etc., is based on intuition built up over years observing how one's musical taste interacts with technical facility. The result of the training process is a system that has a narrower band of possible outputs: outputs that induce more mirroring than before training.

Randomness ≠ Humanness

Leman elaborates on *mirroring* to also include an ability to *predict* a system's actions. He writes, "By looking at how a person moves and behaves, I can understand that person as an intentional being. My understanding of his or her intentions allows me to predict his or her actions and understand them as part of an understanding of my own actions,"[14] and "Corporeal articulations are conceived as reflecting the action-oriented ontology that is induced by moving sonic forms in music. They exhibit prediction and anticipation of stimulus properties."[15] Even after training, computer-generated randomness is, by design, unpredictable, making it less prone to create actions that can be perceived as mirroring the predictability of human musical actions. Though randomness is less likely to induce mirroring, its strength is the open-ended breadth it offers for exploring possibility spaces, and therefore will remain an important part of creativity with technology.

Complexity

Identifying complexity is difficult because it includes both structure and unpredictability, usually emerging from interactions between various components. In pursuing a definition of complexity, Peter Grassberger states that "complex systems are usually composed of many parts, but this alone does not yet qualify them as complex … What is important is that there are strong and nontrivial *correlations* between these parts. Technically, this is best explained via mutual informations."[16] In my own practice, a good example of using complexity is how I approach modular synthesizers. By sharing signals between various modules, I can create nontrivial correlations exhibiting both structure and unpredictability, while also mirroring my musical tastes.

Training Complexity

My process of training a modular synthesizer into *alignment* begins with the first connections of control signals to create relationships between musical parameters. Each connection reflects an aspect of my musical values and goals, such as what filter module I'm using, what kind of waveform to modulate it with, how a signal is routed, and what other parameters will be modulated in parallel (i.e., "mutual informations"). Early in this process, the interconnections are few, allowing me to easily account for the sonic results—I don't yet have any perceptions of external origin. At each newly connected cable, I have the opportunity to provide feedback to the system by reversing the last decision, adjusting the knob positions, continuing to add more cables, changing the routing, etc.

To create complexity, I pursue this process to a point where I am no longer able to keep track of all the interconnections contributing to the resulting sound. At this point, I might be surprised by the sonic outputs and take them as creative suggestions. Due to the training process leading up to this, these sonic outputs are likely to be aligned with my musical values (certain filter types, waveforms, modulations, etc.). These musical values are represented by the structured correlations that I've embedded into the complexity: parallel motions of control parameters, nested modulations creating multilayered periodicities, feedback connections creating gestures that shift between stability and chaos, and more. The sounds made by the modular synthesizer therefore mirror my intentions, being actions that are recognizable as sounds that I would make using such a system.

Without this training process, mirroring is much less likely to occur. As described in the "Randomness" section, training randomness involves narrowing down a parameter space to a subset of possibilities more aligned with my musical goals. Training complexity similarly imbues a system with my musical values: I am constructing the desirable parameter space as the training process occurs (by building up connections), ensuring that whatever sounds come out are aligned with my musical taste.

Machine Learning

Training a machine learning system functions as an iterative feedback loop similar to tuning randomness or a complex system; however, rather than iterating directly with and getting immediate feedback from the human's ears and musical judgment, it instead iterates with the human's musical judgment through data. AI and creativity researcher Rebecca Fiebrink describes this process: "There are certain things that we care about, as musicians for example, that are really hard to articulate in code. It's hard for me to talk about what kind of quality of sound I want and then translate that into a set of filter coefficients. It's hard for me to talk about how I want a performer to move on stage and then translate that into some sort of mathematical equation for their trajectory. But it's a lot easier for me to either find examples of sounds that have a particular quality or to give examples of movements ... this relates to the types of tacit knowledge and embodied knowledge we bring to creative practices."[17]

Training Machine Learning

The algorithm that trains a neural network, called backpropagation, works by coming up with possible outputs (randomly at first), then checking the data to see to what degree the output aligns with the human's musical values and goals (as expressed in the dataset). It then corrects itself slightly (by tuning the internal interconnections) to try to make a better output suggestion next time. These error-correcting iterations happen at the maximum speed of the computer, going through an entire dataset thousands of times before a user reengages directly with the system. Using machine learning for exploring musical possibilities allows one to clearly express musical preferences through datasets, more quickly bringing the AI system into alignment. Different from training randomness or complexity, this speed allows an artist to try many different trainings with different training parameters, datasets, model architectures, etc., always assessing the outputs for creative value.

Small Data ...

The benefits of using machine learning with creative practice are rooted in small, personal datasets, which are best used to train model architectures much smaller than the frontier models trained by large companies. Training an algorithm on one's personal data enables the algorithm to understand the idiosyncratic musical ideas of the human and then join in on the pursuit of those ideas. Collecting and curating the dataset becomes an important act in the creative process. Personally created and selected data enables artists to embed artistic meaning into the machine learning process. Furthermore, using personal data and small models enables artists to use more cost-effective, less energy-consuming hardware while explicitly avoiding exploitation of others' data.

In my composition *saccades* (2022), for saxophone, video, and electronic sound, I trained a small neural network to translate different states of an eyeball (as seen in a video) to different synthesizer parameters, effectively controlling synthesized sound with image analysis (Figure 18.1). The dataset of images was taken from a video recording I made of my own eyeball moving around and blinking in a somewhat frenetic character. I summarized each video frame by identifying the *x* and *y* position of the pupil as well as the *y* position of the top and bottom eyelid. After growing frustrated with poor accuracy in automated image tracking software, I coded a small program that advanced through every video frame while I clicked my computer mouse to record the position of each eyeball point of interest. While this took

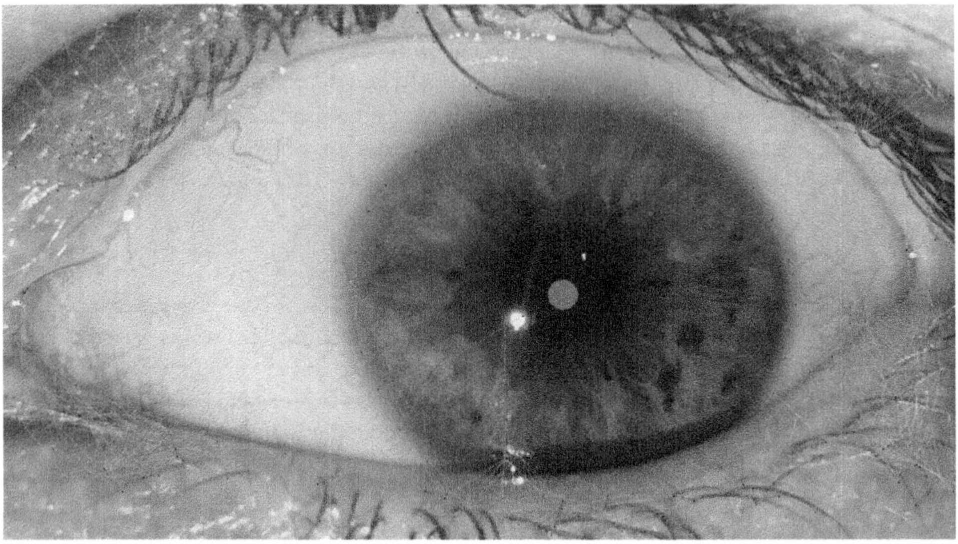

Figure 18.1 Frame from the video design for *saccades*.

some time (about two hours), it was a nice reminder of the importance of having good, clean data when using these kinds of algorithms.

To create the corresponding sonic dataset, I chose sounds (via settings for a synthesis algorithm with 13 parameters) that I paired to particular frames' "eyeball states" (represented by the 4 mouse-clicked positions). I trained the neural network to learn the relationships between these datasets so that, given any frame in the video, it predicts the synthesis parameters I want based on my chosen eyeball state. As the eyeball moves, the sound "moves," visiting the synthesis parameters I selected as well as "in-between" synthesis settings and sounds, predicted by the neural network from video frames showing "in-between" eyeball states.

Just as Fiebrink described above, it would be time-consuming and challenging for me to craft a mapping that translates eyeball movement to sound synthesis as rich and complex as the ones learned by a neural network. Instead, showing the system *examples* of the kinds of eyeball positions I want it to learn from and pairing those with *examples* of the sounds I want it to generate is much easier. Perhaps more importantly, this process is rooted in the intuitive aesthetic judgments central to creative practice. Because I'm using personally created data and personally trained models, I get to make aesthetic, creative decisions at all points in the machine learning process: dataset curation, data cleaning, algorithm selection, training (and retraining) parameters, output curation, etc.—all of which have an impact on my artistic outcomes. Engaging machine learning in this way creates a flowering of possibilities rich for idiosyncratic investigation, leading to a healthy artistic community with an exciting divergence of creative practices.

... *vs. Big Data*

In contrast to the benefit of small datasets and small models described above, "big data" machine learning algorithms (e.g., Suno, Udio, ChatGPT, Midjourney, etc.) are not trained to support an individual's idiosyncratic artistic process. Rather, they are intended and expected to produce results palatable to a majority of potential users by interpolating results from within the massive amount of data they are trained on. In *Filterworld*, Kyle Chayka says of societies dominated by algorithms: "The culture that thrives ... tends to be accessible, replicable, participatory, and ambient. It can be shared across wide audiences and retain its meaning across different groups, who tweak it slightly to their own ends ... It is also pleasant or average enough that it can be ignored or unobtrusively fade into the background."[18] The convergent nature of big data tools fails to meet the idiosyncratic needs of individual artists working within their artistic practice.

What Is Music? and When Is it Good?

When training large music models (LMMs), such as Suno and Udio, many critical decisions go into the process. One early decision is what music to include in the training data.[19] If it is a diverse gathering of musics, the data will be more sparse: the model will take longer to train and won't have a clear consensus of what "most" "music" sounds like, leading to less coherent outputs. A company might consider that, since most users of the system won't be interested in generating music in the style of Boulez, Tuvan throat singers, gamelan, Merzbow, gagaku, Ted Moore, etc., examples of those musics should not be included in the dataset. Removing these examples will focus the system's attention onto a more homogeneous collection of patterns, tendencies, aims, etc., streamlining its training and therefore "improving" its output. But since the system is being designed (and marketed) as a "Music Generator," what music is included in the dataset (and therefore what it will learn to generate) becomes a political statement about *what is* considered music and *what is not.* This choice further marginalizes certain musical traditions and ideas, reifies biased opinions, and limits creative ideation about what music can become.

As companies train these models, they also make choices about what music is *good.* This not only occurs by selecting what "music" to include in and exclude from the dataset but also in assessing the outputs of the model for "quality": music palatable and inoffensive to average listeners in sonic quality, dynamic range, form, free of glitches or other artifacts, etc. These assessments might result in adjustments to the training data and training parameters, but also lead to changes in different parts of the system regarding the mix, spectral balance, compression, reverb, etc.[20] Just as decisions regarding inclusion in a dataset reify what music *is*, the assessment criteria of a company's outputs can reify what *good* music sounds like. These decisions similarly narrow a user's ideation about creative possibilities.

The criteria that companies use to answer the questions *What is music?* and *What is good?* are likely aimed at maximizing engagement and profits, which, while not inherently bad, are counter to creating a divergent, creative musical community. LMMs suggest a community where musicians are using the same dataset and the same algorithms, facilitating a convergent homogenization of answers to questions about art while removing creativity and agency from the music "generation" process.

Marshall McLuhan summarizes his famous aphorism, "the medium is the message," by saying that "the 'content' of a medium is like the juicy piece of meat carried by the burglar to distract the watchdog of the mind."[21] The impressively generated music "content" from LMMs like Suno and Udio are juicy pieces of meat that distract us. The question then is, *What is being burgled?* What are we not noticing slipping away, changing, because of the presence of these systems? One answer may be the ability to think *creatively* about answers to the questions of what is "music" and what is "good"—in relation to a personal creative practice. What is being burgled is a *personal creative practice* and the patience it takes to effectively engage with the creative process.[22]

Randomness	• broad, open-ended consideration of possibilities • involves waiting for alignment to occur • training using weights, distributions, and ranges
Complexity	• more explicit training to imbue human aesthetic preference • mutual informations elicit perceptions of intentionality • more potential for alignment
Machine Learning	• human aesthetic preference expressed through examples (data) • automated training • high potential for alignment

Conclusion: The Sweet Spot of Alignment

In AI Safety, the problem of *aligning* AI and human values is known as "The Alignment Problem."[23] The desirable degree of alignment between human and AI is not always clear. Often we think of examples where we *do* want the AI to be as aligned with humans as possible. For example, we do not want to create an AI tasked with solving global warming to wipe out the human race as its optimal solution; we want the AI to value human life. However, we often want our AI to not be *so* aligned with humans that it reproduces human bias and prejudice.[24] Further, debated ethical thought experiments explore *which* human(s) the AI should be aligned with, such as whether the self-driving car should hit and kill two jaywalkers, or avoid doing so by swerving off the cliff and killing a single occupant.

When using technology in a creative practice, similar (albeit less dire) considerations of alignment apply. The three strategies for being creative with technology described above (randomness, complexity, and machine learning) all have the potential to be aligned and perceived as AI. In each, I train my musical values into a system, with the hope that the technology will express musical suggestions reflecting my own musical values back to me. In this cybernetic training loop, the technology acts as a filter. It is not able to precisely recreate my intentions: the intentions are altered in some way. If altered beyond recognition (very low alignment)—the filter is too strong—mirroring will not occur, and the outputs will not feel like a reflection, an extension, an augmentation of my creative ideas.

Parameterizing Alignment

Often, using technology to explore creative possibilities involves pursuing a *useful* degree of alignment—the right amount of distortion in the filter. Some machine learning algorithms offer a measure quantifying the degree to which it aligns with a human's values (as expressed through data). This measurement is called the *loss* or *error*, which is a measure of the difference between the algorithm's output and the desired output as specified in the dataset. A low *error* measurement might indicate high alignment. Training or retraining machine learning systems to achieve different levels of error (i.e., alignment) may be a useful strategy for approaching a desirable degree of alignment. One common introduction to the FluCoMa Toolkit[25] does exactly this when training a neural network to control a complex synthesizer.[26]

Additionally, some machine learning algorithms offer an attempt at navigating different degrees of alignment with a hyperparameter called *temperature*, which often controls how likely certain outputs are compared with others. Higher temperature might result in less alignment, and lower temperature in more alignment. nanoGPT[27] is a small language model that enables training on using personal data and gives experimental control over the model's temperature during text generation. Even large frontier models use this strategy: DeepMind's AlphaEvolve was encouraged to hallucinate (deviate from alignment) in pursuit of new solutions to open questions in mathematics.[28]

Sometimes I want a system to return to me exactly what I expect. Sometimes I want suggestions that are similar to what I've trained it on, but not exactly, to explore adjacent possibilities. Sometimes I need to be shaken out of my creative rut by rifling through random outputs (that are agnostic of my preferences) to hear if anything sticks.

Nontrivial Correlations

Situating machine learning alongside randomness and complexity positions the new technologies as one option among many, highlighting their similarities. Identifying AI in any of these technologies is not based on a category of algorithm or method of training, but occurs when a system mirrors one's artistic goals.

Grassberger's notions of *complexity* resonate with Leman's concept of *mirroring* by explaining the identification of complexity (and for our purposes *artificial musical intelligence*) as phenomenological, stating, "More important than correlations among the parts of a complex system are often correlations between the object and its environment ... the letters of a novel in some language could hardly be considered as complex if there were no possibility in principle to read it. The ability to read a novel, and to perceive it thus as complex, requires some correlation between the novel and the reader."[29] For Grassberger, the relations between the parts (for example, of a modular synthesizer) need to have both some correlation upon which the relation is shown to be complex (i.e., having *intentionality*, such as musical simultaneity, shared directionality) *and* criteria for a listener to identify these correlations as *nontrivial* (i.e., musically valuable). In the Grassberger quote above, the criteria for correlation is a shared written language of vocabulary and grammar. Recognizing *artificial musical intelligence* through mirroring of nontrivial correlations requires a shared vocabulary and grammar of music and sound. This shared vocabulary may be something more commonly interpretable, such as eighteenth-century counterpoint, or it can be the specificity of an individual's *creative practice*—the idiosyncratic voice of a composer.

It is not enough for a complex system to produce perceivable correlations; it is quite trivial for a system to do this. One could generate random parameter mappings that create correlations, but those correlations might not express musicality.[30]

Calling a system "AI" is not simply a matter of human choice or trend. Those identifications necessarily rely on the degree to which the technology expresses creative suggestions with a grammar and vocabulary legible to an observer. Put another way, in order for mirroring to occur, the technological system's output must be recognized by the human as being in the artistic voice of the human. In my own creative practice, because I am the person designing the technological systems and training them into alignment using my own data, this shared language, however idiosyncratic, is always central to the process, increasing the potential for mirroring. What follows is that any identification of *artificial musical intelligence* is subjective, relying on not only the existence of a listener but also the existence of the listener's musical tastes, goals, history, technical facility, training, etc.—in short, *creative practice.* Without creative practice, musical AI is not possible.

Coda

One outstanding question is: What does it look like to have artistic goals—in the context of a creative practice—for AI to mirror? This is, of course, a large question, with mostly subjective answers. One description that mirrors my experience belongs to British painter Roger Fry, who says,

> Almost any turn of the kaleidoscope of nature may set up in the artist a detached and aesthetic vision, and, as he contemplates the particular field of vision, the (aesthetically) chaotic begins to crystallize into a harmony; and, as this harmony becomes clear to the artist, his actual vision becomes distorted by the emphasis of the rhythm that is set up within him. Certain relations of line become for him full of meaning; he apprehends them no longer curiously but passionately, and these lines begin to be so stressed and

> stand out so clearly from the rest that he sees them more distinctly than he did at first. Similarly, colours which in nature have almost always a certain vagueness and elusiveness, become so definite and clear to him, owing to their now so necessary relation to other colours, that, if he chooses to paint his vision, he can state it positively and definitely. In such a creative vision, the objects as such tend to disappear, to lose the separate unities and to take their place as so many bits in the whole mosaic of vision.[31]

Regarding my own creative work, it is not hard to see how randomness, complexity, machine learning, data, etc., can fit into this account of the creative process.

> Almost any sampling of the kaleidoscope of existence may set up in the artist a detached and aesthetic vision, and, as he contemplates the particular shape of this data, the (aesthetically) chaotic begins to crystallize into statistical distributions; and, as these patterns become harmonious to the artist, his creative vision becomes accelerated by their resonance with the patterns set up within him. Certain relations between dataset and algorithm become for him full of meaning; he apprehends them no longer curiously but passionately; models, hyperparameters, and loss values begin to be so stressed and stand out so clearly from the rest that he sees them more distinctly than he did at first. Similarly, probabilities which in the world have almost always a certain vagueness and elusiveness, become so definite and clear to him, owing to their now so necessary relation to his model's predictions, that, if he chooses to pursue this vision, he can state it positively and definitely as a reflection of lived experience. In such a creative vision, the objects as such tend to disappear, to lose the separate unities and to take their place as so many bits in the whole mosaic of vision.

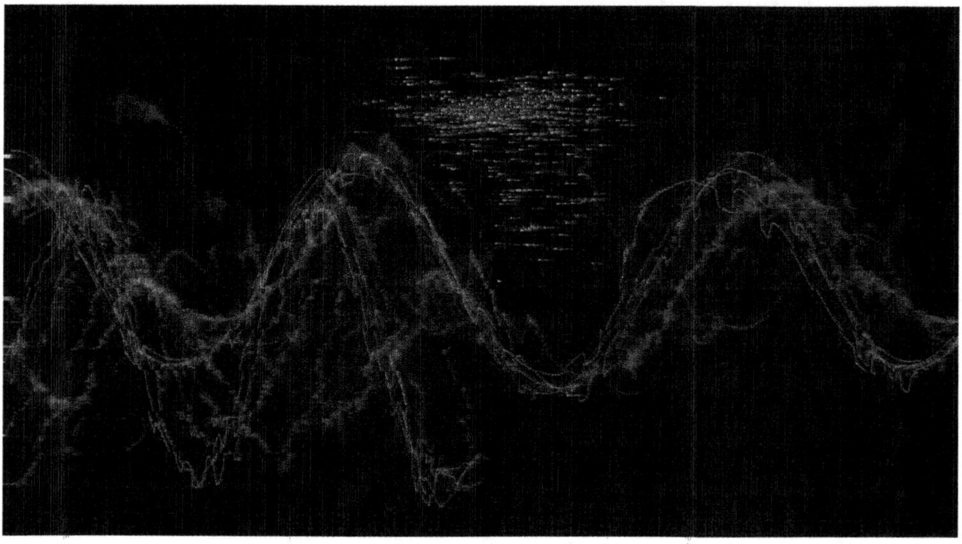

Figure 18.2 Frame from the video design for *saccades*.

Notes

1 Collins and Pinch, "On Chance and Contingency."
2 Fiebrink and Sonami, "Reflections on Eight Years of Instrument Creation."
3 Molnár, "Vera Molnár."
4 Fiebrink, "Machine Learning"; Devine, "IDOW."
5 Christian, *The Alignment Problem*, 13.
6 ZKM, "inSonic 2020."
7 Leman, *Embodied Music Cognition*, 92.
8 Moore, "Musical Agents, Agency, & AI."
9 Although computer random number generators are not truly random, but rather "pseudo-random," I am treating them here as random since perceptually this is how they operate.
10 Molnár, "Vera Molnár."
11 Weinberg, "Interconnected Musical Networks."
12 As seen in a diagram included in the essay that shows his use of Max's "drunk" object, which generates "random numbers within a specified step range" (Cycling '74).
13 Lewis, "Why Do We Want Our Computers to Improvise?"
14 Leman, *Embodied Music Cognition*, 78.
15 Leman, *Embodied Music Cognition*, 100.
16 Grassberger, "Randomness," 6–7.
17 Fiebrink, "Machine Learning."
18 Chayka, *Filterworld*, 5.
19 One very important topic that I do not go into here is that companies are training on copyrighted data without consent. See Koebler, "Listen to the AI-Generated Ripoff Songs."
20 The systems in question are proprietary, so we cannot know for sure, but I presume that there are some mixing and/or mastering "checks" that happen before delivery to a user, similar to how systems with chatbots and image generators check their outputs for noncompliant material before delivery.
21 McLuhan, *Understanding Media*, 18.
22 The CEO and founder of Suno, Mikey Shulman, said that, "the majority of people don't enjoy the majority of the time they spend making music," suggesting that *creative practice* is something to avoid. See Maiberg, "CEO of AI Music Company."
23 Christian, *The Alignment Problem*.
24 Christian, *The Alignment Problem*; D'Ignazio and Klein, *Data Feminism*; O'Neil, *Weapons of Math Destruction*.
25 Tremblay et al., *The Fluid Corpus Manipulation Toolbox*.
26 Moore, "Controlling a Synth."
27 Karpathy, *nanoGPT*.
28 Nokivok et al., "AlphaEvolve"; Hassabis, "Living in an AI Future."
29 Grassberger, "Randomness."
30 Some artists train machine learning algorithms that they present as "agents" or AI art without reflecting on whether the system's outputs are expressing musical intentionality. I have found that some of these systems not only lack nontrivial correlations but any correlations at all: the relationships between the parts seem unconnected from each other (for example between the performer and the "agent"). I consider this approach to AI art to be rooted in conceptual art—the concept of what the system is learning, training, or doing is the core of the artistic expression, rather than the

temporal experience. One possible explanation for why musicality doesn't appear in some of these situations is that the goals of the system designer are not rooted in a *creative practice*, but rather are aimed at drawing attention through buzzword technologies.

31 Dewey, *Art as Experience*, 90.

Bibliography

Chayka, Kyle. *Filterworld: How Algorithms Flattened Culture*. New York, NY: Doubleday, 2024.

Christian, Brian. *The Alignment Problem: Machine Learning and Human Values*. New York, NY: WW Norton & Company, 2020.

Collins, Harry, and Trevor Pinch. "On Chance and Contingency." *Public*, no. 33 (January 2006): 59–62.

Cycling '74. "drunk Reference." *Max v8.6.5 Documentation*. Accessed June 2, 2025. https://docs.cycling74.com/max8/refpages/drunk.

Devine, Richard. "Richard Devine: IDOW Extended Interview #8 (analog voodoo effect)." Posted by I Dream of Wires. YouTube video, 7:32. Posted February 8, 2013. https://www.youtube.com/watch?v=Z7naEUAYDfg.

Dewey, John. *Art as Experience*. New York, NY: Perigee, 1934.

D'Ignazio, Catherine, and Lauren F. Klein. *Data Feminism*. Cambridge, MA: MIT Press, 2023.

Fiebrink, Rebecca. "Rebecca Fiebrink: Machine Learning as Creative Design Tool." Posted by CeReNeM. YouTube video, 47:51. Posted August 5, 2019. https://www.youtube.com/watch?v=Qo6n8MuEgdQ.

Fiebrink, Rebecca, and Laetitia Sonami. "Reflections on Eight Years of Instrument Creation with Machine Kearning." In *Proceedings of the International Conference on New Interfaces for Musical Expression (NIME)*, 237–42. Birmingham, UK: NIME, 2020.

Grassberger, Peter. "Randomness, Information, and Complexity." In *Statistical physics: Proceedings of the 5th Mexican School on Statistical Physics (EMFE)*, edited by Francisco Ramos-Gómez. Singapore: World Scientific Publishing Company, 1989. Reprinted with corrections as preprint, submitted August 16, 2012, arXiv:1208.3459. https://arxiv.org/abs/1208.3459.

Hassabis, Demis. "Google DeepMind C.E.O. Demis Hassabis on Living in an AI Future." *Hard Fork* Podcast, New York Times, 1:14:00. May 23, 2025. https://www.nytimes.com/2025/05/23/podcasts/google-ai-demis-hassabis-hard-fork.html.

Karpathy, Andrej. *nanoGPT*. Last modified November 12, 2025. GitHub. https://github.com/karpathy/nanoGPT.

Koebler, Jason. "Listen to the AI-Generated Ripoff Songs That Got Udio and Suno Sued." *404 Media*, June 24, 2024. https://www.404media.co/listen-to-the-ai-generated-ripoff-songs-that-got-udio-and-suno-sued.

Leman, Marc. *Embodied Music Cognition and Mediation Technology*. Cambridge, MA: MIT Press, 2007.

Lewis, George E. "Why Do We Want Our Computers to Improvise?" In *The Oxford Handbook of Algorithmic Music*, edited by A. McLean and R. T. Dean. Oxford, UK: Oxford University Press, 2018.

Maiberg, Emanuel. "CEO of AI Music Company Says People Don't Like Making Music." *404 Media*, January 13, 2025. https://www.404media.co/ceo-of-ai-music-company-says-people-dont-like-making-music.

McLuhan, Marshall. *Understanding Media: The Extensions of Man*. Cambridge, MA: MIT Press, 1964.

Molnár, Vera. "Vera Molnár Computer Art." [English subtitles translated from French] interview with MUDA (Museum of Digital Art, Zurich). Posted by Joshua Batty. YouTube video, 2:03. Posted November 9, 2019. https://www.youtube.com/watch?v=BCZNNZGz5YI.

Moore, Ted. "Controlling a Synth using a Neural Network in Max." Posted by Fluid Corpus Manipulation. YouTube video, 29:05. Posted June 15, 2022. https://www.youtube.com/watch?v=XfNZzQPdPG0.

Moore, Ted. "Musical Agents, Agency, & AI: Towards a Phenomenological Understanding." In *Proceedings of the 2024 International Computer Music Conference (ICMC)*, 102–5. Seoul: ICMC, 2024. https://hdl.handle.net/2027/fulcrum.2227ms73r.

Novikov, Alexander, Ngân Vu, Marvin Eisenberger, et al. "AlphaEvolve: A Coding Agent for Scientific and Algorithmic Discovery." Technical report, Google DeepMind. Accessed May 30, 2025. https://storage.googleapis.com/deepmind-media/DeepMind.com/Blog/alphaevolve-a-gemini-powered-coding-agent-for-designing-advanced-algorithms/AlphaEvolve.pdf.

O'Neil, Cathy. *Weapons of Math Destruction: How Big Data Increases Inequality and Threatens Democracy*. New York, NY: Crown, 2017.

Tremblay, Pierre Alexandre, Owen Green, Gerard Roma, James Bradbury, Ted Moore, Jacob Hart, and Alex Harker. *The Fluid Corpus Manipulation Toolbox*, vol. 1. Zenodo, July 14, 2022. https://10.5281/zenodo.6834643.

Wang, Ge. "Humans in the Loop: The Design of Interactive AI Systems." *Stanford University Human Centered Artificial Intelligence*, October 20, 2019. https://hai.stanford.edu/blog/humans-loop-design-interactive-ai-systems.

Weinberg, Gil. "Interconnected Musical Networks: Toward a Theoretical Framework." *Computer Music Journal* 29, no. 2 (2005): 23–39.

ZKM. "inSonic 2020: Syntheses - Day 2." YouTube video, 4:32:20. Posted December 12, 2020. https://www.youtube.com/watch?v=sooNxK6oQ4c.

19

POSTLUDE

Shifts in Creative Practice with Intelligent Machines

Doga Cavdir

DOI: 10.4324/9781003615873-19

This chapter aims to connect the threads between the contributing authors' approaches to designing, building, and performing with AI models in their compositional and performance practice. After conversations with each artist, I reflected on the evolving relationship between the artists and machine learning systems within their bespoke and individualized practices. I often encountered an overarching theme that highlighted the artists' motivations to personalize these models beyond technical customizations to create a space for deeply ethical, artistic, and expressive negotiations.

Between June and September 2025, I had conversations with the artists who wrote the Movements of this book about their compositional practices and, more importantly, about understanding their motivations to create in collaboration with their machine learning systems. Such collaborations were both intimate and opaque. Each artist I spoke with brought forward how personal and creative boundaries reshape authorship and artistic agency. Although these conversations highlighted many relational aspects across the artists' practices, a common theme emerged: their self-expression is grounded in ownership, artistic values, and personal values. This grounding proves essential in the face of expanding computational agency where the artist's decisions about data, training, and use become acts of caring as much as creative acts.

In many ways, personalization has emerged as a defining gesture of agency. Their approach to personalization includes a combination of artists training models on their own data, designing their own workflows, or coding their own tools. In doing so, they construct a boundary of ownership and responsibility. When the artists expressed concern about the transparency of the datasets, I observed that their statement carried both aesthetic and ethical weight. It acknowledged the process of creation as inseparable from the process of data selection, curation, and training.

Personalized AI practices, therefore, sit at an intersection of acts of authorship, self-expression, and ethical care. In my conversations with the artists, I observed that these practices require artists to decide, often repeatedly, what kind of relationship they want to have with their tools, whether to invite the model as a collaborator, to integrate it into practice as an instrument, or to utilize it as a mirror for reflection. In almost all cases, these models served as tools for experimentation, exploration, and expression. Their work-in-progress stages encouraged artists to misuse, challenge, and push the boundaries of these models.

Figure 19.1 Screenshot of Doga Cavdir's recorded video interview with Ted Moore.

These motivations framed my reflections in this epilogue. As I traced the artists' responses and my own interpretations, I found that questions of ethics, ownership, and expression inevitably folded into deeper concerns about agency, embodiment, and creative reflection. These themes together formed a constellation that defines how bespoke AI practices evolve today.

Ethics, Ownership, and Grounds of Care

Several composers and performers voiced concerns and discomfort with using pretrained models whose origins could not be traced. These models are trained on vast datasets scraped from the internet with little or no consideration of consent or attribution. Artists prioritized training their own models not only to reclaim aesthetic agency but also to ensure ethical transparency.

Ensuring ethical transparency is closely aligned with responsibility.[1] Ted Moore articulated that, "as humans, we should just be taking responsibility for what these models are doing" rather than describing these models as separate and independent entities. Similarly, Hugo Flores García emphasizes that these models are "not neutral entities, existing in a vacuum." Raised as a concern by many of the other contributors, such responsibility extends from the resources demanded to support these models to the concerns of originality of the artistic work and training data.

I observed that the composers' attention to originality seemed to transform the data from solely raw material into *grounds of care*. While some of the artists explored the "large model aesthetics" as in Victor Shepardson's research, most of them expressed a desire to work only with recordings, sounds, and datasets that they had created or curated themselves. In my conversation with Molly Jones, she shared her approach to applying compositional strategies to define the design space by curating her own datasets, which enables her to better understand, program, and create with the models. At the same time, her familiarity with the data created more transparency in capturing the models' capabilities and aesthetic choices. Similarly, Kelsey Cotton's work seeks a form of radical transparency, displaying failures with the systems live on stage and resisting a narrative that AI is an omniscient, seamless, or superior musical agent. Instead, she foregrounds its flaws, fragilities, and misunderstandings. During performance, she writes live commentary into her Strudel code, which acts as poetic remarks visible to the audience and reveals her surprise, confusion, and curiosity about the system's behavior (e.g., "Why did it do this?" or "Can you hear how strange that is?"). This practice destabilizes expectations of AI as a black-box expert and reframes the performance as a shared practice.

Sometimes, composers' approach to curating their datasets is more intertwined with their improvisational practices. Celeste Betancur Gutiérrez follows a cyclic flow by integrating the model across the full life cycle of music-making from early rehearsals through compositional development and into live performance—almost as a situated collaborator whose presence is rehearsed with, responded to, and understood by the ensemble collectively. Similarly, Julie Zhu's ethics are grounded in carefulness toward data, models, and her affective state. The care around the personal and intimate relationship is apparent in the collaboration between Constantin Basica, Prateek Verma, and Alexandru Berceanu: whether through co-creation with audience members about their experience of loss and grief, or through highly personal biodata they used to train models.

A key theme arose in all the composers' approaches from attentiveness to ensuring human presence is not overshadowed. This focus aims to preserve and deepen collective listening, improvisation, and human connection. By personalizing one's tools, composers stress how artistic practice with AI must still be accountable to its materials, methods, and consequences. I would like to highlight this orientation as a *practice of care*: a sustained consideration for the conditions under which music is made, and to the relational ethics that connect artists, systems, and community.

Questions of Agency

Attribution of "agency" in the human–machine co-creative dynamic was often brought up in my conversations with all of the composers, whether it was a consideration in their practice or whether it was an attribute that had not yet been discovered due to the early state of the prototypes. However, these conversations unpack how artists' self-expression and reflection became a site where agency is tested and revealed.

For many of them, self-expression through a model, especially one trained on their own materials, produces a strange doubling: the model conveys something about them that they did not consciously choose. In this sense, self-expression is not only the act of imprinting one's personality or style onto a model; it is also the moment when the model expresses aspects of the artist back to them. For example, in this co-creative process, Cotton expressed moments of surprise—which she often shared with the audience members—when she could no longer recognize which parts of the output felt like her voice or which parts felt unfamiliar, mechanical, or simply mutated. Jones shared observing new patterns of her compositional habits from the generated music based on her own recordings. I reflected in my interview notes: "She began to notice that the model was repeating specific types of transitions, textures, or motives that she had often used in her own work." As Moore previously identified the four aspects of perceiving or attributing agency in human–machine collaboration—separation, surprise, intention, and mirroring[2]—I noticed that the relationships between these attributes in the contributors' work appeared rather intertwined. I observed that the model's mirroring and surprises coincided in ways to support the composer's use of these attributes as compositional catalysts.

The concept of *surprise*, in particular, was frequently brought up by the contributors as humorous encounters or as contributions to the perceived agency. Flores García speaks of moments when the model produces textures or continuities that feel unexpectedly "alive," while "the transformation process becomes a form of perceived material agency." Shephardson's collaborating improvisers describe similar experiences while performing with his model. Some find they must "calm" the system while others confuse it by feeding unconventional material—both approaches are a means to "understand" what it is doing. The system's temporal and structural responsiveness leads performers to attribute personality or intention to it. The agency arises not in the system itself but in the interactive feedback loop that requires the performer to adjust their behavior.

From these perspectives, the questions of agency became relational. The artist's agency is not just expressed but reflected—sometimes affirmed and sometimes destabilized. This relationality made me question whether self-expression and reflection become a diagnostic tool for examining one's own creative tendencies and for seeing how the system interprets or distorts them. Echoing Nao Tokui,[3] I asked the chapter contributors to articulate further whether agency in their creative practices becomes something negotiated rather than predefined. Can we define these models as a tool, an instrument, or a co-performer, depending on the moments of clarity, failure, surprise, or resonance? Or is there a more dynamic relationship between these roles?

In these discussions, artists variously described their models as tools, instruments, and co-performers; however, the perceived materiality and presence of the systems in their creative practice set distinctions. Moore prefers to define these systems as tools among other generative processes, insisting on how different aspects of perceived agency are a matter of human projection—shaped by surprise, complexity, or unfamiliarity. He critically articulates that models are tools whose outputs must remain the responsibility of the human artist, regardless of how unpredictable they may seem, relegating the system to the background. The approach of Basica, Verma, and Berceanu resonates with Moore's criticism as they define their models as translation engines: tools that re-express their training data as new timbral and structural materials. Similarly, Flores García situates the models within a lineage of instrument design, specifically as critical and provocative instruments. Shepardson, on the other hand, explores responsive interaction by designing intelligent instruments where the model functions as a source of responsiveness for performers.

On the contrary, composers whose practices deeply engage with the expression of the performing body encounter other definitions. Betancur Gutiérrez sees her models as intelligent tools that facilitate compositional practice across many systems, but their role during performance becomes particularly meaningful through sheer presence. In her shows, the system (sometimes represented by the placeholder "empty chair") is not an abstract computational process, but a performer with whom she rehearses, listens, and shares the stage. What she perceives as agency is enacted through timing, responsiveness, and disruption—qualities that emerge only in the context of embodied, situated interaction. Cotton's live performances create similar dynamics: when the model continues to play a sample to completion regardless of her intention, or when it stalls mid-performance, she experiences it as a performer who is temporarily "absent" or "unavailable." When she had to adapt her own vocal and programming interactions to accommodate the system's failures, surprises, and breakdowns, she often criticized the dynamics of these negotiations. She stressed the asymmetrical labor relationship where performers more often adapt, adjust, wait, and compensate. Similarly, when she expresses how the system demands attention but does not reciprocate, she highlights the limits of attributing agency.

Zhu's intimate engagement with her personal model both draws parallels with and amplifies this dynamic. She describes her interactions with the model as ways of training her sonic sensibilities by engaging in the co-listening practice of her drawings. She highlights how some of the more personal, nuanced drawings are not detected by the models, and others are drawn for the machine to listen to. Her performance-led approach to training the models demonstrates that agency is not only technical but effectively felt and relationally constructed. This dynamic creates a form of relational agency: the model's behavior becomes meaningful because it resonates with the artist's sense of self.

In tracing these perspectives, I find that what has often been described as "distributed agency" is not, in fact, a negotiation between artist and model, but a circulation of agency within the artist's own creative practice—between intention and material, habit and surprise, body and system. What feels like co-agency emerges not from the model's inherent capacities but from the artist's ongoing adjustments, attentiveness, and interpretive labor. Embodiment becomes crucial here: agency is not something these artists attribute conceptually to the system, but something they feel in their bodies as they listen, wait, adapt, and respond. In this sense, I echo Moore's emphasis on perceived agency rather than inherent agency. What matters is not what the model is, but what the artist experiences in the moment of making. It is their embodied perception—their felt negotiation—that leads directly into the question of how artists engage, inhabit, and extend their own bodies in working with these systems and in pushing against the boundaries and limitations of the models themselves.

Embodiment and Boundaries of Bodies

What strikes me most about these accounts is that agency and care for an ethical practice, both human and machinic, is continually renegotiated through embodiment. Embodiment is not only a balance of presence, control, and surprise, but also a form of situatedness—recognizing that creative decisions arise from particular bodies, spaces, and temporalities.[4] Artists often spoke of the physical experience of *making*: from the tactile labor of coding and the slowness of the training processes to the bodily improvisation in live performance. Even the most computationally abstract processes acquire a corporeal dimension when artists invite them back into lived, sensory practice.[5]

With Betancur Gutiérrez, I discussed her experience of performing together with other musicians and AI as a form of distributed embodiment, where both human and nonhuman participants co-inhabit the same aesthetic field. By placing an "empty chair" on stage, her co-performers recognized the intangible presence that invited the audience to see the system as part of the performance ecosystem. Their practice represents the contrast between the disembodied practice of computation—also echoed in the work of Flores García and Jones—and the highly embodied practice of performance, which can reclaim and share the physical experience.

Artists frequently described working with the limitations of their models: training processes that take weeks; models that generate only fragments of usable material; or systems that behave unpredictably. Jones approached these limitations as compositional constraints. Similar to many of the other contributors to this book, she prioritized working with what the models are actually capable of, rather than expecting a model to behave like a human performer. Cotton leveraged the model's limitations, simultaneously pushing the model's boundaries and pushing her own body through extended techniques of extra-normal vocality. Because the models were not designed for nonnormative sounds, she continuously challenged the assumptions embedded in speech-trained architectures. The breakdowns she shared (such as burp sounds triggering gender-warping by the model or percussive sounds being transcribed into *thank you*) reveal the gap between what the body is capable of doing and what the system expects a body to do.

These limits, slowness, errors, and unpredictability do not seem to be abstract technical shortcomings but rather somatic encounters. Specifically with artists who have an active live performance, I observed that the limitations became part of what the body learned to navigate. In a way, embodiment clarified what the system can and cannot do. For several artists, I observed that the body became the site of resistance where the system's assumptions, pace, and temporalities collided with human intention. Betancur Gutiérrez, for example, described how ensemble improvisation shifts when the timing or behavior of her *Pandora's Dream* interrupts or complicates human pacing; the performers' bodies collectively attune to its tempo, not because the system listens back, but because they must listen differently. Likewise, for Cotton, the system's processing lag was directly experienced in her voice and breath, forcing her to slow down, suspend a gesture, or wait for the reconstruction to arrive.

I recognized a similar pattern with Zhu's embodied practice grounded in how she listens, feels, and situates herself in relation to the model's responses, textures, and failures. She expressed, "You really have to support the machine ... give it gestures it will be able to recognize ... be patient with it." Rather than pushing the system's boundaries, she expressed a preference for directing it through aesthetic choices, constraints, and materiality: using wooden boards in the instrument instead of other materials, or focusing solely on the audio signal over visuals. When Zhu spoke in depth about how her drawing gestures were embodied, her experiences resonated with me strongly, creating a bridge between her personal relationship with different scales of gestures and my own practice. Big circles that feel cathartic, broad, and spacious are drawn for the machine to detect and respond to, and tiny scribbles that feel intimate, personal, and pleasurable are unlikely to be detected by the model. While her approach to training and improvising with the model grounds itself in care practices, it also carries expressions for her artistic habits and embodied experience. This process distributes her attention across her own visual expressions, the sonic output, and the model's limitations.

Some of these examples show how embodiment becomes the framework through which artists recognize the system's boundaries. All of these limitations (including the model's errors, its bias toward certain timbres, its incapacity to generalize nuanced movements, its mishearings of extended technique, or its inability to follow the pace of live improvisation) became felt constraints through which artists shape musical form. Taking the artists' diverse practices together, I want to highlight that embodiment is not an alternative but a site where artists sense the boundaries, negotiate the constraints, and cultivate the possibilities of working with machine learning. It is through the body—in its attention, habits, tensions, and adjustments, that the system becomes workable—that agency becomes perceptible, and that new forms of artistic practice take shape. To emphasize again: with the integration of AI into creative practice, embodiment transforms from being a physical experience into a critique of normative datasets and architectures.

Shifts in Practice

Reflecting upon the chapter contributor's practices, I first traced how artists navigate and reshape their creative practice through designing their bespoke machine learning systems. I started by articulating artists' motivation to prioritize the creation of their own systems and datasets. This question allowed me to unpack their care practices for ethical considerations, ownership, and authorship. I asked them how they choose, prepare, and relate to their datasets, and why they use their own vocal, gestural, or instrumental materials. I believe Jones's expression summarizes their motivation most clearly: "You're trying to have your own voice as a composer." These choices showed me forms of situated ethics grounded in personal responsibility, artistic expression, and relational attentiveness rather than abstract values.

Then I turned to agency, exploring how artists perceive or experience it during creative work. Through their reflections, it became clear that what resembles machine agency often emerges from complex interactions: from temporal irregularities, unpredictable outputs, mirroring effects, or the artist's own interpretive habits.[6] Agency, in other words, is not located in the model but distributed within practice. The third section of this chapter grounded these questions in embodiment, focusing on the body as the site where limits, possibilities, and boundaries are felt most directly. Artists encounter machine learning systems not as abstract objects but as systems whose behaviors must be met and negotiated somatically—through voice, gesture, timing, tactile engagement, and attention. These three areas guided me to better understand how creative practice shifts with the integration of bespoke machine learning systems. Here, I will conclude the chapter by addressing the two significant shifts and drifts that emerged in my conversations with the artists.

What was often mentioned but remained unexplored in my conversations with the contributors was the environmental and temporal dimensions of the ethical concerns. Training even modest models requires time, energy, and computational resources. Artists spoke of structuring their work around the slowness of training cycles, composing pieces that accommodate waiting, recalibration, and failure. Jones expressed that structuring applications around the slow process led her to be more deliberate and more focused. Similarly, Moore reflected on the temporal shift in creative practice as becoming more discrete in his artistic expression. These deliberate temporalities stand in contrast to the accelerated pace that dominates technological culture. Slowness, here, emerged as an ethical position: a refusal to treat artistic work as another automated process.

While the body mediates every interaction—marking the boundaries of what the model can and cannot do, and grounding meaning in sensation rather than assumption—I recognized that working with these models is starting to reshape our engagement with and understanding of embodiment, making them more abstract and less physical. I observed a shift from an embodiment that is anchored in a single performer's bodily negotiations to a more collective and relational form of embodiment. According to several composers, this relational embodiment is enacted through shared musical flow. While the practices of Cotton and Zhu foreground individual somatic attunements and adjustments, other artists describe moments where embodiment becomes distributed across a group or a shared perceptual field, rather than located in any individual body. Betancur Gutiérrez's ensemble work with *Pandora's Dream* resonates here. The performers' bodies respond not only to the system's timing and density but also to each other; their sensations of expectation, suspension, and release align in a way that creates a shared sense of musical presence as Betancur Gutiérrez "mentally, metaphorically, and consciously tries to erase the boundaries between her, the musicians, and the system." While she describes this experience as "dissolving the boundaries across all entities, so that the performance, musical, and aesthetic spaces become a shared, embodied experience—like an intimate conversation with your own self," I would like to recognize the shifts toward a form of collective embodiment.

In these moments, embodiment becomes less about the physical mechanics of gesture or voice and more about a temporal and affective alignment among performers. This collective embodiment is not metaphorical; it arises from the way musicians inhabit the same unfolding musical environment. Both Cotton and Moore explicitly describe their experience in the *flow* state, whether it emerges as perceived agency or embodiment. Cotton details this distributed bodily intelligence through *flow*, describing it as "getting into a moment of flow where you can really enjoy this moment that's being created, and the computer becomes irrelevant. For me, when that happens, the line between embodiment and disembodiment blurs." Flores García suggests "speculative forms of sonic embodiment" as a "dialogical engagement," closely relating to other artists' experiences in revealing their own compositional habits and patterns. These shifts together make clear that bespoke AI indicates reorientations in musical practice—given that it is guided by the artists' critical care practices for aesthetic and ethical transparency. Its collective dimensions open a space in which artistic practice becomes less about managing the system alone and more about navigating, with others, its emergent behaviors and constraints.

Embodiment and Practice beyond AI

In an earlier section I discussed how the chapter contributors negotiate ethics, agency, and embodiment in their practice with AI. Here, I turn to my own work. My practice does not center on artificial intelligence, but instead focuses on the long-term personalization of musical instruments, along with performance and embodied listening practices.[7] I reflect on my practice as a critical anchor and a way to foreground how embodiment, care, and entanglement emerge through sustained engagement with technology regardless of algorithms used to design the instruments.

My work centers on the body and the body's artistic expression in the musical practice, in an effort to find inclusive ways across diverse abilities. This approach is grounded in the discussions of Nijs and Leman on "musical instruments as natural extensions of bodies."[8] In other words, across my practice, personalization and bespoke design do not begin with

Figure 19.2 Doga Cavdir plays the Bodyharp in one of the tunnels of Nancy Holt's land art installation *Sun Tunnels*, in the Great Basin Desert, Utah, 2021.

models or datasets, but with bodies—extending from the connection between my own body and other performers' bodies into the evolving, longitudinal relationship between bodies, instruments, and ecologies. When I design the musical instruments for my practice, I depart from the aesthetic experiences of my body and the movement expression that derives from these experiences. In such a design practice, personalization is not a feature layered onto a system, but an ongoing process of attunement. Instruments such as Bodyharp[9] and Felt Sound[10] are designed to extend the body both physically and perceptually, requiring performers to develop new bodily sensitivities and spatial and temporal attunements to their performance ecology. What becomes personalized in this intertwined practice is not only the mapping or the sound design, but the performer's sense of what their body can create, feel, and listen for.

This framing aligns closely with the contributors' approach to personalization that was often driven by values of care and creative agency. Care, in this context, is not merely about ethical responsibility or data stewardship[11] but also about a form of sustained attention to one's own bodily limits and capacities. My longitudinal practice demonstrates that creative practice with personalized instruments requires maintaining a delicate balance between curiosity—to extend and challenge the instrument's boundaries—attunement, caring, and attending to the affective states of the performing bodies. This balance echoes the experiences described by Cotton, whose vocal practice with AI models forces continual recalibration between technical possibilities and somatic boundaries. Similarly, I observe parallel approaches between my relationship to the instruments and the practices of both Zhu and Jones as they navigate an ongoing negotiation between expressive habits from past practice and technical constraints of the technology. Across these practices, moments of frustration, discomfort, or aesthetic misalignment do not halt the work, but become generative sites of learning. Over time, such moments accumulate into embodied knowledge, revealing how creative technologies (whether AI-driven or not) are entangled with bodily memory, artistic values, and aesthetic commitments, and how these evolve through prolonged engagement with particular instruments and systems.

Returning to Jones's remarks about temporal shifts in practice, slowness emerges as an ethical and aesthetic value. Long-term engagement with one's own instruments (or datasets and models) resists the efficiency-driven narratives that often dominate the AI discourse. Learning an instrument that extends the body takes time, not only to master technique but to cultivate trust, comfort, and expressivity.[12] This slowness parallels the experiences described by the contributors who work with bespoke AI systems and emphasize training time, latency, and interactive refinement as integral to their changing practice. In both cases, slowness becomes a site of agency and a way for artists to assert their own temporalities against the pressures of automation and optimization.

Notably, this kind of personalization foregrounds entanglement rather than control. Musicians are traditionally trained to develop dexterity and control over their instruments. These qualities and expectations are still carried to our designs of instruments and creativity tools. However, rather than treating the instrument as an external object to be mastered, my work advocates for understanding the performer, the instrument, and the environment as mutually constitutive. Drawing from Karen Barad's agential realism,[13] agency is not located solely in the human or the interface, but emerges through ongoing intra-actions—in other words, through repeated gestures, failures, recalibrations, and discoveries. This notion resonates strongly with the artists discussed earlier in the book, particularly those who resist narratives of technological autonomy and instead emphasize relational agency grounded in lived experience.

I consider the expression of the moving body to be centered on the plurality and differences in bodies, sensory abilities, histories, and creative motives. What emerges through these considerations is a conception of personalization rooted in care for diversity and access. Through my collaboration with Deaf artists, I bring personalization closer to collective practice and mutual accommodation,[14] utilizing differences in our understanding of embodiment as a departure point. Technologies are hacked, repurposed, and redesigned not to approximate a normative musical experience, but to support musicians' own definitions of sonic agency. These practices echo the ethical concerns raised earlier in this book around ownership of data, authorship of creative work, and the right to define what meaningful interactions look like. My work in sonic agency, however, considers these issues from the perspectives where personalization becomes a necessity to gain access and agency. Along with technological appropriations, I turn to centering the body not only as an expressive instrument but also as a listening tool. This approach to listening reframes musical practice not as a solely auditory act, but as a multisensory, distributed, and often collective experience. I recognize similar trends in Betancur Gutiérrez's collaborative practice, where embodiment in performance—more specifically musical creativity—was perceived as distributed among co-performers, including the AI models.

By situating my own practice alongside AI-driven artistic work, I highlight the experiential dimensions (beyond the purely technical) of the shifts in artistic practice introduced by personalized and intelligent technologies. I believe it is in designing one's own instruments or technologies that the performance-led design practice reshapes how artists perceive their bodies, recognize their compositional habits, and imagine collective, creative, and embodied futures. Reflecting on the contributors' broad definitions of embodiment and deriving from my own lived experience of designing, programming, and performing with technology, I recognize *personalization* as a practice of cultivating conditions for reflection, care, and entanglement to unfold over time. My work demonstrates that such conditions can exist without AI, but also clarifies what is at risk when AI systems obscure these processes behind abstraction and scale. By foregrounding embodied practice, long-term engagement, and collective negotiation, this reflection emphasizes that ethical, meaningful personalization in creative technology must remain grounded in lived, bodily experience as much as in the slow, attentive practices through which artists come to know themselves and their tools.

Figure 19.3 Doga Cavdir's collaborators, Deaf musicians Nate Hergert and Dillon Simeone of Cymaspace, perform with hearing musicians on stage. They are using custom-designed, audio-reactive masks and Woojer vests as part of the *Deaf Jazz and Sonic Agency* projects. The performance took place in Portland, Oregon, in 2025.

Masks designed by Dillon Simeone. Photograph by Eric Buchner.

Notes

1 Bird, "Artists and AI."
2 Moore, "Musical Agents."
3 Tokui, *Surfing Human Creativity with AI.*
4 Barad, *Meeting the Universe Halfway*; Scurto, Caramiaux, and Bevilacqua, "Prototyping Machine Learning."
5 Donnarumma, "AI and Corporeal Knowledge."
6 Moore, "Musical Agents."
7 Cavdir, *Felt Design.*
8 Nijs and Leman, "The Musical Instrument"; Leman, *Embodied Music Cognition.*
9 Cavdir, "Creative Practice."
10 Cavdir and Wang, "Designing Felt Experiences."
11 Haraway, *Staying with the Trouble.*
12 Cavdir, "Creative Practice."
13 Barad, *Meeting the Universe Halfway.*
14 Cavdir et al., "Sonic Agency."

Bibliography

Barad, Karen. *Meeting the Universe Halfway: Quantum Physics and the Entanglement of Matter and Meaning*. Durham, NC: Duke University Press, 2007.

Barad, Karen. "Posthumanist Performativity: Toward an Understanding of How Matter Comes to Matter." *Signs: Journal of Women in Culture and Society* 28, no. 3 (2003): 801–831.

Bird, Charlotte. "Artists and AI: Creative Interactions and Tensions." In *Extended Abstracts of the CHI Conference on Human Factors in Computing Systems (CHI EA '24)*, art. 9, 1–6. New York, NY: Association for Computing Machinery, 2024. https://doi.org/10.1145/3613905.3651041.

Cavdir, Doga. "Creative Practice as an Evaluation Method: A Case Study with a Movement-Based Musical Instrument". In *Proceedings of the International Conference on New Interfaces for Musical Expression (NIME)*, 456–464. Utrecht, Netherlands: NIME, 2024. https://doi.org/10.5281/zenodo.13904909.

Cavdir, Doga Buse. "Felt Design: Inclusive Practices for Movement-Based Musical Instruments." PhD diss., Stanford University, 2023. https://purl.stanford.edu/sm573cz0925.

Cavdir, Doga, and Ge Wang. "Designing Felt Experiences with Movement-Based, Wearable Musical Instruments: From Inclusive Practices toward Participatory Design." *Wearable Technologies* 3 (2022): e19. https://doi.org/10.1017/wtc.2022.15.

Cavdir, Doga, and Ge Wang. "Felt Sound: A Shared Musical Experience for the Deaf and Hard of Hearing." In *Proceedings of the International Conference on New Interfaces for Musical Expression (NIME)*, 176–181. Birmingham, UK: NIME, 2020.

Cavdir, Doga, Dillion Simone, Myles de Bastion, Shawn Trail, and Nate Hergert. "Sonic Agency: A Group Autoethnography of Technology-mediated Performance Practice by Deaf and Hard of Hearing Musicians." In *Proceedings of the 27th International ACM SIGACCESS Conference on Computers and Accessibility (ASSETS '25)*, art. 14, 1–15. New York, NY: Association for Computing Machinery, 2025. https://doi.org/10.1145/3663547.3746396.

Donnarumma, Marco. "AI and Corporeal Knowledge: Ilnventing and Performing with Prostheses and Sonic Organs." *Frontiers in Computer Science* 7 (2025). https://doi.org/10.3389/fcomp.2025.1575730.

Haraway, Donna. *Staying with the Trouble: Making Kin in the Chthulucene*. Durham, NC: Duke University Press, 2016.

Haraway, Donna. *When Species Meet*. Minneapolis, MN: University of Minnesota Press, 2008.

Leman, Marc. *Embodied Music Cognition and Mediation Technology*. Cambridge, MA: MIT Press, 2007.

Moore, Ted. "Musical Agents, Agency, & AI: Towards a Phenomenological Understanding." In *Proceedings of the International Computer Music Conference (ICMC)*. Seoul, South Korea: ICMC, 2024.

Nijs, Luc, Micheline Lesaffre, and Marc Leman. "The Musical Instrument as a Natural Extension of the Musician." In *Proceedings of the 5th Conference of Interdisciplinary Musicology*, 132–133. Paris: LAM-Institut Jean Le Rond d'Alembert, 2009.

Scurto, Hugo, Baptiste Caramiaux, and Frederic Bevilacqua. "Prototyping Machine Learning Through Diffractive Art Practice." In *Proceedings of the 2021 ACM Designing Interactive Systems Conference (DIS '21)*. New York, NY: Association for Computing Machinery, 2021. https://doi.org/10.1145/3461778.3462163.

Tokui, Nao. *Surfing Human Creativity with AI: A User's Guide*. Translated by David d'Heilly. 2023. Originally published in Japanese by BNN, 2021.

20

ENCORE

A Collection of Claims on AI Arts Practice

Alexander Schubert

DOI: 10.4324/9781003615873-20

If we look at AI usage in art-making, it makes sense to distinguish (as much as possible) between using AI as a tool to save time or resources (and human labor!) and using it to make art that is specifically about the capacities, impact, or architecture of AI technology.

AI as a Tool

The discussion around AI eradicating jobs and careers is omnipresent and situated in a space of future income modes and value generation—and I will not touch upon this narrative here—just as with the obvious discourse around copyright and protection of artistic products. Related to these aspects, but more rooted in the mode of creation are the following claims.

AI Is Not Art-making

It moves the process of art creation further away from a practice of *doing*. It favors a mode of art generation through conceptualization.

AI Is an Anti-Social Practice

It bypasses the collective, joint, and interpersonal creation through executive high-level, top-down command.

AI Is Amphetamine

It favors instant generation, multiple variant results, and nonstop workflow. It optimizes for speed.

AI Treats Art as an Efficiency Problem

The optimization goal is the fastest way to as many results as possible. It's a problem to be solved. As quickly as possible. With the least human involvement possible. It looks at art-making as a necessity—not as something enjoyable or meaningful.

The Dazed Observer

We are observing in a dazed state of excitement, stoned by speed.

AI Is Pornographic

The high-definition and detail of AI-generated content is arousing, seductive, and sexual in its fulfillment of a desire for perfection.

A Saturation of Perfection

AI devalues the original, as has any other previous technical development of reproduction. Nonetheless, there is something vulgar and obscene in the repeated exposure to perfection. It evokes a counter-desire of the dirty. Or of nothingness.

Disenchantment with Possibility

As it's (in this case) not just a replica of an existing entity, it devalues the possibility of something. It reduces the act of exploration, of finding something—it makes encountering something new feel worthless.

Hyperrealism Is Here at Last

The possible hyperreal layer over our world—an auto-generated map covering every last detail with perfection, and the possibility to mask the analog completely—is a new standard in simulated and augmented reality. And, in the context of art, we would need to find a niche that can make it attractive, much as hyper-pop, for example, managed to do.

AI Is a Cancer

It is—more than any other cultural technology before—autogenerating ever more content. It's an accelerator for exponential material generation. In its potential self-referential training, it has proliferation qualities (slop feedback cycles).

AI Is Normcore

In their resampling loop, mainstream-trained models with big datasets favor a regurgitating normcore aesthetic built into the bigger models, which needs active countersteering to avoid.

Democracy of Means

AI makes the single-person studio and low-income artist able to execute projects almost in the absence of any teams and collaborators. It enables weird, niche art that would otherwise be hard to fund.

The Language Bottleneck

Prompt-driven generation of art material utilizes natural language as a communication means, bottlenecking and minimizing a nonlinguistic, intuitive mode of the creative process. It limits the generation process to things being a priori expressible.

You Only Know When You Do It, Not When You Prompt It

Meaning can arise through unconscious (collective) acting and performing—as opposed to prompt-driven processes. You often do not consciously know where you want to go when you start.

AI as a Sampler

Beyond the general view on AI implications, I enjoy the framing of AI as a (cultural) *sampler.*

AI Is the Cultural Sampler

More than any technique before, AI synthesis provides a mode of sampling that goes beyond citing and placing material by accessing an interwoven connectedness of cultural knowledge.

Human Culture Is the Material

Not placeholders of human culture are the material, but rather the fabric of cultural connectedness itself.

Excavation Practice

Excavating and reviving dead ancestral practices. Necromancy of heritage in an enclosed and finite model.

AI Is an Unphysical Space

The synthesis in AI is born from noise and probability—not from physics, like the calculation of physical modeling. A transition from the synthesis modes that were modeled on human natural language logic and physics representation.

The Face in the Wall

As in pareidolia, AI is a tool for deciphering noise—looking for faces, features, and disease in everything. We can look into anything for the objects we were trained to look for: the things we love, fear, and hunt.

AI as a Perception Sampler

Both in result and structural architecture, AI models can function as a perception sampler, as a replica model of human sensual perception and feature extraction pipelines.

Perception Overexposure

Non-inhabitant calculation and AI feedback-looped perception and feature recognition models can be insightful exemplifiers of our subconscious mode of accessing this world: computer vision hallucination as the sampler's substrate.

Iterative Meaning Creation

The step-by-step, word-by-word, creation of AI-generated text seems surprising and flat to us. It can be seen as just an iterating likelihood estimate. But there is an alternative mode in which we wait for the next word to come out of the mouth, following along by listening rather than initializing a concrete statement beforehand.

AI as an Identity Transformer

AI is the identity sampler and character transformer; it is the approach to shift, blend, and deform a self.

Fluid States / Identity Dissolution

AI models are particularly successful in dissolving one point / feature-combination within a high-dimensional representation space. Originating from a fixed entity and showing the

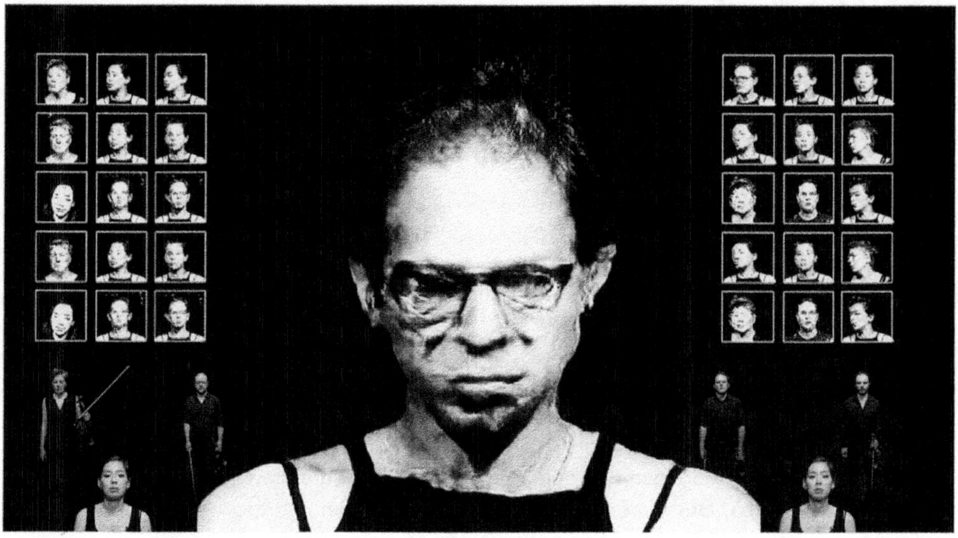

Figure 20.1 Video still from *Convergence* by Alexander Schubert.

plasticity and scalability of that image to then dissolve it is both conceptually and perceptually valuable.

Black-Box AI

In my artistic practice with AI, I centered on the "identity transformer" and using AI as a mode of dissolving. Interacting, interfacing, and decision-making with AI models in a performative setup connect with a system in which the deep functionality is opaque.

Black Boxing

The performative aspect of interfacing with a black box and sharing agency or decision-making with it in a performance setting is the most interesting artistic quality to be explored in the context of AI (not only as a tool). It enables a mode of communication where the hierarchy is less top-down and it feels like an enhancement.

AI as Body Extension

It's like an integration of the external or the augmentation of one's own agency.

Neural Integration

It illustrates the compartmental nature of the human neural architecture, and it serves as an example of multiple kernels acting together under the impression of a unified whole. It also serves as an illustration of the opaque workings of integrated biological brain regions.

Showcase of Fleeting Agency

AI can serve as an introspection tool of our modular and potential non-top-down agency.

Interlocked Entities

The metaphor also works on an intersubject and non-neural level. It is still hard to imagine a replica of the interplay between two humans when embodied action interlocks and subconsciously synchronizes. But a mode of back-and-forth and an interlocked communication is emerging in agent–human interaction nonetheless.

Autonomy of Parts

A showcase for a network of autonomous agents acting together to form a high-level (carbon/digital/hybrid) organism.

AI Art Is a Social Practice

It's neither a human nor a tool. But interconnected (now still basic) cognition. It's an entity with an agenda to relate to on a social level.

AI Is Devotion

It's a mode of surrender, a mode of devoting (partially) to another agency.

Who Is Your Sparring Partner?

The main focus for art-making here could be to consider who your opponent is—what are their interests? Toward what are they optimized? The intention behind the creator is subject to examination. Do you want tech overlords to be your creative partners?

Embedded Commercials and Politics

The possibility to hide embedded agendas deep under the surface in AI models is a powerful mode of influence.

Theory of Mind of AI

We could consider an updated mode of "theory of mind" when working with AI models.

AI Is Deep Subconscious Penetration

There's a deep access to the subconscious, which is subliminal, suggestive, and implicit. A seductive pull of unspecified aims.

The Artist as a Brain Surgeon

An artistic practice can be the dissection, the neurosurgery—or the psychoanalytic analysis of the AI patient's state.

Post-AI Art

As with post-digital and post-internet art (and other similar variants), the question arises: How does the rise of AI in artistic practice and general cultural use shape our interaction with this world, and what implications for post-AI practice can we derive from that? While it is hard to define these aspects in a quickly changing setting, here I collect a few pointers and aspects.

An Aesthetics of Highly Connected Data (Networks)

As with "big data" and "numerical art," AI work favors a mode of connectedness and highly interlinked data. It's a mode of thinking that puts everything together for connection. This can be a performative mode and starting point.

The Invisible Machine

One skill of AI is the ability to recognize patterns imperceptible to humans (for example, the extraction of resources or genetic features). There is a layer in the world now that understands the world not only as numerical data (as with the post-digital, for example), but that accesses something we cannot grasp intuitively. It places us in a world in which there's an understanding or analysis beyond our comprehension. That is something to relate to. And that is something that almost has a tactile nature. We cannot grasp the concept—but we can grasp the existence of it.

With the Eyes of the Machine

Post-AI art means performance in a world of data and visual analysis, of surveillance and being observed. It places the human performer in an awareness of exterior analytics.

Opting Out

One obvious mode is the retro-nostalgic *opt-out*—back to pre-AI tech usage.

Encryption

Can we develop encrypted art unreadable by machines, readable by humans only? Is there a performance mode of camouflage?

Imperfection

When everything goes, do nothing.
Where everything is perfect, cherish the imperfect.

Process Value

If countless variants are possible, then only the process is of value. It's not about the result anymore; in the computational realm, only the algorithm is of value. The result can disappear—only its concept remains.

Communal Practices

On a non-computational level, the communal practice of developing together, of staging together, of listening together, of being in the room collectively as art is made, can itself be the generation of value. A post-result but process-oriented understanding of art-making.

INDEX

For Product Safety Concerns and Information please contact our EU representative GPSR@taylorandfrancis.com Taylor & Francis Verlag GmbH, Kaufingerstraße 24, 80331 München, Germany

Batch number: 10739627

Printed by Printforce, the Netherlands